Ritual and Speculation In Early Tantrism

SUNY Series in Tantric Studies

Paul E. Muller-Ortega, Editor

André Padoux

Ritual and Speculation in Early Tantrism

Studies in Honor of

André Padoux

edited by

Teun Goudriaan

State University of New York Press

Published by
State University of New York Press, Albany

Printed in the United States of America

For information, address State University of New York
Press, State University Plaza, Albany, N.Y., 12246

Production by Leslie Frank-Hass
Marketing by Theresa A. Swierzowski

Library of Congress Cataloging-in-Publication Data

Ritual and speculation in early tantrism: studies in honour of André
Padoux / edited by Teun Goudriaan.
p. cm. — (SUNY series in tantric studies)
Includes bibliographical references and index.
ISBN 0-7914-0897-3 (alk. paper). — ISBN 0-7914-0898-1 (pbk.
alk. paper)
1. Tantrism—Doctrines. 2. Tantrism—Rituals. I. Padoux,
André. II. Goudriaan, Teun. III. Series.
BL1283.845.R48 1991
294.5′514—dc20 91-10169
CIP

10 9 8 7 6 5 4 3 2 1

CONTENTS

Preface

Ritual engagement or abstract speculation about supreme truth? The title of this book, by juxtaposing *ritual* and *speculation*, is expressive of one of the most intriguing characteristics of the Hindu tradition: the conviction that philosophy and ceremonial activity are not two separate compartments—as a modern outside observer might be inclined to think—but that, on the contrary, they should be applied in constant interaction so as to fecundate each other. The study of Tantric literature, especially of the earlier period of remarkable religious inspiration is apt to illustrate this point in various ways.

The contributors to this book have dealt with several aspects of the subject in their own way, in accordance with their distinctive preferences. They have not been asked to follow a particular line of argument; it seemed better to allow them full freedom within the range suggested by the general title. The result is a many-sided orientation from the viewpoint of several Tantric schools; there may be a certain emphasis on the speculative aspects but the ritual structure is never entirely lost sight of.

The articles have been arranged in alphabetical order by the names of the authors. It is a happy coincidence that the first article, by Hélène Brunner, offers an encompassing study of the relation between "wisdom" and "action" in the Śaivāgama tradition, where these two concepts figure with special prominence. Śiva himself has two *śaktis* called *jñāna* and *kriyā* ('wisdom' and 'action'). Brunner argues for the originality of this twofold expansion of power with respect to later conceptions of three or more Śaktis. The main part of her article is devoted to an inquiry after the relationship of doctrine and rituals as described in the Āgamas. It appears, surprisingly, that the two often are in clear disagreement with each other, the ritual usually being older than the transmitted philosophy.

Richard Davis and Vrajavallabha Dviveda have approached a similar topic—the relation between God Śiva and His worshipper in the ceremonial entourage—from different angles. Davis, who concentrates on the Āgamic tradition, also departs from the two aspects of knowledge and ritual, from which context he describes the ideology behind the worshipping priests' divinization. The latter's temporary assumption of the powers of a Śiva is acted out in the ritual of daily worship that therefore "discloses knowledge through action." Dviveda, after retracing the ideal of "becoming a god" to the Brāhmaṇas, gives a description of what actually is done and recited in various types of worship, with special reference to the *Parā* form and lower varieties. He refers mainly to the Yoginīhṛdaya, and to Trika and Krama sources. The chapter was translated from the original Sanskrit by Gérard Colas of Paris.

The Vaiṣṇava (Pāñcarātra) system of meditation and worship (especially its higher form, internal worship) is the subject of a thorough scrutiny by Sanjukta Gupta. For the Pāñcarātra, release by enlightenment depends on divine grace, but "has to be earned by constant *sādhanā*." In *sādhanā* or yoga, the religious ideology of the school is directly experienced by visual and phonic representation.

Midway between Āgamic Śaivism and the Trika system usually associated with Kashmir is Alexis Sanderson's chapter, which throws new light on the position of the Mālinīvijayottara, an oft-quoted but also often misunderstood source of inspiration for Trika adepts. By force of arguments, Sanderson shows that the reputed monism of this Tantra in fact has been superimposed on to the text by its interpreters. The first part of the article contains a useful summary of dualist and monist positions with regard to the soul and its destiny.

Paul Muller-Ortega discusses the theory and meditational practice of the nondual Śaivism of Kashmir with regard to continuous cosmogonic manifestation as expressed by the sixteen vowels of the Sanskrit alphabet. He attempts a new interpretive approach by means of reference to the terminology of "holomovement" put forward by David Bohm in his "Wholeness and the Implicate Order."

Another comparative vista is opened by Raffaele Torella, who concentrates on the influence exerted on the Pratyabhijñā philosophy by the rigorous argumentation of the Buddhist logicians. Although the speculative presuppositions of the two systems seems to be diametrically opposed—the multiplicity of dharmas versus the cosmic Self—a "cross correspondence" can be detected in them, as certain themes developed by the Buddhist logicians are reflected in the argumentations of the Śaiva philosophers.

The development of the yogic tradition in the monistic Śaiva school is studied by Navjivan Rastogi. He discerns three divisions: the threefold (later, fourfold) *upāya-yoga* established in the Mālinīvijayottara, the sixfold Śaiva yoga, and the threefold gradation of gross, subtle, and ultimate applied in the Netra Tantra. Still, there is a continued fidelity to Patañjali's eightfold system, although it has been transformed to a specific Trika yoga that culminates in the ultimate freedom of "supreme agency."

Special aspects of the Śaiva tradition are treated by Teun Goudriaan and Minoru Hara. The former presents a translation of Svacchanda Tantra 11, 91-126, which contain a doctrine of "stages of awakening" or stations on the soul's journey to its ultimate destination. He tries to connect this perspective with statements from the Mahābhārata. Hara examines passages from Kauṇḍinya's commentary on the first of the Pāśupata Sūtras, relating to the qualifications of an applicant for initiation, the interpretation of yoga as *saṃyoga*, and aspects of the theory of the means of valid knowledge. The treatment of these subjects by Kauṇḍinya reveals indebtedness to a simple and early form of Sāṃkhya unrecorded in the classical sources of that school.

Two contributions, those by Gudrun Bühnemann and Jan Schoterman, deal with Kaula sources in a philological way. Bühnemann concentrates on the system of preliminary recitation of a mantra by the sādhaka who wants to identify with it. To this end, she gives an annotated translation of one of the most authoritative sources on the subject, the fifteenth chapter of the Kulārṇava. A quite different text, the as yet unedited Kubjikā Upaniṣad, is the subject of Schoterman's contribution. He discusses its remarkably composite character and convincingly shows the Atharvavedic nature of its oldest layer. It is a matter of great regret that Schoterman could not live to witness the publication of this book.

This volume has been dedicated by the authors as a token of respectful recognition and friendship to one of the foremost French Indologists of our time, who is among the most devoted and thoughtful expounders and interpreters of the Tantric tradition.

André Padoux was born April 13, 1920, at Peking, where his father occupied a diplomatic post. After obtaining his "licence ès lettres" (including a certificate on Chinese) as well as a juridical "licence" at Lyon 1939, he began the study of political science in Lyon and Paris, which he finished successfully (in the diplomatic section) in 1946, despite the interruption caused by World War II. His diplomatic career took a start with a three years' service as a member of the French delegation to the UNESCO, in which function he attended several of its conferences. In November 1949 he was appointed cultural attaché at the French Embassy in Norway and Reader in French at the University of Oslo. From 1953 to 1959, he was active in a similar function in the French Embassy in India at New Delhi.

In the meantime, he made a thorough study of Indian culture and literature, especially Sanskrit literature. Already about the year

1940, he discovered the rich tradition of Indian thought, and in 1946 he commenced (encouraged by Jules Bloch) the study of Sanskrit and Indian culture at the Institut de Civilisation Indienne of the University of Paris, under the guidance of Louis Renou. Also in Oslo, he continued his Sanskrit studies under Georg Morgenstierne, and added Hindi to his program. He also oriented himself on general problems of semantics and poetics, following inter alia the courses of Alf Sommerfelt. In New Delhi, where his Sanskrit studies were pursued further, he met Lilian Silburn who encouraged him to study Abhinavagupta's oeuvre, especially his commentaries on the Parātriṃśikā, which Padoux read with the famous modern Trika adept, Pandit Lakshman Joo, at Srinagar in 1958 and 1959.

André Padoux's academic career dates from November 1959, when he was appointed attaché de recherche at the CNRS (National Centre of Scientific Research). Since 1957, he worked (under the supervision of Olivier Lacombe and Louis Renou) on his doctoral thesis "Recherches sur la symbolique et l'énergie de la parole dans certains textes tantriques," which was published in 1963 and submitted April 1964. This book, which underwent a second edition in 1975, is among the most-favorably judged and most-often quoted modern Indological studies. In Paul Eduardo Muller-Ortega's words: "an encyclopedic work . . . one of the first systematic and in-depth treatments of the notion of the Supreme Word . . . a book that combines thorough scholarliness with a lively and active sympathy for the material." The book is now accessible in a revised English version (see the list of publications, No. 40). As a secondary thesis, Padoux delivered a partial translation of Abhinavagupta's Parātriṃśikāvivaraṇa. In the meantime, he had been appointed conseiller culturel (cultural advisor) at the French Embassy in Laos, where he stayed till August 1964. In September of that year, he became director of the French Insitute at Frankfurt am Main in Western Germany, where he also lectured on modern French poetry. His last diplomatic function was fulfilled at the French Embassy in Hungary from 1969 until November 1972.

From the beginning of 1973, Padoux continued his academic career at the CNRS, as chargé de recherche (until 1978), maître de recherche (until 1984), and directeur de recherche (from October 1984 to his retirement on October 1, 1989). From January 1982 to December 1989 he directed the equipe de recherche (research team) No. 249 of the CNRS, entitled "L'hindouisme, textes, doctrines, pratiques." In 1982, he was elected a member of the Comité National de la Recherche Scientifique, section Langues et Civilisations Orientales, a position he still occupies. Since 1975, he also has been a member of the Scientific Council of the National Institute of Oriental Languages and Civilizations (Conseil Scientifique de l'Institut National des Langues et Civilisations Orientales).

In several countries of the West, Indology is under pressure due to a lamentable tendency of government administrations to economize on "marginal" academic disciplines. Padoux, as a member of the Comité National de la Recherche Scientifique, continues to defend with energy the cause of French Indology. As director of the equipe de recherche, he led its coordination and the invigoration of Āgamic and Tantric studies in France. Under his guidance, the Equipe proved to provide a high-quality seminar on the European level, in which several non-French members participated regularly or occasionally.

Those who have the privilege to know Padoux personally, have been impressed by his friendliness, his cultured style, his honesty and meticulous correctness, his high scientific standard, and his readiness to assist young Indologists, both French and non-French. In publications and reviews, he always combines impartial judgment with a respectful approach. It is our earnest hope that Dr. Padoux will for a long time continue to serve the interest of Orientalism and humanity at large by scholarly publications, wise advice, and protection of the high standard of French Indology—assisted in all these things by Mrs. Padoux's gentle wisdom.

It is a pleasant duty to thank Gérard Colas for his constant assistance and practical advice during the preparation of this book. We also thank SUNY Press for broadmindedly accepting the manuscript for publication and carefully guiding it to completed form.

Teun Goudriaan

Publications by André Padoux

1. *Recherches sur la symbolique et l'énergie de la parole dans certains textes tantriques.* (Publications de l'Institut de Civilisation Indienne de l'Université de Paris, fasc. 21). Paris: de Boccard, 1963; revised second edition, 1975.

2. "Le śivaïsme du Cachemire." In *L'Hindouisme,* ed. A-M. Esnoul, pp. 479-505. Paris: Fayard-Denoel, 1972.

3. "*Mantra* et *yantra-maṇḍala,*" Preface to the French translation of G. Tucci, *Théorie et pratique du maṇḍala.* Paris: Fayard, 1974.

4. "Le śivaïsme du Cachemire: présence et rôle de l'énergie." *Revue Philosophique* (1974): 45-64.

5. *La Parātrīśikālaghuvṛtti d'Abhinavagupta, texte traduit et annoté* (text and translation with notes). (PICI, fasc. 38.) Paris: Institut de Civilisation Indienne, 1975.

6. "Le bouddhisme tantrique" and "Le bouddhisme au Tibet." In *Le Bouddhisme,* ed. L. Silburn, pp. 293-328 and 383-386. Paris: Fayard, 1977. Reedited in *Le bouddhisme hors de l'Inde.* Paris: Stock and Plus, 1980.

7. "Un terme technique du *mantraśāstra: vidarbha.*" *Journal Asiatique* 265 (1977): 345-349.

8. On Mantras and Mantric Practices in the Agni Purāṇa." *Purāṇa* [Varanasi] 20 (1978): 37-65.

9. "Some Suggestions on Research into *Mantra.*" *Indologica Taurinensia* [Torino] 6 (1978): 235-239.

10. "Contributions à l'etude du *mantraśāstra.* I: La sélection des *mantra —mantroddhāra.*" *Bulletin de l'Ecole Française d'Extrême-Orient* (BEFEO) 65 (1978): 65-85.

11. "Contributions à l'étude du *mantraśāstra.* II: *nyāsa*—l'imposition rituelle des *mantra.*" BEFEFO 67 (1980): 59-102.

12. *L'énergie de la parole, cosmogonies de la parole tantrique.* Paris: Le Soleil Noir, 1980.

13. "About *Japa.*" In *Ludwik Sternbach Felicitation Volume,* ed. J. P. Sinha, pp. 593-601. Lucknow: Akhila Bharatiya Sanskrit Parishad, 1981.

14. "A Survey of Tantric Hinduism for the Historian of Religions." *History of Religions* [Chicago] 20 (1981): 345-360 (review article).

15. "Un *japa* tantrique: Yoginīhṛdaya III, 171-190." In *Tantric and Taoist Studies in Honor of R. A. Stein*, ed. M. Strickmann, pp. 141-154. Bruxelles: Institut Belge des Hautes Etudes Chinoises, 1981.

16. "Le Yoginīhṛdaya et la Dīpikā d'Amṛtānanda: quelques problèmes." *Bulletin d'Etudes Indiennes* 1 (1983): 73-78.

17. "Une méthode indienne de maîtrise du temps." *Chronos* [Paris] 1 (1983): 69-90.

18. "L'Hindou, son médecin et son monde." *Critique* 443 (1984): 300-305 (on two books by Sudhir Kakar).

19. "Le monde hindou et le sexe—symbolisme, attitudes, pratiques." *Cahiers Internationaux de Sociologie* 76 (1984): 29-49.

20. Review of J. Schoterman, *The Ṣaṭsāhasrasaṃhitā, Chapters 1-5, Indo-Iranian Journal* 28 (1985): 139-145.

21. "L'énonciation créatrice—l'aller et retour de la parole." *Confrontations* [Paris] 13 (1985): 99-110.

22. "On the Spiritual Aspects of Mudrās." *The Indian Theosophist* [Varanasi] 82, (1985, Thakur Dr. Jaideva Singh Felicitation Number): 72-78.

23. "L'Inde et ses religions." In *Mythes et croyances du monde entier, ed. A. Akoun a.o. IV: Les mondes asiatiques*, pp. 67-74. Paris-Turnhout: Lidis-Brepols, 1985.

24. Edition of *Mantras et diagrammes rituels dans l'Hindouisme.* Paris: Editions du CNRS, 1986.

25. "*Vāmakeśvaratantrāntargataṃ yoginīhṛdayam*," *Ṛtam* [Lucknow] 16-18 (1984-86): 251-257.

26. "Tantrism—Overview," "Hindu Tantrism," "Hindu Tantric Literature," "Vīraśaivism," and "Pratyabhijñā." In *Encyclopaedia of Religions*, ed. M. Eliade, New York: Macmillan, 1986.

27. "On Some Aspects of Tripurasundarī's Worship According to Yoginīhṛdaya—the Role of *Bhāvanā*." In *Navonmeṣa, M. M. Gopinath Kaviraj Smṛti Granth*, vol. 4, pp. 120-128, Varanasi, 1987.

28. "Contributions à l'étude du *mantraśāstra*. III: *Le japa*." *BEFEO* 76 (1987): 117-164.

29. "Un rituel hindou du rosaire (Jayākhyasaṃhitā, chapitre 14)." *Journal Asiatique* 275 (1987): 115-129.

30. "Temples hindous et prêtres de la Déesse." *Revue de l'Histoire des Religions* 204 (1987): 61-70.

31. Two articles [in French] on Tantrism. In *Atlas des Religions.* Paris: Encyclopaedia Universalis, 1988.

32. "Mantras, What Are They?" (Conclusion) In *Understanding Mantras,* ed. H. P. Alper, pp. 295-318. Albany: SUNY Press, 1989.

33. "La présence imaginaire de la parole dans le corps—perspectives indiennes." In *La Voix,* ed. R. Lew and F. Sauvagnat (*Actes du Colloque d'Ivry du 23 janvier 1988*). Paris: La Lysimaque, 1989.

34. "Les écritures du sanskrit." In *Atlas de Littératures.* Paris: Encyclopaedia Universalis, 1990.

35. Articles [in French] on Mantra and Tantrism. In *Supplément 1990.* Paris: Encyclopaedia Universalis, 1990.

36. "The Body in Tantric Ritual: the Case of the *Mudrās.*" In *The Sanskrit Tradition and Tantrism,* ed. T. Goudriaan (*Contributions of the panels of the VIIth World Sanskrit Conference, Leiden 1987,* vol. 1), pp. 66-75. Leiden: E. J. Brill, 1990.

37. "Introduction." In *L'Image Divine. Culte et méditation dans l'hindouisme,* ed. A. Padoux, pp. 1-7. Paris: Editions du CNRS, 1990.

38. "Image mentale, méditation et culte dans la Śrīvidyā: quelques exemples tirés du Yoginīhṛdaya." In *L'Image Divine. Culte et méditation dans l'hindouisme,* pp. 89-98. Paris: Editions du CNRS, 1990.

39. "Renoncer à rêver le renoncement." *Corps Ecrit* [Paris] 34 (1990).

40. *Vāc: The Concept of the Word in Selected Hindu Tantras.* (English version of No. 1; trans. Jacques Gontier). Albany: SUNY Press, 1990.

41. "Yoga and Ritual." In *Studies in Indology: Professor Rasik Vihari Joshi Felicitation Volume,* ed. A. Kumar and others. New Delhi: Shree Publishing House, 1988-89.

In the Press

42. "The Fourfold *upāya* According to Abhinavagupta's Tantrāloka." In *Abhinavagupta and the Synthesis of Indian Culture.* Boston.

43. "The Tripurā or Saubhāgya Darśana and Tripurasundarī's Cult" (communication to the Sixth World Sanskrit Conference, Philadelphia, 1984).

44. "Śivaisme et hétérodoxie: à propos de 'sectes śivaites hétérodoxes'." In *Un renoncement bien tempéré,* ed. S. Bouez. Paris.

45. "Mantric Practices and the Nature of Mantric Utterance." In *S. S. Janaki Shastyabdapūrti Volume,* Madras.

46. "Parole et délivrance—une mystique à base phonématique." *Cahiers de l'Herne* [Paris].

47. Reviews of publications on Indian religions. In *Journal Asiatique* (1981-1984); *Archives de Sciences Sociales des Religions* (since 1983); *Revue de l'Histoire des Religions* (since 1983); *Bulletin d'Etudes Indiennes* (since 1983).

Chapter One

Jñāna and Kriyā:

Relation between Theory and Practice in the Śaivāgamas

Hélène Brunner

Introduction

The Pair *Jñāna-Kriyā* at Different Levels

There is perhaps no Indian school where the pair of concepts "knowledge" and "action" (*jñāna* and *kriyā*) is given such prominence as with the Śaivas, especially in these branches of Śaivism that are more or less directly based on the Āgamas and go by the name of *Southern* and *Northern Śaivism.*[1] Here, we will deal exclusively with the first, technically called *Śaiva-Siddhānta,*[2] but much of what will be said applies to the Northern school as well.

It is but natural to start with Śiva, whose inherent Power (Śakti) usually is described as having two sides: one called *Power of Knowledge,* Jñāna-Śakti or Dṛk-Śakti; the other *Power of Action,* Kriyā-Śakti.[3] These Powers are not separate, being only the two complementary aspects of the unique infinite Power of the God, called simply *spiritual power* (Cicchakti)[4] when considered as a whole. This Śakti is sometimes likened to the effulgence of the Sun-Śiva,[5] and in this perspective the God is the *dharmin* and His Power, the *dharma.* But their inseparability is always insisted upon: Śiva would be nothing without His Śakti, is different from Her[6] only in appearance, so that perhaps we should better say that the two Powers we are speaking of "constitute" Śiva. Whatever the case, the fact that we wish to stress is the polarization of Śiva's Power in two directions and only two. This bipolarization may well be lost sight of when one considers the numerous lists of three, five, eight, nine, sixteen, and more Śaktis,[7] each with a particular function, that we find in the Āgamic literature. In fact, these extensive lists most certainly represent a later development of the doctrine, which introduced subtle distinctions within the Śakti concept and tried to connect them with all kinds of triads, pentads, and so on, met with in the cosmology or ontology of the school. Even the very common list of three, which begins with a Will or Wish (Icchā) logically anterior to Jñāna and Kriyā, is decidedly less satisfactory than the simple division into two; for the "power to know" is not the knowledge, nor is the "Power to act" an action, so that one fails to see any necessity for imagining a "Power to will" (even less a Will, as usually understood). On the contrary, the division into Jñāna and Kriyā is natural. It is almost always the one given at the outset of the considerations on Śakti, and sometimes the only one ever mentioned. Besides, it is reflected in the definition of the soul itself. As is well known, the Āgamas maintain that the essential nature of the soul (*ātman, aṇu*), which manifests itself when the soul is freed from the bonds that prevent it to shine, is exactly the same as that of Śiva, with the sole difference that the soul has been liberated from its bonds at a given moment and by the grace of Śiva, whereas Śiva is eternally free.[8] Now, the most usual and much repeated description of the soul is given in a few words in the Mṛgendra (vp, 2, 5): *caitanyaṃ dṛk-kriyārūpaṃ tad asty ātmani sarvadā* ("in the *ātman* exists at all times a spiritual [power] (*caitanyam* is here synonym of *cit* generally used) consisting in Vision and Action").[9] No other Power is ever mentioned. We feel therefore justified to ignore the complications of the later doctrine and consider both Śiva and the liberated souls as unlimited masses of Power, or Energy, susceptible to manifest themselves in two directions, knowledge on the one hand, action on the other hand.

At this level, the terms *jñāna* and *kriyā* refer to powers.[10] Their expression, or actualization, is the unlimited knowledge that God has of the universe and the unbounded action He may exert on this universe; that is, His omniscience (*sarvajñatva*) and His omnipotence (*sarvakartṛtva*). This one may accept as a general view; but a serious difficulty presents itself when one tries to understand this actualization more precisely. As far as Kriyā is concerned, we are told that it is by Her mere presence that She acts on the *bindu*, the subtle matter which, when so "excited," gives birth to the realities that constitute the world.[11] And we know the form that the resulting activity is taking: they are the well-known "five actions" of Śiva, which we shall talk about presently. But what about Jñāna? Even if we admit that the action of presence, as a rule attributed to Kriyā, in fact concerns the Śakti as a whole, it remains to understand what sort of knowledge Śiva is supposed to have through the play of this Power. We would spontaneously think of some transcendent knowledge, without any relation to ordinary human knowledge, and it might be that some masters of the Siddhānta have upheld views of this kind. But this is not what we actually read. The rare explanations we find in our texts are quite naive and matter of fact: in the same way as a weaver cannot carry on his trade without knowing all about the threads, and so forth, God has to know the objects on which He exerts an action. Because His action is unbounded (he is *sarvakṛt*), His knowledge must be unlimited too,[12] but it is not essentially different from human knowledge.

Another problem concerns the timing, if we may say so, of the manifestation of these divine faculties. According to Kashmirian philosophers, this manifestation is progressive, from the supreme Śiva, where Jñāna and Kriyā are not differentiated, to lesser aspects of the God, where one or the other shines particularly. This vision implies a certain anteriority, and hence superiority, of Jñāna with respect to Kriyā (and even a different conception of Kriyā),[13] which is not belied by the other teachings concerning the Śakti. Now, the Siddhānta, which in many respects seems to have preserved an older form of the Śaiva thought, teaches nothing of the sort concerning Śiva.[14] Sure enough, some texts do explain the three states that the God seems to assume (*laya, bhoga, adhikāra;* or *śakta, udyukta, pravṛtta;* or *niṣkala, sakala-niṣkala, sakala*) by differences in the condition of the Śakti, which is at rest, so to speak (or closed like a bud), in the first case; ready to act in the second; and fully active in the third.[15] But this conception does not entail any dissymmetry in the manifestation of Jñāna and Kriyā, still less any hierarchy between them. Neither does the description, given in several texts, of a progressive unveiling of these Powers in the soul on its journey toward liberation, which moreover is quite another story. So far as Śiva is concerned, there can be, according to the Siddhānta, no superiority, or anteriority, of one of His two Śaktis on the other; at least, theoretically. In fact, a certain partiality for one or the other may be observed in some passages where the texts are not busy with formal definitions. Sometimes, Jñāna-Śakti is spoken of as if She could be identified with Cit, the undifferentiated Śakti, or even directly with Śiva, and therefore appears to hold a superior position.[16] But in the majority of cases, the partiality for Kriyā is striking. For instance, the three above-mentioned conditions of the Śakti are attributed to Kriyā alone by the Ratnatraya,[17] and it is the commentator, Aghoraśiva who explains that by implication Jñāna also is meant, as both are inseparable. More often, it is indirectly that we perceive the greater interest for Kriyā, by the use of the single word *Śakti* when Kriyā-Śakti is clearly meant, as if this Power of Action were the essential aspect of Śiva's Power.[18] We certainly are not far from the mark if we suggest that Śiva was conceived as a Power, without specification, but with the idea of action in the foreground, long before this Power was described as having two sides, Jñāna and Kriyā. And this is quite natural, for the creatures—say, men—experience (or believe they do) the Power of God through some effects, the causes of which they attribute to definite actions of this God, whereas they are not directly aware of His knowledge. The latter is only inferred from His actions. Typically, when a Śaiva master wishes to establish the existence of two infinite Powers in Śiva, he always starts with the evidence of the Power to act and deduces from it, as its necessary condition, the Power to know.[19] We have seen earlier the special conception of Jñāna implied by this way of reasoning.

A last observation may be useful: the word *Jñāna* in this context is often replaced by *Dṛk* (one can then speak of "the Power of Vision"), never by *Vidyā*.

But let us come back to Śiva and his activity concerning the universe. The Siddhāntins maintain that this activity has no motive other than the ultimate liberation of the souls (the *aṇus*); to wit, the removal of the impurity (*mala*, or *āṇavamala*, "impurity of the soul"), which, from no conceivable beginning, "covers" their natural infinite Power, making them ignorant as well as impotent. For this removal, they say, cannot take place without the souls being given both a body (gross and subtle), and a world to live in, consuming their past *karman* and generating a new one. Through the experiences that the souls will undergo in their successive births, their *mala* will "ripen" and be finally ready to be removed.[20] This is why, and only why, Śiva creates the worlds: a series of "pure" worlds manifested out of a very subtle matter called *bindu*; and a series of "impure" worlds, permeated by the same *bindu* but manifested out of a less subtle matter called *māyā*.[21] Both *māyā* and *bindu* are eternal, both are external to Śiva, and both—but especially *bindu*—are sometimes considered as Śaktis of the God. We shall come back later to this peculiar Śakti of a nonspiritual nature. Having created the worlds, Śiva maintains them in existence for a while, then destroys them at a given moment, only to create them anew—one cycle in this process widely encompassing any known puranic period. The three acts just referred to (*sṛṣṭi*, *sthiti*, and *saṃhāra*) are attributed to the supreme God by all the theistic schools in India, but the Śaivas add two more, concerning, not the whole universe like the first three, but only the souls: Grace (*anugraha*) by which Śiva gives them liberation by loosing them from the *mala*, and Obstruction (*rodha, nirodha, tirobhāva, saṃrakṣaṇa*), by which He maintains them in the worlds—or, to use the technical language of the school, sees that they consume the fruits of their *karman*[22]—and hence ensures their continued association with the products of *māyā* (or *bindu*, if they have already exhausted their *karman*). Grace is said to be the operation of Anugraha-Śakti (Salvific Power), and it takes the form of a *dīkṣā*, which is an act of Śiva, even when it is performed through the agency of a human guru. Obstruction is the operation of Rodha-Śakti (or Nirodha-Śakti—also called Tirodhāna-Śakti, Tirobhāva-Śakti and Vāmā), and it takes the form of various hindrances, which at first sight appear to be added by a malign power to the natural obstacle represented by the *mala*. These two Śaktis, however, are not different: they are but two aspects that the unique Śakti of Śiva—naturally Kriyā-Śakti, but the texts speak only of "Śakti"—assumes in succession with regard to each soul. Rodha-Śakti acts as explained before so long as the *mala* of this soul is not ripe, performing an act that seems to be a punishment but is already a grace in disguise; and She automatically turns into Anugraha-Śakti as soon as the *mala* is ripe, ready to be removed through *dīkṣā*.[23] We come then to the number five for the operations (*kriyās*) of Śiva, each of them associated with one of the Faces of Sadāśiva.[24]

Now, within the activity called *creation* (*sṛṣṭi*), there is a definite operation of Śiva that is of special interest to us: the handing down by God to the men (we shall thereafter forget all the other sentient beings, on earth or elsewhere, and especially those who, living in the "pure" world, beyond *māyā*, know nothing of human predicaments and cares) of his Science, called the *Science of Śiva* (*śivajñāna*), or simply but with the utmost veneration *The Science* (*jñāna*).[25] It takes the form of a body of specific instructions, which the God first revealed to some chosen divine Beings, who handed them down to the men, via a series of intermediaries forming a kind of descending ladder. At the bottom of this ladder, the men receive this teaching in the form of texts, called *Tantras* or *Āgamas*.[26] These texts therefore have Śiva as their author; and though their content has suffered a progressive simplification during the handing down process, to allow for the decreasing faculties of the recipients, it is assumed that they are composed of the very words of Śiva and nothing else.[27] The Āgamas on that account are fully authoritative, as no other scripture (including the Vedas) could be.[28] They are the present God makes to men to lead them toward salvation. For all the other ways, taught in various schools and supposedly salvific, are only blind alleys in the eyes of the Śaivas, or at best roads to some paradises from where the soul necessarily will have to descend.

Returning now to our enquiry, it is clear that, in the present context, the word *jñāna* refers not to the operation of knowing, but to the totality of the information that the devotees of Śiva have to know if they want to attain liberation; that is to say, identity with Śiva. This body of knowledge comprises ritual techniques (mainly), philosophical doctrines, rules of right conduct, details on the composition of the subtle body, and so on.[29] The word *jñāna* therefore is better rendered by "science," rather than "knowledge." Not surprisingly, we find it often replaced by *vidyā*. Now, if we look for a corresponding *kriyā* to this all-comprehensive *jñāna*, it seems that the best candidate would be this "action" of men that consists in the use made by them of this divine gift; that is to say, the practice of the *śāstra* in the broadest sense, beginning with the study of all the teachings without distinction. But we usually do not find such a couple in evidence.

Leaving Śiva and the Āgamas for a moment, we must now consider the human soul, where we find the pair *jñāna-kriyā* as a pale reflection of the one which exists at the highest level. As we already saw, the soul, whose nature is the same as Śiva's, has been reduced to a state of total infirmity by the stain (*mala*) that "covers" its natural powers. To undergo the experiences we have spoken of, and that alone will permit the ripening (and future removal) of this *mala*, the soul of necessity must acquire a minimum of capacity. This is the role of two of the "realities" (*tattvas*) which, engendered by the *māyā*, are parts of the subtle body that the soul is given at the beginning of a new creation: the first one, called *kalā-tattva*, tears up, as it were, a bit of the *mala*, unveiling in part the Power of Action of the soul; whereas the second, called *vidyā-tattva*, slightly reveals the Power of Knowledge, thus enabling the soul to receive (later, and through the working of other *tattvas* like *buddhi*) the necessary information from what will be its environment. Such is the gist of the process—as described for instance in the Mṛgendra[30] and generally accepted by the school—that transforms a wholly impotent being into an agent and a knower. The soul is now endowed with a minute part of its own natural *śakti*, which presents the same dichotomy of knowledge and action as the one we find in the unlimited Power of Śiva or the liberated soul. Only, the dichotomy seems to have here a greater reality; and, what is more disconcerting, the (theoretically) perfect symmetry between knowledge and action recognized in the infinite Śakti seems to have been lost.

The acquisition of the two limited faculties is in effect accomplished in two successive stages—for the *vidyātattva* is begotten by the *kalātattva*, and only after the Kriyā-Śakti has been partly uncovered—whereas it was understood and will always be affirmed that Kriyā-Śakti cannot go without Jñāna-Śakti, so that any unveiling of the one should entail a simultaneous and similar unveiling of the other.[31] This violation of the general law is difficult to account for. Let us for the moment only note that, here too, *kriyā* is given prominence over *jñāna*: the soul, it seems, must acquire the capacity to act before the "wish to know" arises in it.

Whatever explanation we may accept on this point, it remains that the couple formed by the limited knowledge and the limited action of an ordinary man is the reproduction, at a lower level, of the perfect pair constituted by the infinite knowledge and the unbounded action of Śiva and the liberated souls. And this is true whether we consider the two faculties in themselves or in their actual expression.

Statement of Our Problem: Doctrine versus Action According to the Āgamas

The preceding considerations have provided us with a general frame in which to inscribe the limited problem we especially intend to deal with and that concerns the interplay of knowledge and action within the Śaiva Scriptures. This problem can be approached from two different directions: pursuing the soul's epos, we could ask ourselves what are—or what should be, according to the texts—the respective parts that man's two faculties, knowledge and action, must play in his journey toward the goal; or we can consider the texts in themselves and, deviating from the line we have followed up to now, attempt to examine the connection between their theoretical and their practical teachings. We shall adopt the second viewpoint, for the enquiry it will lead to is of greater interest for the study of Śaivism. We shall keep the first question in mind, however, and try to give it an indirect answer while busying ourself with the second. Let us then turn to this problem; to wit, the relation between the doctrine (*jñāna, vidyā*) taught in the Āgamas, and the rituals (*kriyā*) described in the same works.

First of all, attention should be called to the shift in meaning we impose on the word *jñāna*: from the all-comprehensive Science represented by the Āgamas themselves, we pass to only a fraction of it, the doctrine, that is to say, the intellectual conceptions about God, the souls, the world, and so on, formulated by our texts.

Whereas in its larger sense, the knowledge given by Śiva to humankind can in no way be divorced from action, as it comprises the ritual procedures, the right conduct, and so on, in its limited sense of "doctrine," its links with action are no longer evident and can rightly be questioned. It is to this task we shall now address ourself, forgetting for a while all the other meanings of the word *jñāna*.

Some further precisions on the two terms under investigation are needed, taking into account the formal organization of the Āgamas.[32] As is well known, some of them distribute their teachings into four "quarters" (*pādas*): *jñāna-* or *vidyā-*, *kriyā-*, *caryā-*, and *yoga-pāda* (in any order), which respectively deal with doctrine, rituals, right conduct, and yoga. It is often suggested that such is the normal situation, and that all the Āgamas which do not answer this description have lost such or such *pādas*. Without attempting to criticize this hypothesis for the moment, we shall simply ask ourselves whether we can rely on this subdivision for the definition of the two terms of our enquiry: do *jñāna* and *kriyā* correspond respectively to the contents of *jñānapāda* and *kriyāpāda*?

Let us begin with the term *kriyā*. If we look into the contents of those (rare) Āgamas that do possess the four *pādas*,[33] we are struck by the fact that the content of the section called *kriyāpāda* is highly variable. Some Āgamas, like the Suprabheda, list in their *kriyāpāda* all the rituals connected with the temple, but exclude from it those (*dīkṣā*, etc.) that concern the disciples and that they include in their *caryāpāda*. Conversely, an Āgama like the Kiraṇa[34] describes the *dīkṣā* and related rituals in its *kriyāpāda*, but deals with the establishment of images (*pratiṣṭhā*) and similar rituals in its *caryāpāda*. And it is in the *yogapāda* of the same Kiraṇa that we find all the rites connected with death, which, quite naturally, in the other texts are described in the *caryāpāda*. In the same *yogapāda* we also find with some surprise the very typical ritual called *lifting of the marks* (*liṅgoddhāra*); that is, the rite that someone coming from another sect must go through to join the Śaiva sect, and which is usually dealt with in connection with *dīkṣā*. These few examples will be enough to show that it would be a serious mistake to circumscribe the concept of *kriyā* by relying on the classification offered by some chosen texts. One must simply take the word in the general sense of "ritual act," whatever the object and beneficiary of this act and whatever the section where it may be described in such or such Āgama.

This state of affairs should in no way disturb us. It shows only that the subdivision of the teachings of Āgamas (so rarely met with in the extant works) is quite artificial and probably rather late;

and that we should refrain from explaining automatically, on the strength on some formal declarations found in the Āgamas,[35] the absence of *yogapāda* and *caryāpada* (we will leave the *jñānapāda* aside for the moment) in the texts we have by loss of material in the course of time. It is more realistic to admit that, in most cases, the different rituals were first given one after the other, in a logical order perhaps, but without any attempt of classification, and that they only later were forced into prelabeled drawers.

Now about the term *jñāna*, in the sense of "doctrine," or "philosophy." When the text is divided into four *pādas*, we naturally have to look for this doctrine in the *jñānapāda* (frequently called *vidyāpāda*); and we actually find it explained there, more or less clearly, more or less precisely. In the present condition of the majority of the texts, however, no such subdivision exists, or only a (questionable) splitting into a modest *vidyāpāda* and a huge *kriyāpāda*. Shall we then have to limit our study to the rare Āgamas that possess a *vidyāpāda*? If such were the case, the results of our investigation would carry little weight. Fortunately, the situation is not so hopeless, for the texts deprived of a doctrinal section are not on that account without any doctrinal teaching. Much such information is given in the course of ritual descriptions, either in the form of whole chapters,[36] or of groups of verses, or again of stray allusions, all the more precious as they are unsystematic. And this happens even in the texts provided with four *pādas*. Besides, some rituals are transparent as to the ideas that lie behind them and open for us, in this way, interesting and often unexpected vistas on the doctrine. This however happens rarely, and most of the rituals we come across are on the contrary completely opaque—a disturbing fact on which we will have to come back.

We are now in a position to start our enquiry. We shall proceed by asking ourselves two questions: first, is there any tight and regular correspondence between the set of beliefs overtly or covertly accepted by the Āgamas and the ritual edifice they describe? second, which of the two, knowledge or ritual, has priority over the other, inspiring it as it were?

Such an enquiry is set with all kinds of difficulties. Some of them are purely psychological, coming from our own cultural conditioning. We would spontaneously maintain that one thinks before acting—and derive from this fact, insufficiently analyzed, much too easy an answer to the second question—and certainly opine that the ritual therefore must be a faithful expression of the theoretical convictions, a positive answer to the first question, which also betrays a naive confidence in the internal unity of our texts. This first obstacle to an impartial appreciation of the Āgamas is not insuperable, but should not be overlooked.

The most serious difficulties, however, are objective and come from the Āgamas themselves. We do not think here of the absence, in such or such text, of this or that type of information, but of the lack of consensus among our sources. Even if we know well that each Āgama constitutes a whole in itself,[37] the fact that they are put together in a corpus connected with a definite school makes us expect a measure of mutual agreement. What we find is rather disappointing. So far as the ritual is concerned, the diversity is somewhat masked by the enormous mass of the material we have to investigate; and after all, diversity in this domain is but natural, for each group of devotees, starting from a common heritage, may well have invented its own techniques, and it is rather the too great similarity that gives cause for reflection and betrays contacts, imitations, rewritings. But in the field of doctrine, one would anticipate a certain homogeneity, because the school is known to be marked off from the Northern school by a peculiar philosophy. It is therefore a matter of astonishment to find differences among the texts important enough to forbid speaking of *the* Āgamic doctrine.[38] And there are signs that show that the diversity was even greater in the past and has been obliterated by the loss of some texts (probably those furthest from what has become the "orthodox" philosophy) and by the repeated alterations to which the works that have come down to us have been subject.

In the light of what has just been said, it seems that the only safe method for solving our problem is to examine the texts separately, especially (but not solely) those which have their four *pādas*, and give the result for each of them. It is possible however both to simplify and to extend the enquiry, by choosing to take into consideration, in the *vidyā* section, only the teachings shared by the majority of the extant Āgamas or the tenets that, having been expounded with the utmost clarity by the great masters of the ninth to twelfth centuries,[39] have finally been accepted by the school and constitute what we call the *orthodox* philosophy. This means that we shall leave aside almost all the isolated teachings. Such a limitation is to be regretted, but actually is a necessity; besides, it will not impair our work too much, for the consensus is large enough to allow a fruitful investigation. One should only keep in mind that this investigation does not cover the whole range of the extant texts. In any case, these texts are much too numerous and most of them too voluminous to be examined in toto, and a choice therefore is unavoidable. Our selection results simply from our past research. Without attempting to start a fresh enquiry, we shall bring together the various observations made in the course of our Āgamic studies regarding the problem we wish to tackle and that actually have made us sensitive to this problem.

Summing up, we shall compare, on the one hand, the set of theoretical views that have gained authority in the school from a certain time onward and represent, not *the* doctrine of Āgamas, but the last stage of Āgamic philosophy; and, on the other hand, the body of rituals preserved in a broad selection of the texts available to us. It goes without saying that the details of our enquiry cannot find place in a limited paper; only the results will be given, with a few examples to illustrate them. In spite of all these limitations, we hope to be able to provide a convincing account of the situation.

On the Agreement between Doctrine and Ritual

The Declarations of the Texts

To begin with, one must note that the texts themselves affirm that the ritual and the doctrine they teach agree with each other. The contrary indeed would be astonishing, if we remember that each Āgama is supposed to represent a complete (though contracted) version of the Science of Śiva, formulated by the God Himself, and as such is exempt of imperfection, hence of contradiction. And even if we do not share this conviction of the faithful regarding the unblemishedness of the Āgamas, we can be sure that the authors of our texts tried their best to approximate as well as possible the ideal of perfect homogeneity between the different teachings of a given work. It then is quite normal that they should insist on this agreement. Such general declarations may be found anywhere, but they are met most frequently in the introductory chapters. Let us for instance quote the Mṛgendra, where it is announced in the *vidyāpāda* that the utilization (*viniyoga*) of the three fundamental categories there defined (*pati, paśu, pāśa*) will be explained in the *caryā-*, *yoga-*, and *kriyāpāda*.[40] And of course the commentators are always keen, especially when it is not obvious, to show that the agreement is perfect.

Evidence of Agreement

That the preceding claim is not vain is copiously evidenced. We however shall deal only briefly with this part of our demonstration, for most of the readers are convinced in advance of the reality of the agreement between the doctrine and the ritual, and it is not necessary to insist. A few indications therefore will suffice.

Let us first consider the most fundamental tenets of Śaiva-Siddhānta: the conception of Śiva (*pati*), of the soul (*paśu*), and of the bonds of the soul (*pāśa*)—these latter being the congenital stain (*āṇavamala*), the *karman*, and the productions of the *māyā*. No ritual, at least as understood by the commentators, seems at first sight to contradict the philosophical view regarding these categories. For instance, it is said that God is infinite and all-pervasive. Consequently, when He is to be "invited" (ritual of *āvāhana*) in a certain image in order to be worshipped, He is first given a "body" of *mantra*, supposed to be able to "condense" the Energy that is God Himself and allow Him to be shifted, as it were, and brought into the place where one wishes Him to be.[41] A similar process is used for any spatial displacement of the soul—which, in spite of the term *aṇu* by which it is designated, is also all-pervasive and infinite. Another instance of conformity is offered by the ritual of *dīkṣā*, which takes into account quite satisfactorily the different bonds of the soul to be purified, with their specific characteristics, and shows very clearly that, at the end of the rite, the liberated soul is equal to Śiva.[42] And so on.

If we now think of the details of the doctrine, we find them in many cases accurately illustrated by the rites. For instance, the throne of Śiva, on which the God is made to sit during the cult, is often built systematically and in good order with the thirty-six "realities" (*tattva*) which are the bricks of the material world, so that one may clearly understand that it represents this universe.[43] At the top, just below Śiva, we find sitting a number of eminent Beings, like the Vidyeśvaras, whom we know to be exalted souls, living in the purest worlds, together with some Śaktis, whose nature it is more difficult to ascertain.[44] In a still more precise way, the ritual of *dīkṣā*, already alluded to, makes use of all the constituents of the universe, considered as included in the particular "road" (*adhvan*) that the guru has chosen, among the six possible ones, for this purificatory journey of the soul that is called *dīkṣā*. It is even only with reference to the *dīkṣā* that one can rightly understand the meaning of "the six roads" (*ṣaḍadhvan*), so often mentioned among the specific tenets of Śaivism. These instances could be multiplied easily.

We are thus inclined to admire the solidity of the whole construction and conclude in favor of a satisfying homogeneity between the doctrinal teachings of the Āgamas and the structure and content of the rituals they propound. With a precision, however: the agreement concerns the doctrine actually taught by the Āgamas, not the one accepted by the Tamil school of Śaiva-Siddhānta.[45]

Evidence of Disagreement

The optimistic picture derived from the preceding considerations unfortunately cannot stand a more detailed and critical examination of our texts. We are now going to show up the main defects and cracks of the seemingly solid Āgamic building, arranging these anomalies according to their nature and origin. This negative part of our criticism will be given more weight than the positive part, for the need to convince is greater, and also on account of the greater diversity of the remarks we shall be led to make.

Cases of Open Disagreement

We shall first of all deal with the most easily perceived of these anomalies: a discrepancy between the doctrine held by a given Āgama and the ritual instructions given in the same text.

There are some cases of patent contradictions. For instance, one may cite the Raurava which, in its chapter on *dīkṣā* (belonging to *kriyāpāda*), describes the "path of *tattvas*" (*tattvādhvan*) as made of thirty-six *tattvas*,[46] whereas in several passages of the *vidyāpāda*, only thirty are recognized.[47] In fact, the contradiction is not so much between doctrine and practice as between two theoretical teachings, for the chapter on *dīkṣā* we are alluding to is devoted to theoretical considerations only, the description of the ritual itself is altogether absent. We shall point to other similar cases later. Another inconsistency of the same text is less obvious but nonetheless characteristic, bearing as it does on an important triad of *tattvas*, not belonging to the list of thirty (or thirty-six), but offering a new scale into which the latter find place: *ātmatattva*, *vidyātattva*, and *śivatattva*—as per the usual sequence, the one retained by the "orthodox" school. Now, the *vidyāpāda* of the Raurava, which mentions them in a descending order, gives the list: *śiva-*, *ātma-*, *vidyā-*, which is original in placing the *ātmatattva* in the intermediate place;[48] and it also defines them in a peculiar way, which agrees with this sequence. But when these very same *tattvas* appear in the ritual of *pavitrārohaṇa*,[49] the formula is "from *ātmatattva* to *śivatattva*" (in a certain case), or "from *śivatattva* to *ātmatattva*" (in another case), that shows that it is the usual sequence, implying a quite different conception of these *tattvas*, which is accepted in this ritual. We hold this disagreement between the two sections of Raurava as much more revealing than what at first sight may appear to be the case; for this triad of *tattvas* finds in the ritual (especially that of *pratiṣṭhā*) a regular use, which testifies of the importance it once must have had in the ontology of the school and no longer corresponds to the feeble attention it is given in the "orthodox" texts. It might be that the *vidyāpāda* of Raurava has preserved an old vision that it would be interesting to try and trace in other works too.[50]

Further instances of the same inconsistency could be cited, most of them of less weight: variations, in the same Āgama, in the distribution of the *tattvas* among the five *kalās* (these are "parts" of *bindu*, the subtle matter of the universe) as explained in the *vidyāpāda* and as evidenced in the ritual; ascription, by the *vidyāpāda*, of a definite function to a certain Face of Sadāśiva, when the ritual has another version, and so forth.

In most cases, the opposition between doctrine and ritual does not take the form of a patent contradiction, but rather of dissymmetry: either the ritual makes use of notions totally absent from the doctrinal part; or (less frequently), some teachings of doctrinal nature are given that do not find place in the ritual, though they could and are actually used in rituals described in other texts.

Instances of the first type are many. Let us cite the Mṛgendra where the most important *dīkṣā* makes use of the path of the five *kalās*[51] (see earlier), whereas the *vidyāpāda* totally ignores these realities.[52] Something similar happens with the Raurava, with this difference that the author to whom we owe the last chapters of the work (evidently added at a later stage) was conscious of the absence in the *vidyāpāda* of any teaching concerning the *kalās* and tried to compensate for this omission by introducing in the chapter on *dīkṣā*[53] some (incomplete) information about them. Unfortunately these details are of no use there, since the ritual of *dīkṣā*, as already noted, is not even sketched; but they are useful for the understanding of the ritual of *antyeṣṭi* given in the preceding chapter. It is clear that the Raurava in its ancient (we dare not say "original") form knew nothing of the *kalās*. Nor did it know anything in general of what is called the "sextuple path" (*kalās, tattvas, bhuvanas, varṇas, padas* and *mantras*), described in the same chapter on *dīkṣā*.[54]

The opposite situation prevails in another series of texts, which have a very simple procedure for *dīkṣā* without the "purification of the six *adhvans*" that characterizes others, although they somewhere else include a development on this sextuple path. This is the case with the Suprabheda, which gives an account of the six *adhvans* in its *vidyāpāda*, even though four of them do not correspond to any ritual, and which awkwardly inserts (obviously in an interpolated fragment) some precisions concerning the five *kalās* in the very chapter on *dīkṣā* that has no use for them, no more than any other chapter on ritual.[55] The case in some ways resembles that of the Raurava, but actually is worse, as here a certain ritual of *dīkṣā* is effectively described, which comes in sharp contrast with the useless teaching placed in its midst, and as this teaching about the five *kalās* is in contradiction with the *vidyāpāda*, where the *kalādhvan* is made, not of the five *kalās* of the *bindu*, but of the thirty-eight *kalās* of Sadāśiva.

Another theoretical teaching that sometimes is given and never systematically used is the conception of five *ātmans*,[56] which still could have influenced the *dīkṣā*, had it been accepted when this ritual was built.

Masked Opposition

All the preceding cases consist of formal clashes, expressed in the wording of the texts and therefore susceptible to be found out by a mere compilation of words or formulas. They are not very numerous, for the evident reason that the Śaiva masters who wrote, rewrote, or altered the Āgamas at different stages did their best, as suggested earlier, to make them appear convincingly homogeneous, adding the missing (or what they considered missing) information, and alas most probably suppressing this or that teaching that they deemed out of line. We shall consider with greater attention the unavowed or unrecognized contradictions that we readers have to trace by a detectivelike investigation, helped not a little by the persistence, in the ritual, of fossilized formulas that appear to have come unchanged from a hoary past.

In a first category, we shall place oppositions masked by superficial agreement. These could have been dealt with in the preceding section, were not the agreement so heavily insisted on that the reader is at first carried away by the proferred explanations and only on second thought sees the difficulty. Let us take as an example the rite of *āvāhana*, that is, the invitation of the Supreme Śiva (or any God or Goddess) in a given receptacle, usually a material image. We have already noted as a positive indication that the way this action is performed suits the conception that the school has of Śiva, taking into account in particular His pervasiveness and infinity. This is the impression derived from the most elaborated texts, especially the *paddhatis*. Now, we come across less-sophisticated descriptions that seem to reflect a state of affairs when the divinity so "invited" in the image apparently was not conceived in this way, but as a mass of Energy that the practitioner could lay his hands on and move according to his wish. The rites that follow the *āvāhana* confirm this frame of mind. In effect, once brought into the image, this God or Goddess has to be "fixed" (rite of *sthāpana*), made "present" (*sannidhāna*), "detained" (*nirodhana*) so that He cannot escape, and finally "enveloped" (*avakuṇṭhana*) to become hidden to others. It is almost certain that this series of actions was first conceived in the context of the cult of the *sādhaka* (a person we shall meet again and whose unique aim is to win the power of a chosen deity), and in old times concerned any divinity, not especially Śiva. Besides, the material image most probably was an impermanent one, like a *sthaṇḍila* (elevated platform made of sand or grains), a *liṅga* made of dough, a pot of water, and so on. Hence the necessity of *āvāhana* (in the literal sense) and the rites immediately following. When this very same sequence of actions, with the same denominations, became a normal part of the cult of Śiva, whoever the practitioner, whatever the context or the aim, it had of course to be reinterpeted to suit the new situation. And it was; but with some uneasiness in the explanations, which indirectly substantiate our hypothesis that these rites are not coeval with the conception of Śiva upheld by the Āgamas. We are not contending that they are out of place in the cult of the supreme God, only that they certainly have not been invented by persons having in mind the greatness, the all-powerfulness, the uniqueness of Śiva; it is in this respect that they are opposed to, or at least in bad harmony with, the philosophy of the school. And they are still less-adapted to the worship on a permanent image, which the God, after He has been introduced by the ritual of "establishment" (*pratiṣṭhā*), is never supposed to leave and therefore cannot be "invited" into, in the normal sense of the word, no more than He can be "dismissed" from it (rite of *visarjana*). Here, too, the Śaiva masters are not at a loss for explanations, which they too often mix with the ones that they offer to get out of the first difficulty and that anyhow do not solve all the problems.[57]

In still more glaring contradiction with the general conception of Śiva are the numberless protective and purificatory rites that precede or follow the cult of Śiva proper and that inevitably arouse perplexity in those who imagine the cult as a pure manifestation of devotion. Why are there so many precautions to defend the place of worship against malevolent beings? Why are there so many offerings to placate them? Why perform these apotropaic rites to efface the evil eye from the image of God after the temple *pūjā*? Why all that, and so many other similar procedures, since Śiva, ever-present in the permanent images, and all-powerful, surely could see to His own and the place's protection? But we shall speak later of this category of rites.

Other cases may be cited with respect to the conception of *karman*. The Śaivas share the general view of *karman* as the result of past actions, adding as a precision that these actions were accomplished by the individual in the "impure worlds"; that is to say, the part of the universe that has taken its origin in *māyā* and is therefore situated below the *māyā-tattva*. They often insist that the only way for an individual to get rid of this bond is to "consume" it totally, in the form of various "fruits," a seemingly impossible task, which nevertheless is accomplished during the ritual of *dīkṣā*, through the power of mantras. In the case of "liberating *dīkṣā*" (*nirvāṇadīkṣā*, which is *the dīkṣā* when no other precision is given), this consumption is total, with the exception of the *karman* whose effects are manifested in this life (*prārabdha-karman*).[58] As we have said earlier, the rite broadly tallies with the theory. Still we may mention some discrepancies: (1) In its most elaborated form, which also is the commonest (the one we find in Pūrva-Kāmika, Mṛgendra, the *paddhati* of Somaśambhu, etc.), the ritual takes the soul along one of the "six paths" (*adhvans*) we have spoken of, from the bottom of the universe up to the level of Śiva, ensuring at each level the simultaneous consumption of *karman* by all the bodies that the soul, in the absence of *dīkṣā*, would have taken on in succession for this purpose. Now, the rites are repeated exactly in the same way at each level, though the uppermost among them (two among five, if the path of *kalās* is chosen) belong to the pure worlds, beyond *māyā*, where no *karman* is supposed to exist. The commentators perceive the incongruity and, in accordance with some texts, speak of "pure *karman*" in these domains[59]—a notion not easy to admit. (2) In the same context of *dīkṣā*, one meets rather often with the affirmation that the past *karman* has been "burned up" by the rite;[60] and though such a contention may be supported by a passage of the Kiraṇa, everywhere quoted,[61] it clashes with the fact that the ritual, as usually described, shows the consumption of the past *karman*, not its burning up. Only the seeds of future *karman* are burned. (3) Some texts describe a ritual called *reanimation of karman* (*karma-sañjīvana*), that the guru must perform when he has given a *dīkṣā* to a wrong recipient. The obvious meaning, openly accepted by some unsophisticated texts, is that the *karman* which had been annihilated by the *dīkṣā* (either consumed or burned up, but in this context the second vision prevails) is restored, and hence, the effect of the rite cancelled. This of course creates some difficulty, since it goes against the affirmation that the *dīkṣā* brings a real change and therefore is irreversible; so much so that the Mṛgendra for instance prefers to reject the direct meaning, interpreting the rite as a *prāyaścitta* intended to avert the bad consequences of the fault made by the guru.[62] This solution of the difficulty, all but convincing, betrays the uneasiness of some Śaiva masters faced with what we consider to be residual rites introduced long ago within the Āgamic body of rituals without much thought, and too firmly rooted to simply be eliminated when the philosophical reflexion developed. In any case, it seems clear that, in the last two examples, we are faced with a conception of *karman* that is different from that which the school advocates.

A similar difficulty is aroused by another rite which is part of the elaborated *dīkṣā*: the offering by the guru, to different divinities, of the subtle body of the pupil who is being initiated (the rite is called *puryaṣṭaka-samarpaṇa*). We have explained elsewhere,[63] first, that this rite supposes a simpler conception of the subtle body than the one commonly accepted by the school, and second, that it was first devised as a *dīkṣā* by itself and only later has been incorporated into a complex ritual where its necessity is anything but evident.

We may adduce a last case in the same category. It concerns a rite that comes at the end of this long purification, called *nirvāṇa-dīkṣā*, and consists in the solemn enumeration, by the guru, of the six Perfections now possessed by the soul.[64] These are no other than the Perfections of the Supreme Śiva: Omniscience, Contentment, and so on. Now, the rite is called *guṇāpādana*, the direct meaning of which is "production of the *guṇas*." One understands naturally that they are given as a kind of gift; and this interpretation is confirmed unambiguously by the mantras recited at that time, each one accompanied by an oblation in the fire: "Oh *ātman*, be omniscient!" The name of the rite (or the verbs by which it is introduced), the mantras, and the fact that, as a rule, an oblation accomplishes something, all that seems to prove that, at this stage of the *dīkṣā*, the soul gets perfections it did not possess before. But this openly contradicts an important tenet of Śaiva-Siddhānta; to wit, that the soul essentially is equal to Śiva and appears as such once its bonds have been removed. Since the *dīkṣā* has effected this purification (the soul later will be joined with some impurities connected with its body to eat up its *prārabdha*, but at this stage it is perfectly free from any stain), the "being-Śiva" (*śivatva*) must reveal itself spontaneously and at the same time the Perfections that characterize this condition—and this, without any ritual to "produce" them.

Such is the theory of *guṇābhivyakti*, specific to our Śaivas. This is why the commentators refuse the normal interpretation of the preceding ritual and explain that it is intended only to make known to the world the new greatness of the soul. In fact, the ritual comes probably from a sect which, though accepting the equality of the liberated soul with Śiva (*śivasamatā*), did not advocate the theory of *abhivyakti*: either the Pāśupatas, or the Mahāvratas, or (less likely) the Kāpālikas, for all of them satisfy this condition.[65]

We may group in a second category the cases where a ritual injunction is ambiguous enough to admit of contradictory interpretations. Many of them are concerned with Śakti, and the ambiguity comes from the fact that the Āgamas are not quite clear about the ontological status of what they speak of as Śakti. As already hinted at, the most influential among them—those we have called *orthodox*—know two quite different supreme Śaktis (both occasionally termed *Parā*): the own Śakti of Śiva, inseparable from Him, and the "external" Śakti, of unconscious (*jaḍa*) nature, whom Śiva acts upon ("excites," as the texts say) to create the world. The latter, which is no other than the *bindu*, several times mentioned[66] (we may write Bindu, as it is often likened to a Goddess), is the *materia prima* of the pure worlds and pervades the rest of the universe as well. She is called Parigrahaśakti (the Śakti "chosen," or "seized," or "espoused"),[67] but she has other names too: Mahāmāyā, Kuṭilā, and Kuṇḍalinī being the most frequent. Such is the vision generally shared by the great masters of the past and that one may expect to be reflected in the ritual.

Let us take as our first example the "construction" and worship of the throne (*āsana*) of Śiva, which comes as a necessary preamble to the cult of Śiva Himself. This throne is made of mantras, each of them, once recited, assuring the presence of a certain reality. Now, the first Power to be invoked, at the bottom of the throne, generally is the "Sustaining Power" (*ādhāraśakti*), upon which all the rest is piled up.[68] This Śakti is sometimes identified with the gigantic Tortoise that the Purāṇas (and the Āgamas as well) describe as the support of the world, but this poetic vision presents no difficulty. The difficulty lies in the nature of this particular Power: which of the two Śaktis recognized by our school is the Ādhāraśakti? Logically, we would say Kuṭilā, because the throne itself is made up with the very *tattvas* issued of, or pervaded by, this subtle matter, and actually it is what we read sometimes.[69] But many commentators understand Her to be the Kriyāśakti, whom we know to be a form of the own Śakti of Śiva.[70] There seems to be a way of reconciling the two points of view: decide that Kriyāśakti, in this context, simply is a synonym for *Bindu.* Though this solution would have the support of some texts,[71] it does not remove every difficulty; for the mere fact that the name Kriyāśakti was introduced in the list of synonyms of Bindu testifies of conflicting doctrines about this reality, that the ritual descriptions seem to ignore.

An ambiguity of the same kind, though much more annoying, concerns the very consort of Sadāśiva. This Goddess plays a role in several rituals, among which we shall retain, as most characteristic, the worship of the throne, just spoken of, and the establishment of the *liṅga* (*liṅga-pratiṣṭhā*). At the end of the *āsanapūjā*, before the God is invited and made to sit by Her side, She is invoked, under the name of Manonmanī, on the receptacle of the lotus that constitutes the uppermost part of the throne and surrounded by eight Śaktis installed on the petals. Opinions already vary about these eight, some authors connecting them with the eight Vidyeśvaras (who are always considered as exalted souls, not as aspects of Śiva), whereas others consider them as different forms of the Supreme Śakti.[72] But here we are interested only in Manonmanī, the "wife" of Sadāśiva. Is She the personification of Śiva's own inherent Śakti? Or something else? The texts are silent on this point. The case of *pratiṣṭhā* is slightly more complex. Outwardly, this ritual consists in the junction of the *liṅga* with its "pedestal" (*pīṭha*), by way of a series of rites deliberately suggesting a coitus. In truth, it is the union of the two divinities represented by the material objects. And since we read in quite a number of texts, as an introduction to this ritual, that "the *liṅga* is Śiva, the *pīṭha* is Śakti"—or some equivalent formula, usually given without any further precision—it may be said that the essence of *pratiṣṭhā* is the union of Śiva with Śakti. All Āgamas agree with this general definition.[73] The difficulty begins when we try to determine the nature of this Śakti. The ritual, as generally described, gives no clue. The mantras recited respectively on the *liṅga* and the *pīṭha*, or on the two vases containing the water that will be poured over these two objects, are respectively that of Śiva and that of a goddess called Manonmanī, or Gaurī, or Umā,[74] without any reference to one or the other of the two Śaktis (Śiva's own, and the Bindu) recognized by the theologians of the school. So that we have the same representation as the one met with in the *āsanapūjā*—not surprising, as the material *pīṭha* is nothing but the concretisation of the mantric *āsana.* And both rituals pose the same problem: who is the Goddess who plays the part of the consort of Śiva? Here, too, as with Ādhāraśakti but for different reasons, it seems that the logic would rule out the inherent Śakti of Śiva. How could She be represented by a Goddess seated on the lotus before the God is invited, as they are inseparable? Above all, how could She be invoked in the *pīṭha*, before the *pratiṣṭhā* is accomplished, without Śiva also being present, and Śiva in the *liṅga*, without Her being present? It would be more satisfactory to understand Manonmanī (or Gaurī, etc.) as a form of Bindu, because the name Parigraha-Śakti, given to Bindu, evokes the status of a Wife and we often read that, from the union of Śiva with this Goddess, the worlds are born.[75] But unfortunately no text even says so in the present context. On the contrary, some Āgamas identify Manonmanī with the inherent Śakti of Śiva.[76] And, what is more disturbing, all the commentators agree in explaining the word *Śakti*, in the stock phrase given earlier, by Kriyāśakti. They probably rely on another declaration, found in several Āgamas and often quoted, that "the *liṅga* is Jñānaśakti, the *pīṭha* is Kriyāśakti";[77] but, as this formula raises new difficulties,[78] we shall not linger over it and simply recognize our incapacity to decide, with the sole help of the texts we know, whether Manonmanī is the own Śakti of Śiva, or Bindu. There is even a third possibility, which looks rather attractive, though we have never seen it even hinted at: the consort of Śiva could be an independent reality pertaining to the domain of the Conscious (*cit*), either an exalted soul, like so many other Śaktis who intervene here and there in the ritual, or the most eminent member of a category "*śakti*," that some Āgamas count among the fundamental ones (*padārthas*). This last view does not fit the orthodox philosophy of the school, but this is surely not a sufficient reason to reject it. So, the question of the identity of Manonmanī remains unsolved for the moment. It should be investigated in as many texts as possible, but there is a high probability that no solution will come out, which could be acceptable in all cases. From this failure, however, one should not arrive at the conclusion that the rituals we are concerned with (*āsanapūjā* and *pratiṣṭhā*) are faulty, in the sense that they are unable to choose between conflicting doctrines about the Śakti. More probably, these rituals, especially the second, were essentially conceived long before the doctrines about Śakti first saw the light, in circles of devotees totally innocent of the subtleties of the later philosophy, and for whom it was enough to know that the God had a Wife (whatever Her ontological status), represented by this object we call *throne* or *pedestal*. The few indications that the later texts consider necessary to add pose more questions than they solve. We may add here that the South Indian temples recognize, in agreement with some Āgamic instructions,[79] three forms of Śiva's Śakti: the Yogaśakti who, as the *pīṭha*, is ever-united with the God (Himself the *liṅga*) in the *garbhagṛha*; the Bhogaśakti ("the One to be enjoyed"), represented by a movable statue in the room that just precedes this inner sanctuary; and the Vīraśakti ("the Heroic One"), who reigns in Her own sanctuary. In spite of inevitable attempts, on the part of late commentators, at paralleling this triad with Icchā, Jñāna, and Kriyā,[80] it seems that here we are faced with quite another vision, which probably is more or less inspired by village cults and agrees with the temple ritual much better than the theoretical classifications we have considered up to now.

Instances of the same type are not lacking, we have called attention to a few of them in a prior work, to whom we refer the readers.[81] In some cases, an ambiguity leads finally to a modification of a ritual. We have found, for example, a passage of the *paddhati* of Aghoraśiva, where this author introduces in the *dīkṣā* a rite that his model (the *paddhati* of Somaśambhu) does not mention and that does not tally with the doctrine advocated by this famous dualist master; and this unhappy addition is in all probability caused by a misinterpretation of the ambiguous term *śakti-tattva* in the corresponding fragment of the Kāmika.[82] The parallel word *śiva-tattva* (meaning sometimes Bindu, sometimes the Supreme Śiva) is also frequently responsible for irritating enigmas.

We have kept for the end the most important ambiguity, which results in the utter impossibility to connect even the more eloquent among the rituals with either monism or dualism. It really is disconcerting to discover that we cannot establish the dualism of our school through the rituals it teaches. No detail of the cult of Śiva, no phase of the *dīkṣā*, clearly speaks in favor of one or the other of the two doctrines that traditionally oppose the Śaiva-Siddhānta to the Kashmir Śaivism. We do see that the soul, during the *dīkṣā*, is progressively freed of its bonds finally turned into "a" Śiva, with all the Perfections that pertain to the God Himself. But there is no ground to affirm with the sole aid of the ritual that "this" Śiva remains independent and does not merge into the Supreme Śiva, nor that the bonds (*pāśa*) that prevented the real nature of the soul to manifest itself have a reality different from that of the God. The ritual could be performed exactly in the same way, were the *pāśa* only apparently separate from Śiva, and the soul no other than the God. And this actually is the case: the *dīkṣā* is described in some treatises accepted as their own by the Northern school—for instance the Svacchanda-Tantra—in exactly the same way as it is in the Kāmika, the Mṛgendra, or the Somaśambhu-paddhati which all belong to Śaiva-Siddhānta.[83] Of course there are some verses in the Svacchanda that try to prevent a dualistic (or rather pluralistic) interpretation of the ritual, but they may have been added at a later stage; and it is usually the commentator who persuades us that we are reading a monistic Tantra.[84] Actually, the probability seems high that the ritual of *dīkṣā* as described in the books we mentioned was first conceived in accordance with a pluralistic view, which accounts more directly for many details. But, even if this were true, the fact that this ritual has been preserved almost without change in a school that rejects this philosophy is eloquent in itself, betraying as it does the comparative independence of even the most elaborate and systematic rituals with respect to doctrine. The observation naturally applies to the (rare) Āgamas, like Ajita and Suprabheda, which teach what looks very much like a monism: their philosophical portion, if genuinely theirs (that is, not the result of a late alteration of the texts) does not show itself in the ritual—at least we could not perceive any connection or only dubious ones.[85]

Case of Totally Opaque Rituals

We have so far confined ourself almost exclusively to a limited category of rituals: the daily cult (*nityapūjā*) and the *dīkṣā* and connected rites, which are described both in the texts solely concerned with private worship (the one that is performed, for their own benefit, by the initiated Śaivas) and in the texts dealing principally with temple ceremonies. We can put in the same class the most characteristic phases of the installation of images (*pratiṣṭhā*) and perhaps a few occasional ceremonies like the *pavitrārohaṇa*. The common mark of these rituals is that, in a sense, they express a certain doctrine, so that we could expect them to reveal in their structure or in their details the main tenets of the school. They therefore were the first to be investigated.

Now, the Āgamas, especially those dealing with temple life, are crammed with a number of rituals, either independent or included in the preceding ones (or for that matter in any other), which by nature have a much looser connection with philosophy. They of course bear the Śaiva mark: the mantras used are Śaiva, and the various divinities invoked belong to the vast Śaiva family. One could even say that these rituals, because of the very number of the divinities they involve, and the spirit that breathes through them, in a way are more characteristically Śaiva than those we have studied until now. But the Śaivism they express is not linked with any definite philosophy. It is not the place here to analyze one such ritual in detail, noting at every step the doctrinal elements that are implied by the acts of which it is made. But were this work done, what would emerge as presupposed convictions would consist only in very general beliefs, some shared by all the theistic schools in India, others more specifically Śaiva. We may cite among the first ones the belief in a God (here, Śiva) who is unique, all-powerful, aloof but still ready to help His true devotees, and whom one must satisfy, not only by the display of devotion and the practice of virtues, but through specific offerings to be made according to rule; side by side, the uncontradictory conviction that the other Forces that govern the world should have their share of attention, even if they occupy secondary posts; and of course a solid faith in the power of mantras, as well as a certain knowledge of their handling. Among the more specific ones are the conviction that Śiva may be won over through special techniques, especially repetitions of His mantras, a science totally independent of any theory on the nature of speech,[86] accompanied by asceticism and eventually yoga practices; and that one in this way can get rid more or less totally of the limitations of human nature, acquiring thus extraordinary powers and, in the best case, the status of Śiva. One should also mention the belief in the existence of a huge scale of worlds, which offer a vast range of enjoyments, and of a number of powerful Beings, who may be either benevolent or malevolent and are accessible through their specific mantras. The law of *karman* is naturally accepted, special stress being laid on the misfortunes that ensue from forbidden acts. It would be difficult, we think, to discover more precise convictions behind the rites we have in mind; to wit, all the rituals destined to correct ritual mistakes (*prāyaścittas*) or to avert the dangers brought by misbehavior or by the play of external factors (*śāntis* of all kind); the worship of the Planets and especially powerful divinities like the fierce forms of Śiva, Gaṇeśa, Caṇḍeśa, or the Mothers, as well as a number of minor ones. A lot of isolated rites of the same kind are parts of the daily *pūjā*, of the *dīkṣā*, of the *pratiṣṭhā*: elimination of Obstacles in the beginning of the *pūjā* (private or other); protection of the ritual site by means of divine Weapons; averting of the evil eye at the end of the temple cult; repeated oblations in the fire in the form of *prāyaścittas*; placating of various Powers by means of *balis*; and so on. The list could be lengthened almost indefinitely, and there is no exaggeration in contending that these rituals make up the bulk of most Āgamas, especially those devoted to temple activity.[87]

As a conclusion to this part of our study, we may say the following:

1. Only a few rituals are linked by nature to specific doctrines, and even they do not always correspond to the accepted tenets of the school—some betraying forgotten doctrines, some admitting of different interpretations.

2. The vast majority of rituals are perfectly indifferent to the specific philosophy of the school and therefore assumedly older than the elaboration of this philosophy.

On the Primacy of Ritual

We started from the reassuring image of a logical Āgamic construction, where doctrine and ritual were in full agreement. Then we showed up one after another the various faults of the system, and finally came to the rather pessimistic conclusion we have just voiced, and that, while answering negatively to the first question posed at the beginning, suggests also the answer to the second. We are now going to pursue the same direction in showing that this situation is not the consequence of any degenerative process, but can be explained simply by the almost exclusive interest in ritual the Śaivas of old seem to have evinced. It is clear that the authors of our texts were concerned primarily with ritual techniques, and it is this body of techniques that they meant to preserve by writing the Āgamas. The concern with doctrine came later and reflections of philosophical nature were generally grafted (often awkwardly) on an already extant construction. Of this, we can adduce many proofs.

We can begin with the remark that 80 percent at least of the content of extant Āgamas (the majority as yet unpublished) deals with rituals. Of course entire sections on doctrine may have been lost. But such losses should not be overestimated; and it is highly probable that, from the very beginning, the practical teachings (especially ritual procedures, but also rules of behavior and perhaps yoga) were by far the most abundant, if not the sole ones. Besides, if some *vidyāpādas* actually have been lost, this is a proof, on the one hand, of the little use the Śaiva masters had of them, as they failed to protect and copy these parts of the manuscripts, and, on the other hand, of the comparative autonomy of ritual toward doctrine, as the ritual largely has been preserved, both in writing and practice.

Let us at this juncture insist on the fact that the details of the doctrine which necessarily had to be known by the practitioners for the right performance of the rites—for instance, the form of the divinities that had to be meditated on, the list of the worlds where the soul might happen to take a body during the process of *dīkṣā*, and above all the teachings concerning the origin, formation, and recitation of mantras—always are given as a normal part of the *kriyāpāda* when there is no *vidyāpāda*,[88] and even sometimes when there is one.[89]

One must also give some attention to the explicit declarations of several commentators that all the teachings of the Āgamas are subservient to ritual, or that the theoretical knowledge is necessary for the efficacy of ritual practices (considered as essential).[90]

Significant too is the extreme importance attached by our texts to the proper performance of the rites, whereas they hardly speak of the proper understanding of the doctrine. At every step we meet with detailed statements of the dangers that threaten the practitioner —or, in case of temple cults, the prince himself, and the country at large—when a ritual is done in the wrong way or a forbidden action is performed, and of the possibility of averting these awful consequences by a "repairing act" (as we like to call the *prāyaścittas*), in preference to "expiations"). The occasions for transgression are countless,[91] but all concern definite ritual actions, or more generally, activities governed by a rule contained in the Āgamas. Similarly, the *prāyaścittas* are extremely varied, from a short recitation (*japa*) of a single mantra to elaborate rituals extending over several days, but they are acts and solely acts. If it is objected that the preceding remarks simply express the law of *karman*, we shall insist in pointing out that it is often affirmed that one may act (and hence sin) with the body, the speech, and the mind,[92] but that nevertheless in practice only the first two categories are taken into consideration in the context of *prāyaścitta*. This perhaps is natural, because a wrong thought or opinion is less easily detected than a vocal or physical mistake. But what about the act of teaching? It is an vocal activity and, as such, could be an occasion for sinning; still it is never considered this way; the sole transgressions mentioned in this context concern the neglect of regular holidays; and the sole dangers spoken of come from external polluting factors like dogs or from disturbing ones like earthquakes or cyclones.[93] And we do not hear of any threat on a Śaiva who goes about spreading a doctrine that does not fit exactly with the one contained (or supposedly implied) in the Āgama he is connected with, so long as he does not speak ill of Śiva, his guru, and the Āgamas. Can we not say then that our texts are obsessed with ritual and set really little value on theory?

Side by side with the teachings concerning transgressions,

we can put the rule that strictly forbids the "mixture of Tantras" (*tantrasaṅkara*). It is important to note that this interdiction is always given in a ritual context. For instance, we read in the Kāmika that, when the rites concerning a temple have been started with a certain Tantra, they must be carried on with the very same Tantra until the end—from the initial ploughing to the cult.[94] This basic rule implies that there were differences in the procedures between the Tantras (or Āgamas) and that each of them was self-sufficient. But the habit of mutual comparison and borrowing must have become current at a certain time, for the Kāmika and other treatises add that one however may take from another text what is missing in his own, provided one sticks to the Āgamas of the Siddhānta.[95] Anyhow, what we wish to point out is that no similar rule is given concerning the doctrine, though it does not seem worse to recognize that the philosophy perhaps was not exactly the same in all the Āgamas than to admit that their practices were different; and a warning not to mix doctrinal elements would have been neither groundless nor useless.

Let us now consider the well-known rule of secrecy, which forbids any master to allow any uninitiated person (a *paśu*) to study the Āgamas[96] or even to listen to them from a distance.[97] It is usual to explain this interdiction by saying that the Āgamas, enunciated by Śiva, are too holy for a *paśu* to hear or read. We think it likelier that the group that had recorded its ritual procedures in a certain text (for such probably was the way the Āgamas were composed) was not ready to let others be acquainted with them; they actually were keys of power and their diffusion would have endangered the party. For it is a fact that a big part of the Āgamic teaching aims at the physical security and well-being of the group concerned, through rituals both protective and aggressive, which we would call *magical* and were better kept secret. Assuredly the theology was not concerned.

The above rule of secrecy is given a better light if put side by side with the restrictions imposed on a person who apparently was never really trusted, a new convert. After a ceremony that was intended to efface all traces of former initiations, he could be given a full *dīkṣā*—that is to say, obtain potential liberation; but he was forbidden to practice, either for himself or for the benefit of others—and even not allowed to know—the special mantras of the group he had just entered. Such at least are the instructions given by the Mṛgendra, whose commentator characteristically remarks: "This means that they [the converts] have no right to utilize the section on ritual (*kriyākāṇḍa*), which has been transmitted (*āmnāta*) in view of mastering the mantras."[98] Such restrictions (which also imply a modified form of *nityapūjā*) may be summed up by saying that these converts could not be either *ācāryas* or *sādhakas*.

We may insert here some considerations on this particular initiate, the *sādhaka*,[99] whose very importance in the Āgamas supports our thesis. He is the one who, after his *dīkṣā*, attaches himself to a definite divinity (his "chosen deity," *iṣṭadevatā*), devoting all his time and energy to win over this God or Goddess, by means of meditation (*dhyāna*), cults (*pūjās*), fire sacrifices (*homas*), and especially lengthy recitations of His or Her mantras (*japas*). This practice (*sādhana*), sometimes of a kind better known from extreme marginal sects,[100] often implies a severe asceticism. It is done in a secluded place and must be pursued up to the advent of what is called *success* (*siddhi*, or *mantrasiddhi*), which consists in the complete mastering of the mass of Energy represented by the chosen deity. The *sādhaka* henceforth is free to make use of his power at will, but the kind of *siddhi* thus acquired varies according to the intensity of *sādhana* and the nature of the divinity involved, ranging from the possession of some supernatural powers to a total divinization. Most of the Āgamas that deal with private worship (and definitely seem to convey an older vision of the Śaiva religious activity than the ones devoted to temple rituals) were written having especially the *sādhakas* in view. This is the case with the Mṛgendra and the Mataṅgapārameśvara, both published. But the *sādhaka* is conspicuous in many others as well, including some texts interested mainly in temples, like the Kiraṇa;[101] and his importance has lasted up to a time (two or three centuries ago?) when a change of outlook occurred and he was put at the back of the stage, if not totally ignored. Now, this *sādhaka* was solely busied with rituals, he had nothing else to do, even was forbidden to comment on the Āgamas; and the rituals he was engaged in often were long, difficult, even dangerous. The qualities required from a candidate to the aspersion (*sādhakābhiṣeka*) that allowed an already initiated Śaiva to enter this path were for this reason those demanded from a warrior and a yogin combined: courage, endurance, enterprise, and so on, as well as more common moral virtues. The list is really impressive,[102] and if we compare it to the list of qualities required from an *ācārya*, or demanded of a candidate to the *nirvāṇadīkṣā*, we cannot but conclude that it was deemed easier to become a guru than to become a *sādhaka*, and still easier to aim "only" at liberation. Because of his social status and authority and his privilege, shared by no other initiate, to give *dīkṣās* and *abhiṣekas*, the *ācārya* of course was considered the highest among the Śaivas of a definite group, but the *sādhakas* came immediately after and were regarded with reverence. Will not this fact indirectly disclose the high value our Śaivas set on ritual—even on private ritual, in the context of which the *sādhaka* is to be understood?

A short incursion into the problem of liberation (*mokṣa*) will not yield different results. According to the orthodox doctrine, mainly derived from the above-mentioned Mataṅgapārameśvara and Mṛgendra, the *sādhaka* is allowed to enter his particular path only after a full *dīkṣā* has rid his soul of all impurities—save a small fraction, deemed necessary for him to pursue his practice. In other words, he must be almost liberated (of course potentially, but this does not matter for our purpose) before launching into the conquest of powers or of perfection. A sharp difference is thus asserted between *mokṣa* and *siddhis* (or *bhukti*), the first being, in a strange manner, a prerequisite for the second.[103] Now, it is almost certain that this vision is a late one. We have many signs showing that the *sādhaka* of old was not conceived as an already liberated person. The liberation on the contrary was at the extreme end of his way, being nothing else but the perfect divinization (the "becoming-Śiva") he could expect from a sustained practice. At that time, the theories connected with the nature of the soul that we have presented as "orthodox" and that have informed the conception of *dīkṣā* had certainly not gained authority. When philosophical reflection developed, a part of the worshippers of Śiva—the Pāśupatas, for instance—seems to have stuck to the old conception of the *sādhaka* and understood the liberation as something to be gained through practice. Our Śaivas, on their side, although accepting exactly the same conception of *mokṣa* (identification with Śiva), maintained that the essential nature of the soul was the same as Śiva's; and they had to decide only about the proper means to unveil this true nature. The majority of the Siddhāntins saw no other possibility than a direct intervention of Śiva's Grace, in the form of *dīkṣā*[104] and they justified (perhaps a posteriori?) their opinion by saying that the main obstacle to liberation, the *āṇavamala*, was a substance (*dravya*), which only an action from the most powerful agent could possibly remove.[105] Other traditional means of liberation, such as true knowledge, asceticism, devotion, and so on were rejected as ineffective. So, the liberation was still obtained by an action, but the activity was no longer man's (the *sādhaka*'s) but God's—a change that certainly would deserve consideration. Parallel to this mainstream, however, was another current (perhaps influenced by nondualistic schools) that maintained that *āṇavamala* was but another name for ignorance and that the natural means to liberation consequently was knowledge (*jñāna*)[106]—or, still better, a combination of *jñāna* and *dīkṣā*, which reminds us of the doctrine of *jñānakarma-samuccaya*.[107] This second current, from the thirteenth century onward, has developed into the rich philosophy known by the name of (Tamil) *Śaiva-Siddhānta*.[108] But what exactly did the authors of that particular Sanskrit school mean by *jñāna* in the present context? We would spontaneously exclude the mere intellectual understanding (even followed by inner conviction) that may be derived from the study of the doctrinal sections of Āgamas, but think of a knowledge of an experimental nature, obtained through one's own efforts and therefore, in a way, akin to action. Unfortunately, confusion reigns supreme in this matter; for the texts do not usually give any precision on this point, and commentators are not missing, who understand *jñāna* as a purely theoretical knowledge.[109] As for the guru himself, the one who gives the *dīkṣā* and comments on the Āgamas, the general opinion is that he must be expert in the rituals and "have knowledge" —with the same ambiguity in the word *jñāna* as already mentioned.[110]

This brief investigation in a very complicated and important question provides double support to our claim that *kriyā* was considered as essential: (1) a direct one, as we have shown that the mainstream of our school was definitely oriented toward action, even in its conception of liberation and of the way to liberation; (2) an indirect one, as no sufficent effort was made in the Āgamic literature to clarify the concept of *jñāna*, even on the part of those who prized it highly and viewed it as a worthy companion to *kriyā*, which testifies to the little attention the Śaiva masters generally gave to knowledge.

In a quite different perspective, we would like to mention a detail that bears witness to the sense of brotherhood the masters felt toward the persons who followed the same ritual practices as theirs: according to the Mṛgendra, a three days' break in the teaching course must be observed when such a colleague dies—as much as for a brother or a disciple.[111] No allusion is made to those who may accept the same philosophy.

Another confirmation of this almost exclusive concern with practice can be found in what we know of the differentiation of Śaiva sects from a common trunk (which it seems justified to assume) into four main branches, the list of which is given, with little variation, in many Āgamas, as well as in the Purāṇas or other literary works. The commonest of the Āgamic classification lists the following schools: Śaiva, Pāśupata, Soma (or Somasiddhānta), and Lākula.[112] Now, it is known that these sects were characterized mainly by the behavior of their adepts, the marks they wore, the observances they used to follow. From the Āgamas we learn that they had special Tantras of their own. And these works, now lost, were of all evidence dealing with ritual, because when warning the *ācāryas* against the "mixing of Tantras" (which always occurs in the context of ritual, as already told), our texts specify that it is particularly forbidden to mix the Śaiva Tantras, "which are mild, or good (*saumya*)," to Lākulas or others, "which are fierce or bad (*raudra*)."[113] Certainly, doctrinal oppositions did exist between these sects, but they were not at the center; and one may doubt whether those that the Śaivas insist upon and that concern the origin of the divine Perfections got by the soul at the time of liberation[114] actually were at the root of the differentiation of sects. Rather did they not come to be recognized only later? For, as far as we know, the non-Āgamic texts never mention them. In contradistinction to this ancient splitting, the separation between a dualistic and a nondualistic school within the Āgamic tradition itself (which stands for the "Śaivas" of the preceding list) seems to have been made on philosophical grounds. This however perhaps is more an appearance than a reality, given that some Āgamas of the Śaiva-Siddhānta (known as a dualistic school) seem to hold a monistic position, whereas there were dualistic interpretations of some Tantras now considered as belonging to the Kashmir school (known as nondualistic).[115]

An Attempt at Explanation

What are the preceding considerations amounting to? Of course our aim was not to discredit the Āgamas as a whole. Neither did we expect to make a revelation in pointing to the decidedly ritualistic bias of these texts. We intended only to bring to light two undeniable facts: first, that the Āgamas, as we know them, do not answer the expectations of those who would like to see theory and practice going hand in hand, the first guiding the second, the second giving the first a concrete expression; second, that a cluster of heterogeneous indications impose the idea that what really is important for these texts, on the part of man as well as on the part of God, is action. We are now going to reflect a little longer on this situation, and see in particular whether our judgment was not warped by the alterations, several times hinted at, to which the texts have been subject.

Alterations of the Text

First of all, we have to establish the fact and the significance of these alterations. It may be unpleasant for a Śaiva devotee to hear that the Āgamas in general, but especially those which are most famous in the South, have been deeply altered, sometimes to such an extent that we have a new work under an old title. But this is a fact, which can be denied only by those who have never read the Āgamas or who place in them a blind faith, exclusive of critical mind. The proofs we can adduce are many.

1. There are literal repetitions: the same verses or groups of verses are found in different Āgamas—a fact that is impossible to account for if we refuse the idea that someone, at a given moment, has inserted in the manuscript of a text fragments of other texts.[116]

2. There are evident alterations, in the form of introductions, within a text, of new teachings alien to its general spirit: sudden praise of the Vedas, whereas these Scriptures in a previous section of the text had been ranked among the inferior treatises—a peculiarity we find in the Uttara-Kāmika and elsewhere;[117] theoretical information that does not fit with the doctrine already acknowledged—like the passage on the five *kalās* in the Suprabheda;[118] ritual descriptions that duplicate previous ones, giving for an act already described new techniques borrowed from elsewhere—like several of the last chapters of the printed Raurava;[119] minor details, perfectly useless, and probably inserted to follow a fashion.

3. Some texts contain chapters that cannot possibly date from the early period of the composition of Āgamas, either because they allude to social divisions unknown from the majority of texts—for instance, to the superclass of Ādiśaivas, eulogized in the Suprabheda, the Pūrva-Kāraṇa, the Uttara-Kāmika, and so on,[120] or because they deal with divinities or practices specific of South India, as is the case with Uttara-Kāmika and Uttara-Kāraṇa (both considered to be true continuations of the Pūrva part of the same work) and many other Āgamas,[121] or on account of their iconographic descriptions, corresponding to images that have appeared at a comparatively late time, or because they insist on conceptions that we know to have crept in late,[122] under the influence either of Vedānta or of *śākta*

modes of worship—as Suprabheda, Uttara-Kāraṇa, Acintyaviśvasādākhya,[123] and others do—or contain discussions and justifications in quite a *paddhati*-like style, a feature of the Pūrva-Kāmika.[124]

4. A few texts are most certainly based on ancient *paddhatis*, though they claim to be Upāgamas, like the Acintyaviśvasādākhya, already mentioned.[125]

5. In some Āgamas, the style, and sometimes the addressee, changes from one part of the work to another, a peculiarity of the Raurava.[126]

6. Finally, one is struck by the number of anomalies concerning quotations: total absence of quotations or even of references (at least, in our present state of knowledge) of a given text in the old literature, as is the case with Suprabheda and others; ancient quotations not to be traced in the extant texts having the same name, as the quotations from Kāmika by Abhinavagupta,[127] of Pauṣkara by Rāmakaṇṭha,[128] and so on; ignorance, on the part of old commentators, of Āgamas that, in their present condition, contain precisely the information that these masters had to derive from secondary literature.[129]

This brief account, which could be enlarged considerably, shows sufficiently that a part at least of the Āgamic literature has undergone drastic changes. Before examining how this situation prevents a simple solution to the problem we have posed, let us reflect for a while on the circumstances that may have permitted or fostered the alterations to which we have pointed.

To begin with, how could any master dare to bring any change in works that his tradition accepts as Scriptures, revealed by Śiva, and made of Śiva's words? This argument against the modifications of Āgamas seems at first sight to carry some weight. Still, we cannot reject evidence and refuse, on the strength of the theoretical untouchability of the Āgamas, to recognize as such the changes they clearly have undergone. We just have to accept the facts as they are, and acknowledge, even if reluctantly, that not all Śaiva masters had faith enough in their tradition to respect the literality of the texts they inherited. No doubt, some of them were genuinely sincere in their initiative and felt that, in the same way they were allowed to take from any of the twenty-eight Āgamas the details of a ritual that were missing from their own (but how old could such a rule be?),[130] they could "complete" the text as well.[131] A few of them must have been perfectly aware that the texts they had at their disposal had already suffered modifications on the part of their predecessors, and they did not see why they should refrain doing the same, if there was a good reason to do it. One has to remember that an *ācārya* is a representative of Śiva on earth, giving for instance *dīkṣā* in the name of Śiva: could he not in the same spirit modify the Āgamas? Finally, some of these gurus certainly had no faith at all, and felt no scruple manipulating the texts or writing them anew; all they wished to do was to put the Āgamic teachings in the reigning fashion or simply to produce a scriptural reference for a rite they deemed efficacious or for a rule serving their purpose. When one knows that a fake Kāmika was written (published, and even commented on) right in the middle of the nineteenth century, for the sake of a process, by a gurukkal who believed the true Kāmika to be irretrievably lost,[132] one cannot reject automatically the possibility of a similar "creation" having occurred earlier.[133] After all, is not this story a very old one? The question that we should ask is perhaps the opposite of what we are presently asking ourselves: when did the Āgamas begin to pass for the Word of Śiva? Probably not at once, but only when their authors were long forgotten. Did not the first alterations occur at that time, when the texts were declared to be so many refractions, through different auditors, of the one indivisible Science of Śiva? For their essential unity had then to be demonstrated. This however is an insoluble problem that we shall leave out.

But, how could modifications of existing texts (new productions pose no real difficulty) be done practically, as any alteration of a text has some chance to last only if it affects all the existing copies of the same text? We must come back in mind to times of old, when each Āgama was the propriety of a given line of teachers.[134] This Āgama was in the hands of the guru in the form of a manuscript, and it is reasonable to assume that this document was unique and copied again only for the sake of preservation, when its material support (bark of tree, palm leaf, etc.) was in too bad a condition, and not for the sake of multiplication. Naturally, contacts nevertheless occurred between parallel spiritual families, comparisons were done between their texts, followed by addition in this or that Āgama—probably on the occasion of its recopying on a new support—of material borrowed from others. This we have to assume if we want to understand the kinship evidenced by several texts, as well as the literal repetition of whole passages. Now, so long as the copies of a certain text were few and preserved within a limited group of devotees, any change was possible. When the number of copies increased, this operation of course became more difficult, but that it was made anyhow is confirmed by the variation in the content of the manuscripts that we have; for instance, some manuscripts of a given Āgama contain chapters that the others, even those in good condition, do not possess.[135] Hence the confused situation we find nowadays.

Ancient Situation

Even reduced to its minimum, a partial reworking of the texts, our hypothesis can explain a lot of the more or less obvious contradictions between doctrine and practice that we have noted in the second part of our study, as well as the contradictions among different articles of doctrine or different rituals; for the changes we are assuming were not necessarily brought up in a perfect manner and, even if the original texts were devoid of contradictions, dissymmetry was sure to creep in, on account of awkward or repeated alterations.

But were the texts in their original form models of homogeneity? This is a most important question, to which we unfortunately can give only hypothetical answers.

Some Āgamas, even in their present condition, display a satisfying homogeneity between their doctrinal and practical teachings. This is the case with the Mataṅgapārameśvara and, in a lesser measure, with the Mṛgendra—both pertaining to the category of Upāgamas, both dealing with private worship, and both, as we have seen, having four *pādas*, with a logical distribution of the matter among them. We are inclined to see in these two texts instances of works written by learned gurus of old—probably heads of *maṭhas*—for the instruction of their disciples. According to inscriptions, the repute of these masters generally was high, and they had the esteem of princes. We must therefore credit them with intelligence, erudition, and all kinds of moral virtues, and expect from them well-built works, concerned with philosophical problems and devoid of patent contradictions. That such works may have passed for Upāgamas at a given moment is quite possible, but we naturally shall never learn this from inscriptions. In any case, the two texts just mentioned are not very old,[136] but as they were commented upon in the tenth or eleventh century,[137] they naturally are earlier by one or two centuries. Perhaps it is from this category of Āgamas that the Siddhānta earned its reputation of giving stress on knowledge;[138] and probably it is from them also that the models for *pūjā* and *dīkṣā*, which imply training in yoga and presuppose (especially the second) a definite ontology, were introduced in the common daily ritual after Soma-śambhu[139] and in some way or other gained access to the Āgamas dealing with temple worship, where they often clash with the other rituals.[140]

With the exception of Kiraṇa,[141] all these temple-oriented Āgamas either have no *vidyāpāda* (separate or not, the question is not there), or (for a few of them) have *vidyāpādas* ill-assorted with the ritual section. In some cases, there is no possibility even to guess how the original text could have looked, either because of the evident alterations[142] or because of the indubitable loss of one or several sections. In most cases however, the texts as we have them seem to have suffered no important changes; and they require no complement, especially no theoretical teachings beyond the few elementary ones we may find here and there: the rituals that are described stand by themselves or rest on beliefs so common that there is no need to specify them. Some of these rituals seem to be very ancient and most of them have probably come from sources altogether different from the decidedly intellectual works concerned with private ritual that we have just mentioned. They no doubt were conceived by unsophisticated groups of devotees, who were content with simple modes of worship and gave little thought to the ontological status of the divinities they invoked, or the real nature of the contact they could have with them.[143] It is this category of texts we had in view in putting forward the theory that no precise philosophy was to be looked for behind the rites and that our investigation of the eventual harmony between doctrine and practice had finally no raison d'être. After an attempt to moderate this verdict by taking into account a minority of Āgamas of a different type, we reiterate it with greater force. This must on no account be mistaken for a negative opinion on the Āgamas; it is only the acknowledgement that in many milieus and for many centuries the important thing was not to understand the world, but to be able to act efficaciously on it. To achieve this aim, man had to ensure for himself the help of all conceivable Forces, the greatest of which, for Śaiva devotees, was that of Śiva. It is but natural that the conception such people had of their God was in keeping with their turn of mind: Śiva's Power essentially was a Power to act, Kriyāśakti.

Conclusion

But let us come back to the pair *jñāna-kriyā* with which we started. Of its innumerable avatars, we have retained three, which play an important role in the Āgamic literature.

1. Jñāna and Kriyā as Powers, aspects of Consciousness as such, Cit. They are infinite in Śiva and in liberated souls, finite in ordinary man.

2. Jñāna as the all-comprehensive Science of Śiva, as He gives it to men, or rather as men receive it—for the appellation of "knowledge" reflects most probably their own view point, meaning all that *they* have to know. (On the part of Śiva, this *jñāna* cannot represent His total knowledge, even if we think of the Āgamas as they were first spoken by Him; and their handing down to beings other than Himself rather proceeds from His Kriyā.) This *jñāna* is but a half-pair, so to say, as we have seen that its natural complement, in the form of the use men must make of the Āgamas, is not commonly referred to by the word *kriyā*.

3. *Jñāna* as the doctrine, or philosophy, coupled with *kriyā* as ritual action—each of the two representing a division of the Āgamas, the mutual relation of which we have questioned.

As we have observed already, there is a complete alteration in the meaning of *jñāna*—not only a change of level and extension—when one passes from the second to the third case; and there is a gap too between the first and the second. It would be totally wrong to consider the Science of Śiva represented by the Āgamas as the expression of His Jñāna-Śakti (we have just said that it is rather an expression of His Kriyā); and it would be equally wrong, though for other reasons, to see in the doctrine (*jñāna*) upheld by the Āgamas (assuming that there is a definite one) the essence of the total Science (*Jñāna*) embodied in these texts. On the side of *kriyā*, the distortion is less glaring, but in any case, our successive pairs fail to give any impression of unity. If we have nevertheless considered them together in the same study, it is not that we were carried away by the mere words; our motivation is deeper. For, behind all these heterogeneous uses of the terms *jñāna* and *kriyā*, we can recognize a fundamental opposition, deeply ingrained in the mind, that takes its source in our human experience and informs all our conceptions. The world is, if we may say so, divided by us vertically into two halves: the domain of thought and the domain of action. And we generally lean on this side or that, though of all evidence we have one foot in each. We should not then be astonished if, against all logic, the same schools that praise the *vidyāpādas* of the Āgamas and insist that knowledge (whatever meaning they give to the word, which is magical as such) is the best instrument man possesses to reach liberation, give also Jñāna-Śakti precedence on Kriyā-Śakti when they consider the Powers of Śiva. This is the position of the Tamil school, which it has developed and still maintains at the cost of a right understanding of the Āgamas. The lack of interest its representatives evince toward the rites is such that they apparently have never realized that the rituals, which have continued being performed almost without change over many centuries and which they accept as their own, bely in many respects the doctrine that they stick to.[144] Our Āgamic Śaivas, on the contrary, often showed a regrettable neglect for the *vidyāpādas*, declared that liberation was to be attained through an action (of man, perhaps, in the pre-Āgamic times, of God in the mature school), and, of the two Śaktis of Śiva, they obviously were more impressed, whether they admitted it or not, by the Power to act, Kriyā-Śakti. It is clear however that they cannot be qualified as blind "activists," no more than the others could be spoken of as pure theoricians. But the respective partiality of the two schools for one side or the other of Śiva is undeniable. We assuredly have a more balanced view in the Kashmir Śaivism which, although giving Jñāna a certain superiority over Kriyā at Śiva's level, sees no divorce between reflection and action, and whose highest speculations were always nourished by a sustained practice. Our friend André Padoux, to whom this paper is dedicated, knows this well, since the speculations on speech that were the main object of his research, though belonging by right to philosophy, interest eminently practical action and thus are at the meeting point between Jñāna and Kriyā.

Notes

1. It might be useful to remind our readers that these convenient appellations do not indicate the birthplace of the two schools, but the country where they finally took root.

2. Let us insist on the fact that *Śaiva-Siddhānta*, or simply *Siddhānta*, is the name given by the Āgamas themselves to the school they represent. We shall use the term here in this sense, not as a designation of the later and partially different Tamil school that goes by the same name.

3. *Jñānakriyātmikā sāpi nityā nityoditā prabhā* (Pau 1, 39a, speaking of Śiva's Śakti); *dṛk-kriyātmakam aiśvaryaṃ yasya taddātrapūrvakam /*

īśvaraḥ so'tra mantavyaḥ śaktidvayayutaḥ prabhuḥ // (ŚRS 8, from *Parākhyā*); *sarvajñānakriyā-rūpā śaktir ekaiva śūlinaḥ* (MK, 25b); *jñāna-kriyā-svabhāvaṃ tattejaḥ śāmbhavaṃ jayati* (TPr, 2b); and so on. The pair however is ignored by some texts, like *Suprabheda*.

4. A more-faithful translation for *Cit* is "Consciousness"—Consciousness without object. But as the opposite of *cit* is *acit*, the inert, that covers all the material realities, we feel that our translation is acceptable. Its advantage is to tally, better than "Consciousness," with the second member of the compound, "Power".

5. *Ananyāpi vibhinnātaḥ śambhoḥ sā samavāyinī / svābhāvikī ca tanmūlā prabhā bhānor ivāmalā* // (RT, 301b-302a), a verse that Aghoraśiva introduces with the following words: *itthaṃ śakti-śaktimator ātmāntaratvābhāve'pi dharmi-dharmatayā bhedaṃ pratipādyopasaṃharati*. Same comparison in Su, vp, 1, 45b-46, describing Manonmanī, who is the Śakti of Sadāśiva: *tasyaiva vāmapārśve tu ādiśaktir manonmanī // vahner uṣṇatvavac chaktir avinābhāvinī vibhoḥ / śaktihīne śivo nāsti śivahīnā na śaktikā //* Similar vision in Pāñcarātra texts (see LT, 8, 8).

6. Śiva is pure knowledge, independent of any object; Śakti is the same but dependent on objects: *parānapekṣaṃ rūpaṃ yad vijñānaṃ śivasaṃjñitam / tasya śaktiṃ parāpekṣaṃ rūpam āhur vipaścitaḥ* (RT, 288b-289a). See also note 5, last quotation.

7. Lists of three: Icchā, Jñāna, Kriyā; or Raudrī, Jyeṣṭhā, Vāmā (often but wrongly identified to the preceding ones, in this order); or Ādiśakti, Manonmanī, Bhavānī (respectively of Śiva, Sadāśiva, Maheśa: PKām, 2, 157b-158a); or Yoga-, Bhoga-, Vīra-Śakti (in quite another context: see later); and so on. List of five: Parā, Ādi, Icchā, Jñāna, Kriyā (Vāt, 1, 24-27). List of eight: Īśānī, Āpūraṇī, Padmī, Vāmā, Mūrti, Hāriṇī, Jananī, Rodhayitrī (MatP, vp, 4, 6a and 15b); and so on. One may note the heterogeneity of these appellations, some of them being personified concepts, whereas others (like Jyeṣṭhā) are names that come apparently from an older layer of Śaivism, where they were applied to individual potent goddesses.

8. *Muktātmano'pi śivāḥ kintv ete tatprasādato muktāḥ / so'nādimukta eko vijñeyaḥ pañcamantratanuḥ* // (TPr 6). Quotations could be multiplied.

9. The commentators quote this line, either to insist that this power always is present and unlimited in scope (a precision given by the following line), or simply to affirm the double nature of *caitanya* (or *cit*). In the latter case, they quote only the first *pāda*.

10. *Kriyāyā hetubhūtatvāt kriyāśaktiś cid eva yat /* (RT, 139b). Commentary by A.: *nātra kriyāveśaḥ kartṛtvam, api tu kriyāyāṃ śaktatvam eva; tataś ca ayaskāntaśakter ivāyasi śivaśakteḥ sannidhimātreṇa bindāv eva kriyāveśo'taḥ kriyāhetubhūtatvāt jñānaśaktir eva kriyāśaktir ucyate* (note the gloss of Cit by Jñānaśakti). The same *Ratnatraya* explains elsewhere that the inalterable Śakti (Cit) neither wishes nor knows nor acts but is called Icchā, Jñāna, and Kriyā because She achieves these effects: *icchākāryam anicchāpi kurvāṇecchā cid avyayā/ jñānam ajñānarūpaivam akriyāpi kriyā tathā //* (190).

11. See note 10. Note that the *bindu*, when excited by Śiva (for this is the usual way to express the action of Śiva's Śakti on this subtle *materia prima*) produces only the "pure" worlds (see later); but it pervades the impure" as well. More on *bindu* farther on.

12. See note 19.

13. RT, 129b-130a, states the above opinion within a passage (126-133) where the author criticizes the view according to which Kriyāśakti is identical with Bindu.

14. With a few exceptions, like TPr, 28-30, reflected in Īśgd III, pp. 10-11, śl. 74b-80.

15. *Śaktodyuktau pravṛttaś ca kartā trividha ucyate/ śakteḥ pravṛttibhedena bhedas tasyopacārataḥ//* (ŚRS 14, verse attributed to Mṛg by this work and others; see Mṛg II, Bhatt, p. 255, the readings of which we have retained). The *Ratnatraya* alludes to the corresponding conditions of *bindu*: *tatrākṣubdhe bhaved bhogo bindau ānandarūpini/ kṣubdhe'dhikāro devasya layo'tikrāntabindukaḥ // ekaiva khalu cicchaktiś śivasya samavāyinī/ trividhopādhi-saṃbhedāt layabhogādhikāriṇī //* (RT, 179-180). Elsewhere the same work describes these three states in detail, using the two other sets of adjectives (262-279). The *śakta* state, for instance, *tatra śakto bhaved ādyo niṣkalaśiva-saṃjñitaḥ / tasmin mukulite vāste kriyākhyā śaktir aiśvarī //*. A slightly different vision in Pau, I, 40-42.

16. See, for instance, our remark in note 10. Also, *jñānātmikā parāśaktiś śambhoḥ* (SiŚe, p. 147). For the identification with Śiva, see note 6, and perhaps Rau, vp, 3, 33b, *jñānaśaktiḥ śivā nityā* (printed version: *nitya-*).

17. See the last fragment quoted note 15.

18. For example, SārK, 23, 13b and commentary.

19. Thus, *ityevaṃ devadevasya sarvakartṛtvam īritam / etena sarvakartṛtvena sarvajño'vāpyate patiḥ //* (MK, 33b-34a, supported by Mṛg,

vp, 5, 13). Commentary by A.: *jñānaṃ vinā kuvindādīnāṃ kartṛtvādṛṣṭeḥ bhagavataḥ sarvakartṛtvataḥ sarvajñatva-siddhir ity uktaṃ prāk.*

20. For a general presentation of this doctrine, see our introductions to SP 1 and SP 3, and Brunner 1988a. See also the French translation of the *vidyāpāda* of *Mṛgendra* by Michel Hulin.

21. Actually the impure worlds are not created directly by Śiva, but by Ananta, the highest of the almost liberated souls, called Vidyeśvaras, who is His delegate for all the actions affecting the domain of *māyā*. The half-verse always quoted in support of this rule is *śuddhe'dhvani śivaḥ kartā prokto'nanto'site prabhuḥ* / (Kir, vp, 3, 27b).

22. *Tirobhāvo yathānurūpād bhogād apracyāvaḥ* (Mṛg, vp, 2, 3, N.K.'s *vṛtti*).

23. See Mṛg, vp, 7, 11-12 (with *vṛtti* and *dīpikā*); and SP 3, pp. vii-viii.

24. The five functions of Śiva are described in many texts. See for instance, Mṛg, vp, 2, 3-4 and chapters 4-5. RT, 262 gives them in a nutshell: *sa tayā* (i.e., *śaktyā*) *jaḍam ākramya sṛjaty avati hanti ca / tirodhayati bhagavān anugṛhṇāti cātmanaḥ //*. We may incidently remark that the last two operations could be deemed superfluous. As we have seen, Grace is already is at work in the creation and maintenance of the world and so is Obstruction, which amounts to binding the soul with the "fruits" of its *karman*. The latter is especially difficult to distinguish from *sthiti*, and this may be the reason why there is some hesitation in the correspondence of *sthiti* and *rodha* with definite Faces. Usually, *sthiti* is attributed to Tat-Puruṣa and *rodha* to Vāmadeva, but the opposite distribution also occurs.

25. See Mṛg, vp, 1, 1b: *jñānaṃ śṛṇuta suvratāḥ* (sentence proferred by a guru addressing his disciples), with the following commentary by N. K., *jñāyante'nena vidyā-caryā-kriyā-yogā iti jñānaṃ śāstram.* In almost all the introductive verses of the Āgamas, a similar sentence will be found, for instance: *śaivaṃ jñānaṃ pravakṣyāmi tac chṛṇudhvaṃ samāhitāḥ* (Rau, vp, *upodghāta*, 21). The *śivajñāna* (or *patijñāna*) removes all the bonds, thus manifesting the *śivatva* of the soul: *athātma-mala-māyākhyā-karma-bandha-vimuktaye / vyaktaye ca śivatvasya śivāj jñānaṃ pravartate //* (ŚRS, 2, from Svā; the last *pāda* is quoted very often). It therefore gives *mukti* and *bhukti*, whereas its opposite, the *paśu-jñāna* (the science having *paśus* for its authors) gives neither, only evanescent pleasures that have little to do with the true *bhukti*. The latter consequently maintains the soul in its condition of *paśu*

(bound soul)—hence another analysis of the word *paśujñāna*. A good master is naturally: *śivaśāstra-samāyuktaḥ paśuśāstra-parāṅmukhaḥ* (Su, cp, 1, 54b; almost the same line in *Vāyavīyasaṃhitā*, quoted in KD, p. 30).

26. Collectively called the *śāstra*, or even the *śruti*. No difference is made between the two terms *Tantra* and *Āgama*, the first being preferred in the Scriptures, but the second having finally prevailed. The myth of the "descent" of the Āgamas from Śiva to humankind is told in almost every Āgama, in a chapter entitled *Tantrāvatāra*, which as a rule lists all the Āgamas (and sometimes the Upāgamas) and generally adds some indications on the particular line of "hearers" connected with the Āgama to which it belongs; a shorter account is in Mṛg, vp, 1, 20-27. In some texts, only the last teaching is given (e.g., MatP, vp, 1, 28-33).

27. See Mṛg, vp, 1, 27.

28. In spite of the fact that the Vedas too (and all other scriptures as well) have Śiva as their author. See Brunner 1981.

29. See the beginning of note 25 (commentary on Mṛg). This explanation by N. K. would suffice to reject the idea expressed by Sivaraman (1973, p. 386) that the treatises where this Science is embedded are collectively called *jñāna* "by reason of the primacy of *vidyā[pāda]*." Such a view is totally foreign to the spirit of the Āgamas.

30. Mṛg, vp, 10, 1-10, esp. 4-5 (intervention of *kalātattva*) and 8-9 (role of *vidyātattva*).

31. See ibid., *dīpikā* ad śl. 5: Aghoraśiva raises the difficulty and gives an answer that is far from satisfactory.

32. We shall not make any distinction between the so-called Mūlāgamas (numbered 28) and the so-called Upāgamas (200 and more), for it is almost certain that some works of the second group are earlier than some of the first (at least, in their present condition). And we shall also leave aside the distinction between the ten Āgamas styled "Śaiva" and the eighteen styled "Raudra," because the tradition (issued from Kashmir) according to which they would teach, respectively, a dualism and a dualism-cum-monism is not supported by the texts we have (Brunner 1985b). For a general description of the Āgamic literature, see Gonda, MRLS, chapters 11-12. List of Āgamas and Upāgamas in Rau, vol. 1, chart facing p. xviii.

33. Four extant Āgamas have them: *Suprabheda* and *Kiraṇa* (both

Mūlāgamas); *Mṛgendra* and *Mataṅgapārameśvara* (both Upāgamas). It seems that the *Pauṣkara* (an Upāgama), only whose *vidyāpāda* is published, did possess four *pādas* too. The *Raurava* (a Mūlāgama) has a *vidyāpāda* followed by a *kriyāpāda* that contains a mixture of practical instructions of all kinds. It might have possessed four *pādas*, however, if we rely on vp, 1, 4. An unpublished manuscript claims to contain the *vidyāpāda* of the *Kāmika*, but it does not seem to be genuine, so that we have to put the most famous (in our times) of the Āgamas among the enormous class of texts that are constituted by an undivided mass of ritual teachings, interspersed with information of different kinds.

34. For an analysis of *Kiraṇa* and of *Suprabheda*, see Brunner 1965 and 1967.

35. The statement that the Āgamas comprise four *pādas* is found in the *Kāmika* (PKām, 1, 108b: *catuṣpāda-yutāny eva*—said of the Tantras of the Siddhānta in general). But we read it mainly in the texts that are actually so divided, and where it concerns only the particular Āgama in which it is found: see Mṛg, vp, 2, 2 (*tripadārthaṃ catuṣpādam*); MatP, kp, 5, 3b-4a (in the description of a good *ācārya*); Su, kp, 21, 6b-7 (same context); Su, kp, 2, 26b, in the course of the description of the *Suprabheda* itself as one of the 28 Āgamas; *kriyādi-jñānaparyantam atraiveha pradṛśyate / idaṃ śāstram anenaiva suprabhedam iti smṛtam //*. We have already noted (Brunner 1967, p. 34) this curious declaration, which, if genuine, would constitute a proof that the division into four *pādas* was indeed exceptional. This hypothesis seems to find support in the existence of an old list of texts especially called *saṃhitās*, given for instance in the commentary of *Aghoraśivācāryapaddhati* (AP, p. 369) and that comprise *Mṛgendra, Mataṅga, Parākhya, Raurava*, two *Svāyambhuvas*, and *Kiraṇa*; that is (with some additions), all the texts we know as possessing four *pādas*, except *Suprabheda*. And we actually find in a commentary of *Kiraṇa* (cited DĀ, T. 76, p. 21) the indication that one calls *saṃhitās* the texts where the four *pādas* are clearly distinguished (see also the line attributed to the *Raurava* in Rau, vol. 3, p. 337, line 16). The possibility exists that these remarks have been introduced at a time when almost all Āgamas had lost much of their content, and the preservation of the four *pādas* was a rare thing. We shall however find in the following pages arguments in favor of the first hypothesis. As for the previously quoted statement of the *Kāmika*, it has little value, evidently being a late addition, as are all the chapters giving the full list of Āgamas. An indication of Tirumular that the Āgamas are divided into three parts—*karman, upāsana* and *jñāna* (see Gonda,

MRLS p. 180)—is more interesting, but would show only that the quadripartition is a late fact. For a more detailed study on this question, see Brunner 1991a.

36. The case of *Ajita*, chapter 2. See some general reflections on the subject in Bhatt's Sanskrit Introduction to this Āgama, vol. 1, pp. x-xi. See also note 88.

37. Some indications on the prior independence of each text in Brunner 1988b, pp. 152-153.

38. For instance, both the second chapter of *Ajita* (*Śivasvarūpam*) and the *vidyāpāda* of *Suprabheda* (see Brunner 1967) teach a monistic philosophy, though these two Āgamas pertain to the group of ten called *śivabheda*, supposedly more dualistic than the group of eighteen called *rudrabheda*.

39. Sadyojyoti, Bhojadeva, Rāmakaṇṭha, and Śrīkaṇṭha, who all belong to this period, are famous for the philosophical treatises they have written, eight of which were published with their respective commentaries under the name of *Aṣṭaprakaraṇa*. The first and the third have also commented on Āgamas. See for some details Pandey, *Bhāskarī* vol. 3, pp. xv-xxv, and Bhatt's Introduction to MatP, vol. 2. One must also mention the other commentators on Āgamas, and the commentators on *paddhatis*, whose work extends up to the sixteenth century or so and who on their side have contributed not a little to the clarification and unification of the doctrine.

40. Mṛg, vp, 2, 8. See also MatP, vp, 26, 63 (with commentary), which teaches that *mokṣa* is to be got by the utilization of all four *pādas* together—a combination that naturally implies noncontradiction among these *pādas*. Allusions in one *pāda* of the teachings given in another *pāda* are rare in the texts (Mṛg, yp, 7a), but frequent in the commentaries (MatP, kp, passim).

41. See for instance Aj, kp, 20, 174-178. Commentators make this point clear: *vyāpakasyāpi jīvasya śarīrāvacchedopādhikatvam iva śivasyāpi mantratejo'vacchedopādhivad abhimata-deśāntara-prāptir na virudhyate* / (Appayadīkṣita, ŚC, p. 65; quoted SP 1, p. 191).

42. For a detailed account of *dīkṣā*, see SP3, chapters 1-5.

43. See MatP, kp, 3, 39-51; Kir, kp, 2, 19-22a (quoted in the commentary of Mṛg, kp, 3, 12); ŚC, pp. 44-45 (quoted SP1, p. 155).

44. SP 1, pp. 166-173 and notes. See also infra, pp. 20-21.

45. A few indications on the points of divergence in Brunner

1977, pp. 114-115 and 118-119. See also notes 29 and 108.

46. Rau, kp, 47 (vol. 3 of Bhatt's edition). We seize the opportunity of confessing that we hold as spurious all the *paṭalas* collected in this vol. 3, as well as the last two (45 and 46) of vol. 2—and this, for several reasons.

47. Rau, vp, 2, 6 and 10, 98-101. This discrepancy has been noted by N. R. Bhatt in his Introduction to Rau, vol. 3 (p. xxxviii).

48. Rau, vp, 4, 39-47 (this chapter continues in the Appendix of vol. 1). We read *śivatattva* at line 39a. Same list in Su, vp, 3, 229-230 —but with *śiva* in the lower place (for which a correction is suggested in Brunner 1967, p. 55), whereas we have the "normal" list in Su, kp, 8, 139.

49. Rau, kp, 45, 61. This chapter clearly is more recent than the chapters 1-44 (see note 46). But already in kp, 6, 3, the rite of *ācamana* takes the three *tattvas* in the order *ātman, vidyā, śiva* (at least as the printed text stands).

50. Perhaps *Suprabheda* (see note 48). But this Āgama makes no use of the three *tattvas* in its ritual of *pratiṣṭhā*. Note that these three *tattvas* also have a "pure" form, known in the Northern school (SvT, 4, 403-406 and commentary), and that reminds us of the three *tattvas* that stand at the core of the teachings of *Vṛhaspatitattva*—a text that belongs to old-Javanese literature and is presumably older than the mature texts of Śaivasiddhānta (see Zieseniss 1958, pp. 7-10, 25-34, etc.).

51. Mṛg, kp, 7, 82b-85 and elsewhere (see the Index in our translation).

52. More exactly, it knows them as "portions" of the *bindutattva*, but not as realities permeating the whole universe and serving as a road (*adhvan*) to Śiva. Details in Brunner 1985a, pp. lxii-lxiii.

53. Rau, kp, 47, 43-58.

54. Ibid., śl. 39 sq. In the same chapter, the nature of the soul with its different conditions (*avasthā*) is also given in the most "orthodox" way (that exemplified by the *Kāmika* for instance), although the *vidyāpāda* is silent about it.

55. Su, vp, 3, 235-247 and cp, 4, 39-45 (there the *kalās* are identified with the five *bhūtas:* see SP 3, Introduction, pp. xiv-xv). To be sure, the text mentions a *homa* to these realities, but it makes no

proper use of them during the actual process of *dīkṣā.*

56. PKār, 30, 101-103 and 233-240 defines in succession: *ātman, antarātman, paramātman, tattvātman,* and *bhūtātman* and uses these notions in a *nyāsa;* but they do not appear in the *dīkṣā* (chapter 145). The *Sarvajñānottara* (T. 317, pp. 459 sq) has *bhūta-, antara-, tattva-, jīva-,* and *mantrātman,* with precise indications on these realites. The first three of PKār often are mentioned, and we also have lists of four or five (slightly different) in the Northern school. In this case, it is clear that we are concerned with a notion introduced in the school from outside and not really integrated.

57. Let us briefly clarify our point. The first difficulty is about Śiva as all-pervading and infinite: how to move Him and fix Him in an image? Two possible answers are: first the intervention of a limiting adjunct, in the form of a mantric body, as mentioned earlier; and second, the direct action of the mantra on the image: it manifests Śiva in the same way as a friction manifests the fire in a piece of wood or as the wind inflames it in the *kuṇḍa.* See for instance SP 1, texts quoted p. 191; or Mak, 2, 663: *yathā kuṇḍagataś cāgnir vāyunā paridīpyate / tathaiva śivamantreṇa jāyate bhagavān śivaḥ.* The second difficulty is: how to understand *āvāhana* and the following rites in the case of a permanent image? This is answered by symbolic interpretations (not constant) of the rites, as in SP 1, pp. 190-192, śl. 66b-70a; and the same view is held in Mṛg, kp, 3, 56. An unhappy mixture of explanations are PKām, 4, 350-362; PKār, 30, 199-201. If the answer to the second question is accepted a difficulty remains: why then should *āvāhana* and *visarjana* be excluded in the case of some special *liṅgas* (rule given everywhere) that (according to PKār, 30, 204) have the virtue to "make the God present"?

58. See SP3, Introduction, pp. xxii-xxvi.

59. See SP3, pp. 316-320, note 247, with Sanskrit quotations.

60. See Mṛg, kp, 8, 147.

61. Kir, vp, 6, 13b-14a, given in SP3, p. xxiii, note 40; quoted in the *vṛtti* of Mṛg, kp, 8, 144-145a; in the commentary of RT, 165; etc.

62. Mṛg, cp, 1, 25-26.

63. SP3, pp. 284-288, notes 265 and 267.

64. See SP 3, pp. 396-400 and note 439, with Sanskrit quotations. Also Mṛg, kp, 8, 135b-136a and commentary.

65. See PMNK, 7: *samatā ca samutpatti-saṅkrānty-āveśa-pakṣataḥ /*

abhivyaktiḥ parā gītā buddhivācām agocarā //. The commentator, Rāmakaṇṭha, attributes *saṅkrānti* to the Pāśupatas (in conformity with the commentary of *Pāśupatasūtra* 4, 24) and criticizes it at length (k. 13-41). A master of the sixteenth century, probably relying on some source unknown to us, attributes *utpatti* to the Mahāvratins and *āveśa* to the Kāpālikas. See Brunner 1986, pp. 518-519.

66. See note 11.

67. See for instance RT, 166: *mantrayonir mahāmāya yā parigrahavartinī / śivasya śaktir ākrāntā yayā sarve'pi pudgalāḥ //*. The term is never clearly explained and admits of several interpretations, of which we give only the likeliest.

68. See Mṛg, kp, 1, 4b; Aj, kp, 20, 144a; PKām, 4, 291-292; SP1, p. 155, śl. 47 (where this Śakti is said to have the form of a young sprout (*bījāṅkurākārā*).

69. For instance in the commentary by Trilocana of the verse of SP1 cited in note 68: *bījāṅkurākārāṃ—bījāṅkurāṇām ākāra iva ākāro yasyās sā tathoktā tāṃ kuṭilātmiketi yāvat, tasyā evāṅkuropamānaśravaṇāt /*. Here he cites a passage of the *Kālottara* giving this description, and continues: *asyā hy aśuddhānāṃ jagadaṅkurāṇām ādhāratayā, śuddhāṇām upādānatayā ca, samasta-jagad-adhiṣṭhānataḥ tadākāratvopamānam upapannam / seyam ādhāraśaktiḥ śivaśakty-adhiṣṭhitā kuṭileti //* (T. 170, p. 47-48, slightly corrected with another manuscript). This commentary is copied verbatim by the commentator of Aghoraśiva, Nirmalamaṇi, who recognizes his debt (AP, pp. 90-91). See also Aj, kp, 18, 201-202a, which gives a prayer to Ādhāraśakti, the wording of which suggests a rather inferior status for this divinity.

70. For instance a text inserted by Aghoraśiva in his *paddhati* (AP, pp. 87-88, reproduced in SP1, p. 157, under [47d] where we read: *śaktiṃ kriyām ādhārarūpiṇīm*. Characteristically, Nirmalamaṇi avoids commenting on this fragment (see the preceding note).

71. For instance *Ratnatraya*, which continues in this way the verse quoted in note 67: *seyaṃ kriyātmikā śaktir īśvarī sarvadoditā /* (RT, 167a)—a statement that the commentator, Aghoraśiva, refuses to accept at its face value: *kaiścit bhrāntyā kriyāśaktir aiśvarīti proktā, na tu paramārthataḥ citsamavāyinī kriyāśaktiḥ*. And he is right, as RT itself (126-133) criticizes the view according to which Bindu would be identical with the inherent Śakti of Śiva.

72. See SP1, pp. 166-168, note 1.

73. See Aj, kp, 18, 244: *piṇḍikā tu bhavec chaktir liṅgaṃ tu parameś-*

varaḥ / tayor yā kriyate yogaḥ sā pratiṣṭheti kīrtitā //.Also SP, beginning of section on *pratiṣṭhā* (in SP4, in preparation): *pīṭhaṃ śaktiś śivo liṅgaṃ tadyogas sā śivāṇubhiḥ / (sā = pratiṣṭhā)*.

74. See Aj, kp, 18, 146; SiŚe, p. 530, śl. 128-129. In this ritual, Ādhāraśakti is identified with the stone (*ādhāraśilā*) that is placed on the ground under the *pīṭha*.

75. See Vat, 67-72. Note that this interpretation parallels the vision of the Pāñcarātras who, according to Schrader (quoted by Gonda 1965, p. 187), see Lakṣmī as a "nonspiritual energy" of Viṣṇu.

76. For instance *Suprabheda*, see note 5. But one must be careful, as this text teaches a kind of monism (note 38).

77. See SiŚe, p. 530, śl. 137. Also SP4, chapter 3.

78. Assuming that Jñānaśakti is identified with Śiva Himself, as She sometimes is (see note 16), we still have to interpret the term *Kriyāśakti*, which might mean "Bindu," as we have said earlier. Besides, it is not even certain that this sentence simply duplicates the previous one; for it occurs in the handbooks we have taken as our models after the junction of the *pīṭha* with the *liṅga*, and we perhaps could understand that two stages have to be distinguished in the *pratiṣṭhā*, the first one identifying the separate *pīṭha* with Bindu (in the form of Manonmanī for instance), the second placing Bindu under the domination of Śiva's Śakti in the form of Kriyā (see note 69)—for this Śakti must be now, like Śiva, all-pervading in the object constituted by the *liṅga* firmly fixed to the *pīṭha*. Further discussion in SP4.

79. The handbook *Arcanaprakāśa* (p. 256) cites *Kāmika* and *Kāraṇa* in this context. One should add *Raurava*, which has a whole chapter on this subject (Rau, kp, chapter 65, typically entitled *Kāmakoṣṭha*).

80. This is done even in Rau, kp, 65, 57.

81. See SP3, pp. 257-260, note 222, where the word *Vāgīśvarī* raises similar difficulties, or pp. 172-173, note 23. See also Hulin, trans. of Mṛg I, vp, 1, 1, p. 4, note 2.

82. See SP3, pp. 334-337, note 393.

83. See SP3, p. liv and our trans. of Mṛg II, pp. xv-xvii.

84. See SvT, *paṭ*. 3 and 4. Even the treatment of *āṇavamala* is the same there (4, 127-131) as in the *Somaśambhupaddhati*, for instance, though this impurity of the soul is conceived quite differently in

the two schools: as a *dravya* in the "orthodox" Siddhānta, the removal of which necessitates a positive action of Śiva (the *dīkṣā*); and as spiritual ignorance (Pandey 1963, p. 308) in the Trika (and perhaps in some Saiddhāntikāgamas as well, see the remarks made by Sanderson on the divergence, on this point, between the *Mataṅga-pārameśvara* and its commentary by Rāmakaṇṭha; Sanderson 1985b).

85. Should we hold as an instance of agreement of ritual with a "monistic" doctrine (see note 38) the detail given in Su, kp, 8, 85 that the lotus which constitutes the throne of Śiva and extends in the whole scale of *tattvas* "springs forth from Icchāśakti" (*icchā-śaktyutthitaṃ padmaṃ pṛthivyādi-śivāntakam*)? But as other, definitely dualistic works, sometimes express a similar opinion, such a description hardly can constitute a proof that the doctrine underlying this rite is monistic.

86. This does not mean that the speculations about speech did not find their way into the Siddhānta school: see *Nādakārikā* and its trans. by P. S. Filliozat. But they never had there the importance they had in Kashmir; and moreover, they were certainly unknown to most of the authors of Āgamas. The practice of mantras (for instance as explained in Padoux 1987) to a large extent is older than the theories about them. See also Goudriaan 1978, chapter 2, esp. pp. 68-104, where a variety of magic uses of mantras may be found. Also HTŚL, chapter 8.

87. A glance at the table of contents of Āgamas like *Kāmika, Kāraṇa, Ajita, Kiraṇa, Suprabheda, Makuṭa*, or of *paddhatis* like that of Īśānaśivagurudeva (to mention only published texts) will suffice to convince any skeptical reader of what we are saying.

88. For instance, the fourth chapter of PKām (*arcanavidhi*) contains the *dhyāna* on Sādaśiva (328 sq), a list of epithets of Śiva that constitutes a teaching on *pati* (349-350), an explanation on the symbolism of the Aṅgas (363 sq), and so on. UKām, chapter 23 (on *nirvāṇadīkṣā*) has a description of the six *adhvans*; chapter 24 gives us many informations concerning the Śaivas, the Scriptures, etc. Such instances are countless. Many Āgamas also include teachings on yoga in the description of rituals and all give the "descent of tantras" (*tantrāvatāra*) and the "formation of mantras" (*mantroddhāra*) as a normal part of their *kriyāpāda*. See also note 89.

89. It is especially true of the teachings concerning the mantras that in this case are often divided between the *vidyāpāda*, which

speaks of the origin, nature, number of the almost purified souls named Mantras (as *vācyas*)—a teaching of little use in the ritual—and the *kriyāpāda*, where we find explained the formation of the *mantras* (as *vācakas*) and also, usually on the occasion of a rite implying it, the right utterance of these groups of sounds, and the accompanying yoga exercises. See Mṛg, vp, 4, 6-8 and kp, chapter 1.

90. It is what we read for instance in RT, 7-8a: the knowledge of the "three jewels" (Bindu, Śakti, Śiva) is indispensable for the performance of *dīkṣā* and *pratiṣṭhā; yoga, karman, siddhis,* and *mokṣa* depend on it. It seems that the knowledge referred to here is only theoretical.

91. See for instance the chapter on *prāyaścitta* of UKām (*paṭ.* 30), of PKār (*paṭ.* 106), of Īśgp (pp. 198-202), etc.

92. See Mṛg, kp, 7, 96b-97a, commentary, and SP3, p. 213, texts under [47a] and [47b]. UKām, 23, 190-196 (quoted in SP3, p. 335) calls the three kinds of faults *vidhi-vaikalya, mantroccāraṇa-vaikalya,* and *mano-vaikalya.*

93. See Mṛg, cp, 1, 54-60; in this case, pollution is removed or danger averted by a break in the teaching.

94. PKām, 1, 106 (identical to Mak, 1, 108): *yena tantreṇa cārabdhaṃ karṣaṇādy-arcanāntakam / tena sarvaṃ prakartavyaṃ na kuryād anyatantrataḥ //* This is the normal rule, given in many texts. It is however immediately softened: *kārayed anyatantreṇa noktaṃ cet tu viśeṣataḥ /* (ibid., 107a).

95. See note 94, last part. Also PKām, 1, 113-114a (identical to Mak, 1, 109b-110): *śivasiddhānta-tantreṇa prārabdhaṃ karṣaṇādikaṃ / na kuryād anyaśāstreṇa kuryāc cet tantrasaṅkaraḥ // tantrasaṅkara-doṣeṇa rājarāṣṭraṃ ca naśyati /.* The fault called *tantrasaṅkara* is now limited to the mixture of treatises belonging to different branches of Śaivism. Still less restrictive rules in 58, 24. See also Su, kp, chapter 56.

96. PKām, 1, 111-112: *dīkṣā-vihīna-viprādyās trivarṇāś śūdrajātayaḥ / savarṇādy-anulomāś ca śilpinaḥ kārukādayaḥ // paṭhanti śivaśāstraṃ cet tat pāpān nṛpa-rāṣṭrayoḥ / acireṇa vināśaḥ syāt tasmād rājā nivārayet //.* In fact, we must suppose that, up to a recent time, only the disciples of a given master would listen to the particular Āgama that the latter had in his possession and that he would hand over only to his successor (see Brunner 1988b, pp. 152-153).

97. Mṛg, cp, 31.

98. Mṛg, cp, 1, 27-28 and commentary. See also Īśgd, III, p. 96.

99. On the *sādhaka*, see Brunner 1975; SP3, chapter 6; Mṛg, kp, 8, 220-238 and cp, 1, 75-128a; MatP II, Introduction, pp. xxiii-xxv.

100. See the remarks by Sanderson 1985a, p. 203 and note 119.

101. Kir, cp, chapters 19 and 20.

102. Brunner 1975, p. 430; SP3, p. 501, texts under [1c] and [1d].

103. Let us not imagine that the *sādhana* of the *sādhaka* results in an actualization of *mokṣa*. The view of those who accept the doctrine we are explaining is the opposite: *mokṣa* will come in due time, on account of *dīkṣā* only, after this circuitous road via *bhukti* and in spite of it. See Brunner 1975, pp. 416-421; SP3, pp. 500-503 and notes.

104. A line of *Svāyambhuva* is always cited to defend this thesis: *dīkṣaiva mocayaty ūrdhvaṃ śaivaṃ dhāma nayaty api* (see ŚRS, 69), and in several texts similar expressions are coined on this famous model.

105. See Mṛg, vp, 7, 6-9 and *dīpikā*; TPr, k. 18; RT, 236-237, commentary by A.; Svā, quoted in Īśgd, III, pp. 2-3; SP3, pp. vi-ix; Brunner 1988a, pp. 644-646.

106. One may cite Śrīkumāra's commentary to TPr: see Filliozat 1971, p. 255, lines 15-21. Also perhaps MatP, kp, 1, 2, in spite of the commentary of Rāmakaṇṭha (see the end of note 84).

107. See note 110.

108. See Sivaraman 1973, p. 381 sq, where the author presents, first, the theory of those whom he calls *activists* (pp. 381-383); second, the doctrine of the "Śaiva-Siddhānta"—read: "Tamil school of"—(pp. 383-388). Unfortunately, the passages taken from Āgamas are not always correctly understood, as in note 20, p. 606 (see our note 10), or note 1, p. 600 (for *kaivalya* in *Suprabheda* does not mean *mokṣa*). Let us, at this juncture, refer to a another view held by the Tamil Śaiva-Siddhānta; to wit, that the seeker of liberation has to go successively through all the four *pādas* of the Āgamas (!), the *vidyāpada* alone leading him to the intimate union with Śiva (Devasenapathi, pp. 250 sq and 292). One cannot be further from the Āgamic teaching.

109. For instance, when a text demands that the guru be *tattvavid*, or *jñānavat*, the usual commentary is that he must know the thirty-six *tattvas*. Such interpretation has the support of some Āgamas, for example, SārK, 8, 5: *ajñātvaitāni tattvāni yo dīkṣāṃ kartum icchati / vṛthā*

pariśramas tasya naiva tatphalam āpnuyāt //, where the word *tattva* means either the five *kalās* just mentioned, or the thirty-six *tattvas* that they contain, but certainly not the supreme reality. See also the two lines of Pau in Īśgd, III, p. 99. Sometimes there is a perceptible hesitation: see SP3, pp. 18-19, note 29, where two different explanations of the compound *jñānācāraguṇopetaḥ* are given by Trilocana, the second only (p. 17, [14i]) referring to the knowledge of the essence of Śiva.

110. An anonymous text cited in the commentary of NT, 16, 77-78a: *na kriyārahitaṃ jñānaṃ na jñānarahitā kriyā / kriyā-jñāna-viniṣpannaḥ ācāryaḥ paśupāśahā* sometimes is quoted in the Saiddhāntika treatises. But one more often meets with the instruction that the *ācārya* must know the four *pādas*. See MatP, kp, 5, 3b-4a: *vidyāpādārtha-kuśalaḥ kriyāpāda-gatakramaḥ / yogapāda-kṛtābhyāsaś caryāpādānuvartakaḥ* //, with the commentary for the first condition: *vidyāpādārtha-yogaḥ, samasta-tattvādi-vicārātmakaḥ, tatra kuśalaḥ, kṣamaḥ* /. There is no question of any intuitive or experimental knowledge. See also SP3, p. 17, last three lines of [14f] (from Su, kp, 21, 6b-7).

111. Mṛg, cp, 60a.

112. Su, kp, 56, 1 and cp, 1, 1-2; PKār, 1, 73 and 26, 58b-59a; UKām, 24, 78 sq; Svā, quoted in Īśgd, vol. 3, p. 6. Dī, quoted in DĀ (T. 76, pp. 12-13) has Kāpāla instead of Soma. For the other sources, see Lorenzen 1972, pp. 7-9 (correct there, p. 9, *Svāyambhuva P.* into *Svāyambhuvāgama*).

113. PKār, 1, 77 (partly corrupt); Su, kp, 56, 7: *saumyaṃ raudraṃ dvidhā vatsa śaivaṃ saumyam iti smṛtam / tadanyaṃ trividhaṃ tatra raudram eveti kīrtitam* // and 13: *pūrvaṃ saumyena saṃsthāpya paścād raudreṇa pūjayet / mohena cet kṛtaṃ tena rājarāṣṭraṃ vinaśyati* //.

114. See notes 64 and 65.

115. We are reminded here of the remark of Gonda, concerning Viṣṇuism and Śaivism, that their opposition "related to their socio-ritual differences rather than the theoretic sides of their religion, theology and philosophical foundations" (Gonda 1976, p. 66).

116. Instances in notes 94 and 95. No systematic survey has yet been made, but we have found whole passages common to *Ajita* and *Vātulaśuddha*, *Ajita* and *Cintya*, *Suprabheda* and *Kāmika*, many more still common to *Suprabheda* and *Makuṭa*, and some verses are even identical in *Pūrva-Kāmika* and *Svacchanda* (see our trans. of Mṛg II, p. xvii).

117. See Brunner 1981.

118. See note 55.

119. See Rau vol. 3, p. v, remarks by N. R. Bhatt.

120. Su, cp, 1, 69-76 and elsewhere; PKār, chapter 26; UKām, 24, 6b-7.

121. The chapters on Mahāmārī (the Tamil Maryammā), Śāstā, the Yoga-, Bhoga-, and Vīra-Śaktis are perhaps the most characteristic, but there are dozens of the same kind.

122. For example, a new conception about the so-called *jñāna-dīkṣās* (AVS); references to *sannyāsins* within Śaivas, when old texts speak only of *yatis* (UKār, 17, 26 sq), to the four stages toward liberation, *sālokya* and so forth, especially important in the late Tamil school (Su, yp, 3, 98-100). The case of *Pauṣkara* is special, for this work (of which only the *vidyāpāda* is known, although old references testify of the existence of a *kriyāpāda*) presents a doctrine so close to the "orthodox" that its genuineness may be suspected right away. See also note 128.

123. See note 125.

124. For instance, PKām, 4, 354-358. For more on this Āgama, see note 129.

125. We had first considered this work as the model for *Somaśambhupaddhati* (see SP 3, pp. liii-liv), but from several indications, which we cannot give here, we now draw the opposite conclusion.

126. The *vidyāpāda* (which, it must be noted, has a separate title) is addressed by Ruru to Mārīci and other Ṛṣis; the *kriyāpāda*, by Īśvara to Ruru.

127. References in Rastogi 1987, p. 256.

128. See the remark by N. R. Bhatt in the Introduction of MatP II, p. xi or lxxxiii: we think that the extant *Pauṣkara* (similar to the one commented on by Umāpati in the fourteenth century) not only is "slightly different," but has little to do with its namesake quoted by old commentators.

129. See our remarks concerning *Kāmika* in the Introduction of our translation of *Mṛgendra* II, pp. xiv-xv.

130. See notes 94 and 95.

131. As an instance of the facility with which texts could be

manipulated, let us remind the readers that, some decades ago, when the *Kāmika* was published and seen as consisting in a mere *kriyāpāda*, whereas only the *vidyā-* and *yogapāda* of *Mṛgendra* were known, it was rumored in Tamilnad that the *Mṛgendra* was the *vidyāpāda* of *Kāmika*—without anyone bothering to read this truncated *Mṛgendra*, where precise allusions to the two other parts would have been found.

132. See for details our review of Saskia C. Kersenboom-Story's *Nityasumaṅgalī*, published in IIJ 33, 1990, 121-142. A manuscript of this fake *Kāmika* can be consulted in the British Museum Library, and several copies are still circulating in Tamilnad. It has even been printed in book form.

133. As already suggested, the present *Pauṣkara* might have been born this way, as well as *Acintyaviśvasādākhya* and the last chapters of *Raurava*.

134. See note 96.

135. Let us cite the case of *Raurava*, which offers several instances of this kind: (1) the chapter on *Sūryapūjā*, which exists only in some manuscripts, see Bhatt's Introduction to vol. 1, Appendix 2 (Rau I, p. 196), where the learned editor of Āgamas concludes to a late addition; (2) most of the chapters collected in vol. 3, which come from a variety of sources (list in vol. 3, pp. cii-cv) and often duplicate previous ones. (Incidentally, now that we are in possession of all that passes under the name of *Raurava*, it would be urgent to try and separate the authentic Āgama from the rest.)

136. On account of some of the doctrines mentioned in the *vidyāpāda*, either for approval or for criticism. See Hulin's Introduction to his translation of Mṛg I, pp. v-vi (with references to other authors).

137. By father and son: see Bhatt's Introductions to Mṛg II, p. vi and to MatP II, pp. xii-xiv, with the complements given in Sanderson 1985b. Both works are named and even quoted by Abhinavagupta in TĀ, see Rastogi 1987, Appendixes 1, 4, 5 (pp. 253-284) and MatP II, pp. 488-489.

138. See Zieseniss 1958, p. 124.

139. Through Aghoraśiva. Somaśambhu himself seems inspired mainly by *Mṛgendra* and *Svacchanda*. See our Introduction to SP3.

140. See Brunner 1990. Let us note that even these "intelligent" rituals comprise rites that must come from very ancient times (like

balis) and that also clash with the rest.

141. See note 34. A serious doubt about the genuineness of the division of *Kiraṇa* into four *pādas* is expressed in Brunner 1991a, p. 265 and note 14 *ibid.*

142. Like *Suprabheda, Kāmika, Raurava.* See earlier.

143. More details in Brunner 1990.

144. Especially on the question of *mokṣa* and of the status of the liberated soul, which the ritual of *dīkṣā* unambiguously demonstrates. See p. 12 above.

Bibliography

General Abbreviations

cp, kp, vp, yp	*caryāpāda, kripyāpāda, vidyāpāda, yogapāda.*
gr.	*grantha* types
BEFEO	*Bulletin de l'Ecole Française d'Extrême-Orient* [Paris]
BEI	*Bulletin d'Etudes Indiennes* [Paris]
BSOAS	*Bulletin of the School of Oriental and African Studies* [London]
IFI	*Institut Français d'Indologie* [Pondichéry]
JA	*Journal Asiatique* [Paris]
KSTS	Kashmir Series of Texts and Studies [Srinagar]
T	Transcript from IFI (with its identification number).

Sanskrit Works and Authors; general surveys

A. Aghoraśivācārya.

Aj *Ajitāgama*, éd. crit. par N. R. Bhatt, Publications IFI No. 24, vol. 1, 1964, vol. 2, 1967.

AP *Aghoraśivācāryapaddhati* (= *Kriyākramadyotikā*), with the commentary (*Prabhā*) by Nirmalamaṇi, Cidambaram, 1927; gr.

Aṣṭ. Pr. *Aṣṭaprakaraṇa*, 2 vols., Devakoṭṭai, 1923 and 1925: vol. 1. *Tattvaprakāśika*, by Bhojadeva, commentary

by A.
Tattvasaṅgraha, by Sadyojyoti, commentary by A.
Tattvatrayanirṇaya, by Sadyojyoti, commentary by A.
vol. 2. *Ratnatraya*, by Śrīkaṇṭha, commentary by A.
Bhogakārikā, by Sadyojyoti, commentary by A.
Nādakārikā, by Rāmakaṇṭha, commentary by A.
Mokṣakārikā, by Sadyojyoti, commentary by Rāmakaṇṭha
Paramokṣanirāsakārikā, by Sadyojyoti, commentary by Rāmakaṇṭha.

AVS — *Acintyaviśvasādākhya*, IFI, T.7, 8, 100, 152.

DĀ — *Dīkṣādarśa*, by Vedajñānaśivācārya, IFI, T.76, 153, 279, 372.

Dī — *Dīptāgama*, IFI, T. 15, 16.

HTŚL — *Hindu Tantric and Śākta Literature*, by T. Goudriaan and S. Gupta (Wiesbaden: Harrassowitz, 1981).

Iśgd — *Īśānaśivagurudevapaddhati*, 4 vols., new ed. (Delhi and Varanasi: Bharatiya Vidya Prakashan, 1988).

KD — *Kriyādīpikā*, by Jñānaśivācārya (Madras, 1929); gr.

Kir — *Kiraṇāgama*, Devakoṭṭai 1932; gr.

LT — *Lakṣmī Tantra*, ed. V. Krishnamacharya (Adyar, 1959).

Mak — *Makuṭāgama* (Madras, 1977); gr.

MatP I — *Mataṅgapārameśvarāgama*, avec le commentaire de Bhaṭṭa Rāmakaṇṭha, éd. crit. par N. R. Bhatt (vol. 1): vp (Pondichéry; Publications IFI No. 56, 1977).

MatP II — *Id.* (vol. 2): kp, yp et cp (Pondichéry: Publications IFI No. 65, 1982).

MK — *Mokṣakārikā*. See Aṣṭ. Pr.

MRLS — *Medieval Religious Literature in Sanskrit*, by J. Gonda (Wiesbaden: Harrassowitz, 1977).

Mṛg I — *Mṛgendrāgama*, vp and yp, with *vṛtti* by Bhaṭṭa Nārāyaṇakaṇṭha and *dīpikā* by Aghoraśivācārya (Devakoṭṭai, 1928).

	Id., trad., introduction et notes by Michel Hulin (Pondichéry: Publication IFI No. 63, 1980).
Mṛg II	*Mṛgendrāgama*, kp et cp, avec la *vṛtti* de Bhaṭṭa Nārāyaṇakaṇṭha, éd. crit. par N. R. Bhatt (Pondichéry; Publications IFI No. 23, 1962). *Id.*, trad., introduction et notes par Hélène Brunner-Lachaux (Pondichéry: Publications IFI No. 69, 1985).
N.	Nirmalamaṇi.
NāK	*Nādakārikā*. See Aṣṭ. Pr. *Id.*, French trans. by P.-S. Filliozat in *BEFEO* 73 (1984): 223-255.
N.K.	Nārāyaṇakaṇṭha.
NT	*Netra Tantra*, with the commentary (*Uddyota*) by Kṣemarāja, 2 vols., KSTS, Nos. 46 and 61, 1926 and 1939.
Pau	*Pauṣkarāgama* (*jñānapāda*) (Madras, 1892); gr. *Id.*, with commentary by Umāpatiśivācārya (Cidambaram, 1925); gr.
PKām	*Pūrva-Kāmikāgama*, new ed. (Madras, 1975).
PKār	*Pūrva-Kāraṇāgama* (Madras, 1921), gr.
PMNK	*Paramokṣanirāsakārikā*. See Aṣṭ. Pr.
Rau	*Rauravāgama*, éd. crit. par N. R. Bhatt, 3 vols. (Pondichéry: Publications IFI No. 18, 1961, 1972, 1988).
RT	*Ratnatraya*. See Aṣṭ. Pr.
SārK	*Sārdhatriśatikālottarāgama*, avec le commentaire de Bhaṭṭa Rāmakaṇṭha, éd. crit. par N. R. Bhatt (Pondichéry: Publications IFI No. 61, 1979).
ŚC	*Śivārcanācandrikā*, by Appayadīkṣita (Devakoṭṭai, 1922).
SiŚe	*Siddhāntaśekhara*, by Viśvanātha (Bangalore, 1971).
SP (1, 2, 3)	*Somaśambhupaddhati*, éd. et trad. par Hélène Brunner-Lachaux, 3 vols. (Pondichéry: Publications IFI No. 25, 1963, 1968, 1977).
SP4	*Id.*, vol. 4, in preparation.

ŚRS — *Śataratnasaṅgraha*, by Umāpatiśivācārya, Tantrik Texts No. 22 (Calcutta, 1944).

Su — *Suprabhedāgama* (Madras, 1928); gr.

SvT — *Svacchandatantra*, with commentary (*Uddyota*) by Kṣemarāja, 6 vols., KSTS, 1921-1943.

Svā — *Svāyambhuvāgama*, IFI, T. 192.

TPr — *Tattvaprakāśika*. See Aṣṭ. Pr.
Tattvaprakāśa (= *id*.), with commentary by Śrīkumāra, Trivandrum Sanskrit Series No. 68 (Trivandrum, 1920).
Id., French trans. (with Introduction and summary of the two commentaries) by P.-S. Filliozat, JA, 1971, pp. 247-295.

UKām — *Uttara-Kāmikāgama* (Madras, 1909); gr.

UKār — *Uttara-Kāraṇāgama* (Madras, 1927); gr.

Vāt — *Vātulaśuddhākhya* (or *Āgamarahasya*) (Bangalore, 1958).

Studies

Brunner, Hélène. 1963, 1968, 1977a, see SP.

———. 1965. "Analyse du *Kiraṇāgama*," *JA*: 309-328.

———. 1967. "Analyse du *Suprabhedāgama*," *JA*: 31-60.

———. 1975. "Le *sādhaka*, personnage oublié du śivaïsme du Sud," *JA*: 411-443.

———. 1977. "Importance de la littérature āgamique pour l'étude des religions vivantes de l'Inde." *Indologica Taurinensia* [Torino], vols. 3-4 (1975-76), pp. 107-124.

———. 1981. "Le Śaiva-Siddhānta, 'essence' du Veda," *Indologica Taurinensia* [Torino], vol. 8-9 (1980-81), pp. 51-66.

———. 1985a. See Mṛg II.

———. 1985b. "On the Threefold Classification of Śaiva Tantras." *Proceedings of the Fifth World Sanskrit Conference*, New Delhi.

———. 1986. "The Pāśupatas as Seen by the Śaivas." *Sanskrit and World Culture*, Schriften zur Geschichte und Kultur des Alten Orients, vol. 18, Berlin, pp. 513-520.

———. 1988a. "Esclavage et Libération selon la perspective des Āgama śivaïtes." *Philosophy and Culture*, vol. 4, Montreal, pp. 641-650.

———. 1988b. "L'ācārya śivaïte: du *guru* au *gurukkaḷ*." *BEI*, No. 6: 145-176.

———. 1990. "*Ātmārthapūjā* versus *Parārthapūjā* in the Śaiva Tradition." In T. Goudriaan ed., *The Sanskrit Tradition and Tantrism*, Leiden: Brill, pp. 4-23.

———. 1991a. "The four *pādas* of Śaivāgamas," in: *S. S. Janaki Felicitation Volume*, Madras: Kuppuswamy Research Institute, in the press.

———. 1991b. "Place of Yoga in Śaivāgamas," in: *N. R. Bhatt Felicitation Volume*, in the press.

Devasenapathi, V. A. 1960. *Śaiva Siddhānta*. University of Madras.

Filliozat, P.-S. 1971 and 1984. See TPr and NāK.

Gonda, J. 1976. *Viṣṇuism and Śivaism, a Comparison*. New Delhi.

———. 1977. See MRLS.

Goudriaan, T. 1978. *Māyā, Divine and Human*. Delhi.

———. 1981. See HTŚL.

Lorenzen, D. N. 1972. *The Kāpālikas and Kālāmukhas*. New Delhi.

Padoux, A. 1987. "Contributions à l'étude du Mantraśāstra III: le *japa*." *BEFEO*, 76: 117-164.

Pandey, K. C. 1954. *Bhāskarī*, vol. 3. Lucknow University.

———. 1963. *Abhinavagupta*, 2d ed. Chowkhamba Sanskrit Studies. Varanasi.

Rastogi, N. 1987. *Introduction to the Tantrāloka*. Delhi, Varanasi, Patna and Madras.

Sanderson, A. 1985a. "Purity and Power among the Brahmans of Kashmir." *The Category of the Person*. Cambridge University Press, pp. 190-215.

———. 1985b. Review of Bhatt's editions of MatP II and *Rauravottarāgama*. *BSOAS*, 48: 564-568.

Sivaraman, K. 1973. *Śaivism in Philosophical Perspective*. Delhi, Patna, and Varanasi.

Zieseniss, A. 1958. *Studien zur Geschichte des Śivaismus. Die Śaiva-Systematik des Vṛhaspatitattva*. New Delhi.

Chapter Two

On Puraścaraṇa: Kulārṇavatantra, Chapter 15

Gudrun Bühnemann

Introduction

The Kulārṇavatantra (KT), written between the eleventh and fifteenth centuries A.D.,[1] is considered one of the most important texts of the Kaula school of Śāktism. A large number of manuscripts of this text are known,[2] and it is quoted extensively in Tantric literature,[3] although often these quotes cannot be traced in the printed edition of the text.[4] The most popular edition of the KT is that by Tārānātha Vidyāratna, which is based on several manuscripts and first appeared in 1917. A second, slightly revised edition came out in 1965 and was reprinted in 1984. Chapters 1 and 2 have been edited again from a large number of manuscripts and provided with a Swedish translation by Carlstedt in 1974. In 1983 Rai brought out a complete but rather free English translation of the text.

This chapter provides an annotated translation of Chapter 15 of the KT, which deals with the 'preliminary ritual' (*puraścaraṇa*) for making a mantra effective (*siddha*). The chapter is significant because it presents in a concise manner important details and beliefs connected with the recitation of mantras (*japa*). It was written at a stage when the technicalities of mantraśāstra had been fully developed and were generally accepted. The author therefore did not find it necessary to give detailed explanations. Therefore the treatments of the sixty defects of mantras (KT 15.65-70) and of the diagrams used to determine the suitability of a mantra for a particular person (15.78-96) are extremely brief and can be understood only with the help of other sources. Among such texts, the Śāradātilaka (ŚT) by Lakṣmaṇa Deśikendra with Rāghavabhaṭṭa's Padārthādarśa (PĀ) (written in 1494 A.D.) is very helpful, as it provides many parallel passages; we should mention further the Tantrarāja (TR) with the commentary Manoramā by Subhagānandanātha (composed 1603-1604 A.D.) and partly by Prakāśānandanātha, and Chapter 64 of the Nārada-Purāṇa. Verses from Chapter 15 of the KT are quoted in a number of texts; for example, Kṛṣṇānanda's Tantrasāra (TS)[5] (seventeenth century), Vidyārṇavatantra (VT), attributed to Vidyāraṇya Yati (compiled before 1726),[6] Puraś-caryārṇava by Pratāp Siṃha Sāh Dev, king of Nepal who ruled from 1774 to 1776/77,[7] and Mantramahārṇava by Mādhavarāya Vaidya (compiled at the end of the nineteenth century).[8] In addition to these quoted verses, a number of verses of this chapter occur with different readings in other texts. These are commonly quoted stanzas for which the original source cannot be determined.

The Sanskrit text of Chapter 15 has been reproduced here from Vidyāratna's edition of the KT, 1965. I have compared it with the following two editions: Kûlârṇava (*sic*) Tantra, ed. Târânâtha Vidyâratna, Calcutta and London 1917, and Kulārṇavatantra, ed. Jīvānanda Vidyāsāgara, Calcutta 1897, and with four manuscripts preserved at the Bhandarkar Oriental Research Institute, Puṇe: No. 1113/1886-92 = A, No. 1114/1886-92 = B, No. 38/A1882-83 = C, and No. 449/1884-86 = D (dated 1726). Chapter 15 occurs in all these sources without major variants in the text.

Chapter 15 begins with a eulogy on the practice of *japa*, which is considered a sacrifice (*yajña*) superior to other sacrifices and a means of attaining the four goals of human life (3). Along with the ritual worship of the gods (*pūjā*), the offering of water libations (*tarpaṇa*), fire sacrifice (*homa*), and the feeding of Brahmins (*brāhmaṇa-bhukti*), *japa* is said to form one of five limbs of the 'preliminary ritual' (*puraścaraṇa*), which makes a mantra effective (*siddha*) (8). A *siddha-mantra* then can be successfully employed for desire-oriented (*kāmya*) rites. One of the conditions for a mantra to become effective is that it be received from a preceptor who has perfected the mantra himself and that it be transmitted through a regular initiation ritual (14-15). Mantras that have been heard accidentally or taken from books are useless (20-21).

For *japa*, the text recommends certain places (22-30), materials for preparing the seat (32-33), and yogic postures for sitting (34). Among the rites preceding the repetition of the mantra are the worship of the Lord of the lamp (*dīpanātha*) (31), *prāṇāyāma*, and along with it the purification of the elements (*bhūtaśuddhi*) (35-45), and *nyāsa* (46-47). The rosary may vary in the number of beads (fifteen, twenty-five, twenty-seven, thirty, or fifty beads). When counting the beads, the worshipper is advised to use different fingers for different results (48-52).

The actual ritual of *japa* begins with a declaration (*saṃkalpa*) on the part of the worshipper that he is now going to repeat mantra X and ends with the offering of the *japa* to the deity (53). Of the three kinds of *japa* (aloud, in a low voice, and mental), the mental repetition is considered best (54). The repetition should be neither too fast nor too slow (55).

When taking up *japa* of a mantra, the impurities at the beginning and end of the recitation (called *jātakasūtaka* and *mṛtakasūtaka* in analogy to terms used in *dharmaśāstra* in connection with the birth and the death of a human being) are to be removed (57-58). Before repeating a mantra, one should know the esoteric meaning of the seed syllables (*mantrārtha*), the "consciousness of the mantra" (*mantra-caitanya*), and the *yonimudrā* (59). This *mudrā* and/or the ten purificatory rituals (*saṃskāra*), which consist of special ways of reciting or purifying the syllables of the mantra (71-72), are employed to remove the sixty possible defects of a mantra. These defects consist mostly of unsuitable arrangements of syllables or an unsuitable number of them (65-70).

For the period of the *puraścaraṇa* the worshipper should observe a special diet (74) and should not accept food from another person, lest half of the fruits of the rite go to that person (75-77). To find out whether a mantra is suitable for a person, the text refers to six diagrams. In the case of the *akathahacakra* (78-85) and the *akaḍamacakra* (86), the syllables of the alphabet are assigned to the squares of a diagram. Beginning with the first letter of the person's name, one counts the squares and assigns categories to them until one arrives at the square in which the first letter of the mantra occurs. The mantra is accepted or rejected on the basis of the category assigned to the square. In the case of the *nakṣatracakra* (87-88) and the *rāśicakra* (89-91), the syllables of the alphabet are assigned to the twenty-seven lunar mansions and to the zodiac signs, respectively. Beginning with the lunar mansion-(lunar) zodiac sign of one's birth, one assigns different categories to the squares of the diagrams until one arrives at the square in which the first letter of the mantra occurs. According to the category, the mantra is accepted or rejected. In the case of the *ṛṇidhanicakra* (92-93), one counts the numbers assigned to the squares of the diagram, beginning with the square in which the first letter of the worshipper's name occurs up to the square in which the first letter of the mantra occurs, and adds the numbers. Then, beginning with the square of the first letter of the mantra, one counts up to the square of the first letter of the name and adds those numbers. After a mathematical procedure the number of the worshipper and that of the mantra are compared. If the number of the mantra is larger, the mantra is considered to be "indebted" to the worshipper from a past life and should be accepted as its repetition is likely to yield quick results. If the number of the worshipper is larger, the mantra should be rejected. In the case of the *kulākulacakra* (94-96), the fifty syllables of the alphabet are classified according to the five elements. One checks whether the letters of the person's name and those of the mantra belong to the same element or to elements that are "friendly" with each other. If the letters are "unfriendly," the mantra should be rejected. There is no indication whether all six diagrams are to be employed with respect to the mantra one wants to adopt. Certain mantras are said to be exempt from this procedure altogether (97-99).

The chapter concludes with a number of general rules regarding the *puraścaraṇa*. It stresses exclusive concentration on the mantra, ritual purity, and mental discipline (103-114).

Chapter 16, which deals with the procedure of desire-oriented (*kāmya*) rites, contains a few more references to topics related to *mantraśāstra*. But it merely lists terms without explaining their meaning. Thus, 16.17ab mentions the *nidrā* and *bodha* forms of mantras, and 16.17cd and 40-44 the three sexes of mantras, topics treated for example also in ŚT 2.57cd-63.

Survey of Contents of KT, Chapter 15

Introduction (frame story) (1-2)
Praise of *japa* (3-6)
The five limbs of the *puraścaraṇa* (7-12)
On perfecting mantras (13-21)
Description of suitable places for the *puraścaraṇa* (22-30)
Worship of the Lord of the lamp (31)
Recommended seats and postures (32-34)
Prāṇāyāma with *bhūtaśuddhi* (35-45)
Nyāsa (46-47)
The two kinds of *akṣamālā* (48-53)
Modes of recitation (54-56)
The two impurities (*sūtaka*) of a mantra (57-58)
The necessity of knowing the *mantrārtha*, *mantracaitanya*, and *yonimudrā* (59-64)
The sixty defects of mantras (65-70)
The ten purificatory rituals (*saṃskāra*) for removing these defects (71-73)
On food (74-77)

Diagrams for determining the qualities of mantras (78-99):[9]
akathahacakra (78-84)
akaḍamacakra (85-86)
nakṣatracakra (87-88)
rāśicakra (89-91)
ṛṇidhanicakra (92-93)
kulākulacakra (94-96)
mantras to which these diagrams need not be applied (97-99)
Miscellaneous rules for the *puraścaraṇa* (100-114)
End (frame story) (115)
Colophon (115+)

Text of the Kulārṇavatantra, Chapter 15

pañcadaśa ullāsaḥ /
śrīdevy uvāca /
kuleśa śrotum icchāmi puraścaraṇalakṣaṇam /
sthānāhārādibhedaṃ ca vada me parameśvara // 1

īśvara uvāca /
śṛṇu devi pravakṣyāmi yan māṃ tvaṃ paripṛcchasi /
tasya śravaṇamātreṇa mantratattvaṃ prakāśate // 2

japayajñāt paro yajño nāparo 'stīha kaścana /
tasmāj japena dharmārthakāmamokṣāṃś ca sādhayet // 3

sarvapādān[10] parityajya mantrapādaṃ[11] samabhyaset /
apramādād bhavet siddhiḥ pramādād aśubhaṃ phalam // 4

bhogāpavargasaṃkalpakalpavrataśubho japaḥ /
japadhyānamayaṃ yogaṃ tasmād devi samācaret // 5

ābrahmabījadoṣāś ca niyamātikramodbhavāḥ /
jñānājñānakṛtāḥ sarve praṇaśyanti japāt priye // 6

saṃsāre duḥkhabhūyiṣṭhe yadīcchet siddhim ātmanaḥ /
pañcāṅgopāsanenaiva mantrajāpī vrajet sukham // 7

pūjā traikālikī nityaṃ japas tarpaṇam eva ca /
homo brāhmaṇabhuktiś ca puraścaraṇam ucyate // 8

yad yad aṅgaṃ vihīyeta tatsaṃkhyādviguṇo japaḥ /
kuryād dvitricatuḥpañcasaṃkhyāṃ[12] vā sādhakaḥ priye // 9

kurvīta cāṅgasiddhyarthaṃ tadaśaktau sa bhaktitaḥ /
taṃ ced aṅgaṃ vihīyeta mantrī neṣṭam avāpnuyāt // 10

annaiś caturvidhair devi padārthaiḥ ṣaḍrasānvitaiḥ /
subhojiteṣu vipreṣu sarvaṃ hi saphalaṃ bhavet // 11

samyaksiddhaikamantrasya pañcāṅgopāsanena ca /
sarvamantrāś ca sidhyanti tvatprasādāt kuleśvari // 12

upadeśasya sāmarthyāt śrīguroś ca prasādataḥ /
mantraprabhāvād bhaktyā ca mantrasiddhiḥ prajāyate // 13

siddhamantrād guror labdho mantro yaḥ siddhibhāg bhavet /
pūrvajanmakṛtābhyāsān mantro vā śīghrasiddhidaḥ // 14

dīkṣāpūrvaṃ kuleśāni pāraṃparyakramāgatam[13] /
nyāyalabdhaś ca yo mantraḥ sa ca siddho na saṃśayaḥ // 15

māsamātraṃ japen mantraṃ bhūtalipyā tu[14] saṃpuṭam /
kramotkramāt sahasraṃ tu tasya siddho bhaven manuḥ // 16

triṣaṣṭyakṣarasaṃyuktamātṛkākṣarasaṃpuṭam /
maṇḍalaṃ pūjayen mantrī[15] mātṛkāvarṇam uccaran // 17

mātṛkājapamātreṇa mantrāṇāṃ koṭikoṭayaḥ /
japitāḥ syur na saṃdeho yataḥ sarvaṃ tadudbhavam // 18

anekakoṭimantrāṇi cittākulakarāṇi ca /
mantraṃ gurukṛpāprāptam ekaṃ syāt sarvasiddhidam // 19

yadṛcchayā śrutaṃ mantraṃ dṛṣṭenāpi [c]chalena ca /
patre sthitaṃ vā cādhyāpya tajjapaḥ syād anarthakṛt // 20

pustake likhitān mantrān vilokya prajapanti ye /
brahmahatyāsamaṃ teṣāṃ pātakaṃ vyādhiduḥkhadam // 21

puṇyakṣetraṃ nadītīraṃ guhā parvatamastakam /
tīrthapradeśāḥ sindhūnāṃ saṃgamaḥ pāvanaṃ vanam // 22

udyānāni viviktāni bilvamūlaṃ taṭaṃ gireḥ /
devatāyatanaṃ kūlaṃ samudrasya nijaṃ gṛham // 23

sādhaneṣu praśastāni sthānāny etāni mantriṇām /
atha vā nivaset tatra yatra cittaṃ prasīdati // 24

sūryasyāgner guror indor dīpasya ca jalasya ca /
goviprakūlavṛkṣāṇāṃ saṃnidhau śasyate japaḥ // 25

gṛhe śataguṇaṃ vidyād goṣṭhe lakṣaguṇaṃ bhavet /
koṭir devālaye puṇyam anantaṃ śivasaṃnidhau // 26

mlecchaduṣṭamṛgavyālaśaṅkātaṅkavivarjitaḥ /
ekāntapāvane nindārahite bhaktisaṃyute // 27

svadeśe dhārmike deśe subhikṣe nirupadrave /
rājabhaktajanasthāne nivaset tāpasāśraye // 28

rājānaḥ sacivā rājñāṃ puruṣāḥ prabhavo janāḥ /
caranti yena mārgeṇa na vaset tatra mantravit // 29

jīrṇadevālayodyānagṛhavṛkṣataleṣu ca /
nadītaḍāgakūpeṣu bhūchidrādiṣu no vaset // 30

dīpanātham ayaṣṭvā yo japapūjādikaṃ caret /
tatphalaṃ gṛhyate tena tasyāyāsaḥ phalaṃ bhavet // 31

vaṃśāśmadharaṇīdārutṛṇapallavanirmitam /
varjayed āsanaṃ dhīmān dāridryavyādhiduḥkhadam // 32

tūlakambalavastrāṇāṃ siṃhavyāghramṛgājinam /
kalpayed āsanaṃ dhīmān saubhāgyajñānavṛddhidam // 33

padmasvastikavīrādiṣv āsaneṣūpaviśya ca /
japārcanādikaṃ kuryād anyathā niṣphalaṃ bhavet // 34

dvādaśāvartayan buddhyā praṇavaṃ tu trimātrakam /
muñcet piṅgalayā vāyum antaḥsthaṃ recako bhavet // 35

ṣoḍaśāvartayan[16] tāraṃ pūrayed bāhyamārutam /
śanakair iḍayā baddhvā pūrakaṃ parikīrtitam // 36

dvādaśāvartayan[16] tāraṃ vāyuṃ madhye ca kumbhayet /
śoṣayed vāyubījena dehaśoṣaṇam īritam // 37

punaś ca pūrvavad vāyuṃ virecyāpūrya kumbhayet /
dahed dahanabījena dehadāhanam īritam // 38

punaś ca pūrvavad vāyuṃ virecyāpūrya kumbhayet /
śivakuṇḍalinīyogasyandanāmṛtadhārayā /
āpādamastakaṃ devi plāvayet plāvanaṃ bhavet // 39

japadhyānaṃ vinā 'garbhaḥ sagarbhas tadviparyayāt /
agarbhād garbhasaṃyuktaḥ prāṇāyāmaḥ śatādhikaḥ // 40

tapāṃsi tīrthayātrādyā makhadānavratādayaḥ /
prāṇāyāmasya tasyaite kalāṃ nārhanti ṣoḍaśīm // 41

mānasaṃ vācikaṃ pāpaṃ kāyikaṃ vāpi yat kṛtam /
tat sarvaṃ nirdahec chīghraṃ prāṇāyāmatrayaṃ śive // 42

dahyate dhmāyamānānāṃ[17] dhātūnāṃ ca yathā malam /
tathendriyāṇāṃ dahyante doṣāḥ prāṇasya saṃyamāt // 43

prāṇāyāmair viśuddhātmā yad yat karma karoti hi /
tat tat phalaty asaṃdehas tv aprayatnena vā kṛtam // 44

āgamoktena mārgeṇābhyāsaṃ nityaṃ karoti yaḥ /
devatābhāvam āpnoti mantrasiddhiḥ prajāyate // 45

yo nyāsakavacacchandomantraṃ japati taṃ priye /
vighnā dṛṣṭvā palāyante siṃhaṃ dṛṣṭvā yathā gajāḥ // 46

akṛtvā nyāsajālaṃ yo mūḍhātmā prajapen manum /
bādhyate sarvavighnaiś ca vyāghrair mṛgaśiśur yathā // 47

akṣamālā dvidhā proktā kalpitākalpiteti ca /
kalpitā maṇibhiḥ kḷptā mātṛkā syād akalpitā // 48

ādikṣāntākṣavarṇatvād akṣamāleti kīrtitā /
anulomavilomābhyāṃ gaṇayen mantravittamaḥ // 49

ekaikam aṅgulībhiḥ syād rekhābhir daśadhā phalam /
maṇibhiḥ śatasāhasraṃ māṇikyānantam ucyate // 50

triṃśadbhiḥ syād dhanaṃ puṣṭiḥ saptaviṃśatibhir bhavet /
pañcaviṃśatibhir mokṣaṃ pañcadaśyābhicārake /
pañcāśadbhiḥ kuleśāni sarvasiddhir udīritā // 51

aṅguṣṭhena ca mokṣaḥ syāt tarjanī śatrunāśinī /
madhyamāṃ dhanadāṃ vidyāt śāntikarmaṇy anāmikā /
kaniṣṭhā stambhany ākarṣaṇy aṅgulī suprakīrtitā // 52

etaj japiṣyāmīty ādau saṃkalpya mantravittamaḥ /
sthirāsano japitvātha devyai sodakam arpayet // 53

uccair japo 'dhamaḥ prokta upāṃśur madhyamaḥ smṛtaḥ /
uttamo mānaso devi trividhaḥ kathito japaḥ // 54

atihrasvo vyādhihetur atidīrghas tapaḥkṣayaḥ /
akṣarākṣarasaṃyukto yo mantraḥ sa na sidhyati // 55

manasā yaḥ smaret stotraṃ vacasā vā manuṃ japet /
ubhayaṃ niṣphalaṃ devi bhinnabhāṇḍodakaṃ yathā // 56

jātasūtakam ādau syāt tadante mṛtasūtakam /
sūtakadvayasaṃyukto yo mantraḥ sa na sidhyati // 57

ādyantarahitaṃ kṛtvā mantram āvartayed dhiyā /
sūtakadvayanirmukto yo mantraḥ sarvasiddhidaḥ // 58

mantrārthaṃ mantracaitanyaṃ yonimudrāṃ na vetti yaḥ /
śatakoṭijapenāpi tasya siddhir na jāyate // 59

suptabījāś ca ye mantrā na dāsyanti phalaṃ priye /
mantrā[ś] caitanyasahitāḥ sarvasiddhikarāḥ smṛtāḥ // 60

caitanyarahitā mantrāḥ proktā varṇās tu kevalam /
phalaṃ naiva prayacchanti lakṣakoṭijapād api // 61

mantroccāre kṛte yādṛk svarūpaṃ prathamaṃ bhavet /
śataiḥ sahasrair lakṣair vā koṭijāpe na tat phalam // 62

hṛtkaṇṭhagranthibhedaś ca sarvāvayavavardhanam /
ānandāśru ca pulako dehāveśaḥ kuleśvari /
gadgadoktiś ca sahasā jāyate nātra saṃśayaḥ // 63

sakṛd uccārite 'py evaṃ mantre caitanyasaṃyute /
dṛśyante pratyayā yatra pāraṃparyaṃ tad ucyate // 64

ruddhaḥ kūṭākṣaro mugdho baddhaḥ kruddhaś ca bheditaḥ /
bālaḥ kumāro yuvakaḥ prauḍho vṛddhaś ca garvitaḥ // 65

stambhito mūrcchito mattaḥ kīlitaḥ khaṇḍitaḥ śaṭhaḥ /
mandaḥ parāṅmukhaś chinno badhiro 'ndhas tv acetanaḥ // 66

kiṃkaraḥ kṣudhitaḥ stabdhaḥ sthānabhraṣṭaś ca pīḍitaḥ /
niḥsneho vikalo dhvasto nirjīvaḥ khaṇḍitārikaḥ // 67

suptas tiraskṛto nīco malinaś ca durāsadaḥ /
niḥsattvo nirjito dagdhaś capalaś ca bhayaṃkaraḥ // 68

nistriṃśo ninditaḥ krūraḥ phalahīno nikṛntanaḥ /
nirvīryo bhramitaḥ[18] śapta ṛṇakliṣṭo 'ṅgahīnakaḥ /
jaḍo ripur udāsīno lajjito mohito 'lasaḥ // 69

ṣaṣṭy etān mantradoṣāṃś ca yo 'jñātvā prajapen manum /
siddhir na jāyate tasya lakṣakoṭijapād api // 70

kathyante daśa saṃskārā mantradoṣaharāḥ priye /
jananaṃ jīvanaṃ paścāt tāḍanaṃ bodhanaṃ tataḥ // 71

abhiṣeko 'tha vimalīkaraṇāpyāyane tathā /
tarpaṇaṃ dīpanaṃ guptiḥ saṃskārāḥ kulanāyike // 72

śāṇollīḍhāni[19] śastrāṇi yathā syur niśitāni vai /
mantrāś ca sphūrtim āyānti saṃskārair daśabhis tathā // 73

bhakṣyaṃ haviṣyaṃ śākādi vihitāni phalāny api /
mūlaṃ śaktuṃ yavānāṃ ca śastāny etāni mantriṇām // 74

yasyānnapānapuṣṭāṅgaḥ kurute dharmasaṃcayam /
annadātuḥ phalaṃ cārdhaṃ kartuś cārdhaṃ na saṃśayaḥ // 75

tasmāt sarvaprayatnena parānnaṃ varjayet sudhīḥ /
puraścaraṇakāle ca kāmyakarmasv apīśvari // 76

jihvā dagdhā parānnena karau dagdhau pratigrahāt /
mano dagdhaṃ parastrībhiḥ kāryasiddhiḥ kathaṃ bhavet // 77

indvagnirudragrahadṛgvedārkadikṣaḍaṣṭasu /
ṣoḍaśamanubāṇābdhitithitrayodaśasv api // 78

likhet ṣoḍaśakoṣṭheṣu mātṛkārṇān vicakṣaṇaḥ /
svanāmādyakṣarād yāvan mantrādyakṣaradarśanam // 79

siddhādīn kalpayen mantrī kuryāt sādhyādibhiḥ[20] punaḥ /
catuścaturvibhāgena siddhādīn gaṇayet punaḥ // 80

siddhasiddho japāt siddho dviguṇāt siddhasādhyakaḥ /
siddhasusiddho 'rdhajapāt siddhārir hanti bāndhavān // 81

sādhyasiddho 'tisaṃkleśāt sādhyasādhyo nirarthakaḥ /
sādhyasusiddho bhajanāt sādhyārir hanti gotrajān // 82

susiddhasiddho 'rdhajapāt tatsādhyas tu yathoktataḥ /
tatsusiddho grahād eva susiddhāriḥ svagotrahā // 83

arisiddhaḥ sutaṃ hanyād arisādhyas tu yoṣitam /
tatsusiddhaḥ kulaṃ hanti svātmānaṃ hanti tadripuḥ // 84

siddhārṇā bāndhavāḥ proktāḥ sādhyās te sevakāḥ smṛtāḥ /
susiddhāḥ poṣakā jñeyāḥ śatravo ghātakāḥ smṛtāḥ // 85[21]

bāndhavā navabāṇaikāḥ syur dviṣaḍdaśa sevakāḥ /
vahnirudrasutāś caiva dvādaśāḥ poṣakāḥ smṛtāḥ // 86

prā-pa-lā-bho-pa-ṭu-prā-hyaṃ-ru-dra-syā-dri-ru-ruḥ-ka-ram /
lo-ka-lo-pa-pa-ṭu-prā-yaḥ-kha-lau-yo-bheṣu bheditāḥ /
varṇāḥ kramāt svarāntau tu revatyaṃśagatau tadā // 87

janma sampad vipat kṣema[ḥ] pratyariḥ sādhako vadhaḥ /
mitraṃ paramamitraṃ ca janmādīni punaḥ punaḥ // 88

vā-laṃ-gau-raṃ-khu-raṃ-śo-ṇaṃ-śa-mī-śo-bhetirāśiṣu /
krameṇa bheditā varṇāḥ kanyāyāṃ śādayaḥ smṛtāḥ[22] // 89

lagno dhanaṃ bhrātṛbandhuputraśatrukalatrakāḥ /
maraṇaṃ dharmakarmāyavyayā dvādaśa rāśayaḥ // 90

svarāśer mantrarāśyantaṃ gaṇanīyaṃ vicakṣaṇaiḥ /
ajñāte rāśinakṣatre nāmādyakṣararāśitaḥ // 91

nāmādyakṣaram ārabhya yāvan mantrādimākṣaram /
tridhā kṛtvā svarair bhindyāt tadanyad viparītakam // 92

kṛtvādhikam ṛṇaṃ jñeyam ṛṇī cen mantravittamaḥ[23] /
svayam ṛṇī cet tan mantraṃ japet[24] pūrvam ṛṇī yataḥ // 93

pañca hrasvāḥ pañca dīrghā bindvantāḥ saṃdhisambhavāḥ /
kādayaḥ pañcaśaḥ ṣakṣasahāntāś ca prakīrtitāḥ // 94

vāyvagnibhūjalākāśāḥ pañcāśallipayaḥ kramāt /
mahīsalilayor mitram[25] anilānalayor api /
śātravaṃ vaiparītyena maitraṃ sarvatra cāparam // 95

parasparaviruddhānāṃ varṇānāṃ yatra saṃgatiḥ /
varjayet tādṛśaṃ mantraṃ nāśakṛt tat kuleśvari // 96

ekākṣare tathā kūṭe traipure mantranāyake[26] /
strīdatte svapralabdhe ca siddhādīn naiva śodhayet // 97

mantrasiddhopadiṣṭeṣu caturāmnāyajeṣu ca /
mālāmantreṣu deveśi siddhādīn naiva śodhayet // 98

nṛsiṃhārkavarāhāṇāṃ prāsādapraṇavasya ca /
sapiṇḍākṣaramantrāṇāṃ siddhādīn naiva śodhayet // 99

mano 'nyatra śivo 'nyatra śaktir anyatra mārutaḥ /
na sidhyati varārohe lakṣakoṭijapād api // 100

vādārthaṃ paṭhyate vidyā parārthaṃ kriyate japaḥ /
khyātyarthaṃ dīyate dānaṃ kathaṃ siddhir varānane // 101

dhanārthaṃ gamyate tīrthaṃ dambhārthaṃ kriyate tapaḥ /
kāryārthaṃ devatāpūjā kathaṃ siddhir nu jāyate // 102

amedhyena tu dehena nyāsaṃ devārcanaṃ japam /
homaṃ kurvanti cen mūḍhās tat sarvaṃ niṣphalaṃ bhavet // 103

viṇmūtratyāgaśeṣādiyuktaḥ karma karoti yaḥ /
japārcanādikaṃ sarvam apavitraṃ bhavet priye // 104

malināmbarakeśādimukhadaurgandhasaṃyutaḥ[27] /
yo japet taṃ dahaty āśu devatā sujugupsitā // 105

ālasyaṃ jṛmbhaṇaṃ nidrāṃ kṣutaṃ niṣṭhīvanaṃ bhayam /
nīcāṅgasparśanaṃ kopaṃ japakāle vivarjayet // 106

atyāhāraḥ pralāpaś[28] ca prajalpo niyamāgrahaḥ[29] /
anyāsaṅgaś ca lolyaṃ[30] ca ṣaḍbhir mantro na sidhyate // 107

uṣṇīśī kañcukī nagno muktakeśo gaṇāvṛtaḥ /
apavitrottarīyaś cāśucir gacchaṃś ca no japet // 108

jāḍyaṃ duḥkhaṃ tṛṇacchedaṃ vivādaṃ vā manoratham /
bahis tu dehavāyuṃ ca japakāle vivarjayet // 109

śāntaḥ śucir mitāhāro bhūśāyī bhaktimān vaśī /
nirdvandvaḥ sthiradhīr maunī saṃyatātmā japet priye // 110

viśvāsāstikyakaruṇāśraddhāniyamaniścayaiḥ /
saṃtoṣautsukyadharmādiguṇair yukto japen naraḥ // 111

sugandhipuṣpābharaṇavastrādibhir alaṃkṛtaḥ /
tasya hastagatā siddhir nānyasya japakoṭitaḥ // 112

tanniṣṭhas tadgataprāṇas taccittas tatparāyaṇaḥ /
tatpadārthānusaṃdhānaṃ kurvan mantraṃ japet priye // 113

japāt[31] śrāntaḥ punar dhyāyed dhyānāt[32] śrāntaḥ punar japet /
japadhyānādiyuktasya kṣipraṃ mantraḥ prasidhyati // 114

iti te kathitaṃ kiṃcit puraścaraṇalakṣaṇam /
samāsena kuleśāni kiṃ bhūyaḥ śrotum icchasi // 115

iti śrīkulārṇave nirvāṇamokṣadvāre mahārahasye sarvāgamottamottame sapādalakṣagranthe pañcamakhaṇḍe ūrdhvāmnāyatantre puraścaraṇādikathanaṃ nāma pañcadaśa ullāsaḥ //

Translation

Chapter Fifteen.

The venerable Goddess said:

1. O Lord of the *kula*, I wish to hear about the nature of the preliminary ritual (*puraścaraṇa*).[33] O highest Lord, also tell me the details of [suitable] places, food items, and other things [related to this ritual].

The Lord said:

2. Listen, O Goddess, I shall tell you what you ask me. By merely hearing this [speech] the real nature of a mantra becomes manifest.

3. In this world there is no other sacrifice superior to the sacrifice of *japa*;[34] therefore one can attain by *japa* [the four goals of human life, viz.] [religious] merit, worldly prosperity, sensual pleasure, and liberation.

4. Leaving all [other] recitations (*vāda*) aside, one should practice the recitation of a mantra. From care[ful practice] comes success, from carelessness an unfavorable result.

5. *Japa* is good for a [religious] observance having the objective of worldly enjoyment and liberation. Therefore,

O Goddess, one should practice [this] yoga that consists of *japa* and meditation (*dhyāna*).

6. O beloved one, by *japa* all [mistakes] are destroyed; those caused by transgression of rules, done knowingly or unknowingly, including mistakes [committed] with respect to the syllable *Oṃ*.

7. If one desires success for oneself in this worldly existence, which is full of suffering, one should recite a mantra [and] attain happiness by the worship with five limbs (*pañcāṅga-upāsanā*)[35] alone.

8. *Pūjā* [performed] daily at the three prescribed times,[36] *japa* as well as offering of water libations (*tarpaṇa*), fire sacrifice (*homa*), and feeding of Brahmins are called the *preliminary ritual* (*puraścaraṇa*).[37]

9-10. If one limb [of the above five limbs of the *puraścaraṇa*] is lacking, *japa* [should be done] twice the number of [repetitions prescribed for] that [limb];[38] or, O beloved one, the performer of the ritual should make the number [of repetitions] two, three, four, or five times[39] [that]. And to make the limbs [of the *puraścaraṇa*] complete, he should devoutly do [this] if he is unable to perform [a limb]. For if a limb is lacking, the reciter of the mantra will not obtain the desired [objective].

11. Everything is achieved, O Goddess, when the Brahmins are well fed with food of four types [and] substances having six different tastes.[40]

12. And for one who has perfected one single mantra in the proper way by means of the worship with five limbs, all mantras become perfected by your grace, O mistress of the *kula*.

13.[41] The perfection of a mantra is caused by the power of transmission (*upadeśa*) [of the mantra], the venerable preceptor's grace, the effect of the mantra, and the [reciter's] devotion.

14. [Only] a mantra that has been received from a preceptor who [himself] has perfected the mantra can be perfected. Or else, a mantra will quickly grant success due to practice [of *japa*] performed in previous lives.

15. O mistress of the *kula,* also that mantra doubtlessly will be perfected which has been received in the proper way through initiation (*dīkṣā*) performed in a traditional manner.

16. One should repeat the mantra enclosed at the beginning and end (*saṃpuṭa*) by the syllables of the *bhūtalipi*[42] 1,000 times in regular and reversed order for one month; [thereby] one perfects the mantra.

17. The reciter of the mantra should worship the *maṇḍala*[43] enclosed at the beginning and end by the syllables of the alphabet connected with the sixty-three[44] syllables by uttering the [respective] syllable of the alphabet.

18. By the mere repetition (*japa*) of syllables [of the alphabet] doubtlessly crores of crores of mantras are repeated [automatically] because every [mantra] has originated from these [syllables].

19. The many crores of mantras confuse the mind. Only that mantra which has been received through the preceptor's grace grants all success.

20. The *japa* of a mantra causes harm if the [mantra] has been heard accidentally, or transmitted through a glance or deceit, or written on a leaf [of paper, etc.].

21. Those who look up mantras written in a book [and] repeat [them] commit an offence equal to the murder of a Brahmin, which causes disease and sorrow.

22-24.[45] A sacred place, the bank of a [sacred][46] river, a cave, the top of a mountain, areas around sacred bathing places, the confluence of rivers, a sacred forest, pure[47] gardens, the root of a Bilva tree, the slope of a hill, a temple, the sea shore, one's own house: these are the places recommended for the practices of reciters of mantras. Or else, one may stay wherever the mind is at peace.

25. *Japa* is recommended in the proximity of the sun, fire, preceptor, moon, a lamp as well as water, a cow, Brahmin,[48] and the *kula* trees.[49]

26.[50] One should consider the merit [of *japa* done] in [one's] house as being a hundredfold; [the merit of *japa* done] in a cows' stable is 100,000 times [that], in a temple 10 million times [that], [and]in the proximity of Śiva [i.e., in his temple] infinite.

27-28.[51] Free from fear and terror of barbarians, evil people, wild beasts, and snakes, one should live in one's own country, which [should be a] solitary [place], pure, free from blame, endowed with devotion, [or] in a virtuous country, which is abundant in alms, without disturbances, a place where the people are loyal to the king, a refuge for ascetics.

29. The knower of mantras should not live in an area where kings, officials, ministers, [and] influential people move about.

30. Further, one should not live in abandoned temples,[52] gardens, houses, [and] under trees, [near] rivers, ponds, wells, [and] in subterranean shelters, and so on.

31. One who performs *japa, pūjā,* and other [rituals] without having worshipped the Lord of the lamp (*dīpanātha*)[53] has the fruits of these [rituals] taken away by the [Lord of the lamp]; for him [the worshipper], the [only] result is [his] fatigue.

32. The wise man should avoid a seat made of bamboo, stone, earth, wood, grass, or twigs, which causes poverty, disease, and sorrow.

33. The wise man should prepare a seat of cotton or woolen fabric; [or he should prepare as a seat] the skin of a lion, tiger, or deer, which promotes good welfare and increase of knowledge.

34. And having seated oneself in a posture like the lotus [posture] (*padmāsana*), svastika [posture] (*svastikāsana*), or hero [posture] (*vīrāsana*) one should perform *japa*, worship, and other [rites]; otherwise [one's efforts] will be fruitless.

35. Repeating the syllable OṂ mentally twelve times, [each repetition] having a length of three smallest time units, one should exhale the air inside [one's lungs] through the right nostril (*piṅgalā*): [this] is the exhalation.[54]

36. Repeating the syllable OṂ sixteen times, one should inhale the outside air slowly by closing the left nostril (*iḍā*):

[this] is called *inhalation.*

37. And repeating the syllable OṂ twelve times, one should retain the air in between [the inhalation and the exhalation]. [While retaining it] one should dry up [one's body] by [reciting] the wind seed syllable (*bīja*) (= YAṂ): [this] is called *drying up the body.*

38. And again, having exhaled the air as before, having inhaled, one should retain [the air]. [While retaining it] one should burn up [one's body] by [reciting] the fire seed syllable [= RAṂ]: [this] is called *burning up the body.*

39. And again, having exhaled the air as before, having inhaled, one should retain [the air]. [While retaining it] one should bathe [the body] from the feet to the head with the stream of nectar flowing from the union of the *kuṇḍalinī* with Śiva, O Goddess: [this] is called *bathing.*

40. *Prāṇāyāma* without *japa* and meditation (*dhyāna*) is "sterile" (*agarbha*); "pregnant" is the opposite of that (i.e., *with japa* and meditation).[55] The "pregnant" (*prāṇāyāma*) is a hundred times better than the "sterile" one.

41. Austerities, [activities] like pilgrimages [and] sacrifices, charitable acts, [religious] observances (*vrata*), and so forth, these are not worth even a sixteenth part[56] of this ["pregnant"] *prāṇāyāma.*

42. Three [cycles of] *prāṇāyāma,* O auspicious one, quickly burn up any offense committed mentally, verbally, or physically.

43.[57] Just as the impurity of metals is burnt up when the [metals] are heated in a fire and blown upon, the defects of the sense organs are burnt up by *prāṇāyāma.*

44. Whatever act a man who has purified himself by *prāṇāyāmas* performs doubtlessly bears fruit as an act done effortlessly.

45. One who practises [*prāṇāyāma*] regularly according to the method prescribed by the Āgamas [= Tantra] attains a divine state, [and] perfection of [his] mantra is achieved.

46. O beloved one, seeing one who repeats [his] mantra with the *nyāsa*[58] as [his] armor and with [the knowledge]

of *chandas*,[59] obstacles run away like elephants having seen a lion.

47. The fool who repeats [his] mantra without having applied a network of *nyāsas* [on his body] is harassed by all [kinds of] obstacles like a young deer by tigers.

48. The rosary (*akṣamālā*) is said to be of two kinds: created and uncreated. The created one is made of beads; the uncreated one [consists of] the syllables of the alphabet.

49. It is called *a-kṣa-mālā* because it consists of the bead-like syllables from *a* to *kṣa*. The excellent knower of mantras should count [these] in regular and reversed order.

50. A single [result] is produced by [counting the number of repetitions] with the fingers; the result is tenfold [when counting] by [drawing] lines [on the ground, wall, etc.]; it is 100,000-fold [when counting] with precious stones; it is said to be infinite [when counting] with rubies.

51. [By counting] with thirty [beads] money is obtained, [by counting] with twenty-seven [beads] prosperity, [by counting] with twenty-five [beads] liberation; [counting] with fifteen [beads] [is recommended] for black magic (*abhicāra*), [counting] with fifty [beads], O mistress of the *kula*, is said [to grant] all attainments.

52. And by [using] the thumb [in counting] liberation is attained; the index finger destroys enemies; one should consider the middle finger as granting money; the ring finger [is useful] for rites of pacification (*śānti*), the little finger is said to be the finger for [the rites of] immobilization (*stambhana*) [and] attraction (*ākarṣaṇa*).[60]

53. Having first made the declaration (*saṃkalpa*)[61] [as follows:] "I shall perform *japa* of this [mantra]," the excellent knower of the mantra should repeat the mantra [sitting] in a firm posture and then offer [the *japa*] to the Goddess along with water.[62]

54.[63] The *japa* [done] aloud is said to be the lowest; the one [done] in a low voice is considered medium; the mental one is the highest, O Goddess. [Thus] the *japa* has been described as being of three varieties.

55. If [the repetition] is too fast, it causes disease; if too slow, it diminishes the ascetic power. The mantra whose syllables are mixed up cannot be perfected.

56. Both [practices], reciting a stotra mentally or repeating a mantra aloud, O Goddess, are useless like water in a broken vessel.

57. In the beginning [of the recitation] there is the impurity [arising] on birth (*jātasūtaka*), at the end of it the impurity [arising] on death (*mṛtasūtaka*).[64] The mantra which is accompanied by both impurities cannot be perfected.

58. Having freed the mantra from the [impurities] at the beginning and end [of the recitation], one should repeat [it] with devotion. The mantra that is free from both impurities grants all success.

59.[65] One who does not know the "meaning of the mantra" (*mantrārtha*),[66] the "consciousness of the mantra" (*mantracaitanya*),[67] [and] the *yonimudrā*[68] will not succeed even after 100 crores of repetitions.

60. Those mantras whose seed (*bīja*) is dormant, O beloved one, do not yield a result. Those [mantras] that are [repeated] along with "consciousness of the mantra" are considered as granting all success.

61. But mantras without "consciousness" are called mere syllables. They never yield a result even after 100,000 crores of repetitions.

62. That state which appears at once when the mantra is pronounced [with "consciousness"], that fruit does not result from even 100, 1,000, 100,000, or 10 million repetitions [of the mantra without "consciousness"].

63-64. Even with a single utterance of a mantra with "consciousness," the nodes of the heart and the throat[69] are pierced, all limbs are strengthened, tears of joy, goose-flesh, possession of the body, and stammering speech arise suddenly without doubt, O mistress of the *kula*. In cases where [such] signs are seen, there [the act] is said to be in accordance with the tradition.

65-70. And one who repeats a mantra without knowing

the following sixty defects[70] of a mantra will not succeed even after 100,000 crores of repetitions.

[A mantra can be] (1) "obstructed" (*ruddha*);[71] (2) "having false syllables" (*kūṭākṣara*);[72] (3) "perplexed" (*mugdha*);[73] (4) "bound" (*baddha*);[74] (5) "angry" (*kruddha*);[75] (6) "broken" (*bhedita*);[76] (7) "young" (*bāla*);[77] (8) "adolescent" (*kumāra*);[78] (9) "youthful" (*yuvaka*);[79] (10) "grown up" (*prauḍha*);[80] (11) "old" (*vṛddha*);[81] (12) "proud" (*garvita*);[82] (13) "restrained" (*stambhita*);[83] (14) "insensible" (*mūrcchita*);[84] (15) "intoxicated" (*matta*);[85] (16) "tied" (*kīlita*);[86] (17) "broken" (*khaṇḍita*);[87] (18) "deceitful" (*śaṭha*);[88] (19) "slow" (*manda*);[89] (20) "turning the face away" (*parāṅmukha*);[90] (21) "cut" (*chinna*);[91] (22) "deaf" (*badhira*);[92] (23) "blind" (*andha*);[93] (24) "inanimate" (*acetana*);[94] (25) "servile" (*kiṃkara*);[95] (26) "hungry" (*kṣudhita*);[96] (27) "immobilized" (*stabdha*);[97] (28) "fallen from its place" (*sthānabhraṣṭa*);[98] (29) "tormented" (*pīḍita*);[99] (30) "without affection" (*niḥsneha*);[100] (31) "deprived of parts" (*vikala*);[101] (32) "fallen to pieces" (*dhvasta*);[102] (33) "lifeless" (*nirjīva*);[103] (34) "having [its] enemies destroyed" (*khaṇḍitārika*);[104] (35) "asleep" (*supta*);[105] (36) "disregarded" (*tiraskṛta*);[106] (37) "low" (*nīca*);[107] (38) "dirty" (*malina*);[108] (39) "difficult to approach" (*durāsada*);[109] (40) "without essence" (*niḥsattva*);[110] (41) "conquered" (*nirjita*);[111] (42) "burnt" (*dagdha*);[112] (43) "unstable" (*capala*);[113] (44) "frightening" (*bhayaṃkara*);[114] (45) "pitiless" (*nistriṃśa*);[115] (46) "censured" (*nindita*);[116] (47) "cruel" (*krūra*);[117] (48) "fruitless" (*phalahīna*);[118] (49) "destroying" (*nikṛntana*);[119] (50) "powerless" (*nirvīrya*);[120] (51) "revolved" (*bhramita*);[121] (52) "cursed" (*śapta*);[122] (53) "pressed by debt" (*ṛṇakliṣṭa*);[123] (54) "limbless" (*aṅgahīna*);[124] (55) "dull" (*jaḍa*);[125] (56) "hostile" (*ripu*);[126] (57) "indifferent" (*udāsīna*);[127] (58) "ashamed" (*lajjita*);[128] (59) "deluded" (*mohita*);[129] (60) "inactive" (*alasa*).[130]

71-72. O beloved one, I name the ten purificatory rituals (*saṃskāra*)[131] that remove the defects of mantras. [The following are] the purificatory rituals, O mistress of the *kula*: (1) creating (*janana*),[132] (2) giving life (*jīvana*),[133] then (3) striking (*tāḍana*),[134] (4) awakening (*bodhana*),[135] then (5) consecrating (*abhiṣeka*),[136] then (6) cleaning (*vimalīkaraṇa*),[137] and (7) strengthening (*āpyāyana*)[138] as well as (8) offering water libations (*tarpaṇa*),[139] (9) kindling (*dīpana*),[140] [and] (10) concealing (*gupti*).[141]

73. Just as weapons are sharpened when rubbed on a

whetstone, mantras attain brilliance by means of the ten purificatory rituals.

74.[142] The following [food items] are recommended for reciters of mantras: eatables,[143] sacrificial food (*haviṣya*),[144] vegetables, and so forth, also prescribed fruits, [bulbous] roots, [and] barley flour.

75. Nourished by his food and drink [the reciter] acquires religious merit: to that donor of food doubtlessly goes half the fruits and to the performer [of the rite] the [remaining] half.

76. Therefore the wise man with all efforts should avoid the food of others at the time of the "preliminary ritual" as well as [at the time] of desire-oriented rituals, O mistress.

77. When the tongue is burnt by the food of others, when the hands are burnt by accepting [gifts or remuneration], [and] when the mind is burnt by [thoughts of] others' wives, how can there be attainment of one's goal?

78-80.[145] The wise man should write the syllables of the alphabet in sixteen squares [in the following order of the squares:] 1, 3, 11, 9, 2, 4, 12, 10, 6, 8, 16, 14, 5, 7, 15, [and] 13. Beginning with the first letter of his name [and counting] until he sees the first letter of the mantra, the knower of mantras should assign [the categories:] *siddha* and so on,[146] [to the squares]; again he should form (*siddha* and so on) [prefixed] with [the categories] *siddha* and so on.[147] Again he should count *siddha* and so on in the divisions of four [prefixed with the categories *sādhya*, *susiddha*, and *ari*].[148]

81. [A mantra that is identified as] *siddha-siddha* is perfected by *japa* [of the prescribed number], *siddha-sādhya* by double [the number of *japa* prescribed], *siddha-susiddha* by one-half [of the prescribed number]; *siddha-ari* destroys relatives.

82. *Sādhya-siddha* [is perfected] with much difficulty; *sādhya-sādhya* is useless; *sādhya-susiddha* [is perfected] by dividing [the number of repetitions];[149] *sādhya-ari* destroys those belonging to one's family line.

83. *Susiddha-siddha* [is perfected] by one-half [of the number of *japa*], and its *sādhya* [= *susiddha-sādhya*] [by the

number] stated [earlier];[150] its *susiddha* [= *susiddha-susiddha*] [is perfected] by merely adopting it;[151] *susiddha-ari* destroys those belonging to one's family line.

84. *Ari-siddha* destroys the son, and *ari-sādhya* the wife, its *susiddha* [= *ari-susiddha*] destroys the family; its 'enemy' (*ari-ari*) destroys oneself.

85.[152] The syllables of the *siddha*[-mantras] are called *relatives*, the *sādhyas* are considered servants; one should consider the *susiddhas* supporters; the enemies (*ari*) are considered destroyers.

86. [The squares] 9, 5, and 1 [of the *akaḍamacakra*] are 'relatives' [= *siddha*]; 2, 6, and 10 are 'servants' [= *sādhya*]; 3, 11, 7, and 12[153] are considered 'supporters' [= *susiddha*].

87.[154] The syllables [of the alphabet] divided [into the following groups] are assigned to the lunar mansions (*nakṣatra*) in [regular] order:[155] *prā*[= 2]-*pa*[= 1]-*lā*[= 3]-*bho*[= 4]-*pa*[= 1]-*ṭu*[= 1]-*prā*[= 2]-*hyaṃ*[= 1]-*ru*[= 2]-*dra*[= 2]-*syā*[= 1]-*dri*[= 2]-*ru*[= 2]-*ruḥ*[= 2]-*ka*[= 1]-*raṃ*[= 2]-*lo*[= 3]-*ka*[= 1]-*lo*[= 3]-*pa*[= 1]-*pa*[= 1]-*ṭu*[= 1]-*prā*[= 2]-*yaḥ*[= 1]-*kha*[= 2]-*lau*[= 3]-*yo*[= 1]. But those two [syllables] ending in *svara* [= *anusvāra/visarga: aṃ/aḥ*] form part of the [lunar mansion] Revatī.

88. [Beginning with the lunar mansion of one's birth and counting up to the lunar mansion in which the first letter of the mantra occurs, one should assign the categories] birth, wealth, calamity, welfare, opponent, fulfiller, slayer, friend, and best friend, [then] again birth, and so on.

89.[156] The syllables [of the alphabet grouped as][157] *vā*[= 4]-*laṃ*[= 3]-*gau*[= 3]-*raṃ*[= 2]-*khu*[= 2]-*raṃ*[= 2]-*śo*[= 5]-*ṇaṃ*[= 5]-*śa*[= 5]-*mī*[= 5]-*śo*[= 5]-*bha*[= 4] are assigned to the zodiac signs (*rāśi*) in [regular] order; [the syllables] *śa* and so on[158] are assigned to Virgo.

90. The twelve astrological houses (*rāśi*)[159] are the ascendant (*lagna*),[160] money, brother, friend, son, enemy, wife, death, religious merit, activity, gain, [and] loss.

91. Beginning with their own [lunar] zodiac sign, wise men should count up to the zodiac sign in which the first letter of the mantra [occurs]. When the lunar mansion [in the case of the *nakṣatracakra*] and the zodiac sign [in the

case of the *rāśicakra*] are not known, [they] should begin with the zodiac sign in which the first letter of the name [occurs].

92-93.[161] Beginning with the first letter of the name [one should add all numbers given in the diagram] up to the first letter of the mantra. Having multiplied [the sum] by three, one should divide [the product] by seven. Having performed the reverse [process],[162] one should consider [the number] that is larger as *ṛṇī*. If the mantra is *ṛṇī*, it is best, because it is "indebted" (*ṛṇī*) from before;[163] if [the worshipper] himself is *ṛṇī*, he should give up that mantra.

94-96.[164] The fifty syllables [of the alphabet] specified as the five short vowels, the five long vowels, the diphthongs (*saṃdhisaṃbhava*) along with the *anusvāra* (*bindu*) put at the end,[165] those [syllables] beginning with *ka* and so on in groups of five, those ending in *ṣa, kṣa, ḷa,*[166] *sa,* [and] *ha* in sequence are wind, fire, earth, water, [and] ether. There is friendship between the earth and water, also between fire and wind. In the opposite cases there is enmity. The other one [= ether] is a friend to all. Where there is a combination of syllables that are opposed to each other [with respect to the governing elements], one should reject the mantra, O mistress of the *kula*, as it is destructive.

97. In the case of a one-syllabled mantra, a *kūṭa*[167] [mantra], a mantra of Tripurā, one given by a woman,[168] (and) one obtained in a dream, one should not test for *siddha* and so on, O mistress of the mantras.

98. O mistress of the gods, one should not test for *siddha* and so on in the case of [mantras] taught by persons who have perfected the mantra, those originating from the four *āmnāyas*,[169] and *mālāmantras*.[170]

99.[171] One should not test for *siddha* and so on in the case of mantras of Nṛsiṃha, the sun, Varāha, the *prāsāda* (*bīja*),[172] OṂ, [and] mantras having *sapiṇḍa*[173] syllables.

100. If one's mind is in one place, Śiva in another, Śakti in another, [and] the breath in another, [the mantra] cannot be perfected, O you with fine hips, even after 100,000 crores of repetitions.

101. If knowledge is acquired for the sake of debate, if

japa is done for the sake of another, if charity is given for the sake of fame, how can there be success, O you having a beautiful face?

102. If one goes to a place of pilgrimage for the sake of [obtaining] money, if one performs austerity out of hypocrisy, if one worships the gods with a [selfish] motive, how can there be success?

103. If ignorant people perform *nyāsa*, worship of gods, *japa*, [and] fire sacrifice with an impure body—all that will be fruitless.

104.[174] A ritual like *japa* or worship performed with traces of excrement and urine, and so on [on the body],[175] all that becomes impure, O beloved one.

105. If one performs *japa* with unclean garments, hair, and so forth, and with a bad smell in the mouth, the extremely disgusted deity burns him up immediately.

106. At the time of *japa* one should avoid laziness, yawning, sleep, sneezing, spitting, fear, touching the lower limbs,[176] [and] anger.

107. A mantra is not perfected on account of these six: overeating, exertion, gossip, adherence to [unsuitable] rules, company of others, and fickleness.[177]

108.[178] One should not perform *japa* with the head covered with a turban, with a robe[179] on, naked, with untied hair,[180] surrounded by attendants, wearing an impure upper garment, in an impure condition, [or] while walking.

109. At the time of *japa* one should avoid dullness, sorrow, tearing grass,[181] quarreling, daydreaming, and passing wind.

110. O beloved one, one should perform *japa* being calm, [ritually] pure, moderate in eating, sleeping on the ground [at night], being devoted, [with sense organs] controlled, free from the pairs of opposites [i.e., indifferent to heat and cold, etc.], with a tranquil mind, observing silence, [and] with one's mind controlled.

111-112. A man endowed with faith, belief in God, compassion, trust, restraint [of mind], and determination,

[and] with qualities like contentment, zeal, and piety, [and] adorned with fragrant flowers, ornaments, and garments should do *japa*. Success lies in his hand, not [in the hand] of another man [not conforming with these qualities] in spite of crores of *japa*.

113. One should repeat the mantra, O beloved one, being devoted to it, putting one's life in it, with a concentrated mind, being absorbed in it, [and] following the meaning of its words.

114. When tired of *japa*, one should meditate; when tired of meditation, one should do *japa*. The mantra of one who combines *japa* and meditation, and so forth, is perfected quickly.

115. Thus I have told you briefly something about the characteristics of the "preliminary ritual" (*puraścaraṇa*), O mistress of the *kula*. What more do you want to hear?

Thus [ends] the fifteenth chapter (*ullāsa*), called the description of the *preliminary ritual*, and so on, in the venerable Kulārṇava, which is the door to liberation and salvation, the great secret doctrine, the very best of all Āgamas, [a work consisting of] 125,000 *anuṣṭubh* units (*grantha*), in the fifth section, in the Ūrdhvāmnāya-Tantra.

Notes

I would like to thank the Japan Society for the Promotion of Science, Tokyo, and Professor M. Tachikawa, Nagoya, for the support and assistance that enabled me to research this paper.

1. Date according to Carlstedt 1974, p. 66.

2. Cf. the *New Catalogus Catalogorum*, gen. ed. V. Raghavan, vol. 4 (Madras, 1968), pp. 244-245.

3. Cf. the *New Catalogus Catalogorum*, vol. 4, pp. 245-246.

4. On the several editions of the KT, cf. Goudriaan in Goudriaan and Gupta 1981, p. 93.

5. For example, p. 29, 22-27 = KT 15.75-77; p. 79, 8-13 = KT 15.45-47.

6. The upper limit for the composition of this text is fixed by a date of a manuscript, cf. Śāstrī 1944, p. 3. For quotes, cf. VT 1,

p. 442, 15-17 = KT 15.20-21; VT 1, p. 447, 24 = KT 15.16.

7. For example, p. 424, 15-20 = KT 15.75-77.

8. For example, p. 15, 1-23 = KT 15.1-3ab, 6-7, 8-10, 12-17, 18-21, 56cd, 74-77, 100-103, 105.

9. This section is totally omitted in manuscript A and placed at the end of the whole chapter in manuscripts C and D.

10. Read *-vādān* with A, fol. 59a.9; B, fol. 90a.6-7; D, fol. 182a.7.

11. Read *-vādaṃ* with A, fol. 59a.9; B, fol. 90a.7; D, fol. 182a.7.

12. Read *-khyaṃ*.

13. Read *-gataḥ*.

14. Read with v.l. in the text and D, fol. 183b.2, *-lipyarṇasaṃpuṭam*.

15. Reading suggested by the editor; text reads *mantraṃ*.

16. Suggested reading *-vartayaṃs*. The form *-vartayan* has been retained by the copyists in analogy to the reading in verse 35a.

17. Text reads *dhmārya-*.

18. Read with D, fol. 188a.5, *-taḥ*.

19. Text reads *-ṇollo-*.

20. Read with ŚT 2.130 and v.l. in the KT, edited by Vidyāsāgara, *siddhādibhiḥ*.

21. The editor omits verse 85 in counting. The verses have been renumbered.

22. Reading follows the v.l. in the footnote; text reads *-tā*.

23. Read with v.l. in the text: *mantra uttamaḥ*.

24. Read *tyajet* (cf. v.l. in the text *tyajed*).

25. Read with B, fol. 95b.1, and C, fol. 64a.6, *maitram*.

26. Suggested reading (cf. also v.l. in the text), *-nāyike*.

27. Read with A, fol. 61b.11, *-daurgandhya-*.

28. Read with v.l. in the text, A, fol. 62a.1, and C, fol. 63a.13 (cf. also the reading in the HYP, quoted note 177), *prayāsaś*.

29. Read with D, fol. 189b.4 and v.l. in the text (cf. also the reading in the HYP quoted in note 177), *niyamagraha*.

30. Read with A, fol. 62a.1, C, fol. 63a.13, and D, fol. 189b.5, *laulyaṃ*.

31. The correct *sandhi* form is *japāc*.

32. The correct *sandhi* form is *dhyānāc*.

33. Verse 8 defines the five parts of this ritual, which is performed to perfect a mantra.

34. For the exalted position of *japa*, cf. also Bhagavadgītā 10.25c: *yajñānāṃ japayajño 'smi*, and MSm 2.85ab: *vidhiyajñāj japayajño viśiṣṭo daśabhir guṇaiḥ* (these places are also quoted by Padoux 1987, p. 118).

35. That is, the "preliminary ritual," the five limbs of which are mentioned in verse 8.

36. That is, in the morning, at noon, and in the evening.

37. Of these five parts of the *puraścaraṇa*, the *pūjā* is to be performed three times every day; the other four parts are to be performed for a mixed number of times: the number of offerings of water libations (*tarpaṇa*) to the deity is one-tenth the number of *japa*; the number of offerings in the fire (*homa*) is one-tenth the number of water libations; the number of Brahmins fed is one-tenth the number of offerings in the fire.

38. For example, 1,000 offerings in the fire prescribed in a ritual can be substituted by 2,000 repetitions of the mantra.

39. According to one's caste the number of performances can be two, three, four, or five times the prescribed number; cf. PĀ, p. 660, 11, and TS, p. 36, 5-16.

40. The feeding of Brahmins (*brāhmaṇabhojana*) is valued very highly here and makes up for shortcomings in the ritual.

41. Verses 13-14 occur also in PĀ, p. 661, 21-24 (quoted from an unknown source).

42. Bhūtalipi is not a script here but an arrangement of forty-two syllables of the alphabet in the following specific order (cf. ŚT 7.1-4):
First group: a i u ṛ ḷ
Second group: e ai o au
Third group: ha ya ra va la
Fourth group: ṅa ka kha gha ga
Fifth group: ña ca cha jha ja
Sixth group: ṇa ṭa ṭha ḍha ḍa

Seventh group: na ta tha dha da
Eighth group: ma pa pha bha ba
Ninth group: śa ṣa sa

43. Is this maṇḍala formed by writing the sixty-three syllables in a circular way?

44. Are these also the sixty-three syllables of the alphabet? For a tradition accepting sixty-three or sixty-four *varṇas*, cf. introductory verse 3, preserved in some recensions of the Pāṇinīya Śikṣā:

triṣaṣṭiś catuḥṣaṣṭir vā varṇāḥ sambhavato matāḥ /
prākṛte saṃskṛte cāpi svayaṃ proktāḥ svayambhuvā //

(cf. Ghosh: Pāṇinīya Śikṣā, p. 49). The sixty-three *varṇas* are

twenty-one vowels: a ā ā3 i ī ī3 u ū ū3 ṛ ṝ ṝ3 ḷ
e e3 o o3 ai ai3 au au3
twenty-five stops (*sparśa*): ka kha ga gha ṅa
ca cha ja jha ña
ṭa ṭha ḍa ḍha ṇa
ta tha da dha na
pa pha ba bha ma
ya ra la va śa ṣa sa ha (= 8)
four yamas: kk (e.g., in *palikknī*), kkh (e.g., in *cakkhnatuḥ*),
gg (e.g., in *aggni*), ggh (e.g., in *nigghnanti*)
anusvāra: aṃ
visarga: aḥ
jihvāmūlīya: ḥka (-kha)
upadhmānīya: ḥpa (-pha)
duḥspṛṣṭa: ḷ3.

45. Verses 22-24ab occur also in ŚT 2.138-139 (with v.l.), verses 22-23 (with v.l.) in TS, p. 28, 5-10 (quote from the Yoginīhṛdaya).

46. Cf. PĀ, p. 117, 15-16: *nadītīraṃ puṇyanadītīram*. Verse 30 prohibits *japa* on the bank of a river.

47. For *vivikta* (usually, 'solitary'), 'pure' in this context; cf. PĀ, p. 117, 17.

48. The objects and persons mentioned in this verse are regarded as suitable to receive worship. They are also known as *pūjāsthāna* or *pūjāpāda*.

49. The nine kula trees are listed in KT 11.68. They should be worshipped as the *kulayoginīs* are believed to live in them (KT 11.66).

One is not allowed to sleep under them (KT 11.67).

50. Verses 26-28 (with v.l.) occur in TS, p. 28, 11-16 (quote from the Yoginīhṛdaya).

51. Verses 27-30 occur also in PĀ, p. 118, 6-13, and VT 1, pp. 413, 32, through 414, 3 (quoted from "Yāmala").

52. Ruined buildings are believed to be inhabited by evil spirits.

53. The worship of the Lord of the lamp (*dīpanātha*) occurs at the beginning of the Tantric *pūjā*. PKS 3.7 prescribes the formula (*bīja* syllable): *raktadvādaśaśaktiyuktāya dīpanāthāya namaḥ* and an offering of a handful of flowers.

54. Verses 35-39 describe briefly the rite of the purification of the elements (*bhūtaśuddhi*) of the reciter's body. The physical body is believed to be destroyed by drying it up and burning it; a new divine body is created and bathed in nectar flowing from the *sahasrāracakra*.

55. For a similar distinction, cf. ŚT 25.20:

prāṇāyāmo hi dvividhaḥ sagarbho 'garbha eva ca /
japadhyānādibhir yuktaṃ sagarbhaṃ taṃ vidur budhāḥ //

56. For the stereotype expression "not worth a sixteenth part," see also MSm 2.86; cf. Goudriaan in Goudriaan and Gupta 1981, p. 30.

57. This verse occurs in MSm 6.71 (with v.l.).

58. *Nyāsa* is the assignment of alphabets, parts of mantras, and so on, to various parts of the body, which thereby is believed to be invested with divine power and made secure.

59. That is, the meter that expresses the inner rhythm of the mantra.

60. The ritual immobilization of an enemy and the attraction of a desired person or object belong to the acts of black magic (*abhicāra*).

61. According to the *dharmaśāstra*, every ritual act is to begin with a declaration (*saṃkalpa*) of the place, time, aim, and method of the ritual act one is going to perform. The rite is considered fruitless without such a declaration.

62. At the end of the repetition of the mantra, the *japa* is visualized as offered into the left hand of a goddess (or into the right hand of a god) by simultaneously pouring water on the

idol['s hand] and reciting the verse:

guhyātiguhyagoptā tvam gṛhāṇāsmatkṛtaṃ japam /
siddhir bhavatu me deva tvatprasādāt tvayi sthite //
(PĀ, p. 306, 11-12).

63. Verses 54-56 also occur in TS, p. 33, 24-25; 33, 28 and 33, 31 (quoted from an unidentified source).

64. In analogy to the concept of the two kinds of impurities (*aśauca*) arising for members of a family on the occurrence of birth or death, which are explained in the *dharmaśāstras* (cf. Kane 4, pp. 269 ff.), the *mantraśāstra* describes the impurities arising at the beginning and end of the repetition of a mantra. For details about these impurities, cf. Puraścaryārṇava, pp. 526, 20-527, 9 (which quotes verses from the KT that cannot be located in the printed edition). The impurities of the mantra are removed by reciting the mantra 7 times or 108 times with the syllable OṂ at the beginning and end (cf., e.g., TS, p. 34, 24-26, quoting "Kāsasaṃhitā").

65. Verses 59-64 occur also in TS, pp. 34, 28-35, 7 (with v.l., quote from the "Kāsasaṃhitā").

66. *Mantrārtha* refers to the esoteric meaning of the respective letters of the *bījas* of the deity of the mantra (cf. PrT, pp. 419, 11-420, 22). According to the Puraścaryārṇava, p. 526, 17, this meaning is to be explained by the preceptor.

67. There are different interpretations of *mantracaitanya*. For four interpretations, see PrT, p. 418, 4-26. According to an unknown source quoted in Puraścaryārṇava, p. 528, 12-15, it consists of the knowledge that the deity has the form of the mantra, the preceptor the form of the deity, one's self the form of the preceptor, and the mantra the form of one's self.

68. The *yonimudrā* is employed to remove the defects of the mantras listed in verses 65-70. It is one of the *mudrās* of Haṭhayoga, similar to *mūlabandha*. According to PĀ, p. 95, 14-16, it is accompanied by visualizing the syllables of the mantra ascending from the *mūlādhāracakra* to the *brahmarandhra*, meditating, retaining the breath, repeating the mantra 1,000 times, and visualizing the syllables as descending from the *brahmarandhra* to the *mūlādhāra*.

69. The location of the nodes *brahmagranthi*, *viṣṇugranthi* (and *rudragranthi*) in the *anāhatacakra* (heart), *viśuddhicakra* (throat), [and *ājñācakra*, space between the eyebrows] is described in the commentary called Jyotsnā on HYP 4.70-76. In Haṭhayoga these nodes

are pierced by the practice of *prāṇāyāma*.

70. Verses 65-69 enumerate the sixty possible "defects" of mantras, although some of the names (e.g., "young" or "grown up") do not seem to indicate defects but rather the author's intention to enumerate all possible types of mantras. The defects are to be removed by performing the *yonimudrā* (see note 68) or the ten purificatory rituals listed in verses 71-72. I am not aware of any other text that lists sixty defects of mantras. ŚT 2.64-108 and NP 64.14-19 list forty-nine defects (although Mantramahodadhi 24.97 refers to the ŚT listing fifty defects); N, p. 166, 2, refers to fifty defects without mentioning any source. TR 1.75-81 lists only twenty-five defects. This text follows a different tradition regarding the interpretation of the defects.

As the KT does not give any explanation as to what these defects consist of, explanations had to be looked for in the earlier-mentioned sources. I follow the tradition of the ŚT and NP and the explanations given in the PĀ (on the ŚT) and in VT 1, pp. 30 ff., which comments in detail on the passage from the ŚT. In cases where no explanations were found in these texts, I consulted the TR.

71. According to ŚT 2.72 and NP 64.22, a mantra is *ruddha* when the earth seed syllable LAṂ is inserted twice at the beginning, middle, and end. For further details, cf. PĀ, p. 84, 8-17.

72. According to ŚT 2.94a and NP 64.44, a mantra is *kūṭa* (or *niraṃśaka*) when it consists of one syllable. VT 1, p. 35, 14, explains that although consisting of many syllables, it is considered as monosyllabic (bahvakṣarātmakaṃ bījaṃ kūṭaḥ / sa bahvakṣaro 'pi ekākṣara eveti jñeyo niraṃśakaḥ /). But see also verse 97a.

73. I am unaware of any text explaining the meaning of *mugdha* in this context.

74. I am unaware of any text explaining the meaning of *baddha* in this context.

75. *Kruddha* may be the same as *atikruddha*, which is explained in ŚT 2.101 as a mantra of twenty-eight or thirty-one syllables.

76. According to ŚT 2.83 and NP 64.34, *bhedita* is a mantra having in the middle two nouns terminating in the dative or ablative plural ending *-bhyas*,and having VAṢAṬ at the beginning and HRAḤ in the middle.

77. According to ŚT 2.89a and NP 64.39c, *bala* is a mantra consisting of seven syllables.

78. According to ŚT 2.89b and NP 64.39d, *kumāra* is a mantra consisting of eight syllables.

79. According to ŚT 2.84c and NP 64.40a, *yuvaka* is a mantra consisting of sixteen syllables.

80. According to ŚT 2.89d and NP 64.40ab, *prauḍha* is a mantra consisting of forty syllables.

81. According to ŚT 2.90 and NP 64.40cd-41ab, *vṛddha* is a mantra consisting of 30, 64, 100, or 104 syllables.

82. According to TR 1.75c, *garvita* is a mantra that has not been received in a regular initiation.

83. According to ŚT 2.78 and NP 64.28cd-29ab, *stambhita* is a mantra having PHAṬ and LA in the middle and PHAṬ and LA twice at the end.

84. According to ŚT 2.86cd and NP 64.36cd, *mūrcchita* is a mantra having PHAṬ in the middle.

85. According to TR 1.78a, *matta* is a mantra that has not been obtained from a preceptor but has been taken from a leaf [of a manuscript].

86. According to ŚT 2.77 and NP 64.27-28ab, *kīlita* is a mantra not having the following syllables at the beginning, middle or end: HAṂSAḤ, HAUṂ, AIṂ, HAṂ, SAḤ, PHREṂ, HŪṂ, HRĪṂ, namāmi.

87. According to TR 1.79a, *khaṇḍita* is a mantra that one repeats (by mistake) incompletely.

88. I am not aware of any text explaining the meaning of *śaṭha* in this context.

89. According to ŚT 2.93d and NP 64.44b, *manda* is a mantra of ten syllables.

90. According to ŚT 2.73d-74 and NP 64.24, *parāṅmukha* is a mantra that has KLĪṂ at the beginning and HRĪṂ or KROṂ at the end and that does *not* have KLĪṂ in the middle, HRĪṂ at the beginning, or KROṂ at the end.

91. According to ŚT 2.71 (NP 64.20cd-21 differs), *chinna* is a mantra that has YAṂ at the beginning, middle, or end and that is connected with HRĪṂ or has HRĪṂ separate or contains HRĀṂ, HRĪṂ, HRŪṂ, HRAIṂ, or HRAUṂ three, four, or five times.

92. According to ŚT 2.74d-75, *badhira* (also called *karṇahīna*) is a mantra *not* having HAṂ or SAṂ at the beginning, middle, or end.

93. According to ŚT 2.76 and NP 64.26, *andha* (also called *netrahīna*) is a mantra that consists of five syllables and does *not* contain RA, HA, or SA.

94. I am not aware of any text explaining the meaning of *acetana* in this context.

95. I am not aware of any text explaining the meaning of *kiṃkara* in this context. B, fol. 93a.15; C, fol. 62b.12; and a v.l. in the text read *kekara*, which is found in ŚT 2.86b and NP 64.17c and is explained as a mantra of four syllables (ŚT 2.94d and NP 64.45cd).

96. According to ŚT 2.97cd-98a and NP 64.48, *kṣudhita* (also called *kṣudhārta* or *kṣudhātura*) is a mantra of twenty-four or twenty-seven syllables.

97. I am not aware of any text explaining the meaning of *stabdha* in this context.

98. According to ŚT 2.104cd-105ab and NP 64.53cd-54ab, *sthānabhraṣṭa* is a mantra having sixty-five to ninety-nine syllables.

99. According to ŚT 2.108cd and NP 64.58ab, *pīḍita* is a mantra of more than 1,000 syllables.

100. According to ŚT 2.106b-107ab and NP 64.55cd-56, *niḥsneha* (also called *atiniḥsneha*) is a mantra of 91, 100, 150, 200, or 300 syllables.

101. According to ŚT 2.105cd-106a and NP 64.54cd-55ab, *vikala* is a mantra of thirteen or fifteen syllables.

102. According to ŚT 2.87d-88 and NP 64.38cd-39ab, *dhvasta* (also called *pradhvasta*) is a mantra that consists of eighteen or nineteen (NP: twenty) syllables and contains OṂ (NP: KLĪṂ), HRĪṂ, and KROṂ.

103. I am not aware of any text explaining the meaning of *nirjīva* in this context. The text gives as v.l., *nirbīja*, which is found in ŚT 2.67c and NP 64.17a and is explained as a mantra having NAMAḤ at the end, SVĀHĀ in the middle, and *not* having the syllables VAṢAṬ, HUṂ, PHAṬ, and HAṂ, and SA (ŚT 2.91cd-92 and NP 64.42-43ab).

104. I am not aware of any text explaining the meaning of *khaṇḍitārika* in this context.

105. According to ŚT 2.84 and NP 64.35ab, *supta* (also called *suṣupta*) is a mantra of three syllables, not having HAṂSAḤ.

106. According to ŚT 2.82 and NP 64.33, *tiraskṛta* is a mantra having DA or HŪṂ in the middle and PHAṬ twice at the end.

107. I am not aware of any text explaining the meaning of *nīca* in this context.

108. According to ŚT 2.81 and NP 64.32, *malina* is a mantra having the syllable MA four times at the beginning, middle, and end.

109. I am not aware of any text explaining the meaning of *durāsada* in this context.

110. According to ŚT 2.94c and NP 64.45a, *niḥsattva* (also called *sattvahīna*) is a mantra of two syllables.

111. According to TR 1.76c, *nirjita* is a mantra that cannot be perfected because of the reciter's stock of bad karma from previous lives.

112. According to ŚT 2.79 and NP 64.29cd-30ab, *dagdha* is a mantra having RA and VA combined seven times at the end.

113. I am not aware of any text explaining the meaning of *capala* in this context.

114. I am not aware of any text explaining the meaning of *bhayaṃkara* in this context.

115. According to ŚT 2.91a and NP 64.41cd, *nistriṃśa* is a mantra of nine syllables having OṂ at the beginning or end or both.

116. I am not aware of any text explaining the meaning of *nindita* in this context.

117. According to ŚT 2.102 and NP 64.51, *krūra* (also called *atikrūra*) is a mantra of thirty or thirty-three (NP: twenty-eight or thirty-one) syllables.

118. I am not aware of any text explaining the meaning of *phalahīna* in this context.

119. I am not aware of any text explaining the meaning of *nikṛntana* in this context.

120. *Nirvīrya* is probably the same as *hṛtavīrya* (ŚT 2.86cd) and *hatavīrya* (NP 64.37ab), which refer to a mantra ending in PHAṬ.

121. *Bhramita* may be the same as *bhrānta* (NP 64.37cd-38ab) and

hīna (ŚT 2.87a-c), referring to a mantra having PHAṬ four times at the beginning, middle, and end.

122. I am not aware of any text explaining the meaning of *śapta* in this context.

123. I am not aware of any text explaining the meaning of *ṛṇakliṣṭa* in this context.

124. According to ŚT 2.100 and NP 64.50, *aṅgahīna* is a mantra of twenty-six, twenty-nine, or thirty-six syllables.

125. I am not aware of any text explaining the meaning of *jaḍa* in this context.

126. TR 1.75d classifies as *śatru* (= *ripu*) a mantra belonging to the category of *ari*-mantras (see verses 81-85 of this chapter of the KT).

127. I am not aware of any text explaining the meaning of *udāsīna* in this context.

128. I am not aware of any text explaining the meaning of *lajjita* in this context.

129. According to ŚT 2.97ab and NP 64.47cd, *mohita* is a mantra of thirty-two syllables.

130. I am not aware of any text explaining the meaning of *alasa* in this context. Suggested reading with TR 1.76d is *ahasa* 'without HA and SA' (see Subhagānandanātha's commentary on TR 12.19-20: *ahasāḥ hakārasakārarahitāḥ*).

131. The following ten rites are supposed to remove the defects of the mantras, which are mentioned in the preceding list. As the KT does not give details about the rituals, I refer to the explanations in ŚT 2.114-122.

132. *Janana* is the extraction of the syllables of the mantra one by one from the alphabet.

133. *Jīvana* is the recitation of each syllable of the mantra separately prefixed by the syllable OṂ.

134. *Tāḍana* means that, having written down the syllables of the mantra, one should sprinkle each syllable with sandal water while reciting YAṂ.

135. *Bodhana* means that, having written down the mantra, one should touch it with as many red oleander flowers as there

are syllables in the mantra while repeating RAṂ.

136. *Abhiṣeka* means that, according to the regulations found in one's own Tantric tradition, one should sprinkle the syllables of the mantra with water mixed with as many twigs of the Aśvattha tree as there are syllables in the mantra.

137. *Vimalīkaraṇa* means that contemplating the mantra one should burn its three impurities with the recitation of the "light" mantra, OṂ HRAUṂ.

138. *Āpyāyana* is the sprinkling of each syllable of the written mantra with water mixed with Kuśa grass.

139. *Tarpaṇa* means that, having uttered the mantra, one offers water to it by saying, "I satiate mantra X."

140. *Dīpana* is the prefixing of OṂ HRĪṂ ŚRĪṂ to the mantra.

141. *Gupti* is keeping secret the mantra that one repeats.

142. This verse occurs with v.l. in ŚT 2.140.

143. ŚT 2.140a reads *bhaikṣyam*, food obtained by begging (in the case of a *brahmacārin* or a *yati*; cf. PĀ, p. 118, 15).

144. That is, food to be offered to the fire as an oblation in connection with *vratas*, not *śrāddhas* (cf. PĀ, p. 118, 19). On *haviṣya*, see Kane 2, p. 681, and 4, p. 149, note 343.

145. Verse 80ab occurs also in ŚT 2.130ab. For verses 80-84, see also TR 1.49cd-55 with v.l.

Verses 78-85 deal with the *akathahacakra*, which is named after the syllables *a-ka-tha-ha* written in the first square. This diagram is used to determine the qualities of a mantra in respect to a particular worshipper. The four squares of the diagram (= I-IV) are subdivided into four squares each in the following manner:

1	2	3	4
I		II	
5	6	7	8
9	10	11	12
IV		III	
13	14	15	16

The syllables of the alphabet from *a* to *kṣa* (cf. TR 1.48b and ŚT 2.129c) are assigned to the squares from the first squares of groups I-IV to the fourth square of these groups. Illustration 1 shows this diagram reconstructed according to the Manoramā, pp. 8, 16-9, 20, on TR 1.45cd-48ab.

अकथह १	उङप २	आखदळ ३	ऊचफ ४
ओडव ५	लृझम ६	औढश ७	लॄञय ८
ईघन ९	ऋजभ १०	इगधक्ष ११	ॠछब १२
अःतस १३	ऐठल १४	अंणष १५	एटर १६

Illustration 1. *Akathahacakra.*

The method of assigning the categories *siddha*, etc., to the squares is not specified in the text of the KT. It seems that the major square (= I, II, III, or IV) in whose subdivision the first letter of the worshipper's name occurs is called the *siddha* group. It has the subdivisions *siddha-siddha, siddha-sādhya, siddha-susiddha,* and *siddha-ari.* Beginning with the major group (I, II, III, or IV) containing the initial letter of one's name, one assigns in clockwise direction the categories *siddha, sādhya, susiddha,* and *ari* to the major squares. Then, beginning again with the subdivisions containing the initial letter of the name, one assigns the categories *siddha-siddha,* etc., clockwise to the subdivisions within that major square, following the same pattern for the subdivisions within the other major squares. One then locates the square containing the first letter of the mantra. From the category assigned to the major square and the subdivision containing the letter, one determines whether the mantra is suitable for repetition by a particular person following the judgments given in verses 82-84.

146. That is, *sādhya, susiddha,* and *ari.*

147. The subcategories formed with *siddha* are *siddha-siddha, siddha-sādhya, siddha-susiddha,* and *siddha-ari.*

148. The subcategories formed with *sādhya* are *sādhya-siddha,*

sādhya-sādhya, sādhya-susiddha, and *sādhya-ari*. Next are the subcategories formed with *susiddha*: *susiddha-siddha, susiddha-sādhya, susiddha-susiddha,* and *susiddha-ari*. The subcategories formed with *ari* are *ari-siddha, ari-sādhya, ari-susiddha,* and *ari-ari*.

149. For this interpretation of *bhajanāt*, see Piṅgalāmata, quoted in PĀ, p. 105, 9: tatsusiddhaḥ sārdhajapāt.

150. That is, with reference to *siddha-sādhya* = double the number of *japa* prescribed. See also Piṅgalāmata, quoted in PĀ, p. 105, 10: tatsādhyo dviguṇāj japāt.

151. For this meaning of *grahāt*, see ŚT 2.130c: susiddhaḥ prāptimātreṇa.

152. Verse 85 occurs also in ŚT 2.131 with v.l. Verses 85-86 apparently refer to the *akaḍamacakra*, a diagram of twelve squares to which the syllables of the alphabet are assigned. Again the number and sequence of the syllables is not specified. PĀ, p. 107, 15, and Mantramahodadhi 24.21 state that the syllables from *a* to *ha*, omitting the vowels *ṛ, ṝ, ḷ,* and *ḹ*, are intended. The diagram is named after the syllables *a-ka-ḍa-ma*, which occur in the first square. Illustration 2 shows this diagram reconstructed on the basis of contemporary prints.

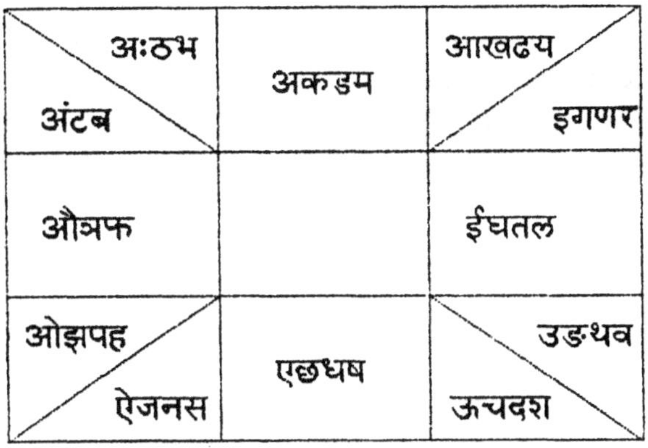

Illustration 2. *Akaḍamacakra.*

Beginning with the square that contains the first letter of the worshipper's name (see Mantramahodadhi 24.22), one should assign in a clockwise direction the categories *siddha, sādhya, susiddha,* and *ari* until one arrives at the square that contains the first letter of the mantra. Thus, if the initial letter of the mantra occurs in squares

1, 5, or 9 (1 referring to the square containing the first letter of the worshipper's name, and so on), the mantra is regarded as *siddha,* in squares 2, 6, or 10 as *sādhya,* in squares 3, 7, or 11 as *susiddha,* and (cf. the reading quoted in note 153) in squares 4, 8, or 12 as *ari.*

153. This verse erroneously assigns square 12 to the category "supporter" (*susiddha*). The following reading provided as v.l. to the text of the KT is preferable as it also accounts for the category *ari*: vahnirudramunayas tu poṣakā dvādaśāṣṭa [ka] caturas tu ghātakāḥ / "3, 11, [and] 7 are 'supporters' [= *susiddha*], but 12, 8, [and] 4 are 'destroyers,' [= *ari*]."

154. Verses 87-90 occur also in ŚT 2.124cd-128. Verses 87-88 deal briefly with the *nakṣatracakra,* where the syllables of the alphabet are assigned to the twenty-seven lunar mansions. The KT mentions the number of syllables to be written in each square but does not give details about the sequence of certain groups of syllables like *kṣa, ḷa,* and *ha*. Illustration 3 shows this diagram reconstructed on the basis of contemporary prints. I follow the instructions of PĀ, p. 99, 25, where it is said that the last square of Revatī contains the syllable *ḷa* [and the *anusvāra* and *visarga*] and that the syllable *kṣa* is not to be written separately, but is included in *ṣa,* which is assigned to Uttarā Bhādrapadā. Beginning with the lunar mansion of one's birth, one assigns the following categories: (1) birth, (2) wealth, and so forth (see verse 88). According to verse 91, one may begin with the lunar mansion in which the first letter of one's name occurs if the lunar mansion of one's birth is unknown. If the initial letter of the mantra occurs in squares 1 [= birth], 3 [= calamity], 5 [= opponent], or 7 [= slayer] (see PĀ, p. 101, 4), the mantra should be rejected; all other squares are auspicious.

155. The scheme of numbers assigned to the consonants in verses 87 and 89 is given in the following table according to PĀ, p. 99, 17-23. commenting on ŚT 2.124cd-125ab. PĀ ascribes it to Vararuci.

1	2	3	4	5	6	7	8	9
k	kh	g	gh	c	ch	j	jh	ñ
ṭ	ṭh	ḍ	ḍh	ṇ	t	th	d	dh
p	ph	b	bh	m				
y	r	l	v	ś	ṣ	s	h	

Each consonant is assigned the number at the top of the column in which it occurs. Vowels are only for pronunciation; they have no numerical value. In the case of conjunct letters, only the value of

अश्विनी अ आ	भरणी इ	कृत्तिका ई उ ऊ	रोहिणी ऋ ॠ ऌ ॡ	मृगशिरा ए	आर्द्रा ऐ	पुनर्वसु ओ औ	पुष्य क	आश्लेषा ख ग
मघा घ ङ	पूर्वा फाल्गुनी च	उत्तरा फाल्गुनी छ ज	हस्त झ ञ	चित्रा ट ठ	स्वाती ड	विशाखा ढ ण	अनुराधा त थ द	ज्येष्ठा ध
मूल न प फ	पूर्वाषाढा ब	उत्तराषाढा भ	श्रवणा म	धनिष्ठा य र	शतभिषा ल	पूर्वा भाद्रपदा व श	उत्तरा भाद्रपदा ष स ह	रेवती ळ अं अः

Illustration 3. *Nakṣatracakra*.

the last letter is considered; e.g., *pra* = *r* = 2.

156. Verses 89-91 deal with the *rāśicakra*, where the syllables of the alphabet are assigned to the zodiac signs from Aries to Pisces. Illustration 4 shows this diagram reconstructed on the basis of contemporary prints and the authority of PĀ, p. 102, 9-12.

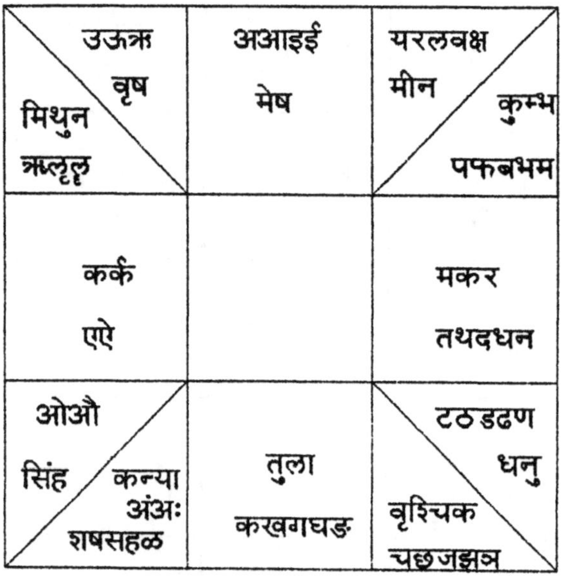

Illustration 4. *Rāśicakra*.

According to this text, the syllables *ya, ra, la, va,* and *kṣa* are assigned to Pisces (although the text says that the house of Pisces should contain only four syllables). Contrary to the statement in PĀ, p. 99, 3f., where the syllable *kṣa* is considered part of the syllable *ṣa* (see note 154), *kṣa* occurs separately here. The syllables *aṃ, aḥ,* plus *śa, ṣa, sa, ha,* and *ḷa* are assigned to Virgo. Counting from one's (lunar) zodiac sign to the square in which the first letter of the mantra occurs, one assigns the twelve astrological houses to the squares and determines their significance for the mantra from the names of the houses (see verse 88). If the initial letter of the mantra occurs in houses 6 [= enemy], 8 [= death], or 12 [= loss], the mantra is to be rejected (see PĀ, p. 102, 16). If one's zodiac sign is not known, one may start from the zodiac sign in which the first letter of one's name occurs.

157. For the numbers corresponding to the consonants, cf. PĀ,

p. 102, 7-8, and note 155, table of consonants.

158. According to PĀ, p. 102, 9, the remaining syllables are *ṣa*, *sa*, *ha*, and *ḷa*.

159. *Rāśi* is used here as a synonym for *bhāva*, astrological house.

160. That is, the sign rising on the horizon at the time of birth. In a horoscope it is assigned to the first square, which is related to a person's body and health.

161. For verses 92-93, cf. TR 1.56-57 with v.l. These verses deal with the *ṛṇidhanicakra*, where numbers are assigned to the letters of the worshipper's name and to the letters of the mantra. This diagram is not described in the KT but it is treated in PĀ, p. 110, 9-22. It consists of six rows of eleven squares each. The upper row contains the numbers assigned to the letters of the mantra (vowels and consonants separated). Rows two to five contain the syllables of the alphabet and the bottom row has the numbers assigned to the letters of the worshipper's name. Illustration 5 shows this diagram reconstructed on the basis of contemporary prints and the authority of PĀ, p. 110, 9-22.

१४	२७	२	१२	१५	६	४	३	८	८	९
अ	इ	उ	ऋ	ॡ	ए	ऐ	ओ	औ	अं	अः
क	ख	ग	घ	ङ	च	छ	ज	झ	ञ	ट
ठ	ड	ढ	ण	त	थ	द	ध	न	प	फ
ब	भ	म	य	र	ल	व	श	ष	स	ह
१०	१	७	४	८	३	७	५	४	६	३

Illustration 5. *Ṛṇidhanicakra*.

Beginning with the square in which the first letter of the worshipper's name occurs, one counts in alphabetical order to the square in which the first letter of the mantra occurs. The numbers assigned to the squares in the bottom row of the diagram are added, the sum is multiplied by three, and the product is divided by seven. The number thus obtained is called *sādhakarāśi*. Then, beginning with the square in which the first letter of the mantra occurs, one counts (if necessary, backwards) to the square in which the first letter of the name occurs. The numbers assigned to the squares in the top row of the diagram are added, the sum is multiplied by three, and the product is divided by seven. The number thus obtained is called *sādhyarāśi* or *mantrarāśi*. This method is also described in PĀ, p. 111, 1-6, which quotes the authority of TR 1.56. This verse is identical to KT 15.92 except for a v.l. in *pāda* b.

One compares the number of the name (= *sādhakarāśi*) and the number of the mantra (= *mantrarāśi*) and calls the larger number *ṛṇī*, the smaller one *dhanī*. An *ṛṇī* mantra is a debtor from previous lives (see note 163), a *dhanī* mantra is a creditor (see PĀ, p. 110, 28-29). If the mantra is *ṛṇī*, it should be adopted; but if the worshipper is *ṛṇī*, the mantra should be rejected.

162. That is, counting from the first letter of the mantra to the first letter of the name, multiplying the figure obtained by three, and dividing the product by seven (see PĀ, p. 111, 5-6). According to the Manoramā, p. 10, 22-23, on TR 1.56cd, the figure is to be multiplied by seven and divided by three.

163. According to a belief recorded in TR 1.58cd-61ab (see also Mantramahodadhi 24.50-51), such a mantra was repeated in a previous life but could not yield a result at that time because the mantra first had to eradicate evil karma. The reciter might have died before the mantra became effective. Therefore, this mantra is considered to be indebted to the reciter from a previous life and will give results quickly in this life. For *japa* done in a previous life, see also KT 15.14.

164. Verses 94-95ab occur with v.l. in ŚT 2.10-11ab. Verses 94-96 deal with the *kulākulacakra*, which is used to determine whether the letters of a person's name and those of the mantra belong to one family (*kula*) or not (*akula*). The fifty syllables (see note 166) of the alphabet are classified according to the five elements (see Illustration 6). If the letters of the person's name belong to the same element as the letters of the mantra or to elements that are "friends," the mantra should be adopted; otherwise it should be rejected.

165. That is, *e, ai, o, au,* and *aṃ*. For this interpretation, see PĀ, pp. 70, 16ff.

166. For the insertion of *ḷa*, see ŚT 2.11d (the text prints *la* for *ḷa*). This text reads *ṣakṣaḷasahāntāḥ*, which is preferable to the reading *ṣakṣasahāntāś ca* in KT 15.94 where *ca* is inserted for metrical reasons. The fifty syllables of the alphabet referred to in the verse are the

वायु	अग्नि	भू	जल	आकाश
अ	इ	उ	ऋ	लृ
आ	ई	ऊ	ॠ	ॡ
ए	ऐ	ओ	औ	अं
क	ख	ग	घ	ङ
च	छ	ज	झ	ञ
ट	ठ	ड	ढ	ण
त	थ	द	ध	न
प	फ	ब	भ	म
य	र	ल	व	श
ष	क्ष	ळ	स	ह

Illustration 6. *Kulākulacakra.*

five short vowels: *a, i, u, ṛ, ḷ*; the long vowels: *ā, ī, ū, ṝ, ḹ*; the diphthongs and *anusvāra*: *e, o, ai, au, aṃ*; six groups of five syllables each; and *ṣa, kṣa, ḷa, sa,* and *ha.*

167. The commentary Naukā on Mantramahodadhi 24.58d explains *kūṭa* as a mantra consisting of a group of consonants (*kūṭo vyañjanasamūhaḥ*).

168. N, p. 164, 26-30, comments: a mantra given by a distinguished woman who is learned and a preceptor.

169. Five and four *āmnāyas*, i.e., "literary traditions," are named in KT 3.7 and 3.9-10.

170. A *mālāmantra* is usually a mantra exceeding twenty syllables (see the discussion in PĀ, p. 112, 3-15).

171. Verse 99 occurs also in TS, p. 6, 7-8 (quote from the Siddhasārasvata).

172. The *prāsāda-bīja* is HAṂ.

173. Are these mantras whose syllables are closely related or belong to the same group (*sapiṇḍa*)? Or are these mantras whose syllables contain conjunct consonants (*piṇḍākṣara*)? PĀ, p. 112, 1, reads *piṇḍa* (instead of *sapiṇḍa*), which is explained in TR 35.28a as a one-syllabled mantra. One-syllabled mantras already have been

mentioned in verse 97.

174. Verses 104-106 occur also in TS, p. 30, 9-14.

175. According to the rules of *dharmaśāstra*, one should clean oneself after passing urine and stool.

176. See also ŚT 7.121. According to PĀ, p. 412, 7, these are the limbs below the navel.

177. Similarly, HYP 1.15 states six obstacles in yogic practice: overeating, exertion, excessive talk, observance of [unsuitable] disciplines, promiscuous company, and unsteadiness:

atyāhāraḥ prayāsaś ca prajalpo niyamagrahaḥ /
janasaṅgaś ca laulyaṃ ca ṣaḍbhir yogo vinaśyati //

178. Verse 108ab occurs also in KT 11.18ab. Verse 108 occurs also in TS, p. 31, 30-31 (quoted from an unidentified source).

179. That is, a long garment covering the body from the shoulders to the feet.

180. When performing religious rites the hair is supposed to be tied in a knot.

181. This refers to the nervous habit of tearing grass with the hand while performing *japa* outside in the open. See MSm 4.71, where meaningless actions like tearing grass, biting nails, etc., are forbidden.

Bibliography and Abbreviations

Carlstedt, G. 1974. *Studier I Kulārṇava-Tantra.* Uppsala.

Chakravarti, C. 1931-32. *Kulārṇava Tantra—Its Extent and Contents.* Annals of the Bhandarkar Oriental Research Institute 13.206-211.

Goudriaan, T., and S. Gupta. 1981. *Hindu Tantric and Śākta Literature.* Wiesbaden.

HYP: *Haṭhayogapradīpikā. Text, Commentary, Translation.* The Adyar Library Bulletin 36.1972.

Kane, P. V. ²1968-77. *History of Dharmaśāstra*, 5 vols. Poona.

KT: *Kulārṇavatantra.* Introduction by A. Avalon, readings by M. P. Pandit, Sanskrit text ed. T. Vidyāratna. Calcutta and London, 1965 (revised ed.).

Text with English translation by Ram Kumar Rai. Varanasi, 1983.

Mantramahodadhi: *Mantramahodadhiḥ saṭīkaḥ*. Bombay, 1983 (reprint).

Mantrayogasaṃhitā: *Mantra-Yoga Saṃhitā*, edited text with English trans. Ram Kumar Rai. Varanasi and Delhi [2]1982.

MM: *Mantramahārṇava: Mantramahārṇavaḥ . . . mādhavarāyavaidyasaṃgṛhītaḥ*. Bombay, [2]1984.

MSm: *Manusmṛti*, with the Sanskrit commentary *Manvartha-Muktāvalī* of Kullūka Bhaṭṭa, ed. J. L. Shastri. Delhi, 1983.

N: *Nityotsava of Umānandanātha* [Supplement to Paraśurāma-kalpasūtra], ed. A. Mahadeva Sastri, revised and enlarged by Swami Trivikrama Tirtha. Baroda, [4]1977.

Nāṭyaśāstra: *Nāṭyaśāstra of Bharatamuni with the Commentary Abhinavabhāratī by Abhinavaguptācārya*, ed. M. Ramakrishna Kavi. Baroda, vol. 1, [2]1956; vols. 2-4, 1934-1964.

NP: Nārada-Purāṇa. *Atha nāradīyamahāpurāṇaṃ prārabhyate*. Bombay, 1923.

PĀ: *Padārthādarśa* by Rāghavabhaṭṭa; see ŚT.

Padoux, A. 1987. "Contributions à l'étude du mantraśāstra III. Le japa." *Bulletin de l'École Française d'Extrême-Orient* 77: 117-164.

Pāṇinīya Śikṣā, ed. and trans. M. Ghosh. *Pāṇinīya Śikṣā or the Śikṣā Vedāṅga Ascribed to Pāṇini*. Calcutta, 1938.

PKS: *Paraśurāmakalpasūtra with Rāmeśvara's Commentary*, ed. A. Mahadeva Sastri, revised and enlarged by S. Y. Sastri Dave. Baroda, [3]1979.

PrT: Prāṇatoṣiṇī. *Śrīrāmatoṣaṇa-Bhaṭṭācāryyeṇa tantraśāstrāt saṃkalayya viracitā*. Calcutta, [3]1898.

Puraścaryārṇava of His Majesty Shri Pratap Sinh Sah Dev King of Nepal, ed. late Pt. Muralidhar Jha. Delhi, 1985 (reprint).

Śāstrī, S. S. 1944. *Iconography of Śrī Vidyārṇava Tantra*. Bangalore.

ŚT: Śāradātilakatantra. *Śāradā-Tilaka Tantram*. Text with Introduction ed. A. Avalon. Delhi, 1982 (reprint).

Tantrābhidhāna: *Tantrābhidhāna with Bījanighaṇṭu, Bījābhidhāna, Mantrārthābhidhāna, Varṇabījakoṣa, Mudrānighaṇṭu*, ed. P. Bhattacharya. Delhi, 1983 (reprint).

TR: *Tantrarājatantra*, ed. L. Shastri. Calcutta, 1926.

TS: Tantrasāra. *Tantrasāraḥ mahāmahopādhyāyaśrīkṛṣṇānandavāgīśabhaṭṭācāryaviracitaḥ*. 2 Fasc. Banaras, 1938.

VT: Vidyārṇavatantra. *Shrividyarnavatantra,* ed. R. C. Kak and Harabhatta Shastri, 2 vols. Srinagar, 1932-1937.

Chapter Three

Becoming a Śiva, and Acting as One, in Śaiva Worship

Richard H. Davis

A proper Śaiva *āgama* should stand on four feet (*pāda*): the feet of knowledge (*jñāna*), ritual action (*kriyā*), proper conduct (*caryā*), and disciplinary practice (yoga). The *jñānapāda* describes how the world is; it sets forth, in metaphysical and theological terms, the fundamental order of the universe as envisioned by Śaiva-Siddhānta. The *kriyāpāda* prescribes how one should conduct oneself in that world, utilizing the most powerful and efficacious forms of action. (The other two sections, though necessary, clearly are subordinate to the first two.) And just as the feet of knowledge and ritual action are equally necessary to a complete, self-standing Āgama, Śaiva texts insist that an aspirant who wishes to advance within the world of Śiva must exert himself both to know that world and to act properly and effectively within it.[1]

Though sharing this ideal of mutuality, Śaiva texts do disagree over whether knowledge or ritual action is more important for gaining the highest ends. Some Āgamas clearly grant a greater role in the attainment of liberation to knowledge. "Devotees gain liberation solely through knowledge," asserts the Ajitāgama.[2] "As for a ritual like worship, it gives only worldly results such as divine status." Other treatises, by contrast, stress the necessity of ritual action. Aghoraśiva uses the analogy of a cataract covering the eye to support this position. Because the cataract is a physical affliction, recognition alone is not sufficient to remove it; physical action in the form of medical treatment also is required. So, too, the fetters that cover the soul are substantive, and one must remove them through ritual activity, not through knowledge alone.[3]

Even when such texts advance the primacy of one over the other, however, they still concede the necessity of the lesser as well. As Ajitāgama continues, "When Śiva the Lord of All Gods is worshipped, he grants knowledge and devotion."[4] Ritual actions like worship are crucial, in the view of this Āgama, because they give rise to knowledge; without ritual practice, the requisite knowledge might never arise. Conversely, the advocates of action recognize that correct knowledge is required for proper comprehension and practice of ritual. Although Nārāyaṇakaṇṭha holds that the ritual of initiation (*dīkṣā*) is the singular key to liberation, he adds this proviso: "It is not possible to perform initiation without knowledge, because knowledge provides the means of determining the inherent form of bound souls, fetters, and the Lord, indicates how to accomplish all paths of attainment, and reveals the greatness of the Mantras, the Mantreśvaras, and others."[5] Without correct knowledge, one's ritual practice will be shaky and finally fruitless.

Other texts assert the equal necessity of knowledge and action. Śivāgrayogin quotes an unnamed Āgama source to this effect: "Knowledge devoid of activity is not the preeminent means of attainment (*pradhāna*), nor is activity devoid of understanding the preeminent means. Therefore, successful attainment of liberation arises only through both of them together, just as a bird does not fly without two wings."[6] Or, to use another analogy: "Like rice mixed with honey, or like honey mixed with rice, austerities (*tapas*) and knowledge combined make an excellent medicine."[7] Whether it is a matter of rising like a bird to a higher level of attainment or medically treating the malady of bondage, the Śaiva aspirant needs to make full use of both conscious powers of knowing and acting. In the Śaiva-Siddhānta view, these are not two separate pathways leading to the same end, but rather are two interrelated and complementary constituents of a single path.

Such claims of mutuality are all fine and good, but what does this mean in practical terms? How does ritual action engender knowledge, as Ajitāgama says? Is proper knowledge necessary to the performance of ritual, as Aghoraśiva and Nārāyaṇakaṇṭha aver? In this essay, I propose to investigate these questions in terms of practice, by considering some aspects of daily worship (*nityapūjā*) as it is formulated in Śaiva Āgamas and related Siddhānta texts.[8]

Daily worship is a ubiquitous Hindu ritual form by which devotees of a divinity regularly offer tokens of their respect and adoration to that deity embodied in an image or icon. It is the most common and recurrent ritual action of Hindu temples and, in many respects, paradigmatic for the entire system of temple ritual that developed in early medieval India. During this period, each Hindu order articulated its own version of *pūjā*, suitable for the particular god or goddess each held as preeminent and adapted to its own particular theological convictions. The Śaiva-Siddhānta school,

I argue, reformulated Śaiva *pūjā* in such a way that it acts as a virtual précis of Śaiva-Siddhānta theology, a daily catechism in action for worshippers who undertake it with diligence and mindfulness. To perform *pūjā* properly as the Śaiva texts prescribe it, then, both requires theological knowledge and engenders it, such that the worshipper's knowledge and practice ripen integrally through a daily regimen. To demonstrate this, I will focus on the matter of emission and reabsorption as they are enacted within daily worship.

1

According to Śaiva philosophy, Śiva performs five fundamental activities (*pañcakṛtya*) that shape and activate the universe. Of these, the two highest relate primarily to the soul: he "veils" (*tirobhāva*) the true nature of things from bound souls, and he grants "grace" (*anugraha*) to souls when they are ready for it, liberating them from bondage. His other three activities bring about the complex oscillations, the perpetual comings and goings, of the substantive worlds in which souls reside: emission (*sṛṣṭi*), maintenance (*sthiti*), and reabsorption (*saṃhāra*). Maintenance, a stabilizing action, is relatively unimportant in the dynamic cosmology of Śaiva-Siddhānta. Emission and reabsorption, by contrast, are central. They are the activities by which Śiva acts as the ultimate instrumental cause of all cosmic movement.

Emission and reabsorption are ubiquitous principles of the manifest cosmos and so may be observed in many different domains. The paradigmatic example is the recurring emission and reabsorption of the *tattvas*, the "suchnesses" that constitute material being, out of and back into their source-substances *māyā* and *mahāmāyā*. For Śaiva cosmology, *māyā* is the material cause of our world. (*Mahāmāyā*, the source-substance of the "pure realm," is of less direct concern to us inhabitants of an "impure" cosmos.) *Māyā* is real and substantive (*vastutā*), not illusory, and it is ontologically separate from Śiva. At the onset of each creation, *māyā* is undifferentiated and pervasive. Śiva then agitates *māyā* with his appointed powers and causes it to emit, in orderly sequence, the differentiated thirty-one *tattvas* of the impure realm. Although *māyā* is subtle, its derivative *tattvas* become increasingly tangible until we reach the five material elements (*bhūtas*), among which Earth (*pṛthivī*) is the most highly differentiated and gross of all *tattvas*. These differentiated *tattvas* enter into multiple combinations with one another, together constituting what we recognize as our ever-fluctuating world of *saṃsāra*. At the time of reabsorption or dissolution (*pralaya*), each *tattva* remerges into its source, until all are reintegrated into *māyā*. Quiescent, unitary *māyā* then awaits another emission.

As with the emanation of the *tattvas*, any movement along the "path of emission" (*sṛṣṭimārga*) involves a transformation from unity to differentiation, from one to many, from pervasiveness to increasing particularity. By contrast, the "path of reabsorption" (*saṃhāramārga*) reintegrates that which has become separated; it reinstates the unity lost through differentiation. Emission indicates a movement from subtle (*sūkṣma*) to gross (*sthūla*), from pure to impure, from superior to inferior; reabsorption indicates the converse. Emission and reabsorption also relate to the disposition of things in space. The path of emission is represented visually as a descending motion from high to low, or as a radiating movement proceeding outward from a center toward peripheries. Reabsorption ascends or moves inward toward a center.

The cosmic processes of emission and reabsorption, then, govern a bundle of contrastive terms, interconnected by two converse paths of movement.

unity		differentiation
integration		disintegration
subtle	——emission——→	gross
pure		impure
superior	←——reabsorption——	inferior
high		low
center		peripheral

The rhythm of the manifest universe is an oscillation back and forth between these opposite poles, under the direction of Śiva and his animating powers.

These cosmological principles are a matter of Śaiva knowledge. The Āgamas reveal to us these patterns of transformation, which might otherwise be obscured from our ordinarily limited powers of cognition. In *pūjā*, the same principles become a matter of action as well. Emission and reabsorption are embedded as an organizing logic within the ritual of worship, just as they are embedded in the cosmos as a whole. The Śaiva worshipper is called upon to enact repeatedly the movements of emission and reabsorption himself, which are at the same time the activies Śiva performs to animate the cosmos.

2

The Āgamas often begin their accounts of daily worship with an important directive: śivībhūya śivaṃ yajet. For dualistic Śaiva-Siddhānta, which maintains that souls and Śiva are and forever remain ontologically distinct, this does not mean that a worshipper should 'become Śiva' or merge with Śiva. (*śivasāyujya*) before worshipping him, because that would be asking him to accomplish the metaphysically impossible. Seeking to attain identity or consubstantiality with the Lord Śiva might be appropriate for a monist worshipper, but a Śaiva-Siddhāntin aspires rather to reach a state of separate but equal 'Śivaness' (*śivatva*). This is, in fact, the Śaiva-Siddhānta definition of *mokṣa*: a liberated soul becomes an autonomous theomorphic entity, distinct from Śiva but with all his powers and qualities. It is 'equivalent to Siva' (*śivasāmya*) or 'has the same form as Siva' (*śivarūpatā*). In daily worship, too, the Āgamas prescribe that the worshipper must first become *a* Śiva to worship Śiva. But how does he do that?

In his normal condition, the worshipper undertaking *pūjā* is unlike Śiva in two fundamental respects: the worshipper is immersed in impurities and lacks Śiva's powers. His soul inhabits a body made up of the various differentiated *tattvas* of the manifest cosmos, which are considered inherently impure. And with the innate capacities of the soul suppressed by fetters, his diminished powers of knowledge and action pale in comparison to Śiva's omniscience and omnipotence. Before one may worship Śiva one must address both these deficiencies through a rite of self-purification (*ātma-śuddhi*). Performed near the commencement of *pūjā*, self-purification is the means by which a worshipper transforms his own body for the purpose of ritual. First he empties his body of its impure material constituents with a set of purificatory actions, then he superimposes mantras invoking Śiva's powers onto all parts of the body. In this way the body is made over into a "divine body," a pure body composed of mantras or powers. As Śiva acts in the world by means of the mantras that constitute his body, so the worshipper creates for himself a parallel mantra body that will enable him to perform all subsequent acts of ritual.

To remove the impurities of the body requires two steps. First the worshipper must reabsorb all the *tattvas* of his "subtle body" (*sūkṣmaśarīra*) and then collapse and burn the elements of his "gross body" (*sthūlaśarīra*). Together, these two processes result in a profound emptying out of the body, leaving it a kind of empty shell to be filled subsequently with mantras.

The purification of the subtle body is an explicit and straightforward application of reabsorption. The subtle body in its ordinary condition, according to Śaiva-Siddhānta, is composed of the thirty-six differentiated *tattvas* dispersed through the body. In this differentiated state, the *tattvas* are inherently impure; purity exists only in the state of integration, where all material constituents are unified within their two source-substances *māyā* and *mahāmāyā*. Accordingly, the task of the worshipper is to reabsorb the entire constitution of the subtle body into its undifferentiated source. As Aghoraśiva directs him, "In order to purify the subtle body, the worshipper should cause the *tattvas* to be dissolved (*laya*), each into its own source, in an inverse order [to that of their emission], ending with *mahāmāyā*."[9] Through internal visualization (*bhāvanā*), the worshipper makes each *tattva* return into the substance that gave birth to it. "Accordingly, one should visualize Earth reabsorbed into Odor, Water into Taste, Fire into Form, Wind into Touch, Ether into Sound, and these five perceptible qualities (*tanmātra*) into the inert aspect of the Ego (*tamasāhaṃkāra*)."[10] And so on, reversing the order of emission, until the thirty-one *tattvas* of the impure domain are unified in *māyā* and the five *tattvas* of the pure domain reintegrated within *mahāmāyā*.

By reabsorbing all the *tattvas* of the subtle body into their two sources, the worshipper is able to remove a large portion of the impurities that distinguish his body from that of Śiva. Yet other impurities still bind his soul. The impurities of the gross body are identified with the five material elements (*bhūtas*): Earth, Water, Fire, Wind, and Ether. To purify the body of these elements, the worshipper must first imagine each of them as a domain or maṇḍala, characterized by a whole series of features. For instance, Aghoraśiva instructs the worshipper to imagine the Earth mandala as follows: "One should visualize the Earth *maṇḍala* as yellow, firm, square, and decorated with a thunderbolt; it is presided over by its governor Sadyojāta; it is connected with the seed-syllable of Earth, HLAṂ, and with Brahman as its lord (*kāraṇeśvara*), and it has the form of *nivṛttikalā*; it extends from the feet up to the head."[11] The domains are located in the body in the ascending order of reabsorption, with the least pure element, Earth, situated at the lowest part, and the most pure element, Ether, at the highest. The Śaiva texts provide several different specifications of the domains' locations in the body, but all follow the same ascending arrangement.

Each domain also has a number of qualities (*guṇas*), corresponding to the number of *tanmātras* present in each material element. The element Earth contains all five sensory qualities—Sound, Touch, Form, Taste, and Odor. Water has four qualities (omitting Odor), Fire has three, and so on. In purifying his gross body, the worshipper must expel all these qualities from each domain, using for each one an individual "expulsion" (*udghāta*) that follows the path of reabsorption. With an ascending breath along the *suṣumṇā*, the central breath channel, one can remove gradually all sensory qualities. And when this is accomplished, the worshipper imagines that each element has taken on the form of and been neutralized by its contrary element. The element Wind subdues Earth and is in turn subdued by it. Water conquers and is conquered by Fire. Ether takes on the form of the Highest Ether.

With the obstructive forces of the elements thereby curbed, the worshipper may now annihilate them fully. He visualizes a fire arising from his right big toe that burns all the impurities of the elements located in the body. The imagined fire, following the path of reabsorption upward from that toe, purifies his gross body just as the visualized reabsorption of *tattvas* into their source-substances purified the subtle body. With both aspects of his material form suitably cleansed of all impurities, the worshipper then pictures it to himself as a pure, empty frame. "Imagining it completely emptied of all that has the form of a fetter, the worshipper should bathe his entire body, inside and out, with streams of nectar flowing from the upside-down lotus at the top of his crown, penetrating the openings of every capillary, using the MŪLA mantra ending in VAUṢAṬ."[12] All impurities that normally distinguish the worshipper's body from that of Śiva have now been ritually extirpated.

The worshipper must next reconstruct his body as a "divine body" or a "body of powers" (*śāktadeha*), a Śiva-like instrument that will enable one to act as a Śiva within the domain of ritual. To do this, one imposes (*nyāsa*) onto oneself a body of mantras, exactly parallel to the divine body one later will impose onto the *liṅga* that Śiva inhabits. As Kāmikāgama makes clear, "The worshipper should impose mantras onto the divinity just as he does on his body."[13] Whereas purification, aiming at the removal of obstructing constituents from the body, follows the order of reabsorption, the reconstruction of a divine body, involving the superimposition of empowering mantras, follows the converse path of emission.

Kāmikāgama prescribes an elaborate method of reconstruction, appropriate for a priest performing *pūjā* on behalf of others. The priest first imposes onto himself the five *brahmamantras*, then the thirty-eight *kalāmantras*, the six *aṅgamantras*, mantras of the letters of the alphabet; six "limbs" of the alphabet, nine unspecified *tattvas*, and finally the VYOMAVYĀPIN ("space-pervading") mantra. The most important of these, the five *brahmamantra*s, sets the pattern.

The five *brahmamantra*s are identified as the instruments with which Śiva performs his five fundamental activities, and they are said at the same time to constitute his active body. "Śiva's body, beginning with the head, is composed of the five mantras that are appropriate for the five activities: ĪŚĀNA, TATPURUṢA, AGHORA, VĀMA, and SADYOJĀTA."[14] The five mantras may be envisioned also as the five "faces" of Sadāśiva, the most complete manifest form of the divinity. ĪŚĀNA, in this case, is the upraised face of Sadāśiva, TATPURUṢA the eastern face, and so on in a circumambulatory order. The order of mantra placement in both cases corresponds to the relative rank of the activity with which it is associated. Because grace is Śiva's preeminent activity, the ĪŚĀNA mantra that is the instrument of grace is the highest of the *brahmamantras*, whereas SADYOJĀTA used for emission, the least of the five activities, is the lowest.

The worshipper constructing his own body of powers is called upon to impose the same mantras on the corresponding parts of his body, following a descending order: ĪŚĀNA on the top of the head, TATPURUṢA on the mouth, AGHORA on the heart, VĀMA on the genitals, and SADYOJĀTA on the feet. As an alternative, one may prefer to impose the five *brahmamantra*s onto one's own five "faces": ĪŚĀNA on the upraised face (i.e., the top of the head), TATPURUṢA on the easterly face, and so on around the head in the same circumambulatory manner. In either case, it is clear, the priest is imposing onto his own body the most fundamental powers of Śiva himself; he is reconstructing his body as a Sadāśiva.

With the imposition of each subsequent set of mantra powers, the worshipper further constructs and enhances his divine body. In each case, too, the direction of placement follows the path of emission: either descending on the body from head to feet, or proceeding from the center outward (in the case of the *aṅgamantras*). When the metamorphosis is complete, the worshipper has emitted for himself a body parallel to that of Śiva, and with that divine body he may act as a Śiva within the sphere of ritual.

The ritual topography of the worshipper's body, then, follows the logic of emission and reabsorption. Substances or constituents are located from top to bottom with the most subtle and superior highest, the least subtle and inferior lowest. Accordingly, upward movements on or within the body follow the path of reabsorption, whereas descending movements follow the path of emission. Ritual actions aimed at removing things from the body follow an ascending course, and actions that impose or add things to the body move downward. As he transforms his body into a Śiva, a worshipper also replicates or reenacts the patterned cosmic activities of Śiva.

3

Temple space, like the worshipper's body, is organized in Śaiva ritual according to the cosmological principles of emission and reabsorption.

A priest performing *pūjā* on behalf of others must move within and through the temple, a fabricated structure with its own geography and its own organization of images. Moreover, during the course of worship he must construct new ritual spaces within the temple. Two such constructions involve setting up pots of bathing water for Śiva's consecration and visualization of a "court" of subordinate lords surrounding the Śiva *liṅga*. In all ritual spaces, things are arranged in a determinate order. There first of all must be a center. Outer elements are arranged as concentric circuits of spaces around the center, and objects or deities are located within these spaces according to their relation to this emanating source. Movement in such spaces partakes of the same logic: movement from the center outward follows the path of emission, whereas movement from the peripheries inward follows the path of reabsorption. To illustrate this, I will consider the rite of the entourages (*āvaraṇa*).

As Lord of the Cosmos, Śiva typically is surrounded by hosts of gods and other spirits who act as his attendants, guardians, devotees, and agents. Śaiva texts often describe Śiva seated in state on a Himalayan mountain, in the midst of a divine assembly, as the scene in which the Āgamas themselves are first revealed. Likewise, these subordinate gods throng the ritually constructed dwellings of Śiva (often homologized to mountains), covering the outer walls of the temple and inhabiting their own lesser shrines in the courtyards surrounding the main sanctum and its Śiva *liṅga*.

After the worshipper has invoked Śiva into the *liṅga* during daily worship, the Āgamas advise, he should make Śiva feel at home by creating still another court for him. In the rite of the entourages, the worshipper visualizes Śiva seated at the center of a royal court composed of one, three, or five groups of eight deities each in attendance. He envisions each deity according to an appropriate meditation verse, invokes the deity into this mentally constructed form, and then worships it with all proper offerings. Whereas the deities in the subsidiary shrines outside the *garbhagṛha* constitute Śiva's "exterior entourage" (*bāhyāvaraṇa*), the visualized divinities here make up his "interior entourages" (*antarāvaraṇa*), the court within. In both, the attending divinities are placed in a series of emanating concentric circles facing the central *liṅga*, arranged in order of priority with respect to the center. *The liṅga* is the source. "During reabsorption, all beings are reabsorbed into it, and [during emission] they emanate out from it—for that reason it is called *liṅga*. When the *liṅga* is worshipped, all the gods are worshipped."[15]

In the innermost circle, the *garbhāvaraṇa*, the worshipper visualizes the *brahmamantras* and the *aṅgamantras*, direct emanations of Śiva's own body. The inhabitants of this interior entourage, says the Kāmikāgama, "are to be drawn out from Śiva, the *brahmamantras* from his chest, etc., and the *aṅgamantras* from his heart, etc."[16] The worshipper places the Vidyeśvaras, the most eminent of all Śiva's agents (*adhikārin*), in the second entourage. In the third are found the Gaṇeśvaras, a group of divinities best described as forming Śiva's household: his wife Ambikā, his sons Gaṇeśa and Skanda, his mount Vṛṣa, his favored devotees Caṇḍa, Bhṛṅgin, and Naṇḍin, and Mahākāla his primary guardian. Next he places the World Guardians (*lokapālas*)—Indra, Agni, Yama, and that ilk—in the fourth entourage. Assigned to the protection of the directions of this world, the World Guardians are decidedly lower in rank than the Vidyeśvaras, whose domain extends over all the impure worlds. Finally, the outermost entourage contains the weapons that the World Guardians bear: Indra's thunderbolt stands in the east, Agni's spear in the southeast, and so on. As in a human royal court, those whose duty it is to protect the attendants of the court are stationed at its outer perimeter.

All these attending deities share in Śiva's lordship, but in differing degrees. As an imperial king assigns lesser kings to perform the functions of sovereignty in smaller, encompassed portions of the empire, Śiva also employs various powers or agents to enact his universal lordship in specific domains or parts of the world. The court of entourages the worshipper visualizes for Śiva here creates a meditative map of Śiva's hierarchized sovereignty: the emanating, encompassing Śiva *liṅga* at the center, surrounded most intimately by the mantras Śiva uses to act in the world, then by those beings who act as Śiva's agents arranged according to rank, in the order of emission.

Once envisioned, these entourages participate in the services of *pūjā*. Each one is suitably consecrated. When offering food to Śiva, the worshipper also presents it to all the deities of the court, in rank order beginning with the innermost circle. And after all the offerings are completed, they must be dismissed and returned to their source. The worshipper "makes the gods surrounding the *liṅga* get up with the ASTRA mantra and the *mudrā* of reabsorption" and rejoins them with the central embodiment of Śiva.[17]

Acting as a Śiva within the domain of ritual, the worshipper has performed his own activities of emission and reabsorption. He has emitted from the undifferentiated Śiva *liṅga* a visualized instantiation of Śiva's differentiated sovereignty, maintained and honored it during the services of worship, then reabsorbed its constituent parts back into the *liṅga* at the close of *pūjā*. In doing so, not only does one exercise one's own Śiva-like powers, but also embodies ritually the knowledge of Śiva's all-encompassing cosmic lordship.

4

These are not the only cases where the cosmological activities of emission and reabsorption are enacted in the course of daily worship. When the worshipper imposes mantras on his hands, when he constructs a divine throne for Śiva to sit upon during invocation, when he recites the PRĀSĀDA mantra in an ascending manner, when he arranges pots for consecrating Śiva, when he moves through the terrain of the temple—at these moments and others as well, his actions are guided by the logic of emission and reabsorption. The movements of emission and reabsorption are just as ubiquitous in the sphere of ritual as they are in the cosmos itself.

In this way, the ritual of daily worship discloses knowledge through action, in a condensed, reiterative, and compelling way. The ritual prescriptions of the *āgamas* direct the worshipper to focus, over and over, day after day, on the primary principles of the theological world as he acts with and through them in *pūjā*. The domain of ritual thereby becomes a place where one may perceive more immediately, with less interference, the fuller state of things as described in the *jñānapāda*. What the worshipper sees, directly, as they animate his own actions, are the multiple projections of the cosmological and theological foundations of Śiva's cosmos.

Notes

1. This essay recapitulates several arguments developed in greater detail in my monograph, *Ritual in an Oscillating Universe: Worshiping Śiva in Medieval India* (Princeton: Princeton University press, 1991). Research support for this project was provided by a Fulbright-Hays Research Fellowship and a dissertation write-up grant from the Mrs. Giles Whiting Foundation.

2. *Ajitāgama, kriyāpāda* 18.3-4, ed., N. R. Bhatt, *Ajitāgama*, vol. 1 (Pondichery: Institut Français d'Indologie, 1964).

3. *Tattvaprakāśavṛtti* 15, ed. Kameshwar Nath Mishra, *Tattvaprakāśaḥ by Mahārājādhirāja Bhoja with Tātparyadīpikā and Vṛtti Commentaries* (Varanasi: Chaukhambha Orientalia, 1976).

4. *Ajitāgama, kriyāpāda* 18.4.

5. *Mṛgendrāgamavṛtti, yogapāda* 1, ed. Madhusudan Kaul Shastri; *Mṛgendrāgama, vidyāpāda and Yogapāda, with the Commentary of Bhaṭṭa Nārāyaṇakaṇṭha* (Bombay: Nirnaya Sagar Press, 1930).

6. *Śaivaparibhāṣā* 5.12, trans. S. S. Suryanarayana Sastri, *The Śaivaparibhāṣā of Śivāgrayogin* (Madras: University of Madras, 1982). Śivāgrayogin himself is of the knowledge-is-better persuasion.

7. *Śaivaparibhāṣā* 5.12.

8. I am concerned here only with *āgamas* and related texts that advance an identifiable Śaiva *siddhānta* outlook, as it was articulated in Sanskrit texts prior to the time of the Tamil author Mēykaṇṭar. Of course, I do not wish to imply that all *āgamas* present this dualistic, ritualistic vision of the world.

9. Aghoraśiva, *Kriyākramadyotikā*, p. 57. Karunkulam Krishna Sastri, ed., *Kriyākramadyotikā of Aghoraśiva with the Commentary of Nirmalamaṇi* (Cidambaram: Jnanasambandham Press, 1927).

10. Aghoraśiva, *Kriyākramadyotikā*, p. 57.

11. Ibid., pp. 57-58.

12. Ibid., p. 59.

13. *Pūrvakāmikāgama* 4.349. C. Svaminathasivacarya, ed., *Kāmikāgama (Pūrvabhāga)* (Madras: South Indian Archakas Association, 1975).

14. *Mṛgendrāgama, vidyāpāda* 3.8-9.

15. *Ajitāgama, kriyāpāda* 3.17-18.

16. *Pūrvakāmikāgama* 4.456.

17. Ibid., 4.518-519.

Chapter Four

"Having Become a God, He Should Sacrifice to the Gods"

Vrajavallabha Dviveda

The title sentence is found in many Tantra texts with variant readings. The sentence *"Having become a god, he attains the gods"* is stated repeatedly in the first Brāhmaṇa of the fourth chapter in the Bṛhadāraṇyakopaniṣad. And also in the Śatapathabrāhmaṇa, at the beginning of the section dealing with the ceremonies of the new moon and full moon, the sacrificer declares "Now from untruth I arrive at truth" (1.1.1.4) and at the end, "I am what really I am" (1.9.3.23). In the same context it is explained that "Human beings verily are untruth and gods are truth" (1.1.1.4). Thus the meaning of this becomes clear that having abandoned humanhood and assumed godhood, the sacrificer should engage in the oblations, sacrifice, and so on; and that, after the completion of the performance, the sacrificer should return to humanhood. There for this purpose, it is said only: "Verily he should speak truth only" (1.1.1.5) and nothing more. Is not the significance of all these statements that, having assumed the nature of one's own chosen god, one should propitiate gods! How then does a worshipper qualify to be of the nature of a god? As an answer to this inquiry the methods of the purification of the elements (*bhūtaśuddhi*) and of the installation of the breaths (*prāṇapratiṣṭhā*) clearly are visible in the scriptures.

Purification of the Elements

Of these two, the most abbreviated method of purification of the elements[1] is as follows. Having caused to rise from the *mūlādhāra*, with breath retention, the supreme deity Kuṇḍalī, thinner than a lotus fiber; having meditated on it in the aperture of Brahman; having taken the *jīva*, of the form of the flame of a lamp and situated in the heart; and having reached the aperture of Brahman through the path of Suṣumnā, one should unite the *jīva* to Brahman, uttering the mantra OṂ HAṂ SAḤ SO 'HAM. The definition of the purification of the elements is stated as "The cleansing of the elements that form the basis of the body, which is obtained from the conjunction with the unmanifest Brahman, is known as the purification of the elements." Its performance as the foremost in the process of worship (*pūjā*) is taught as necessary by the passage "Since any ritual act, such as *japa* and so forth performed without the purification of the elements is fruitless, one should first perform it." As an answer to the inquiry as to which kind of order should be followed in the purification of the elements that are the basis of the body, it is explained along with the application.

For the body the *ṛṣi* is the self; the meter is the *prakṛti;* the deity is the supreme self; the application is in *japa* to purify the elements of the body.

OṂ, for the germ mantra of the earth, the *ṛṣi* is Brahmā; the meter is Gāyatrī; the deity is Pṛthivī; the application is in *japa* for the purification of the earth element. One should meditate on the abode of the earth[2] as extending from the feet up to the knees, quadrangular, yellow, with a *bindu* and with the germ (*bīja*) LAṂ. It has been said: "The earth element extends from the feet up to the knees. There the domain of the earth is quadrangular, with the germ LAṂ, marked with a thunderbolt and yellow-colored. Having meditated on it, or by this conceived [it] as emanating from the germ, one should purify first the earth."

OṂ, for the germ mantra of Varuṇa, the *ṛṣi* is Hiraṇyagarbha; the meter is Anuṣṭubh; the deity is Varuṇa; the application is in *japa* for the purification of the water element. One should meditate on the domain of Varuṇa as extending from the knees up to the navel, having the shape of a bow, white colored, furnished with a *bindu,* with the germ VAṂ. It has been said: "The water element which extends from the knees up to the navel is the second one. There the domain of Varuṇa is shaped like a bow, marked with a *bindu,* with the germ VAṂ, white colored. Having meditated on this, one should purify the water with it."

OṂ, for the germ mantra of the fire, the *ṛṣi* is Kaśyapa; the meter is Jagatī; the deity is Agni Jātavedas; the application is in *japa* for the purification of the fire element. One should meditate on the triangular domain of the fire, which extends from the navel up to the heart; it is red, furnished with a *bindu,* with the germ RAṂ. It has been said: "The fire element that extends from the navel up to the heart is the third one. This domain called fire is triangular, marked with a lotus, with the germ RAṂ and red colored. Having meditated on this, one should purify the fire."

OṂ, for the germ mantra of the wind, the *ṛṣi* is Kiṣkindha; the meter is Bṛhatī; the deity is Vāyu; the application is in *japa* for the purification of the wind element. One should meditate on the domain of the wind as extending from the heart up to the space between the eyebrows; it is round, has the color of the smoke, has a *bindu*, with the germ YAṂ. It has been said: "The Vāyu element that extends from the heart up to the eyebrows is the fourth one. There the domain relating to Vāyu is round, endowed with a svastika and dark-blue colored, with the germ YAṂ. Having meditated on this, one should purify the wind."

OṂ, for the germ mantra of the ether, the *ṛṣi* is Rudra; the meter is Triṣṭubh; the deity is the supreme self; the application is in *japa* for the purification of the ether element. One should meditate on the domain of the ether as extending from the space between the eyebrows up to the forehead; it is formless, colorless, with a *bindu*, with the germ HAṂ. It has been said: "The ether element that extends from the space between the eyebrows up to the aperture of Brahman is the fifth one. Having meditated on the stainless germ HAṂ, one should purify the ether with this."

Having thus purified the five elements, one should dissolve them in due order in their respective origins as follows: "Having conceived the elements in this manner, one should dissolve them one by one. Having dissolved the earth in the water, the water in the fire, the fire in the wind and this in the ether, one should dissolve the ether in the ego, the ego in the *mahat-tattva*, the *mahant* in the *prakṛti*, and the *māyā* in the self." Thereupon one should dissolve the self, that is, the Puruṣa, into the highest Brahman. And after this dissolution, one should conceive the self as having the nature of the highest Brahman as "I am God and no other. I am nothing but Brahman, not liable to sorrow. I am of the nature of truth, consciousness and bliss and am endowed with the nature of non-differentiation." Then one should meditate on the villainous man (*pāpapuruṣa*) in the body as follows:

> Having become full of pure existence and consciousness, one should conceive the villainous man, dark blue, of the size of a thumb, and situated in the left part of the abdomen; the murder of a Brahman is his head; the theft of gold form his arms; the consumption of intoxicating liquor is his heart; the violation of the teacher's bed form his hips. Being in contact [with people associated] with those crimes form his two legs.[3] Sins are his limbs and

> minor members of the body. Minor offences are the hairs of his body. He is red haired and red eyed. He holds a sword and a shield; he is a fierce man and shines like lampblack.

Having thus meditated on the villainous man and having taken water, one resolves: "Kiṣkindha is the *ṛṣi* of the germ of the wind, which is YAṂ; Jagatī is the meter; Vāyu, the deity. Kaśyapa is the *ṛṣi* of the germ of the fire, whih is RAṂ; Triṣṭubh is the meter; Agni, the deity. Hiraṇyagarbha is the *ṛṣi* of the germ of the water, which is VAṂ; Triṣṭubh, the meter; Varuṇa, the deity. The application is in the drying up (*śoṣaṇa*), burning (*dāhana*), and inundation (*plāvana*) of the villainous man." Then, after repeating sixteen times with an inhalation, YAṂ, which is the germ of the wind, one should conceive the villainous man as dried up by the Wind emanated from this germ. After repeating sixty-four times, with a breath retention, RAṂ, which is the germ of the fire, one should conceive it as reduced to ashes by the fire emanated from this germ. After repeating thirty-two times, with an expiration, VAṂ, which is the germ of the water, one should inundate the ashes of the villainous man. Such is the first method. But elsewhere,[4] following another tradition, the method of drying up and so forth is prescribed after eleven repetitions of all the germs: "The domain of the fire is triangular and furnished with the syllable RAṂ; having repeated eleven times, he should burn the villainous man," etc. The description of drying up, burning, and inundation also is seen in such texts as the Prapañcasāra[5] and so on in connection with the breath control. In this context the author of the Mahārthamañjarī has explained his own verse: "The drying up of the bodies is the destruction of the impurity; the burning is the extirpation of the latent impressions of this [impurity]; the inundation is the purification accomplished by sprinkling the ambrosia of knowledge" (44), as follows in the autocommentary Parimala:

> A certain supernaturalness is to be brought about for the worshippers at the very beginning of the process of worship and that results in the destruction etc. of the covering of impurity. Here "drying up of their bodies" is nothing but the attenuation of the impurity adhering to them, i.e. of the ignorance which is the origin of the sprouts of the transmigration. "Burning" consists in the elimination of the latent impressions, i.e. of the persistence as the essence of the *saṃskāra*-s of the above mentioned

> impurity of their [bodies]. Similarly, "inundation" is the cleansing, i.e. the purification (*pavitrīkaraṇa*), caused by the continuous flow of the knowledge which is the cognition of one's own self, [a knowledge] which is like ambrosia as it gives the delight of the form of the attainment of one's own nature and which arises along with the removal of the ignorance. (p. 111)

By these procedures of drying up, burning, and inundation, the practicer obtains a divine body that is resplendent and virtuous, that is the means to the realization of all the human aims, of which the sins have been destroyed, and that is fit for the propitiation of the deity. And in that (body) the process of installation of the breaths must be effected.

Installation of the Breaths

Having sipped water and controlled the breaths, having taken water, one should take the following resolution: "Of this revered mantra of installation of the breaths[6] the *ṛṣi*s are Brahmā, Viṣṇu, and Maheśvara; the meters are Ṛk, Yajus, and Sāman; the deity is the power of the breaths that is the cause of the production of the universe; the germ is ĀṂ; the *śakti* is HRĪṂ; the pin (*kīlaka*) is KRAUṂ; the application is in the installation of my breaths." Having thus performed the application, one then should perform the assignments (*nyāsa*): *brahmaviṣṇumaheśvararṣibhyo namaḥ*, on the head; *ṛkyajuḥsāmachandobhyo namaḥ*, on the face; *jagatsṛṣṭikāriṇīprāṇaśaktidevatāyai namaḥ*, on the heart; ĀṂ *bījāya namaḥ*, on the sex organ; HRĪṂ *śaktaye namaḥ*, on the feet; KRAUṂ *kīlakāya namaḥ*, on the whole body.

> Aṃ kaṃ khaṃ gaṃ ghaṃ ṅaṃ āṃ pṛthivyaptejovāyvākāśātmane aṅguṣṭhābhyāṃ namaḥ. Iṃ caṃ chaṃ jaṃ jhaṃ ñaṃ īṃ śabdasparśarūparasagandhātmane tarjanībhyāṃ namaḥ. Uṃ ṭaṃ ṭhaṃ ḍaṃ ḍhaṃ ṇaṃ ūṃ tvakcakṣuḥśrotrajihvāghrāṇātmane madhyamābhyāṃ namaḥ. Eṃ taṃ thaṃ daṃ dhaṃ naṃ aiṃ vākpāṇipādapāyūpasthātmane anāmikābhyāṃ namaḥ. Oṃ paṃ phaṃ baṃ bhaṃ maṃ auṃ vacanādānagativisargānandātmane kaniṣṭhābhyāṃ namaḥ. Aṃ yaṃ raṃ laṃ vaṃ śaṃ ṣaṃ saṃ aḥ manobuddhyahaṅkāracittavijñānātmane karatalakarapṛṣṭhābhyāṃ namaḥ.

With the same method one should perform the assignment on the heart, and so forth. Then one should perform the following assignments: ĀṂ *namaḥ,* from the navel down to the feet; HRĪṂ *namaḥ,* from the heart down to the navel; KRAUṂ *namaḥ,* from the space between the eyebrows down to the heart. And one should assign on the heart the seven bodily constituents (*dhātu*) in such a manner as follows: *yaṃ tvagātmane namaḥ, raṃ raktātmane namaḥ; laṃ māṃsātmane namaḥ; vaṃ medasātmane namaḥ; saṃ asthyātmane namaḥ; saṃ majjātmane namaḥ; śaṃ śukrātmane namaḥ.* Then one should perform these assignments on the heart: HRĪṂ *ojasātmane namaḥ;* HŪṂ *prāṇātmane namaḥ; kṣaṃ jīvātmane namaḥ.* And one should proceed with the *vyāpaka,* starting with "*Aṃ, namaḥ,*" "*Āṃ, namaḥ,*" "*Iṃ, namaḥ,*" and ending with the syllable *Kṣa.*

Then having assigned the Śakti of the throne in his heart, having meditated, having worshipped [her] with the mental acts of homage, having held the hand on the heart, with the "gesture of the knowledge" (*jñāna-mudrā*), one should establish the breaths as follows: ĀṂ HRĪṂ KRAUṂ *yaṃ raṃ laṃ vaṃ śaṃ saṃ saṃ haṃ saḥ so 'haṃ prāṇa iha prāṇāḥ;* then ĀṂ HRĪṂ KRAUṂ *yaṃ raṃ laṃ vaṃ śaṃ ṣaṃ saṃ haṃ saḥ so 'haṃ jīva iha sthitaḥ;* again, ĀṂ HRĪṂ KRAUṂ *yaṃ raṃ vaṃ śaṃ ṣaṃ saṃ haṃ saḥ so 'haṃ, sarvendriyāṇi vāṅmanastvakcakṣuḥśrotrajihvāghrāṇapādapāṇipāyūpasthānīhaivāgatya sukhaṃ circaṃ tiṣṭhantu namaḥ,* HRĪṂ *kṣaṃ saṃ haṃ saḥ* HRĪṂ HRĪṂ. One should recite this mantra of installation of the breaths thrice. One should repeat the *praṇava* sixteen times for the fulfillment of the sanctifying ceremonies (*saṃskāra*); that is, the impregnation rite and so on. Then one should conceive one's own body as made of light in such terms: "Let the sanctifying ceremonies, that is, the impregnation rite and so on, be brought forth to the body by this; my body has now become fit to undertake all ritual acts." Then one should perform breath control as follows: having uttered the sixteen vowels *A* and so on, one should inhale the wind (*vāyu*) through the left nostril; having uttered the twenty-five letters from *Ka* onward, one should stabilize the wind with a retention; having uttered the letters from *Ya* to *Kṣa,* one should breathe out the wind. One should proceed thrice in this way. The virtue of this practice of breath control is extolled in the scriptures thus: "Just as the fire burns the defect of the ores, so the interiorized sin is burnt by breath-control."[7]

Through the conjoined performances of the purification of the elements and the installation of the breaths, the worshipper, having become the own chosen god, propitiates afterward the chosen deity.

Three Kinds of Worship

Two kinds of cult (*varivasyā*), external and internal, are described in the treatises of the Tantra. Of these the propitiation of one's own chosen deity (*sveṣṭadevatā*) with external flowers, incense, and so on is known as *external cult;* the propitiation of this deity with the mind engaged in contemplation is known as *internal cult.* In the Kula, Krama, and other traditions one's own self-deity (*svātma-devatā*) is propitiated on the lines of their respective scriptures. And this is yet another kind of worship. This threefold method of worship is described as divided into *parā, aparā,* and *parāparā* in the Yoginīhṛdaya (3.2-4) thus:

> O Gaurī, the daily worship ordained for you is distinguished into three types: *parā, aparā,* and thirdly *parāparā.* The first pertains to the state of nonduality and is experienced by all the sense perceptions. And the second is the worship of the [Śrī]cakra; it is performed by me continually. In such a manner, O Devī, the third is the *parāparā* [situated] in what is full of knowledge. The *parā* worship is known to be the highest."

In this passage one should understand that the external worship is *aparā,* the internal worship is *parā,* and the propitiation of one's own self-deity is the *parāparā* worship.

In the preceding passage the superiority of the *parā* is declared. And in the Śaktisaṃgamatantra, to a question of the Goddess regarding worship, Śiva answers: "Of what use indeed, is the external purification of an earthen jar full of excrement? After the completion of the internal purification one should perform the external purification" (4.11.74-75); and: "After the completion of the internal worship, one should perform the external worship"(4.11.79). The author of the Dīpikā commentary on the Yoginīhṛdaya, on the strength of the statement: "Whatever is about to be prescribed subsequently [as] external, one should perform all that internally" (3.90), concludes: "By this it is pointed out that one should first perform also inwardly the complete external worship." For this very reason such statements are found: "That which is performed continually with external materials like flowers and so on is not the [real] worship, but that which is the supreme state in the nondual splendor, in one's own magnitude is the worship." For, the external worship becomes, as it were, fruitless without the internal cult as indicated by "That worship, where the mind is not appeased while dwelling in the middle of the pure and limitless ocean of consciousness, is similar to a game with a cloth doll played by a girl." For this very reason Śivānanda gives the definition of worship as follows: "Worship is the repose of the objective universe on the ground of consciousness;" and he shows the esoteric purport of the incense, perfume, lamp, and food offering, on the authority of the Bhaṭṭagaṅgādharastotra. And for this very reason the definition of worship is stated in the Mahānayapaddhati thus: "That firm intuition (*parāmarśa*) of the form, the nature of which is supreme and unobstructed, is worship; thus it has been settled by the Lord." And Praśastibhūtipāda declares: "The worship of the wise consists in furthering their own state at the moment of the experience of those gladdening mental states [that are] the pleasing and resplendent appearances visible here." For everything is pervaded by the Goddess, as indicated by: "Whichever lofty consciousness and whichever mental state resplendent with bliss, whichever marvelous form in the universe, all that is the appearance of you, O Goddess." In the following statement of the Āgama scriptures also the word *kriyā* ("ritual act") should be understood as synonymous of *pūjana* ("worship"): "Yoga is not one thing and *kriyā* another; this intelligence which has attained truth in the appeasement of the tendencies of one's own mind, this is named *kriyā*." And as this points only to the *parā* worship, the superiority of the *parā* worship thus is well proven. And it must be known that for this reason the repeated performance of the *parā* worship is very essential to attain fitness for the *aparā* and *parāparā* worship. And in this context, there is a specific application of the purification of the elements and of the installation of the breaths; let wise men understand it from the explanation of these two procedures given previously.

The worship of the external [Śrī]cakra, referred to as *aparā* in the passage of the Yoginīhṛdaya cited earlier, is known as *external cult* (*bāhyavarivasyā*). According to the author of the Dīpikā (3.112) the external worship is that performed with perfume, flowers, and so forth, which are products of the five elements. The author of the Ṛjuvimarśinī commentary on the Nityāṣoḍaṣikārṇava also (p. 134) gives their characteristics on the authority of the Prapañcasāra. This worship is developed variously as five, sixteen, and sixty-four acts of homage.

And the *parāparā* worship has been thus commented on with reference to authority by Amṛtānanda: "Thus the third worship *parāparā* is the repose 'in what is full of knowledge,' i.e. in the splendour full of the above mentioned contemplation of nonduality, 'of the external ritual act,' that which has the form of the worship of enclosures, which are distinct [from the self]. It has been said by the wise: 'Like the offerings of clarified butter poured into fire, by means of worship I abandon the differentiating perception etc. in the splendour full of pure brightness'." In this respect the distinction between the *parā* and *parāparā* worship should be understood attentively and clearly. Of these the worship called *parāparā* is for purifying the impure thoughts of differentiation, whereas in the worship called *parā* everything shines, filled only of pure consciousness.

Thus the worship called *parāparā* is described in the statements of the Jñānendukaumudī: "Abandoning this conscious own self, why should they worship the inert?"[8] of the Mukhyāmnāyarahasyavidhi: "One's own self-deity should be propitiated with one's own real essence, with perfumes etc. perceptible by means of the senses; this itself is the 'great sacrifice' of the knower", in these two statements of the Trikasāra: "Worship is the stream of bliss," "By attaining Śiva and Śakti," and in this statement of the Pūjanastotra: "Oh! a certain agreeable taste."

Inclusion of the Other Types of Worship

Worship is explained as of four kinds—*cāra, rāva, caru,* and *mudrā*—by Maheśvarānanda on the authority of the statement of the Cidgaganacandrikā, which begins with *cārarāva* and so on. It thus is

> Of these, *cāra* is the rule of conduct; *rāva* is the "reflection" (*vimarśa*); *caru* is the first, second, etc.;[9] *mudrā* is the particular mode of dressing and the particular position of hands, feet, etc. which is assumed with one's own body to effect the Parāmeśvara-hood for one's own self. The "great gesture" (*mahatī mudrā*) is entirely included in *rāva* itself. Among these four kinds of worship, it is the *rāva* that is employed chiefly. The performance of others is as leading to that entirely. Hence the intuition (*parāmarśa*) of one's own nature is the supreme worship. And the rest, like perfume, flower, incense, lamp, water destined to washing feet etc., is mere show. Such is the intended meaning. (p. 106)

In this passage Maheśvarānanda declares the supremacy of the *rava*, which is "reflection." As it is possible to include *cāra* and *mudrā* in the external worship called *aparā*, and *caru* in the *parāparā* worship, again the threefold character of the worship finally results from this passage.

In the Buddhist Tantras also the threefold method of worship is explained as "external," "relating to the self" (*adhyātmikī*) (that is, mental, *manomayī*), and "secret" (*guhyā*). Of these it may be said that *external* stands for *aparā*, *relating to the self* for *parā*, and *secret worship* for *parāparā*. It is performed toward the "sacrifice" to one's self-deity. Here the internal purification is the fruit of the *anuttarapūjā*, which is of seven or eleven kinds, and of the contemplation of the *caturbrahmavihāra*.[10] The definition and nature of these can be known from texts such as the Sādhana-mālā. Here the contemplation of the *niṣpanna-krama* is practiced to attain godhood.

In the Trika doctrines the three spiritual means (*upāya*) called *āṇava* (associated to the individual), *śākta* (associated to the energy), and *śāmbhava* (associated to the Lord), and a fourth procedure, the *anupāya* ("absence of means"), are described as the means of recognition (*pratyabhijñā*) of one's nature. It is possible to include them in the same threefold division. It is thus: some *āṇava* means are included in the *aparā* worship, others in the *parāparā*; the *śākta* means are included in the *parāparā* worship; the *śāmbhava* means and the *anupāya* procedure are included in the *parā* worship. In some *āṇava* means, such internal aids as *prāṇa-cakra* are employed, and sometimes women, intoxicating liquor, and meat are adopted among *śākta* and *śāmbhava* means to please one's own self-deity: thus it is appropriate to include all these only in the worship called *parāparā*, and not in the *parā*. The yogin who has entered in the final state of the *śāmbhava* means and in the *anūpaya* procedure is dependent on no external or internal practice other than the intuitive knowledge: thus it is certain that, in such kinds of *śāmbhava* means and *anūpaya* procedure, the *parā* worship is brought about.

Because we have explained the fourfold means elsewhere,[11] we do not endeavor to do it again here. It is merely the threefold worship that we shall briefly describe according to the Scriptures.

Aparā Worship

In the Tantrāloka (6.2-4), while explaining the *āṇava* means called *fixing of the spot*, Abhinavagupta states: "The spot [of worship] is said to be of three kinds: in the breath, in the body, and outside.

Breath is fivefold. In the body, [the spot] is twofold as outward and inward. Outside it is elevenfold: maṇḍala, sacred ground (*sthaṇḍila*), receptacle, rosary, book, *liṅga*, skull (*tūra*), cloth (*paṭa*), painted image (*pusta*), idol (*pratimā*), and form (*mūrti*).[12] Again each of these is manifold." Here Jayaratha explains thus: '*pusta*' is a figure created by smearing etc.; '*mūrti*' is connected with the Teacher etc. The *aparā* worship is the propitiation performed with external [means] such as flowers after the installation of one's own chosen deity in one of the eleven spots just enumerated. In the Siddhayogīśvaramata the gradual superiority of the sacred ground, the skull, and the cloth is explained by "The skull is superior to the sacred ground; the cloth is superior to the skull." On this subject Jayaratha explains both the words *sthaṇḍila* and *tūra*: "The *sthaṇḍila* is a spot of earth selected in view of the 'sacrifice' (*yāga*); the *tūra* is a kind of support sculpted into receptacle etc." (2.43). The definition of the skull along with its fashioning taken from the Siddhātantra should be consulted in the Luptāgamasaṃgraha (Part 2, pp. 199-200). The explanation of the word *maṇḍala* is given in this passage: "A *maṇḍala* is said [to be] the 'essence' (*sāra*); 'Śiva' is indeed meant by the word *maṇḍa*" (Tantrāloka 37.21). And Jayaratha states: "*maṇḍala* is that which gives the *maṇḍa*, i.e. the essence (*sāra*) called *Śiva*; such is the meaning." In this connection it is worth remembering the statement of the Haṃsaparāmeśvara: "All worship should take place on the sacred ground, but *adhivāsana* should not take place there," and the statement of the Siddhānta: "Having fastened firmly the internal *liṅga*, let him worship the external *liṅga*."

Various matters connected with the external worship are taught in passages collected in both parts of the Luptāgamasaṃgraha. During the worship of the ten guardians of the directions, eight guardians are first worshipped in the eight directions in the *maṇḍalas* and so forth. The question regarding the spot of worship of the ninth and tenth guardians thus is answered by the śloka of the Tattvavimarśinī: "One direction is mentioned between the directions of Indra and Īśāna; the other direction is mentioned between the directions of Nirṛti and Ambu."[13] It is known by this that the worship of the presiding deity of the Upper Region must be performed between the directions of Indra and Īśāna and the worship of the presiding deity of the Lower Regions, between that of the Nairṛta and of Ambu. Here the "direction of Indra" is the east and the "direction of Ambu" is the west. The spots of worship of Nandin, Rudra, Gaṅgā, Yamunā, and others are indicated in this statement of the Triśirobhairava beginning with "Thence at the base, from the North." In the same way, the order of the deities of the doors taught in the Triśiromata and in the Vāma- and Siddhānta-matas is explained in the Svacchandodyota (2.24-25). The preparation of the five products of the cow is found in the Parākhyasaṃhitā. Just as in the Svacchandatantra (3.54-55), the sanctifying ceremony of the five products of the cow is worth the attention in the Sātvata-saṃhitā too (7.10, 16.13). The commentary on the same passage also should be consulted.

Discussions on bath, posture, *sandhyā*- service, libation of water, assignment (*nyāsa*), gesture (*mudrā*), purification of the body, selection of site, *adhivāsa* ceremony, pavilion, *arghya* vessel, repetition of the mantra to be mastered, worship, feeding of the fire and so on according to the Siddhāntaśaiva method can be seen in passages of the Kiraṇa, Niḥśvāsottara, Pauṣkara, Mataṅga, Mayasaṅgraha, Raurava, Svāyambhuva, and so forth. A detailed description of the external worship is found in the Kriyā- and Caryāpadas in the Śaiva and other Āgamas. The characteristics of the performance of the *namas* (*namaskāra*) thus are explained in the Pañcārthapramāṇa of the Pāśupatas in connection with the exegesis of the Aghoramantra: "The performance of the *namas* is the act of abandoning of the nature of cause and effect." The "Vedic observances" (*veda-vratāni*) and the "great sacrifices" (*mahāyajñāḥ*) can be looked up in the two (respective) passages of the Yajña-sūtra, and the forty-eight sanctifying ceremonies currently in all the Āgamas and in some Smṛti texts. This subject of the external worship is developed in the appendix of the second edition of the Paraśurāmakalpasūtra, pages 386-395, 428-541; it should be seen there.

Parā Worship

The nature of the drying up, purification of the hands, and 'emerging' (*unmajjana*) is exposed in statements of the Kramavāsanā[14] by way of the directory of the internal "sacrifice." This text now is found printed under the title of Subhagodaya-vāsanā. In this complete text and in the Cidvilāsastava, the same internal cult that consists in symbolical interpretation (*vāsanā*) and that does not depend on external and internal flowers, breaths, and so on is explained as leading to the resting in nondual splendor, in one's own magnitude. In the Jñānadīpavimarśinī unpublished until today, the external and internal acts of homage are explained in all contexts like the worship of the sun during the *sandhyā* service. The nature of these acts of homage also can be seen in statements of the Udayākarapaddhati. The *parā* worship is presented by means of the *anupāya* procedure in the beginning and final *ślokas* of the Vijñāna-bhairava, particularly in the *ślokas* that teach 'concentration' (*dhāraṇā*). Similar interpretation is given for words like *japa, yajana, liṅga,* and so forth in the Gītāniṣyanda, the Bhaṭṭanāyakastotra, and the Pūrvatantra.

The universe comprehending the mobile and immobile is made of "light" (*prakāśa*) and "reflection" (*vimarśa*); thus indeed is the path taught by the Pratyabhijñā doctrine. Because there is no difference between "light" and "reflection" as between the moon and the moonlight, verily everything is full of inseparable "light" and "reflection". The followers of the Traipura tradition also accept this theory. Here as the worshipped and the worshipper and the substances of worship, in fact, are nonexistent, this principle consisting of "light" and "reflection" is worshipped only with mental acts of homage. This indeed is the *parā* worship. It is attained by those who dwell in the path devoid of the three constituents (*guṇa*). Its nature is described in the Yoginīhṛdaya (3.5-7) thus:

> Having meditated on the sandal of the Teacher in the Vāgbhava ("womb-of-speech") [triangle] situated in the great cluster of lotuses (in the brahmarandhra), [this sandal] that nourishes the forms of the universe and that showers supreme ambrosia; agitated by the intoxicating drink of the visualization of the supreme nonduality, engaged in the contemplation of the sound that moves in the cavity of the heart, turned away from the words of the form of differentiation, always turned inward; the contraction being torn asunder by the expansion of *Citkalā*, he is thus extremely resplendent.

The meaning of this passage should be known from its commentary, the Dīpikā. This real nature of the union of Kāmeśvara and Kāmeśvarī, who consist of "light" and "reflection," is propitiated as based upon the form of Kāmakalā, with the ultimate aim of light and of expansion in the nondual great *bindu* that is their symbol.

The *śloka* of the Tantrāloka "*sthānabheda* etc." ("The spot [of worship] . . .") has been cited here at the beginning of the explanation of the *aparā* worship. In this *śloka* it is taught that just as the worship is performed in eleven external substances, so it should be performed in the breath and in the body. In the same passage the eleven external spots are enumerated and in the commentary by Jayaratha they are explained by other statements as well. In the body the worship is performed in two ways, outward and inward. According to other Tantras, that which is effected by means of the awakening of the

Kuṇḍalinīśakti in the spots of the *mūlādhāra* and so on should be known as internal; that which is brought about in the form of the "assignment of the six limbs [of the mantra]," "assignment [performed] to the hands," 'tying of the gesture' (*mudrābandha*), arrangement (*viracana*) of the gesture and so forth on external places like the heart should be known as external; and that which is performed with the internal and external substances of the body should be known as secret. They should be included respectively in the *parā*, *aparā*, and *parāparā* worships.

Breath as fivefold, flows in the different limbs of the body as indicated by "In the heart, it is *prāṇa*; in the anus, *apāna*; in the region of the navel, *samāna*; in the area of the neck, *udāna*; and that which moves in the whole body is *vyāna*"; and it moves inside and outside in the form of the inhalation and exhalation. The yogins, having resorted to the inhalation and exhalation that move inside and outside, perform the method of the *ajapājapa* ("recitation of what is not recited"). Having resorted to the breaths that flow inside the body, they conceive the *kālodaya*, the *varṇodaya*, and the *cakrodaya*. The revered Abhinavagupta explains these methods of *kālodaya* and so on in the sixth and seventh Āhnikas by: "The *kālādhvan* is clearly established in breath etc." (*Tantrāloka* 6.37). In the Buddhist Kālacakratantra this method also is described in detail. This also should be regarded as included in the *parā* worship. Even the *ajapājapa* should be considered as a particular method of *parā* worship.

Parāparā Worship

In the statement of the Yoginīhṛdaya (3.8a): "The worship of one's own self is that which is enjoined with substances pleasing to the senses," the method of *parāparā* worship should be understood, and not that of *parā* because here, for the worship of one's own self-deity, substances pleasing to the senses, external or belonging to the body are employed. The mind, stained by endless latent impressions, indeed follows the wrong path. As its purification is impossible without the cleansing of the differentiating thoughts, a certain new way of worship leading to the pleasing of one's own self-deity has been disclosed in the Vāma, Kula, Krama, and Trika traditions and in the Vajrayāna Tantras, which are capable of provoking equally a fall and an elevation. While purifying the emotions by means of pleasing the senses, it would lead to virtue; while augmenting the attachment to objects, it would lead to vice. As has been said by the author of the Yogabhāṣya: "The river of mind indeed flows in two directions: it flows towards virtue and it flows towards vice" (1.12).

In the fifteenth and in the twenty-ninth Āhnikas of the Tantrāloka the method of worship called *parāparā* basically is discussed through the authority of various texts, respectively as based upon the Vāmācāra and leading to the Kula ritual. In the Kula ritual and in the Vajrayāna texts the substances belonging to the body, termed *five germs, five lamps, five nectars* are adopted as ingredients in the worship. In the Tantrālokaviveka, twelve substances are enumerated as "*Retas, harāmbu* (urine), *rajas, kṣāra* and *nālājyaka, pauruṣa, kṣmābhava,* he-goat (meat), *mīnaja* (fish meat), *śākunīyaka* (bird meat), onion and garlic: such are the auspicious twelve substances" (29.17); and the "five gems" as "I shall explain the *caru* which belongs to the body and difficult to obtain even by the Suras: *śivāmbu* (urine), *retas,* blood (*rajas*), *nālājya, viśvanirgama*" (29.200). Among these, excepting the eleventh and twelfth substances, the remaining substances are grouped under the name of *five nectars* and *five lamps* in the Vajrayāna texts. They are enumerated among the substances belonging to the body. The secret worship[15] accomplished with these is called *parāparā.* In the course of time the pair of substances called *kuṇḍa-golaka* came to be included among the internal substances belonging to the body, as indicated by the Tantrāloka: "He should fill the *arghya* vessel with substances that are the cause and fruit of delight" (29.22). It becomes clear from the study of such texts as the Yoginīhṛdaya that, in the Traipura tradition, only a refined form of internal substances belonging to the body has been accepted.

Conclusion

Thus to answer to the question; How indeed does a practicer, having assumed the nature of a god, qualify to perform the "sacrifice (*yajana*) to the god?" the method of purification of the elements and of installation of the breaths as well as the threefold character of worship called *sacrifice to the god* have been described. Because the statements of various texts and authors collected in Luptāgamasaṃgraha, which consists of two parts, have been quoted here as authoritative, the origin of the references of these statements that have not been indicated, may be known with the help of the Luptāgamasaṃgraha. And here it should be noted that, although there is no need of the purification of the elements and installation of the breaths in the *parā* worship, these two are needed in the *aparā* and the *parāparā* worships. When the worshipper of one's own chosen deity, by means of *aparā* worship in the circle and so forth begs for indulgence on the lines of the commentary of Śivānanda (on Nityāṣoḍaśikārṇava 1.[189]) as

> Your form, the essence of which is self-experienced pure consciousness and that consists of the intuition (*parāmarśa*) of the nonartificial self, has been visualized for an instant as distinct in the circle, caused to shine as having an external objectivity; forgive this momentary lapse of ours, as uttered by the Śrīrahasyaguru: "Let these joyful modifications of my senses be connected with their respective objects, O Lord, [but] let the inconsiderate act that is the loss of the feeling of nonseparation with you not occur, even an instant, even slightly" (Śivastotrāvalī 8.5),[16]

then what is there to say of the practicer who presents mental offerings during a *parā* worship? So it may be said that the method of purification of the elements and installation of the breaths is hidden, in a different way, in the *parā* worship and in its various forms described here; therefore it is well said: "Having accomplished the internal purification, one should perform the external purification" and "One should perform first all external worship inwardly." As compared to the *aparā* worship, this *parā* worship is indispensable at the beginning of the *parāparā* worship also for the purifying of the mental ingredients and so on. For this very reason the superiority of the *parā* worship is declared. The *parā* worship that overcomes the divisions pertaining to space, time, religion, race, and so forth is superior to everything: who indeed would contradict this, whether a theoretician, orthodox or unorthodox, or a follower of the various contemporary theories that represent the traditional or progressive doctrines. Thus truly, it is well said: "Having become a god, he should sacrifice to the gods"; peace!

Notes

1. A brief explanation of the purification of the elements is seen at the end of the Chapter 17 in the Bhūtaśuddhitantra added to the third part of the Tantrasaṃgraha (p. 625). The purification of the elements and the purification of the self are described in the first part of the Īśānaśivagurudevapaddhati (pp. 97-101). The purification of the elements and the installation of the breaths are explained, briefly and extensively, in such texts as the Prapañcasāra

and works related to Dharma-śāstra.

2. Elsewhere also, in all other Tantras, the domain, shape, color, germ, etc. of the elements earth, etc., are explained in the same way.

3. Here are recalled the five crimes described in the Manusmṛti (11.54): "The murder of a Brahmin, the drinking of liquor, theft and the approach of the teacher's wife are called the great crimes, as well as the contact with those guilty of such crimes." The word *saṃyogin* should be understood to mean 'association' (*saṃsarga*).

4. Many methods of this *sagarbha* breath control are explained in the Yogapādas of the Tantras and Āgamas, in the Yoga scriptures and in the Purāṇas.

5. "Or else, by the fifty *mātra* division, according to the rule, he should control the breaths in the body variously purified by the drying up, burning and inundation" (19.25).

6. This process of installation of the breaths is indicated for another purpose, in another way, in the Artharatnāvalī, a commentary on the Nityāṣoḍaśikārṇava; it should be consulted there (p. 155). This process is explained in the thirty-fifth chapter of the Prapañcasāra also.

7. Manu (6.71) declares: "Just as the impurities of the ores that are being melted are burnt, thus the defects of the senses are burnt by the subduing of the breath."

8. The Kaula teachers, those who conform to the Vajrayāna and the Nāthayogins, who hold that "If one can install God, by the greatness of the mantra, in such inert substances as an image, a cloth, a painting, a sacred ground, a skull etc. then how could not His installation take place in this human body, which is filled with consciousness?" worship their own self-deity following the Lākula final teaching quoted by the Tantrāloka: "The body is made of all gods" (15.604).

9. This means liquor, meat, and so forth.

10. Here by the expression *caturbrahmavihāra* the four states of friendship, compassion, joy, and indifference are meant. And these are explained in the Yogasūtra of Patañjali: "Mental serenity arises from the reflection on friendship, compassion, joy and indifference, which have happiness, sorrow, merit and sin as their objects" (1.33) and in the Tattvārthasūtra (7.12) of the Jaina school: "Friendship, joy, compassion and impartiality towards those who

are pure, who abound in good qualities, who are afflicted and who behave improperly."

11. See Vijñānabhairava, 2d ed., Introduction, pp. 15-20.

12. Some dissimilarity is found in the eleven substances enumerated in this statement of the Bhairavakula quoted in the Tantrāloka (27.45-46): One should perform the worship on a sacred ground, in fire, in a cloth, in a *liṅga*, in a vessel, in a lotus, in a maṇḍala, in a *mūrti*, in a jar (*ghaṭa*), in a collection of weapons, in a *ghaṭa* (body?) and in a cord."

13. The same order is indicated in this statement of the Īśānaśivagurudevapaddhati (Part 3, p. 36): "One should know that Brahmā who is the lord of the upper direction, is between Indra and Īśāna, and that Ananta who is the lord of the lower direction, is between Nirṛti and Varuṇa: such is the instruction."

14. In the Mahārthamañjarīparimala (pp. 112-113) three ślokas of the Kramavāsanā of his Paramaguru are quoted by Maheśvarānanda and these are collected in the first part of the Luptāgamasaṃgraha [pp. 29-30] under the same name. The same three ślokas are found in the Subhagodayavāsanā (21, 24, 26), published among the appendices in our edition of the Nityāṣoḍaṣikārṇava: it thus is ascertained that this text does not differ from the Kramavāsanā.

15. The particulars of the *parāpara* worship as described by the Vāma, Kaula, Krama, and other traditions and of the *anuttarapūjā* of eleven kinds described in the Buddhist Tantras should be consulted in our article entitled: "Tāntrikī varivasyā tasyā bhedāś ca" (Sārasvatī Suṣamā, Va. 39, A. 1-4: 132-138).

16. This is the meaning: for the "teacher of the secret," Bhaṭṭotpala, the author of the Śivastotrāvalī, the loss of the feeling of nonseparation from the Lord is not wished, even an instant, even slightly. And the goddess Tripurasundarī, during her propitiation by the worshipper, is being caused for an instant to shine in objectiveness in the Śrīcakra which is an external *maṇḍala* of worship. It is this lapse that is to be forgiven.

Chapter Five

The Stages of Awakening in the Svacchanda-Tantra

Teun Goudriaan

In the Svacchanda-Tantra (SvT), an important early Śaiva Tantra, use is made of a sequence of terms derived from the root *budh-*, 'to awake, to become conscious or aware,' to express a gradation of the conscious subject's spiritual development. The nucleus of this chapter is a translation of SvT 11, 91-126, with the greater part of its commentary where the self's progressive awakening has been described in precise yet imaginative style against the background of the ritual of the great karma-destroying initiation.

Stages of awakening already occur in the Śāntiparvan of the Mahābhārata in a few textually complicated chapters. A comparison of these two sources amounts to a case study of the relation between early Śaivatantra and older religious speculation. On the whole, I have restricted myself to a presentation of these two passages, occasionally referring to older Upaniṣads (Bṛhadāraṇyaka and Maitrāyaṇīya) and other Śaiva sources. Buddhist literature has not been taken into account.

In early Śaivism, similar gradatory systems also have been applied to the yogic concentration upon the self's ascent to the protophonic and supraphonic realms of Śakti and Śiva, and in the monistic-idealistic analysis of the states of consciousness (waking, etc.). These systems have been referred to only succinctly at the end of the chapter. In the course of this investigation, therefore it will appear that the idea of stages of spiritual awakening has been handled in different ways as a conceptual tool to suit different contexts: Sāṃkhya speculation; monotheistic soteriology based on Śaiva ritual and yoga; idealistic psychology. It has been subjected to various types of manipulation, such as extension and systematization, sophistication and reinterpretation. Notwithstanding these differentiations, it is possible to recognize the conceptual pattern from its origin in the Upaniṣads through (and without doubt also beside) the Epic to the early Tantra.

The Stages of Awakening in Mbh. 12, 291ff

At the beginning of Chapter 291 of the Śāntiparvan, Yudhiṣṭhira poses a question to Bhīṣma concerning the difference between the perishable (*kṣara-*), by which one recurs (in saṃsāra), and the imperishable (*akṣara-*) by which one does not recur.[1] For his answer, the grandsire claims no originality; he refers for this subject to an instruction of Karālajanaka by Vasiṣṭha. The exposition is concerned in the first place with a fivefold creative process that will not detain us at the moment. The process results in a system of twenty-four *tattvas*, categories of existence, subsumed under the term *the perishable* (called this because the world of beings perishes in it, *yatredaṃ kṣarate jagat*, 12b). It is also characterized as *mohātmaka-* (35c), which suggests a connection with Māyā. The imperishable is the twenty-fifth *tattva*, which is Viṣṇu (37), the large or cosmic *ātman* (41). He is not really a *tattva*, but is so called because of his association (*saṃśrayaṇa-*) with the *tattvas*; the same in 42d, *nistattvaḥ pañcaviṃśakaḥ*. Nīlakaṇṭha, the Advaitin commentator (seventeenth century), expresses this relation of the Lord with the *tattvas* as *adhiṣṭhāna-* 'control' (cf. *adhitiṣṭhati*, 291, 38b), adding that the causal relation of the Supreme Being and the creation is due to nescience (*ajñāna*) and therefore unreal in ultimate sense. In 293, 43, again, the Mbh. characterizes the perfect form of the Lord who is free from the *guṇas* (the three material constituents of Nature) as the controller (*adhiṣṭhātar*) of nature and the *guṇas*, being the "twenty-fifth."

This unmanifest cosmic being is present in the heart of all beings as an intelligent principle. However, for some unspecified reason this being has lost natural intelligence and undergoes a modification in the course of which he wrongly imagines himself to "possess" nature (*prakṛti*): *vikurvāṇaḥ prakṛtimān abhimanyaty abuddhimān* (291, 41cd). Nīlakaṇṭha (Nīl.) here identifies nature with Avidyā; he further considers the state of being *abuddhimān* as directly connected with the influence of Māyā as appears from his gloss *mūḍhaḥ* 'deluded'; and this in accordance with the *mohātmaka-* of the text itself (see earlier). For him the *abhimāna* consists in a wrong conception of separate individuality: *aham ity ātmānaṃ manyate*.[2] The Prakṛti very probably has to be identified with the 'unawake person' (*abuddhajana*) mentioned in the next stanza (291, 42):

> Tamaḥsattvarajoyuktas tāsu tāsv iha yoniṣu /
> līyate 'pratibuddhatvād[3] abuddhajanasevanāt //

Being combined with [the three *guṇas*:] inertia, lucidity and activity, he is absorbed in our [world of existence] in so many births

by reason of his unawakened state, because
he has dealings with an unawake person.

Nīl. gives an interesting interpretation of *līyate: yonibhiḥ saha tādātmyaṃ prāpnoti* 'he obtains a state of identity with these births,' but he does not comment on the last quarter (*abuddhajana-*). This latter *pāda* is repeated at 293, 1b, whereas the third quarter (*līyate . . .*) literally recurs as 293, 3c. Such repetitions tend to underline the importance of this stanza. They give evidence of the internal cohesion of these at first reading somewhat confused chapters. The term *jana-* for the delusive power is found again at 295, 23, where the *ātman* becomes aware of his real nature (see later).

The last stanzas (43-48) of Chapter 291 show how the cosmic self, "living together" (*sahavāsa-*, 43a) with Prakṛti, undergoes the different modes of existence (*bhāva-*) under the influence of the *guṇas*. In short, this is the perishable with which the twenty-fifth associates himself by a fall from his [innate] wisdom (48). The situation is summarized in 293, 10cd: *abuddhasevanāc cāpi buddho 'py abudhatāṃ vrajet* 'and due to his dealings with the unawake, also the awake reaches a state of unawareness' (but see later).

Chapter 292 contains an expatiation on the same theme. The unawakened self follows the unawake or unintelligent (i.e., nature): *apratibuddhatvād abuddham anuvartate.*[4] He ensnares himself in the *guṇas*, like a chrysalis (*kīṭaḥ kośakāraḥ*, 4ab) in its cocoon. All his experiences of the world—births, illness, diets, study, ritual, and especially all kinds of ascetic observances—are products of his own wrong representation (*abhimāna*, 7e). A similar message is expressed more philosophically in 294, 31: all *tattvas* are created by the internal self (*antarātman*). This imagination is due to [the self's] unawakened state (*asambodhāt*, 24a); in that state, it is created by him for his own amusement (*krīḍārtham abhimanyate*, 28d).[5] All these activities (*kriyāpatham*, 26d) are executed by nature: *prakṛtiḥ kurute devī*, 27a (we are reminded of ŚvetUp 4, 8f.); and this suggests that there is no real difference between the self as creator and nature as performer of these imaginations. The chapter closes with the remark (292, 48cd) that the Imperishable, by loss of his innate intellect (*abuddhi-*; Nīl. *viparyastabuddhi-* 'by confusion of his intellect') imagines himself to be perishable: *akṣaraḥ kṣaram ātmānam abuddhis tv abhimanyate.*

Chapter 293 adds interesting opinions about the nature of the relationship between Prakṛti and Puruṣa. In verse 12-21, Karālajanaka himself formulates (without committing himself to it) a naturalistic, proto-Tantric doctrine that amounts to this: that the interplay between the two fundamental powers is the basic metaphysical principle. Just as the copulation of a man and a woman results in the creation of a new body the constituents of which are partly derived from the father, partly from the mother, in the same way the copulation of Prakṛti and Puruṣa provides for creation and maintenance of the world. In this view, release is irrelevant or does not exist. Vasiṣṭha strongly opposes this view that, according to him, fails to grasp the meaning of the Scriptures. In verses 41 f., he then again comes to speak on the stages of awakening from the viewpoint of Sāṃkhya-Yoga defended by him:

41 Yadā tv eṣa guṇān sarvān prākṛtān abhimanyate /
tadā sa guṇavān eva parameṇānupaśyati //
42 Yat tad buddheḥ paraṃ prāhuḥ sāṃkhyā yogāś ca sarvaśaḥ /
budhyamānaṃ mahāprājñam abuddhaparivarjanāt //
43 Aprabuddham athāvyaktaṃ saguṇaṃ prāhur Īśvaram /

When he represents to himself all the strands of nature,
on that very moment he is the possessor of the strands;
he considers them as the highest.[6]
That which the teachers of Sāṃkhya and Yoga unanimously
proclaim as beyond intelligence, they call the awakening,
of great wisdom, because it avoids the unawake [nature];
but then, the unawakened, [although] unmanifest, they call
the Lord [connected] with the *guṇas.*

These lines are difficult to interpret, but it seems that the 'unawake' (*abuddha-*) nature is closely related to, although here subtly distinguished from, the 'unawakened' (*aprabuddha-*) self, identical with a qualified, *guṇic* (*saguṇa-*, 43b) form of the Lord.[7] Two states of the self therefore are described: the state in which the self identifies with nature and its *guṇas* with which he or she is equipped or possesses (*guṇavān*, 41c, see *prakṛtimān*, 291, 41c); and another state in which the self is realizing that unawake nature should be avoided; the state of the awakening (*budhyamāna-*, 42c). The text seems to emphasize that this awakening [self] still is no other than the *guṇic* Lord, the Avyakta; that is, the twenty-fourth *tattva* (who = Prakṛti, 294, 27a), as may appear from 293, 45:

Yadā prabuddhās tv avyaktam avasthājanmabhīravaḥ /
budhyamānaṃ prabudhyanti gamayanti samaṃ tadā //

When the awakened [sages], in fear of mental states and births,
become awake to the unmanifest as awakening,
they cause it to come to rest [or; equilibrium].

Also verse 46 seems to support the identification of the awakening and the unawakened: *asamyag anudarśanaṃ budhyamānā-*

prabuddhābhyāṃ pṛthak pṛthak . . . 'wrong is the conception of the Budhyamāna and the Aprabuddha as different . . . ' (and, we may add, as a copulating pair, see 293, 19, referred to earlier).[8] The aware (*budha-*), however, realize (*budhyante*, 44d) the Lord as essentially free from the *guṇas* (*nirguṇa-*, 43c) and as their controller, and in this way are awakened (*prabuddha*, 45a).[9]

Summarizing the preceding discourse, we can state that the text in the Chapters 291-293 distinguishes three stages of awakening:

1. The unawakened state, in which the self, being *aprabuddha* (or *abuddhimān*, 291, 41; or *apratibuddha*, 291, 42), identifies with nature that is *abuddha* "unawake."[10] The text denotes the subject of this experience as *the perishable* or *the guṇic Lord* (*saguṇa īśvaraḥ*). He seems to be a modification of the imperishable, Viṣṇu (291, 37), the "twenty-fifth," the cosmic self (291, 41), who by his own free will associates himself with the categories of lower existence. By *abhimāna*, he creates the play of the *guṇas* and identifies with them.

2. The awakening state (*budhyamāna*) in which the realization breaks through that this play of the *guṇas* should be avoided and that the unawake is not the self's real essence. This is said to come to pass while the self still is intimately connected with Nature. The stanzas 293, 41f. might even be interpreted in the direction of idealistic monism: the unawake does not exist outside the Lord's qualified, *guṇic* experience (see Śaṅkara on BhagGītā 13, 2 which we cannot discuss here).

3. The awakened state (*prabuddha*; 293, 10 *buddha*).[11] The word *prabuddha-*, used in the plural (293, 45) denotes those sages who realize the eternal quietude of the unmanifest, the unqualified Lord who is the controller of nature and the *guṇas*, the twenty-fifth (293, 43c-44d):

Nirguṇaṃ ceśvaraṃ nityam adhiṣṭhātāram eva ca //
prakṛteś ca guṇānāṃ ca pañcaviṃśatikaṃ budhāḥ /
sāṃkhyayoge ca kuśalā budhyante paramaiṣiṇaḥ //

Despite the attribution of this insight to the followers of Sāṃkhya and Yoga, there is a Vedāntic tinge to this doctrine: the play of the *guṇas* that leads to delusion is due to the Lord's deceptive self-representation (*abhimānitvam*, 293, 39).

A further extension of this message follows in 294-296, where we also find subtle deviations from the preceding (although the discussants remain the same). At the beginning of 294, Karālajanaka understandably complains that the preceding exposition was too difficult for him. He asks for an elucidation of the triad *buddha, budhyamāna*, and *aprabuddha* (or *apratibuddha*, 294, 4 and 295, 46). Vasiṣṭha in first instance ignores this request and instead gives a digression about yogic practice and *sāṃkhyic* theory. The terms in question recur only a few times, at first at 294, 43, which unfortunately again is difficult to understand:

> Pañcaviṃśo 'prabuddhātmā budhyamāna iti smṛtaḥ /
> yadā tu budhyate 'tmānaṃ tadā bhavati kevalaḥ //

> The twenty-fifth, when of [still] unawakened self,
> is known as the awakening; but when
> he realizes his self, then be becomes isolated [and free].

This stanza contains an extended use of the term *twenty-fifth* that here also denotes the self in a state of bondage. In the state of final realization he is called *kevala*, a Sāṃkhyan term that did not occur in the preceding chapters. The most problematic aspect of the stanza is the variety of readings in the first quarter, but I believe that preferably we should follow the critical text.[12]

The "degradation" of the twenty-fifth, that is, the individual Puruṣa or Jīva (no trace of the latter term in these chapters of the Mbh.; it is used in Nīl.'s commentary) is continued in 295, 10-18, where we read of his absorption into Prakṛti, see 15a-16b:

> Yadā tu guṇajālaṃ tad avyaktātmani saṃkṣipet /
> tadā saha guṇais tais tu pañcaviṃśo vilīyate //
> guṇā guṇeṣu līyante tadaikā prakṛtir bhavet /

> When he retrojects that *guṇic* structure into the unmanifest self,
> then the twenty-fifth is absorbed together with these *guṇas*;
> the *guṇas* are absorbed in the *guṇas*, and then
> there would only be undivided nature.

In 16cd, the same is reformulated as an absorption of the Kṣetrajña into the Kṣetra. Nature thus becomes imperishable (*akṣara-*, 17a, but Kinjawadekar's text reads *kṣara-*, 307, 17). This surprising viewpoint, although in its wording resembling 291, 42 and 293, 3 (*yoniṣu līyate*, there said of "ordinary" experience), rather may be a rethinking of 293, 45 (*yadā prabuddhās*, see earlier); at the same time, it foreshadows the situation of the souls absorbed in primeval Māyā (*pralayākala-*) postulated by the Śaiva Āgamas. However this may be, Vasiṣṭha in Mbh. 12, 295, 20f. continues his description of the awakening of the soul who becomes aware of its fundamental difference from nature's *guṇas* that it despises (not, brings to equilibrium, as in 293, 45 quoted earlier). The stanza 295, 22 not unintentionally begins exactly like verse 15:

Yadā tu guṇajālaṃ tat prākṛtaṃ vijugupsate /
paśyate cāparaṃ paśyaṃ tadā paśyan na saṃjvaret //

When he rejects with repulsion that *guṇic* structure
that belongs to nature, and when he beholds
that other whom one should behold (?),
then he will not regret his vision.

In Chapter 296, still another element is added. In the first stanzas, the status of the awakening is discussed further: according to verse 3, he is called *budhyamāna* (Nīl. repeats his identification with Jīva), because he has a realization of the unmanifest [nature]; that is, as different from himself. In case of absence of even this realization, he is called the *Unawakened* (*apratibuddha-*, verse 4, cf. its use in 291, 42 and 293, 3). The awakening has the status of the "twenty-fifth" (5-7) and is characterized by addiction to worldly existence (*saṅgātmakaḥ*, 5). The awakened, however, is characterized now as the "twenty-sixth," pure, immeasurable, eternal (7c-8b). He is pure awareness (*budhyate kevalam*, 9b) and observes [the play of] the twenty-fifth and twenty-fourth (9cd). He is free from the twenty-five *tattvas* (14). This new truth of the existence of the twenty-sixth, the awake, is then repeated in other wordings that we shall not discuss here.

We can summarize as follows: according to the author of Mbh. 12, 296, the unawake (*aprabuddha*) is primeval nature, in an inactive state of equilibrium, in which the self or soul has temporarily merged. The awakening (*budhyamāna*) denotes that state in which the self, still bound by nature, has become conscious of its own identity versus the natural process. In this state the self is called the *twenty-fifth* or *individual soul* (*puruṣa*; later, *jīva*). The awake or awakened (*buddha; prabuddha*) is the isolated (*kevala*), perfect, twenty-sixth, who exceeds the system of the *tattvas*. One might compare this to the position of the Bhagavadgītā (15, 16f.): (1) *kṣara*; (2) *akṣara* or Puruṣa; (3) Paramātman or Kṛṣṇa. And a similar relationship among these three is expressed even more clearly in Liṅga Purāṇa 1, 28, 7a-c:

Iha ṣaḍviṃśako dhyeyo dhyātā vai pañcaviṃśakaḥ /
caturviṃśakam avyaktam . . .

> Here, the twenty-sixth is the object of meditation,
> the twenty-fifth is the meditator,
> whereas the twenty-fourth is the Unmanifest . . .

The twenty-sixth is identified with Śiva in this text in verse 9.

This doctrine might be described as a superimposition above the Sāṃkhya series of twenty-five *tattvas* and especially above the doctrine of the Lord Viṣṇu as the twenty-fifth held in Mbh. 12, 291 and discussed at the beginning of this article. This "meta-*Sāṃkhyic*" position heralds the development of Tantric speculation on ever-higher spiritual realms. The relation of nature, the individual subject, and the Lord resembles the (more subtle) doctrine of *Pāśa, Paśu,* and *Pati* held by the Śaiva-Siddhānta and other Śaiva schools. Nīlakaṇṭha in his comment on 296, 21 also aptly refers to ŚvetUp 1, 10ab: *kṣaraṃ pradhānam amṛtākṣaraṃ Haraḥ / kṣarātmānāv īśate deva ekaḥ,* "the substrate is the perishable; the imperishable immortal is [the self who is] Hara [Śiva; monistic standpoint?]; the unique God rules over the perishable and the imperishable."

In his concluding speech (296, 41f.), Bhīṣma returns to the doctrine of the twenty-fifth without referring to the still higher principle advocated in the earlier part of the same chapter. This suggests that at least the passage from 294, 1 to 296, 40 is an interpolation containing a restatement of the earlier exposition.[13] At the end, Bhīṣma compares the unmanifest or nescience with a terrible, unfathomable ocean in which the beings are drowned:

> 49 Ajñānasāgaro ghoro hy avyakto 'gādha ucyate /
> ahany ahani majjanti yatra bhūtāni Bharata //.

We conclude that the Chapters 291-296 contain highly interesting, but rather unsystematically presented viewpoints about the relation of nature and the soul. The positions taken in the latter part (294-296) seem to indicate a certain development or, perhaps better, a change of emphasis, with respect to the earlier chapters (291-293). The chief message seems to be that the self obtains release from bondage in nature by grades, characterized as stages of awakening or awareness. This terminology (based upon derivations of the root *budh-*) has been derived partly from the Upaniṣads, although its application in Buddhism also may have been of influence. However, the sometimes rather cryptic way of expression in the Mahābhārata leaves some problems unresolved. One of these is the exact nature of the self's "immersion" in Prakṛti. Does this refer to the ordinary chain of rebirths, including rebirths as unenlightened human beings (*yoniṣu līyate,* 291, 42) or to lower vital forms corresponding to "animal consciousness,"[14] or to total "embryonic" consciousnessless state as suggested by 295, 15f.? As will be seen later (and already hinted at earlier), the Śaiva speculative tradition, here represented by the Svacchanda Tantra, has tried to clarify this uncertainty.

The Svacchanda Tantra on the Stages of Awareness

In its presentation of a theory of stages of awareness (here, I prefer this term to "awakening"), the Svacchanda Tantra (SvT; 11, 83c-84b; 11, 91-126) largely uses and expands the same terminology as applied in the Mahābhārata.[15] The text introduces this doctrine in combination with that of the fivefold Ātman, thus suggesting a close connection between these two theorems, but this relationship is not insisted on although the commentator, the Śaiva Advaitin Kṣemarāja (Kashmir, eleventh century) tries to push it a little further. In the following pages, a translation is given of the relevant text with the exception of the stanzas 101, 103, 117, and 118, together with the greater part of Kṣemarāja's "*Uddyota*" commentary. We do not discuss the doctrine of the Ātmans, except where a reference could not be avoided in the context.[16]

The stanza 11, 83c-84b announces five stages of spiritual awakening:

> Abudhaś ca budhaś caiva budhyamānas tathaiva ca /
> prabuddhaḥ suprabuddhaś ca punaś ca kathayāmi te //

> Also the unaware and the aware, and also the awakening, the awakened and the completely awakened, [these] I explain to Thee.

As is usual in many Tantras, the speaker is Śiva, the addressee is the Goddess, his spouse. After this announcement, the stanzas 84c-90 expound the fivefold *ātman.* We proceed with Kṣemarāja's introductory line to verse 91. Unless otherwise indicated, the commentary is translated in full. For its text, we have to refer to the edition; the text of the SvT itself is given in the notes.

> Then, [the author] comes to the explanation of the types (*bheda-*) 'Unaware' etc.:
>
> (91) And now, O Goddess, I shall explain the Unaware, concisely.
>
> As follows:

> The Supreme Lord, having contracted [the manifested world] in the dissolution of the self of categories and beings which concerns the [lower] realm [from] particularization to earth, during the night of the undifferentiated Māyā, will remain inactive as long as no [sun]rise again [appears].[17]

[These lines] should be connected with what is said later [in verse 95]: "the Unaware abides . . . " *The self* is the individuality (*svabhāva*) of the thirty "categories from particularization to the earth," and of the fourteen [kinds of] "beings" from the immovable up to [God] Brahmā that are dependent upon these [thirty categories].

The *Supreme Lord*, engaged in its [that self's] *dissolution, having contracted* the complete manifested world (*adhva-prapañca-*) that belongs to Māyā, with Lord Ananta at its top[18]—the *undifferentiated*ness of *Māyā* is of such a nature that all different modifications[19] have disappeared; and because everything is asleep[20] it is called *night*; "in" that "night"—*inactive*; that is, not intent on the creation of differentiation, "remains as long as no [sun]rise"—this is the disappearance of the period of the *māyic* night on which [the author] is going to say more later, as long as this will not be in regular progress.

For in its progress He "again" is active, creating the world by introspection (*antarmukhena*). And at that period

> 93ab Also [there is] no existence of pleasure and pain etc.,
> nor of karman for the collection of Ātmans.[21]

Karman, action to be performed; of the *collection of Ātmans*—the totality of *Jīvas* that is to be manifested (*ullāsya-*) by the combination with bodies ranging [in their composition] from particularization (*kalā*) to earth—there is no existence of a body "of pleasure and pain," and so on; that is, a state of profound delusion obtains.

But then, this collection of Ātmans

> 93cd Of deluded self in the sleep of impurity,
> with insight and activity [belonging to] consciousness thwarted,
> 94 does not understand sound or other [objects of sense]
> nor itself, O Beautiful One.

It does not understand its cause, nor its
own position.
95 Because it has no understanding of this all,
its sense[-connected] insight and activity
are lost;
in that [position] it abides unaware
until the dawn of Māyā.[22]

His[23] *self* has been profoundly[24] *deluded,* [that is,] reduced to inertia by *sleep*—the state of sleeping—brought about by *impurity* (*mala-*) that is of the nature of nonillumination (*akhyāti*). For that reason, his full *insight and activity* that consist of *consciousness* are *thwarted.* He is in this condition also because, on account of the dissolution of the world, his [partial] *insight and activity* connected with *senses* are *lost.* And therefore he *does not understand sound and other* [objects of sense], *nor himself* as having the nature of an experiencer; he is even unable to conceive by means of a psychic organism [the awareness:] "thus I am." And also his *cause,* the Supreme Lord who has created such a situation of profound delusion,[25] and his own *position,* shelter; viz. identity with Māyā, he *does not understand. Because* [he] *has no understanding of all this,* therefore this one is *unaware* on account of his nonawakening state. *In that,* that is, in Māyā, he exists (*āste* for *tiṣṭhate*) *until the dawn* which is *of Māyā.* The absence of Sandhi in the expression *māyā-aharmukha* is archaic (*chāndasa*). The word *therefore* has to be understood implicitly on account of [the earlier occurrence in the text of] *because.*

In this way, being thus absorbed in Māyā, the Pralayākala[26] is termed *unaware.* The one who had been called *Ātman* by the text in the stanza "having found shelter in the equilibrium of nature" (*pradhānasāmyam āśritya,* verse 84),[27] he is absorbed in Prakṛti, and thus there is a difference [between that Ātman and this Abudha].

Thus, hereby

96 the unaware has been explained.
Learn now also from Me the aware.

In this case,

when *karman* has come to maturation,
having been uplifted by the Lord's volition
as a ray;

97 Just as the sun extends its grace upon the light
of the eye,
in the same way the Lord extends His grace
upon the *ātmans'* faculties.[28]

The *volition* (*icchā*) of the Lord, who acts in His manifestation as Ananta works in this way that, whenever out of the numberless *karmans* of the *ātmans* a certain "*karman* has come to maturation" because of growth to abundance (*udreka-*) and thus becomes suited to bring about a certain result, it attaches the result of such a *karman* to a particular *ātman.* Having been "uplifted," that is, pulled out from the endless mass of *karmans* by this "volition" that is identical with the *ray* of the text, it is connected with a particular *ātman* for enjoyment. And then He "extends His grace to," that is, He causes to unfold (*unmīlayati*),[29] "the faculties" of particularization and so forth of these same "*ātmans*," by which procedure these *ātmans* begin to partake of understanding such as limited power of action and so on [as will be shown presently].

Kṣemarāja further argues, that the metaphor of the "sun" and the "light of the eye" (which we probably have to understand as the faculty of seeing) shows that the Lord's volition is the sovereign (*bhagavatī*) power from which alone the *ātmans* obtain their insight.

"Only by the grace of that [volition of the Lord], the Ātman,

98 His consciousness being slightly unfolded by
particularization,
a range of activity being shown to him by
[partial] wisdom,
Attachment [appears] to him with its nature
of charming,
characterized by the enjoyment of the objects of
the senses.[30]

Attachment, which has the nature of embracing *the objects of the senses* indiscriminately, continues *charming him*, the Soul (*puṃs-*).

99 Time, certainly, drives him onward[31]
[stretching] from the instant to final dissolution.
Destination (*niyati*), undoubtedly, constantly
attaches him to weal and woe.

100 Without excess, without falling short
for even the thousandth part of an atom;

thus he, being enveloped by the five [sheaths:] particularization, and so on

having attained the status of the Puruṣa
within the category of that name,[32]

exists."

Stanza 101 now gives an etymology of Puruṣa, which will not detain us here. Some short and unessential notes by Kṣemarāja on the stanzas 98 f. also have been omitted. For 101 ff., the commentary, much shorter than on the preceding ślokas, most often has been summarized.

102 In which [status] the Lord Śrīkaṇṭha
through destination, on account of *karman*,
binds the unenlightened (*paśu*), although
unconforming,
with the structure of bondage called the *substrate.*[33]

The commentary explains that Śrīkaṇṭha is the Śiva manifestation that presides over the upward course up to the substrate (*pradhānam*); that is, the twenty-four lower *tattvas.* The bondage itself is the primeval impurity (*āṇava*). Unconforming (*asamañjas*) is explained as "not suitable for projection of the nonself." Stanza 103 now specifies the nature of the bondage by the lower *tattvas,* commented on by Kṣemarāja in conventional Sāṃkhya terminology.

104 Bound in this way, he wanders around
within [the *tattvas*] from Māyā to earth;

being [thus] *bound, he wanders around*: he has recourse to birth after birth.

Therefore, he is called a wanderer because
he wanders again and again [in different births].[34]

For this soul, the 'wanderer' (*saṃsārin*),

105 the objects of sense: sound and so on, are there;
therefore he is called a sense enjoyer.
For him, the objects of sense are the highest,
occurring to him in several varieties,

The objects of sense, such as women; he says that these are "the highest," the most exalted things.

106 and with several *karmic* consequences.
These he enjoys, determined by their mode
of existence.

By their *mode of existence* (*bhāva-*); i.e., their existential nature (*sattā*), *determined*: his psyche infused (*vāsita-*).

Because he enjoys this, he is called an enjoyer.[35]
107 In this field, [he as] its knower,
like a farmer, O Thou of excellent figure,

This field includes the five elements as limit; with *its knower*, the Kṣetrajña is meant. Within the image of the "farmer," the word *field* means 'farming plot'—

he ploughs with the ploughshares of greed,
considering [it in] great affection.[36]

The commentator refers to stanza 105, which equates affection (*abhilāṣa*) with impurity (*mala*). The soul "ploughs the field which is the body with strong 'greed,' preparing it for the sowing of the seed of *karman*." He further notes the metaphoric way of expression in the Tantra.

108 And he sows, in a deluded state of mind,
always the seed of mind, speech and body,
of righteousness and unrighteousness,
spreading it out on all sides.
109 From that, a sprout comes forth
that results in happiness and sorrow.
It grows through desire and wrath
abundantly watered by the water of attachment.[37]

According to Kṣemarāja, the *sprout* is to be understood as the (future) bodies and organs of sense. He describes the relation between happiness and sorrow as "the result which is sorrow, assuming the form of happiness."

110 The place, the time and the age
in which the acts good and bad have been sown—
in the corresponding time, [place and age]
will they obtain their result.

In that time means in the periods of youth and so forth in a future birth.

111 The aware, however, enjoys [results]
of different kinds, conditioned by previous karman;

because he has such a knowledge [of that field]
he is called a knower of the field.[38]

The commentator, who has little to add to this passage, identifies the aware with the type of soul called *Sakala* in the course of his explanation of verses 120-126.

112 Because he has awareness of the objects of the
senses,
therefore he is called the *aware*.

Thus, this *aware* is called by the names of *puruṣa, wanderer, sense enjoyer, enjoyer,* and *knower of the field,* each corresponding to a specific meaning.

When the *puruṣa* develops his thought on this
[situation]
as being undesirable, at that moment
113 he [becomes] the awakening. And now I explain
[that one] to Thee:[39]

The commentary on 120-126 explains that the awakening is touched by the "descent of Śakti" (*śaktipāta*) in an act of grace. The following passage describes the practical, soteriological application of the acquired insight.

When he develops repulsion of the experiences,
the agreeable as well as the disagreeable,
114 and considers them to be unsubstantial,
having recourse to supreme equanimity,
he becomes aware of the realm from Māyā
down to the earth
as an illusory structure.[40]
115 "Sons, friends and the wife, well wishers, own
people, relations;
the material goods obtained by me
in good and sinful ways—
116 all these people will enjoy that [when I am gone]
without misgivings or obstruction;
but I, all alone,
will have to travel to Yama's court."[41]

The next two stanzas describe how the *puruṣa* or *ātman* learns to detach himself from the people around him (he should see them as his enemies, *vairiṇaḥ,* 117b), and even to despise his own body, which is to fall victim to decrepitude and death. Then he concludes his meditation with

119 "Here I am, in this thoroughly filthy [body],
how can I find repose here?"
Thus he should be conscious again and again
with perturbed conscience:[42]

According to the commentator, the words *here I am* imply the realization of the *ātman's* true nature from the Āgamas and other authorities. He does not comment on the term *conscience* (tentative rendering of *cittam*). We have to understand that the self needs the psychic apparatus to generate the salutary realization of its difference from the surrounding world, but this point remains problematic.

120 "How can I become released
from this inescapable round of births?"
Having become thus awakened,
absorbed in that [state], having refuge in it,[43]

The stage of being awakened is reached, says Kṣemarāja, by undergoing the ritual Śaiva initiation.

121 Having liberated himself from all activities
he is then called *released*. Such is the awakened,
hear now from me the completely awakened:
122 When, by the wisdom [conferred] by initiation,
by yoga,
and by right conduct, O Dutiful One,
he has reached the supreme position that is
unassailable, superior to the courses of existence,
123 free from stain or filth, peaceful,
out of reach of the manifested world, unshakable,
superior to causality, omniscient, omnipresent,
124 satiated and eternally [self] aware,
independent, constant, of unassailable limitless
power,
completely awakened, eternal;
125 then the *ātman*, in union with it,
in the possession of its characteristics,
is likewise called *completely awakened*
in accordance with Bhairava's word.
126 But without the initiation,
one is not entitled to perform the Śaiva Yoga.[44]

Here ends the exposition. In his introduction to 127, the commentator again characterizes the preceding passage as "the description of the creation of *tattvas* as subservient to the *ātman*" (he did so earlier in verse 82).[45] He also contends that "the different states (*avasthā*) of the *ātman* are to make clear what is to be avoided and to be accepted" (*heya* and *upādeya*, conventional terms suggestive of the "catechism").

The Śaiva and Epic Perspectives on the Stages of Awakening

Although the general theoretical background (the soul's or self's emancipatory progress; release from Saṃsāra; and also linguistic determination by means of the root *budh-* in verbal forms or derivatives) clearly is the same in the passages just discussed from the Mbh and the SvT,[46] there are also marked differences.

First of all, the SvT presents its wisdom as a speculative background for the all-important Śaiva initiation ceremony; the guru is supposed to provide the initiate with a broad vision of his or her real self, its previous "*saṃsāric* history" and final destination. We might speak of "applied soteriology." The Mbh does not directly presuppose such a cadre; its teaching seems to stand on itself as a theoretical course in higher wisdom, the practical or ritual concomitants of which could be worked out in different ways.

The general subject, we may agree, is the self that in principle is called *ātman* in the Mbh as well as in the SvT (for the latter, see notes 21, 22, and 26), although both texts prefer not to use this term regularly. In the Mbh, the subject usually is circumscribed, very often with the numeral the *twenty-fifth* (in Chapter 296 also the *twenty-sixth*), but also frequently with varieties of the demonstrative pronoun: *ayam* (292, 4d and 32c, etc.), *eṣa* (292, 7d; 293, 3d; etc.), *sa* (294, 24a; etc.), *asau* (296, 13a). The word *ātman* appears in non-compounded form in 292, 24e; 293, 9a (*pañcaviṃśa . . . ātmā*); 294, 12a, 20d, 25d. *Dehin* is found in 293, 33b; *pumān* in 293, 36a. In the analyzed texts there is no reference to the Jīva, although the commentaries use the term; for example, Kṣemarāja on SvT 11, 93 paraphrases *ātmavarga-* with *jīvajāta-* (but he indicates the *ātman* as the subject in 11, 98). Also in the SvT, the experiencing subject is indicated only vaguely and intermittently. *Ātman-* is denoted once in the singular at the end of the passage; the plural *ātmanām* in 97d denotes the collective singular *ātmavarga-* of 93b.[47] There is no reminiscence of the five kinds of *ātmans* that were distinguished subtly in stanzas 82-90. On the other hand, one could argue that there is not much difference in kind between these *ātmans* (who in reality also denote stages in the emancipatory course; they are called respectively the *ātman, antarātman, bāhyātman, nirātman,* and *paramātman*) and the stages of awakening: *Abudha* and so forth. Both theories run parallel to a certain extent, although they certainly do not wholly overlap. The *Budha* "Aware," whose situation is comparable to that of the Bāhyātman (i.e., the *ātman* provided with a material body) of verse 86, also is characterized by a number of other terms: *puruṣa* or *pumān* (100, 112); *paśu* (102, connected with the state of being bound by *pāśa-*, "bonds"); *saṃsārin* (104); *viṣayin* (105); *bhoktṛ* (106); *kṣetrajña* (111). These names therefore denote only a particular stage in the self's progress. The usual type of statement about the experiencing subject generally remains somewhat vague: "then he is called," "he attains the status of," and so on.[48]

An important difference between the SvT and the Mbh is that the former presents a theory of five stages of the awakening self, whereas the Mbh with much less systematization distinguishes only three grades of emancipation. These generally are called *aprabuddha* (or *apratibuddha* or *abuddhimān*), *budhyamāna*, and *prabuddha* or *buddha*. Only the term *budhyamāna* recurs without variety, and also in the SvT, as the pivotal stage in which the spiritual awakening reaches a "takeoff." The following higher course is distinguished in the SvT in two stages called *prabuddha* and (new term) *suprabuddha*. The subtler presentation of the emancipatory stage may have been carried through to provide a theoretical basis for the spiritual hierarchy in the Śaiva community. Also the two lowest stages have in the SvT obtained new names: *Abudha* and *Budha*. Both deserve our special attention. The status of a *Budha*, experienced in bodily existence as an unenlightened being, obtains by far the most attention in the SvT (verses 96-112) as compared to the other stages of awakening. The *Budha* is comparable to the "twenty-fifth" in the Mbh, as appears clearly from the synonyms enumerated in the SvT (see earlier) and the Mbh (12, 294, 35-37); of the three synonyms given for the twenty-fifth in the Mbh: *adhiṣṭhātṛ, kṣetrajña*, and *puruṣa*, the latter two also occur in the SvT as designations of the *Budha*. Kṣemarāja on SvT 11, 120-125, identifies him with the Sakala type of soul of "divided" experience: *sakala eva ca bāhyaviṣayāvabodhād buddha* [read *budha!*] *iti*. This is nothing but a restatement of the words of the Tantra itself (112ab): he is called Budha *viṣayān budhyate yasmāt* 'because he is aware of the sense objects.' This word *aware*, in the sense of 'being conscious of one's immediate environment,' seems here a useful rendering of the adjective *budha-* formed directly from the root *budh-*, 'to be aware,' 'to wake up,' without a participal suffix. This positive expression of the more or less negative sense of *'ātman* bound to a body' may be called a significant innovation, which may have been inspired by Śivasūtra 1, 8: *jñānaṃ jāgrat*. In the chapters from the Mbh discussed here, the term *budha-* occurs twice, both times in the plural, meaning 'the wise' (12, 293, 44b; 294, 15c). The position of the *Budha* in the SvT, however, is no different from the status of the one who in the Mbh is called *apra[ti]buddha* or *abuddhimān*, that is, the twenty-fifth (Puruṣa) who is still in the grip of nature, with this difference, that the Budha is in the grip of Māyā (see verse 114 and later). The term *buddha-*, on the contrary, in the Mbh serves as a synonym to *prabuddha-*, and thus denotes the one who has obtained real insight (293, 10d; 294, 4c; 295, 46a; 296, 7c); in the SvT it does not occur in that function.

The negative counterpart of Budha is *abudha* "unaware." This *abudha-* in the Mbh occurs only once (that is to say, in the analyzed chapters), in 293, 10d: *buddho 'py abudhatāṃ vrajet* (as a consequence of his commitment to Prakṛti); but this is exactly the situation of the Budha in the SvT, not of the Abudha. And because there is no parallel for this *abudhatā* in the Mbh, we should consider its occurrence here as a variant *metri causa* for *abuddhatā*, and we therefore should preferably translate it as 'an unawakened state,' not as 'a state of unawareness' as was done provisionally in the first part of this chapter.

Prakṛti itself is consistently called *abuddha[jana]* in the Mbh; for example, in 291, 42d; 293, 1b, 10c, and 42d; or (only in Chapter 296) *apratibuddha* (6a) and *aprabuddha* (1a). Abudha does not occur as a designation for Prakṛti, nor for the *ātman* who would be (temporarily or originally) absorbed in it. A better parallel for the *Abudha* status in the SvT is provided by BĀUp 4, 8, 11: to mirthless worlds, enveloped by blind darkness, go those people who are without wisdom or insight, the *avidvāṃso 'budho janāḥ* (stem *abudh-*). These "worlds of darkness" indeed are suggestive of the description of the night of Māyā in SvT 11, 91-95, although the expression *andhatamas* does not recur there. Another difference is that the "mirthless worlds" are reached by the individuals after death; there is no vision of cosmic Pralaya in the Upaniṣad. But still, the parallel is interesting, especially when we compare the next words in the BĀUp: *ātmānaṃ ced vijānīyād, ayam asmīti puruṣaḥ*, with SvT verses 119f.: *so 'ham asmi . . . katham atra ramāmi . . . evaṃ prabuddhaḥ*.

In the Śaiva perspective, the Abudha status is intimately connected with the new doctrine of the souls' temporary dissolution in Māyā's womb during Pralaya, the interval between two world periods; a status that can be compared to that of an embryo, although such a comparison is not founded on the text itself. It usually is known in Śaiva doctrinal literature as the state of the *Pralayākala*, 'Undivided in *Pralaya*,' or *Pralayakevala*,[49] characterized by *māyāsāmyam* 'identity with Māyā' (SvT 11, 92a). In this way, the cosmological perspective of the period of rest between two cosmical revolutions has been integrated into the theological-soteriological structure developed by the Śaiva thinkers.

As is well known, the metaphor of sleep and awakening for the period of cosmic quietude and the beginning of evolution is found in several texts. We could mention BĀUp 1, 4, 10: *brahma vā idam agra āsīt; tad ātmānam evāved, ahaṃ brahmāsmīti, tasmāt tat sarvam abhavat. Tad yo yo devānāṃ pratyabudhyata, sa eva tad abhavat* 'Brahman was this [world] in the beginning; it became conscious of itself: "I am Brahman," therefore it became that all. Thus, every godhead that waked up, became also that.' "This notion lives on in Purāṇic cosmogonies where Nārāyaṇa etc. 'wakes up' to create the cosmos, the conception of the Days and Nights of Brahmā, etc.," says Van Buitenen;[50] and he adds most significantly in our context: "the sage can still wake up (*buddha, pratibuddha*) to the higher reality," referring to BhGītā 2, 69. According to the MaitrUp (2, 6), also the created beings, who were unawakened and motionless like a stone, were awakened by Prajāpati who entered into them as wind-breath: *tā aśmevāprabuddhā . . . apaśyat . . . so 'manyata: etāsāṃ pratibodhanāyābhy-antaraṃ praviśānīti.*[51] The cosmic sleep is succinctly described in the famous stanza Manu 1, 5: *āsīd idaṃ tamobhūtam . . . prasuptam iva sarvataḥ* 'this world was existing as darkness . . . as it were asleep on all sides'; and the awakening in the same text, 1, 74: *tasya so* [i.e., god Brahmā] *'harniśasyānte prasuptaḥ pratibudhyate* 'at the end of that period of a day and a night, he wakes up from his sleep.'[52]

In the Mbh chapters analyzed in this chapter, the cosmic awakening is also described (12, 291, 13ff.): after the night of Brahmā, he (who? Brahmā? subject not mentioned) wakes up (*pratibudhyate*, 14) and creates the Great Being, Hiraṇyagarbha, who is known as *Buddhi* or *Mahān* (17). A microcosmic counterpart to this cosmological figure would seem to be the *Mahān ātman* mentioned in 291, 41. Both this *ātman* and Hiraṇyagarbha create worlds (the *Mahān ātman* is called *sargapralayakovida-*)[53] and their situations resemble each other very much: Hiraṇyagarbha, who also is called by many names, is the representant of the highest being in creating or rather emanating the manifest world (*sṛjaty ātmānam ātmanā*, 291, 20), and the *ātman* creates divided experience by his own *abhimāna*, false representation, as was shown earlier. Such macro-microcosmic parallelism suggested or implied in the Mbh, however, is not attempted by the SvT, at least not in the analyzed fragment, although Śaiva monism holds that evolution is nothing else than a self-contraction of the Lord's total awareness. Only Kṣemarāja's commentary on SvT 11, 96-97 might be explained in this way, despite the important role ascribed to "grace."

In short, in Śruti as well as in Smṛti, there are, plenty of utterances that may have inspired the development of the doctrine of the Abudha who has found shelter in the unawareness of *māyic* quietude. But here, a precision is still necessary, because Māyā is not Prakṛti in the Śaiva perspective (despite ŚvetUp 4, 9: *māyāṃ tu prakṛtim vidyāt*).

In the Mbh, the soul's delusion is repeatedly described as identification with the play of the *guṇas* (12, 293, 33f.; 45; 295, 15f.; etc.). In 293, 45, it seems that the high goal is to reach "equilibrium" by realizing the imperishable in the perishable (*yadā . . . avyaktam . . . prabudhyanti, gamayanti samaṃ tadā*), but in 295, 15 the emphasis is different: collecting the *guṇic* structure in imperishable Prakṛti means that the knower of the field would become absorbed in the field. Here, this is not the high goal; on the contrary, one should purify oneself by realizing one's fundamental difference from nature (295, 20: *viśuddho bhavati prakṛteḥ parivarjanāt, anyo 'ham anyeyam iti*). This comes much closer to the emancipatory career of the self in the SvT, where the *pradhānasāmyam* is characterized as the situation of the lowest Ātman (11, 84; see earlier note 27); and although *māyāsāmya* evokes *prakṛtisāmya* or *guṇasāmya* from the Mbh (see note 17), there is an important doctrinal difference. In the Śaiva system of thirty-six *tattvas*, Prakṛti occupies the twenty-fourth place (counted from below) and Māyā the thirtieth place. In the Śaiva perspective, Prakṛti thus stands as a coarser evolute of Māyā, in a sense her "child," as the Old Javanese Vṛhaspatitattva characterizes their relation.[54] Also in the discussed stanzas of the SvT, Prakṛti recedes behind Māyā in teleological importance. The three constituents of Prakṛti, the *guṇas*, although by no means lost in the Śaiva system, are superseded as prime instruments of bondage by the five *kañcukas* "husks": particularization and so forth. The theory of the *Kañcukas* is a subtler and more effective way to express the gradual recession or contraction of the self's original powers. In the analyzed passage of the SvT, the *guṇas* are seldom mentioned. They figure only in verse 103 (not translated here): the Budha is said to be *baddhas triguṇabandhena*, "bound by the bond of the three *guṇas*"; evolution of Buddhi from the *guṇas* was expressed in verse 68.

The Śaiva perspective is widened immensely when compared with the Sāṅkhya of the Mbh. The drama is repeated on a higher stage by means of Māyā and the *Kañcukas* produced by her.[55] This final act is played out in a similar way, indicated by Rāmakaṇṭha:[56] *paramā muktiḥ . . . mahāmāyāpuruṣavivekodayāt,* "the final release consists in the unfolding of the discrimination between the cosmic Māyā and the *puruṣa*" in the state of the Vijñānakevalin "[the self] of mere wisdom." A similar expression is used by Kṣemarāja in his comment on SvT 11, 88: the Nirātman is the Vijñānākala who has "mastered the wisdom of discrimination between Māyā and the *puruṣa-tattva* (*abhyastamāyāpuṃstattva-vivekajñānaḥ*). It should be noted that these Śaiva teachers still use the term *Puruṣa* for the higher self that becomes liberated from Māyā.

A last remark on the Śaiva viewpoint already noted earlier: the whole process of bondage and liberation, here formulated by means of the evolution from Abudha to Budha and the subsequent transformation into the higher states of awakening, is theologically founded on and mystically enclosed by the vision of Śiva's power of grace.[57]

The "Stages" in Other Contexts in the Early Śaivatantra

The philosophical-soteriological viewpoint just discussed is not the only context in which a gradation of stages of awakening occurs. The Śaiva theoreticians applied such a serial progression in at least two other cadres. One of these is to be found also in the SvT, in the long chapter that deals with the ritual of initiation and its immediate background (4, 238f.). The direct context is the concentration on a vivid movement of the internal life principle conceived as Śakti. This yogic procedure, accompanied by progressively subtle pronunciation of the Śakti's mantric form, leads the way to an identification with the Śakti's own resort in the region of the fontanelle and the even higher realm of Śiva: a directly realized course of spiritual emancipation. The term used most frequently in this connection is *uccāra.* From the mantric viewpoint, a description of the process has been given by Padoux:[58] mantra as phonic energy cannot be realized by the adept "without its being pronounced, at least internally, or associated to an internal movement, or a spiritual effort, which participates of the energy that is Word" (my translation). We therefore can distinguish three aspects of *uccāra*: movement, pronunciation, spiritual effort. The first two aspects are known to the dictionaries (e.g., Monier Williams, p. 173: "rising, . . . pronunciation"). Both these aspects are combined in Nārāyaṇakaṇṭha's commentary on MṛgĀg, Kr., 2, 31: *dvādaśāntaparyantoccāritaplutaśāntiparyantaṃ yāvan mantraṃ smaran,* 'mentally reciting the mantra by extending it, causing it to ascend up to the Dvādaśānta [Śiva's place] where the state of peace is obtained.'[59] Padoux (*Recherches*, 327) correctly emphasizes the meaning 'rising' (*montée*). This internal movement that leads to spiritual awakening is described in SvT 4, 233f. where it is called *cāra*, paraphrased by Kṣemarāja as *prāṇavāha* 'movement of the breath." This *cāra* is realized over a distance of thirty-six fingers' breadth, which is the distance from the heart lotus to the resort of Śakti (the fontanelle, according to our commentator). That this upward course is subdivided into three parts is not of immediate relevance to our context. Now, as long as the *tattva* (probably, the Śiva status) has not been found, the moving self will have to descend again (4, 234-237). Follow the remarkable stanzas (238 and 239):

> Śaktyā cādho yadā gacched abudhas tu tadā bhavet /
> hṛdgataḥ punar uttiṣṭhed budhyamānaḥ sa ucyate //
> Śaktiṃ prāpya budho jñeyaḥ, vyāpinyaṃse prabuddhatā /
> atītaḥ suprabuddhas tu, unmanastvaṃ tadā bhavet //

> When he, by the Śakti, goes downward, then he is unaware;
> when he, being in the heart, arises again, he is called *awakening*.
> Having reached the Śakti, he sould be known as *aware;*
> the awakened state occurs in the "penetrating" level;[60]
> having risen above it, he is completely awakened,
> then the mindless state occurs.

The most important feature to note is that the basic unaware state is equalized with the descending course of the moving self that is in this way doomed to a new round of existence within the bodily system. The aware, however, follows the ascending course that is the road to the experience of liberation culminating in the two highest, supraindividual stages. Here also, the self that starts the upward movement is called the *awakening*, but the system of gradation is another as in SvT 11 as appears from the different role of the Budha. Here, *aware* does not mean 'aware of the sense objects' as in SvT 11, 112 discussed in the preceding section, but a stage of continuous wakefulness, a lower variety of "awakened" (*prabuddha*). In other words, *budha* here = *buddha*, and this again suggests that also the descending Abudha is to be interpreted as *abuddha* 'unawakened.' The descending movement indeed does not suggest the quietude of the *māyic* womb, but rather the rebirth into a new existence. Interpreted in this way, the conceptual system can be characterized as perhaps an extended version of the speculations of the Mbh discussed earlier, realistically applied to yogic-microcosmic experience. The extension is realized by a more systematic description of the ascending course (*buddha, prabuddha, suprabuddha*).

This reconstruction can be substantiated by reference to a second source for the passage in question: the unedited Tantrasadbhāva (Tsb; 1, 143f.).[61] In the view of this text (1, 62), the self's motion is brought about by the "fifth Śakti of Śiva". In 1, 148 and 149 (which correspond with SvT 4, 238 and 239 quoted earlier) both manuscripts of the Tsb mention the spiritual gradation *abudhya* (written *abuddhya*)-*budhyamāna-buddha-*, the verb *prabudhyate-suprabuddha*. The use of *buddha* instead of *budha* results in a bad meter (149a: *śaktiṃ prāpya buddho jñeyo*), whereas *prabudhyate* is clumsy in comparison with the refined *prabuddhatā* of the SvT. The Tsb even commits violations of elementary rules of grammar.[62] However, shortly before (1, 145c), the Tsb expressed a more general twofold distinction between the unawakened (*abuddha*) and the awakened (*prabuddha*) in metrically correct form; the *pāda* is not found in the SvT version.

The situation described in the preceding paragraph suggests that the Tsb, despite its linguistic and metrical imperfection, gives the more original version with its *abuddha* and *buddha* for the *abudha* and *budha* of the SvT. The SvT then would contain a more sophisticated rendering of the passage, which was acceptable to those who had enjoyed a thorough grammatical training or at least wished to conform to grammatical standards. The Tsb may have been closer to the Siddha-Nātha tradition that cared less for the niceties of outward expression.

The secondary nature of the SvT version of this passage also is suggested by its relative shortness (six stanzas against eight in the Tsb), which may have been motivated by the wish to avoid unnecessary prolixity.[63] But a definitive assessment can be formulated only after a more extensive study of the mutual relation between these two texts.

Still another application of the terminology of spiritual gradation is in the domain of the analysis of the states of consciousness. The Spanda Kārikās[64] distinguish two situations (*avasthā*): agent (*kartṛ*) and product (*kāryam*). The agent is *akṣaya*; that is, eternal, it cannot get lost. The product is *kṣaya*, destructible (see Yudhiṣṭhira's question after the *kṣara* and the *akṣara* referred to at the beginning of the section from the Mbh discussed earlier). The unaware (*abudha*) agent wrongly thinks that he is destroyed whereas only his effort-relation toward the products is destroyed. The constant realization of his indestructible nature in the three states of consciousness (waking, dream, deep sleep) amounts to his being completely awakened (*suprabuddha*). On first sight, we have here a twofold distinction *abudha-suprabuddha*. But perhaps, *suprabuddha* is only a metrical variant of *prabuddha* (17c: *nityaṃ syāt suprabuddhasya*) because it is not clear why *su-* should be applied as a meaningless subgradation of a twofold contrast. The twofold distinction can be compared to stanza 1, 25 of the same text, where *mūḍha* 'deluded' is contrasted to *prabuddha*. Kṣemarāja, however, in his commentary to the Spanda Kārikās, neatly distinguishes between *aprabuddha* (his rendering of *abudha* in verse 14), *prabuddha*, and *suprabuddha*. His interpretation without doubt is influenced by the positions of the Mālinīvijayottaratantra and the Tantrāloka shortly referred to presently.[65]

The Mālinīvijayottaratantra (2, 43) applied the fourfold series, *abuddha-buddha-prabuddha-suprabuddha*, to a gradation of the waking state only, according to the realization of different stages of identity with the externalized object.[66] This gradation is intimately linked with a theory of four yogic states of identification with the object (*piṇḍa*, etc.) that cannot be discussed here; the reader is referred to the exemplary treatment by Oberhammer.[67] The doctrine has been restated by Abhinavagupta and his commentator Jayaratha in a context of yogic psychology based on monistic idealism.[68]

Notes

1. Same opposition of *kṣara* and *akṣara* in ŚvetUp 1, 1, 8.

2. Nīlakaṇṭha's commentary is quoted from the following edition: *The Mahābhārata with the Bharata Bhawadeepa Commentary of Nīlakaṇṭha*, ed. Pandit Ramchandrashastri Kinjawadekar, vol. 5: *Shanti Parva* (reprinted New Delhi: Oriental Books Reprint Corp., 1979), pp. 610f. The present chapter, 291 of the Pune edition, there is numbered 302.

3. Kinj[awadekar]'s text: *pratibuddhatvād*, which seems to be untenable. No mention of this variant in the Pune edition, probably because only the Avagraha is concerned. Roy (vol. 10, p. 421) translates "in consequence of his forgetfulness." "Absorption" in the *yonis*: also in Kubjikāmata Tantra 16, 29: *yonyārṇave līnam*.

4. The verb *anu-vart-* is used as a synonym for *sev-* of 291, 42d; see also 291, 43d, *guṇān anu nivartate*, and 295, 23bd, *imaṃ janam . . . anuvartitavān*.

5. In Mataṅga-pārameśvarāgama, Vidyāpāda, 4, 37cd, such a function of the "playful Lord" is conceptualized by the Śakti called

Jananī, 'Creatrix' (*Mat.*, ed. N. R. Bhatt, Pondichéry, 1977, p. 94). In the same text (5, 29), *play* is defined as "abandonment of one's own nature" (*svabhāvasya cyutiḥ*) or as a "vibration" (*kṣobha*), see the further exposition in that text.

6. I interpret *parameṇa* in 41d as an instrumental term denoting the secondary object. *Anupaśyati* is a noncommittal term: in 294, 19, the same verb is used for a vision of the Antarātman; also in BhGītā 14, 19ab it denotes a correct insight.

7. See 294, 40ab: *avyakataṃ kṣetram ity uktaṃ tathā sattvaṃ tatheśvaram*, "the unmanifest is called the *field*, and also *lucidity*, and what is the lord." Nīl. here notes, contrary to his expositions discussed in note 9, that the term *the Lord* and its synonyms denote the visible world (*dṛśya-*; ed. Kinj., Chapter 306, 41). An early Śaiva parallel comes from Bali: *caturviṃśatitattvam ca śivāṅgaṃ ca pradhānakam* 'the substrate, the twenty-fourth *tattva*, is also a portion of Śiva' (T. Goudriaan and C. Hooykaas, *Stuti and Stava of Balinese Brahman Priests*, Amsterdam: North Holland, 1971, p. 451). We may further compare the doctrine of Brahman as womb of the universe in BhGītā 14, 3: *mama yonir mahad brahma*, or VāyuPur 4, 17: *avyaktaṃ kāraṇam . . . prakṛtiṃ caiva yam āhuḥ . . . jagadyonim . . . param brahma sanātanam . . . guṇasāmye*.

8. Some manuscripts in 46c read *budhyamānaprabuddhābhyām*, thus separating the awakening and the awakened. I cannot understand the purport of this position, nor of Kinj.'s text (305, 35c): *budhyamānā prabuddhānām*.

9. In this passage, Nīl. recognizes only the free and perfect form of the Lord. In 41-43 (Kinj. 305, 30-32), moreover, he comments upon a text that is different on a few crucial points. The essentials of Nīl.'s position are as follows. (1) In 41b (Kinj. 305, 30b), *abhimanyate* is explained as *hinasti, kāmādīn jayati* 'he attacks [the *Guṇas*], conquers desire etc. . . .'; a parallel for such an "aggressive" meaning of *abhiman* is provided, but the explanation seems far-fetched. (2) In 41cd, Nīl.'s text reads *tadā sa guṇahānyai taṃ param evānupaśyati* 'then, he beholds that Supreme One [or, considers Him as the Supreme], in order to get rid of the *guṇas*.' We might also read . . . *guṇahānyaitam* . . ., "*by getting rid of the guṇas*, one considers," with better sense. Several manuscripts give *-hānyaivam*, with little difference of meaning. (3) In 43a (Kinj. 305, 32a), Nīl. interprets *aprabuddham* passively as *ajñātam* 'unknown'; viz., by the unenlightened. See also note 11. (4) In 43b, Nīl.'s text reads [*-am*] *aguṇam Īśvaram* instead of [*-aṃ*] *saguṇam Īśvaram*. Nīl.: *aguṇaṃ guṇebhyo 'nyaṃ nirguṇam*. The word *Īśvaram* is

explained as *antaryāminam* 'the inner controller.' Several manuscripts of the Southern recension read 43b as *guṇaṃ prāhur anīśvaram* (or, *nirīśvaram*) 'they declare the *guṇas* to be not īśvara.'

It is clear that in Nīl.'s view the whole passage describes only the enlightened self. He (or his text) does not accept a connection or identification of the Lord with the *guṇas*. This interpretation, in my view, should be rejected mainly on the following grounds: (a) Nīl.'s standpoint is out of tune with the broader context discussed in these pages, which clearly refers to an unawakened state of the Lord's self; see, e.g., 294, 40 in note 7 or 295, 10-12 where both *kṣara* and *akṣara* are called *Īśvara* (*ubhāv eveśvarau matau*, 12b). (b) His interpretation of *abhimanyate* is far-fetched (see point 1), besides, it deviates from other occurrences of this verb in these chapters, e.g., 292, 7: *yāni . . . dvandvāni prākṛtāni . . . eṣo 'py abhimanyate, abhimanyaty abhimānāt* 'these dualities of nature . . . he also imagines . . . out of his imagination.' (c) His interpretation of *aprabuddham* in 43a is wrong, see 296, 1ab *aprabuddham athāvyaktam imaṃ guṇavidhiṃ śṛṇu.* The Pune edition in this passage gives very little information on the views of other commentators. In 43a, however, Arjunamiśra is quoted on *aprabuddham*, which he explains as *anutpannavivekakhyātim* in conformity with my own interpretation.

10. The term *aprabuddha-* may have been taken from Maitrāyaṇīya-Up. 2, 6 (ed. Van Buitenen, p. 100), where it is used differently for the primitive state of the unconscious beings who are still without life breath: *Prajāpatir . . . bahvīḥ prajā asṛjata / tā aśmevāprabuddhā aprāṇāḥ sthāṇur iva tiṣṭhamānā apaśyat.* Also here, however, one can maintain that the existence of unconscious nature is the result of the Lord's mental "play": *sa nāramataikaḥ / so 'tmānam abhyadhyāyat.*

11. See the use of *pratibuddha-* in a related context in BṛhĀrUp 4, 4, 13: *yasyānuvittaḥ pratibuddha ātmā, asmin saṃdehye gahane praviṣṭaḥ / sa viśvakṛt.* But *pratibuddha-* is used here in passive sense, "being realized," although we find active translations; e.g., Swāmī Mādhavānanda, *The BĀUp with the Commentary of Śaṅkarācārya*, Almora [3]1950, p. 739: "He who has realised and intimately known the Self"; Paul Deussen, *Sechzig Upanishads des Veda*, Leipzig 1921, p. 478: "Doch wer . . . den Ātman fand, zu ihm aufwachte."

12. To begin with, Arjunamiśra (quoted in the critical edition) seems to interpret the text as: *prabuddhātmā: buddhātmā budhyamāna iti rūpadvayaṃ pañcaviṃśasya . . . buddhatvaṃ tu vivekakhyāter anantaram īśvaras tu nityaṃ buddhaikarūpa iti.* This would be in conflict with 296, 5-7, discussed presently; besides, we would need a connecting particle

in the first half of our stanza 294, 43 between *prabuddhātmā* and *budhyamāna*. But a similar view is held by Arjunamiśra in his commentary on 295, 46: the states of *buddha* and *budhyamāna* are conducive to the knowledge of the *ātman* (*buddhāditraye dvayam ātmajñānaprakāśakam*). Nīl.'s interpretation lies in the same direction; he reads *'prakṛtyātmā*, 'whose self is not of Prakṛti,' and explains as *prakṛtito niṣkṛṣṭaḥ budhyamānaḥ* [this word, he says, is to be interpreted in the active] . . . *jīva eva prakṛtityāgāt kevalo bhavati* "extracted from Pr., awakening, the pure Soul, because of its leaving Pr., becomes isolated.' The result is a clear distinction: *abuddhaṃ prakṛtiḥ, budhyamāno jīvaḥ, prabuddhaḥ kevalaḥ*. This is attractive and in conformity with Chapters 291-293, but conflicts with 295, 10f., as shown presently. Besides, the critical edition gives only the variant *prakṛtyātmā* 'of a self which is Pr.,' not *'prakṛtyātmā*; but the difference is only orthographical. A few unimportant readings were left out of the picture.

13. Besides, the opposition *kṣara-akṣara* is negated in 295, 10. According to that stanza, both nature and the soul are perishable as well as imperishable.

14. This term is applied to the first of six grades of consciousness by Peter Koestenbaum, *The New Image of the Person* (Westport, Conn.: Greenwood Press, 1978), p. 78.

15. J. Gonda, *Medieval Religious Literature in Sanskrit*, History of Indian Literature, II-1 (Wiesbaden: Otto Harrassowitz, 1977), pp. 205f. on the SvT. I have used and translated the text as edited by M. K. Shastri with the commentary Uddyota by Kṣemarāja, 7 vols., Kashmir Series of Texts and Studies (Bombay, 1921-35). SvT 11, 82ff. are in vol. 7, KSTS No. 56, pp. 58-79.

16. An article on the fivefold Ātman in the SvT by the present writter is to appear in the *Wiener Zeitschrift für die Kunde Südasiens* [in English].

17. SvT 11, 91 and 92:

Abudhaṃ ca punar devi kathayāmi samāsataḥ /
tattvabhūtātmasaṃhāre kalākṣityantagocare //
māyāsāmyaniśāyāṃ vai saṃhṛtya Parameśvaraḥ /
nirvyāpāro bhavet tāvad yāvad vai nodayaḥ punaḥ //

With *māyāsāmya*, compare the *sāmya* with Prakṛti repudiated by the awakening soul in Mbh. 12, 295, 38; and also the term *guṇasāmya* in VāyuPur 4, 17 quoted in note 7, and in the SvT itself, 11, 286. For the connection with the sun, see Mbh. 12, 292, 28 *raśmijālam ivādityas tatkālena niyacchati*. See also note 48.

18. This situation is described at SvT 10, 1126f. (ed. KSTS, vol. 5B, p. 470). For Ananta, see also H. Brunner, *Mṛgendra Āgama, Sections des Rites et du Comportement*, Pondicherry: Institut Français d'Indologie vol. 69 (trans. Pondichéry, Pondicherry: Institut Français d'Indologie, 1985), p. 74, note 2.

19. *Vikṛti-*, cf. Mbh. 12, 292, 29: *ātmarūpaguṇān . . . vikurvāṇaḥ*.

20. *Viśvaprasvāpāt*, cf. Manu 1, 5: *āsīd idaṃ tamobhūtam . . . prasuptam iva*; and see later, p. 158.

21. SvT 11, 93ab: *Sukhaduḥkhādyabhāvaś ca hy ātmavargasya karmaṇaḥ*. This Ātmavarga (the totality of selves, not to be confounded with the "five Ātmans") is explained presently by Kṣemarāja. Both text and commentary seem to suggest by their syntax that the collection of Ātmans and karman are identical; I have ignored this in the translation.

22. SvT 11, 93c-95:

Malanidrāvimūḍhātmā ruddhacaitanyadṛkkriyaḥ //
na vijānāti śabdādīn ātmānaṃ ca varānane /
kāraṇaṃ na vijānāti na ca sthānaṃ svakaṃ priye //
sarvam etan na jānāti yato luptākṣadṛkkriyaḥ /
abudhas tiṣṭhate tatra yāvan māyā-aharmukham //

The subject of this passage is not explicit in the SvT. itself. According to Kṣemarāja, it is the "collection of selves," and we have followed him here. In 97d, the Tantra gives *ātman* in the plural, but in the stanzas 98 f. the singular is used regularly. The subject is called *pumān* in 112d, and *ātman* in 125a. I have silently understood *ātman* to be the subject in 98 ff. and already in the commentary on the present stanzas.

23. See the end of the preceding note. All selves are supposed to be of identical essence.

24. *Viśeṣeṇa*, standard explanation of *vi-* in *vimūḍha*.

25. The element *ādi-* has not been translated.

26. Or Pralayakevala, cf. Nārāyanakaṇṭha on Mṛgendrāgama, Kriyāpāda, 8, 96: "although the Ātman who is Pralayakevala is bound by Karman, that [*karman's*] power is thwarted (*ruddha-*, same term as in SvT 11, 93d), . . . that means, its fruition is blocked" (ed. N. R. Bhatt, Pondichéry, 1962, p. 153; trans. Brunner, p. 258).

27. That is, the first of the series of five *ātmans* discussed in the preceding passage of the SvT. Prakṛti is lower than Māyā in the Śaiva hierarchy of *tattvas*.

28. SvT 11, 96-97:

Abudhas tu samākhyātaḥ, budhaṃ caiva nibodha me /
paripākagate karmaṇīśvarecchākaroddhṛte //
prakāśaṃ nāyanaṃ yadvad anugṛhṇāti bhāskaraḥ /
karaṇāny anugṛhṇāti tadvad īśvara ātmanām //

29. See Mṛgendrāg., Vidyāpāda (ed. M. K. Shastri, Bombay, 1930; KSTS No. 50), 7, 12: *yadonmīlanam ādhatte, tadānugrāhikocyate.* Trans. M. Hulin, Pondicherry: Institut Français d'Indologie No. 63 (Pondichéry, Institut Français d'Indologie, 1980), pp. 181f.

30. SvT 11, 98:

Kalonmīlitacaitanyo vidyādarśitagocaraḥ /
rāgo 'sya rañjakatvena viṣayānandalakṣaṇaḥ //

31. Here, I agree with J. W. de Jong's interpretation of *kalayati;* see *Indo-Iranian Journal* 18 (1976): 299. The situation is doubtful in SvT 4, 235.

32. SvT 11, 99-100:

Kālo vai kalayaty enaṃ tuṭyādipralayāvadhiḥ /
niyatir niścitaṃ nityaṃ yojayec ca śubhāśubhe //
paramāṇusahasrāṃśān na ca nyūnaṃ na cādhikam /
puṃbhāvaṃ samanuprāpya tattve ca puruṣāhvaye //

33. SvT 11, 102:

Yataḥ śrīkaṇṭhanāthas tu niyatyā karmataḥ paśum /
pradhānapāśajālena veṣṭayed asamañjasam //

34. SvT 11, 104:

Baddhaḥ saṃcarati hy evaṃ māyādyavanigocare /
saṃsārī procyate tasmāt saṃsared yat punaḥ punaḥ //

35. SvT 11, 105-106:

Śabdādiviṣayā yasmād vidyante viṣayī tataḥ /
viṣayāḥ param ity āha nānābhedair visarpitāḥ //
nānākarmavipākaiś ca bhuṅkte tadbhāvabhāvitaḥ /
evaṃ bhuṅkte tu vai yasmāt tasmād bhoktā sa ucyate //

36. SvT 11, 107:

Tasmiṃs tajjño varārohe kṣetre vai karṣako yathā /
mahābhilāṣam ālokya kṛṣed vai lobhalāṅgalaiḥ //

37. SvT 11, 108-109:

Vapec ca mohabhāvena manovākkāyikaṃ sadā /
dharmādharmamayaṃ bījaṃ pravikārya samantataḥ //
tasmād vai aṅkurotpattiḥ sukhaduḥkhaphalodayā /
vardhate kāmakrodhena siktā rāgāmbunā bhṛśam //

38. SvT 11, 110-111:

Yasmin deśe ca kāle ca vayasā yādṛśena ca /
uptaṃ śubhāśubhaṃ karma tatkāle labhate phalam //
bhuṅkte tu vividhākāraṃ pūrvakarmavaśād budhaḥ /
yasmād evaṃ vijānāti tasmāt kṣetrajña ucyate //

39. SvT 11, 112-113b:

Viṣayān budhyate yasmād budhas tasmāt prakīrtitaḥ /
tad evāniṣṭarūpeṇa yadā bhāvayate pumān //
budhyamānas tu sa tadā, adhunā kathayāmi te /

40. SvT 11, 113c-114:

Yadā jugupsate bhogān śubhāṃś caivāśubhāṃs tathā //
kṛtrimān eva manyeta paraṃ vairāgyam āśritaḥ /
māyādyavaniparyantam indrajālaṃ tu budhyate //

See Mbh. 12, 295, 20 and 22 (partly quoted earlier): *anyo 'ham anyeyaṃ (prakṛtir) iti yadā budhyati buddhimān . . . yadā tu guṇajālaṃ tat prākṛtaṃ vijugupsate, tadā . . . na saṃjvaret.* The latter term, *he will not regret*, must have been inspired by BĀUp 4, 4, 12: *kim icchan . . . śarīram anusaṃjvaret;* and 4, 4, 15: *yadaitam anupaśyati . . . na tato vijugupsate.*

41. SvT 11, 115-116:

Putramitrakalatrāṇi suhṛtsvajanabāndhavāḥ /
yad arjitaṃ mayā dravyaṃ śubhenāpy aśubhena vā //
tad bhokṣyante tv ime sarve nirātaṅkā nirākulāḥ /
ekākī cāham evaiṣa yāsyāmi Yamasādanam //

42. SvT 11, 119:

So 'ham asmi malākīrṇe katham atra ramāmy aham /
nityam udvignacittas tu cintayed vai punaḥ punaḥ //

43. SvT 11, 120:

Kathaṃ muktir bhaved asmāt saṃsārād duratikramāt /
evaṃ prabuddho deveśi tallayas tatparāyaṇaḥ //

44. SvT 11, 121-126b:

Sarvārambhavinirmuktaḥ pramuktaḥ procyate tadā /
prabuddhas tu samākhyātaḥ suprabuddhaṃ tu me śṛṇu //
dīkṣājñānena yogena caryayāpy atha suvrate /
yadā prāptaḥ paraṃ sthānam adhvātītaṃ nirāmayam //
virajo vimalaṃ śāntaṃ prapañcātītagocaram /
niṣkampaṃ kāraṇātītaṃ sarvajñaṃ sarvatomukham //
sutṛptānādisambuddhaṃ svatantraṃ nityam eva hi /
aluptaśaktivibhavaṃ suprabuddhaṃ sanātanam //
tasmin yuktas tadātmā vai tadguṇais tu samanvitaḥ /
suprabuddhaḥ sa evokto Bhairavasya vaco yathā //
na cādhikāritā dīkṣāṃ vinā yoge 'sti śāṅkare /

45. Mṛgendrāg., Vidyāpāda, 12, 32c-33b; cf. also Sāṃkhyakārikā 42 and 56.

46. The abbreviations Mbh and SvT used in this section usually refer only to the discussed fragments: Mbh 12 (Śāntiparvan), 291-296, and SvT 11, verses 91-126.

47. Compare the term *aṇuvarga*, Nārāyaṇakaṇṭha on Mṛgendrāg., Vi., 7, 12.

48. The compounded *-ātman* in SvT 11, 91c *tattvabhūtātman*, has been played down by Kṣemarāja as a characterizing suffix indicating a subject's 'nature' or 'essence' (*svabhāva*). I am not certain whether he is right here; the *bhūtas* (5), *tattvas* (30) and *ātmans* (3) are in the Mālinīvij. Tantra (MVT) stated to be the first three of the five locations of the Śakti's powerful presence (*samāveśa*) to be realized by the initiate. But the sequence is not the same, and Kṣemarāja knew the MVT very well. He certainly would have referred to it if he deemed it necessary. We also may think of the three constituents of the "third *Padārtha*" recognized in Mataṅga-pārameśvara Āg., Vidyāpāda, 2, 16f. (ed. N. R. Bhatt, Pondicherry: Institut Français d'Indologie No. 56, Pondichéry: Institut Français d'Indologie, 1977, pp. 33, xx): *bhūta*, *bhāva*, and *tattva*. The commentator of that text, Rāmakaṇṭha, explains *tattva* as the thirty categories as earlier, *kalādikṣityantāḥ*, born from Māyā, but he deviates in his interpretation of *bhāva*, '364 worlds,' and *bhūta*, the embodied beings born in these worlds. The series *bhūta*, *bhāva*, *tattva* occurs in the SvT itself in 11, 87cd; i.e., in the passage devoted to the five *ātmans*: the *nirātman* is released from *bhūta*[*s*] and *bhāva*[*s*] and has abandoned the *tattva* nature (*tattvadharma*) and the *kalā*. The commentator here connects *bhūta* with the lower material *tattvas*, *bhāva* with the *buddhi*, *tattva*

with *puruṣa*, and with the *kañcukas* as a whole, thus encompassing everything created by Māyā. The commentators therefore disagree with each other about the interpretation of the latter series; besides, it is difficult to harmonize *ātman* and *bhāva*.

49. For a description of this state and the other *avasthās* from the viewpoint of Śaiva-Siddhānta, cf. V. A. Devasenapathi, *Śaiva Siddhānta as Expounded in the Śivajñāna-Siddhiyār and Its Six Commentaries* (Madras: University of Madras, 1960), pp. 232 f.

50. J. A. B. Van Buitenen, *The Large Ātman*, in *History of Religions*, vol. 4 (1964-65), pp. 103-114, quote on p. 109, note 13.

51. *The Maitrāyaṇīya Up.*, ed. J. A. B. Van Buitenen (The Hague: Mouton, 1962), p. 100; translation on p. 127.

52. On the epic and Purāṇic counterparts of the last stanza and their chronological problems, one can still consult with profit E. Frauwallner, *Untersuchungen zum Mokṣadharma*, *JAOS* 45 (1925): 51-67, quote on p. 59, and (with different conclusion) P. Hacker, *The Sāṃkhyaization of the Emanation Doctrine*, *WZKSA* [Vienna], 5 (1961): 75-112, esp. pp. 81, 85. Hacker also notes in such expositions, "clear traces of a constant antagonism between theism and impersonalism" (p. 111).

53. In the text itself, there is no complete parallelism because the *mahān ātman* is identified with the "twenty-fifth" (294, 35) who is the *Kṣetrajña*, and not with the *buddhi* = *Hiraṇyagarbha*. On Hiraṇyagarbha as the life principle, see F. D. K. Bosch, *The Golden Germ*, The Hague: Mouton, 1960, p. 49 f. In the MatPārĀg, Vidyāpāda, 16, 1 f., the cosmic awakening and subsequent creation is a function of Śrīkaṇṭha, an emanation of Śiva on a lower level than Ananta who presides over the worlds created by Māyā. These, however, include the coarse material domain in which the Budha finds himself; see the earlier commentary on SvT 11, 96f., and SvT 11, 102 with its commentary.

54. "Das Produkt (*anak*, literally 'child') des Māyātattva ist das soganannte *pradhānatattva*, eine Vergröberung (*ganal*) des Māyātattva. . . . Dieses [i.e., the Pradhāna = Prakṛti, TG] ist es . . . welches die Bewusstlosigkeit [Ungeistigkeit, *lupa*] des Puruṣa veranlasst," says Alexander Zieseniss, *Studien zur Geschichte des Śivaismus: Die Śaiva-Systematik des Vṛhaspatitattva*. Śata-Piṭaka, vol. 7, Indonesian Section, New Delhi: International Academy of Indian Culture, 1958), p. 33.

55. Māyā is discussed from the Śaiva viewpoint in MatPārAg,

Vidyāpāda, Chapter 8; see Introduction by N. R. Bhatt, pp. xxvif.; also H. Brunner-Lachaux, *Somaśambhupaddhati*, IIIe Partie, Pondicherry: Institut Français d'Indologie 25-III, (Pondichéry: Institut Français d'Indologie, 1977) p. vi.

56. Rāmakaṇṭha's commentary on the Sārdhatriśati-Kālottarāgama, 1, 5, ed. N. R. Bhatt, Pondicherry: Institut Français d'Indologie, No. 61, (Pondichéry: Institut Français d'Indologie, 1979), p. 12. Rāmakaṇṭha further argues that the released state is not yet reached by the realization of the distinction Puruṣa-Prakṛtiguṇas (i.e., the state of *Budhyamāna*) because not all *karmans* have yet been enjoyed in that state. To this effect he quotes the Paramokṣanirāsakārikā, verse 54 (Bhatt, loc. cit.). See also Brunner, *Somaśambhupaddhati*, III (1977), p. xiii.

57. See p. 29 (chapter by Mrs. Brunner).

58. A. Padoux, *Recherches sur la symbolique et l'énergie de la parole dans certains textes tantriques* (Paris, [2]1975), p. 326. The French original: "étant Parole, le mantra, en même temps que conscience, est également son, énergie phonique: . . . il ne peut pas être l'objet d'un prise de conscience par l'adepte, celui-ci ne peut pas fixer sur lui son attention, sans qu'il soit en même temps, au moins intérieurement, prononcé, ou associé à un mouvement intérieur, ou un effort spirituel, qui participe de l'énergie qui est Parole."

59. Translation H. Brunner (see note 18), p. 34: "réciter mentalement le mantra en l'allongeant jusqu'au *dvādaśānta*, c'est-à-dire jusqu'à ce qu'il atteigne l'apaisement." I have translated the variant *-plutaṃ* recorded in the edition by N. R. Bhatt. See also Jayaratha on Tantrāloka 5, 131 quoted by Padoux, op. cit., p. 331; and Padoux, p. 121. Kṣemarāja on SvT 7, 237 emphasizes the aspect of pronunciation: *uccāraḥ karaṇabandhādipūrvaṃ mantrodīraṇam*, quoted by V. V. Dviveda, *Āgama-mīmāṃsā* (New Delhi: L. B. Shastri Kendriya Sanskrit Vidyapeetha, 1982), p. 63, note 1.

60. The *vyāpinī*, a supraaudible level in which the ascending self experiences the Śakti's all-penetrative nature. See Padoux, op. cit., pp. 84, 344.

61. Two manuscripts of the Tantrasadbhāva are known to me: Nos. 1-363 and 5-445 of the National Archives at Kathmandu, Nepal. The manuscripts deviate from each other on some places. Tsb 1, 142-206 (numbering mine) and SvT 4, 234-296 are practically identical. Within this text group, Tsb 1, 142-149 corresponds with SvT 4, 234-239. It is not possible to discuss here the relation between

these two texts in more general terms.

62. Thus, in 148a, *śaktyādhastāt*, "below Śakti," stem *śaktyā-* or irregular *sandhi*; similar phenomena in the Kubjikāmata, see the edition of that text by T. Goudriaan and J. A. Schoterman (Leiden: E. J. Brill, 1988), pp. 57f., 71f. The SvT corrects into a somewhat different statement. In 148c, the Tsb reads *ca punottiṣṭhe[t]*; the SvT, *punar uttiṣṭhet*. An earlier *pāda* is given in the Tsb (1, 146d) as *tṛtīyaṃ śaktinā yutam*, with contamination of masculine and feminine *i*-stems; the SvT (4, 236d) corrects with the help of *tu* into a correct phrase *śaktyante tu tṛtīyakam*; etc.

63. An instance of a similar procedure applied by Abhinavagupta in his Tantrāloka can be found in T. Goudriaan and S. Gupta, *Hindu Tantric and Śākta Literature*, HIL, II, 2, (Wiesbaden: Harrassowitz, 1981), p. 163. However, Tsb 1, 150-206 and SvT 4, 240-296 exactly correspond without any condensation or extension having been applied.

64. *Spandakārikās, The Divine Creative Pulsation*, ed. and trans. Jaideva Singh (Delhi: Motilal Banarsidass, 1980), pp. 79 f.

65. For further treatment of the problem I refer to ibid., p. 89, where no sharp distinction is made between the view of the Kārikās and the commentator's interpretation.

66. Mālinīvijayottaratantra (MVT), ed. M. K. Shastri, KSTS No. 37, (Bombay, 1922). The stanza 2, 43 is quoted by Jayaratha on Tantrāloka (TĀ) 10, 239-240.

67. Gerhard Oberhammer, *Strukturen yogischer Meditation. Untersuchungen zur Spiritualität des Yoga* (Vienna: Österreichische Akademie der Wissenschaften, 1977), pp. 108 ff.

68. TĀ 10, 236 f.; reedited by R. C. Dwivedi and N. J. Rastogi (Delhi: Motilal Banarsidass, 1987), vol. 5, p. 2045. The TĀ itself paraphrases MVT 2, 43 in verses 239c-240b. For a further discussion of the subject, see the competent treatment by Jaideva Singh, *Śiva Sūtras: The Yoga of Supreme Identity* (Delhi, 1979), p. 44.

Chapter Six

Yoga and *Antaryāga* in Pāñcarātra

Sanjukta Gupta*

1.1

In all Tantric religious practice (*sādhanā*), yoga practice, namely visualization in meditation, is an essential concomitant to ritual action. The Jayākhya Saṃhitā (JS) states that the divine energy willed that the performer of religious duties (*karmin*) be released from the ceaseless cycle of death and birth and as a remedy for this condition evolved from herself the mantras. When the *sādhaka*, by performing all the rites connected with his worshipped mantra reaches perfection, the divine *śakti* wills that *sādhaka's* release. At that moment the cosmic omnipotent *śakti* identified with the *mantra-śakti* pervades the *sādhaka's* awareness so that he becomes enlightened by realizing his true identity as pure consciousness. The enlightened *sādhaka*, when all his accumulated *karma* has been duly exhausted, merges into Brahman (JS 3, 20-23). The religious duties of a *sādhaka* include the daily practice of yoga. The same text most categorically declares that the transcendental experience of the true nature of reality arises out of the practice of yoga.

The procedure recorded there is the traditional Upaniṣadic one. The *sādhaka* acquires a reasonable knowledge of the theoretical and conceptual background of the soteriology of his system. Then, when he feels disposed to total renunciation and acutely yearns for emancipation from the cycle of rebirth, the *sādhaka* approaches a suitable guru. The guru through his power of insight determines the spiritual capacity of the initiant and accordingly initiates the latter either with a *nirbīja* mantra or with a *sabīja* mantra of Vāsudeva

---

*It gives me great pleasure to acknowledge my admiration for Professor André Padoux' valuable contribution to the studies of Tantraśāstra. His ongoing research on Mantraśāstra might be supplemented by this chapter on the Tantric Vaiṣṇava ritual and yoga.

leading respectively to *nirbīja* or *asamprajñāta samādhi* and *sabīja* or *samprajñāta samādhi*. According to JS, the former produces only liberation whereas the latter produces both enjoyment and liberation. But we shall see that in fact an advanced *sādhaka* of the latter group is not distinguished from the former. Although JS does not use the Pātañjala yoga terms *samprajñāta* and so on, the descriptions of *sabīja* and *nirbīja samādhis* agree with the Pātañjala terms (Yogasūtra 1, 16-22 and Bhāṣya; JS 5, 5-30; SS 6, 214: *yadā saṃvedyanirmukte samādhau labhate sthitim*).

1.2

The Pāñcarātra asserts that liberation (*mukti*) is attained primarily by enlightenment; that is, the realization of the true nature of one's own self as Brahman. But that enlightenment is brought about by means of prolonged *sādhanā* with the mantra received from the guru at the sādhaka's final initiation. In this sense the system advocates both perfect knowledge (*jñāna*) and the practice of religious rites with mantras (*karma*) as the means to liberation. The dawning of releasing knowledge depends on the grace of the divine *śakti* (JS 3, 19-22). But this grace has to be earned by constant *sādhanā*. The nature of *sādhanā* is clearly such as to make the *sādhaka* always aware of his relationship with his mantra. The central theme of all *sādhanā* is to underscore the sādhaka's identity with that mantra and the deity referred to by it. He also must realize that all mantras and their deities are manifestations of the single transcendent unity of the supreme divinity who fundamentally is identical with the Upaniṣadic Brahman, but assumes a recognizable form out of compassion for his devotees. This form is designated by the mantra as its deity. In the Pāñcarātra view, the mantra is the first polarization of divine oneness into designation and the object designated. Because in ancient metaphysics designation is equated with cognition, mantra is the agent of the deity's perception. Ultimately, cognition and the cognized are the same divine, who has polarized himself by his own will and power. This is done for the benefit of the *sādhaka*, who is here the cognizer, the conscious entity who due to delusion identifies with his intelligence (*buddhi*), the storehouse of human *karma*. In reality there is but one conscious entity, Brahman, and the cognizer is Brahman. Thus the three (cognizer, cognition, and cognized) are one; that is, Brahman. I shall discuss this metaphysics of nondualism later.

In this chapter I shall show how this yoga *sādhanā*, which is an integral part of the *sādhaka's* daily ritual duties, is closely linked with the ideological background of the system. The daily ritual acts performed mentally and physically lead the *sādhaka* to an accurate grasp of this ideology. Its personal experience brings about his release from the cycle of rebirth. Its core is the basic unity of creation. To realize this ultimate unity, the *sādhaka* first learns to analyze empirical diversity. He begins by learning to understand the basic dichotomy, between matter and spirit. Then he learns to analyze his experience by means of a second dichotomy, between experience and its content. Finally, the *sādhaka* must realize the mystery of the nonduality of God, who is both the Upaniṣadic impersonal Brahman and the supreme God with personal qualities of omniscience and omnipotence. The resolution of this mystery lies in the identity of God's *śakti*. *Śakti* supplies the unqualified Brahman with a divine personality and form. It is the cosmic potency, *spanda*, that evolves into the material creation, on the one hand, and all the mantras and their gods, on the other. Vāsudeva, the highest God, is indeed the manifest divine *śakti* (PS 33, 74).

In yoga, the *sādhaka* must first identify himself as the microcosm, then merge his personal microcosmic self with the macrocosm, and finally, being totally immersed in the cosmic *śakti*, the *sādhaka* realizes the oneness of *śakti* and transcendental God and the total unity of creation in the latter.

1.3

The *sādhaka's* daily ritual worship can be roughly divided into five parts: (1) *bhūtaśuddhi*, purification of one's microcosmic body; (2) *nyāsa*, investing one's body with the divine body of the mantra deity,[1] (3) mentally conducting a complete worship of one's god, by offering various ingredients and finally performing a fire sacrifice, which invariably forms the final section of ritual worship; (4) physically worshipping God and performing a fire sacrifice; (5) *japa*, repeating one's mantra with or without a rosary, for a fixed number of times while visualizing the body (*mūrti*) of the deity of one's mantra. The first three parts of the *sādhaka's* ritual are conducted in the imagination only, which requires great concentration and understanding of Pāñcarātra metaphysics. For this, the sect has evolved a method in which several systems of symbolism are piled on each other, making the material very dense for outsiders. The idea of *sādhanā* is to present conceptual matter visually, to facilitate direct experience, as merely knowing the ideology does not lead to *mukti.*

1.4

The Pāñcarātra Āgamas I have used here—the Sāttvata (SS), the Jayākhya (JS), and the Pauṣkara (PS) Saṃhitās—seldom present a systematic account of their religious ideology. Like all early Tantric texts, they concentrate mainly on *sādhanā.* The system adopts Vedic orthopraxy and incorporates in its daily ritual program the five types of sacrifices to be performed daily by a Vaidika brahmin: *brahmayajña, devayajña, bhūtayajña, pitṛyajña and nṛyajña,* but the very first, studying Vedic or religious texts, is replaced by the recitation of *stotras* in praise of the God. Others are juxtaposed to the purely Pāñcarātra rituals and adopted to the sectarian mode. Thus in the SS the *devayajña* forms the last part of daily worship, which is followed by *pitṛyajña, bhūtabali* (*bhūtayajña*), and feeding one or more Vaiṣṇava guests; that is, *nṛyajña.* But at each step the conceptual background is translated in some form of ritual. Thus, the fire is considered to be an emanation (Kālavaiśvānara, i.e., Saṃkarṣaṇa or Ananta, see my paper on Viṣvaksena and so forth, also see later) of the supreme Vāsudeva; *Bhūtas* (spirits) are guarded by Viṣvaksena, and so on.

Clearly, metaphysics is not just for pondering over, but to be applied in *sādhanā.* Understanding monotheistic ideas is not only an intellectual exercise but should be translated into physical and mental acts. The latter are considered vastly superior. They consist of forming mental pictures of ideological concepts. Every single idea is transformed into an image. The typical phrase for this process is *tadbhāvabhāvitātman* ('he whose mind is infused by that image'). In this way, the *sādhaka* performs ritual acts in a special kind of meditation. This is not to say that the more general kind of meditation is not practiced. In daily *sādhanā,* the last obligatory act indeed is practicing that form of yoga in the night before and after sleeping (SS 6, 193-214).[2] But there is hardly any precise information in the Āgamas about the method of such practice, if we except such late texts as the Ahirbudhnya Saṃhitā (AS). To understand some of the oblique remarks, it is absolutely necessary to study such Śaiva-Śākta texts as the Vijñānabhairava, Mahārthamañjarī, or Pratyabijñāhṛdayam. These esoteric elements of yoga are described in the Āgamas in connection with *bhūtaśuddhi* or the contemplative ritual acts that precede the actual offerings. In fact, JS identifies *bhūtaśuddhi* with *samādhi;* that is, yoga (JS 10; SS 2, 72-75; 3).

1.5

The importance of the preparatory contemplative self-purification and the contemplative ritual worship of God is immense. For during both these rituals the *sādhaka* mentally acts out the entire Pāñcarātra soteriology, the nondualism of God's divine power (*śaktyadvayavāda*). God's power is the medium through which, as is remarked earlier, God, the totally transcendental and immutable, manifests creation. The latter is divided in two, pure and impure. The individual (*jīva*) as well falls in the category of impure because, unlike pure conscious entities, that is, the deities, *jīvas* lack the four qualities: *dharma* (righteousness), *jñāna* (knowledge), *vairāgya* (detachment), and *aiśvarya* (power). *Jīvas* have lost these because of their *karma* and delusion, isolation, and transience.

2.1

Pure creation is entirely a manifestation of God's compassion for the individual and consists of mantras and the deities designated by them. It is divided into three categories emanating from each other: transcendental at the top, then subtle, and finally gross. At the highest level is the manifest godhead, Vāsudeva, with his six divine attributes in full display. The first attribute is absolute consciousness or knowledge (*jñāna*) that is free from reference to any object and is the inherent nature of the absolute being. When the will to create dawns on God, there necessarily emanates from Him transcendental speech, which at the next moment in a flash reveals to God all phenomena that will be created. This experience of the entities to be created accounts for God's omniscience. The natural function of the speech-experience is to effect cognition; that is, it is the cognizing or signifying agent (*vedaka, vācaka*) of all phenomena to be created. This changes divine knowledge into referential knowledge, that is, designations with reference to the designated (*vācya*), although the latter still possesses no existence independent of the former. Moreover, this speech that is theologically identified with God's omnipotent power (*sāmarthyaśakti*, SS 2, 63; 2-4), also reveals God's remaining five attributes: power, sovereignty, force, valor, and energy (*śakti, aiśvarya, bala, vīrya*, and *tejas*). In other words, for the first time, God also becomes designated. Thus, at this cosmic stage, God is manifest as the godhead, Vāsudeva, and is revealed to His own knowledge as such. This is known as Vāsudeva's ever-manifest (*nityodita*) state, on which the *sādhaka* can concentrate in deep meditation.

2.2

Vāsudeva is the transcendent state of pure creation composed of mantras (PS 33, 74-86). He next moves into a quiescent (*para*) state in which all dichotomy disappears into His total stillness. The diffusion of all His divine attributes is contracted into its source, divine omnipotence (PS introduces at this point five divine *śaktis*; viz., *prāṇa, icchā, kriyā, jñāna,* and *kāla*; PS 33, verses 19, 117 and 140). This is Vāsudeva's tranquil (*śāntodita*) state. This stage is the source of the quadruple divinity (*caturvyūha*), heralding the imminent conceptual diversification of the pure creation. The diversity is affected by distributing the divine attributes in pairs among the divine manifestations of the quadruple God: Saṃkarṣaṇa (*jñāna* and *bala*), Pradyumna (*aiśvarya* and *vīrya*), and Aniruddha (*śakti* and *tejas*). These three represent the subtle creation, although Aniruddha also embodies the totality of the gross pure creation of mantras and deities.

2.3

This last group, the final stage of pure creation, is distributed in two groups: one of twelve deities, corresponding to the twelve months, and the other of thirty-nine deities, subdivided into three groups of twelve with a primordial deity connected with primordial water (material *śakti*) preceding each group. It is worth noting that pure creation, which moves vertically through the progressive congealment of the stages, repeats the pattern of its progression in the subtle and gross stages. Thus, the four Vyūha gods progress from unity to diversity following the four levels of the yogin's spiritual awareness; viz., *turya*, deep sleep, dream state, and waking state (see later). The three groups of twelve (the Vibhava deities) do the same. They represent the three lower levels of such awareness that are described a three circles, *cakras*; viz., fire, moon, and sun, representing respectively wakefulness, dream, and deep sleep levels. The cosmic deity Padmanābha, sleeping on the couch of the serpent Ananta floating on the primordial water that is *māyā śakti* corresponds to the fourth level, *turya* (SS 9, 98-109). Further, each of the Vibhava deities possesses a fragment of the six divine attributes and thus is a manifestation of the divine *śakti*.

This concludes the account of the pure creation. In late Pāñcarātra texts influenced by the southern bhakti cult, a fourth category: *arcā* or temple images, are added to the three categories, *para*, *vyūha*, and *vibhava*, noted in the SS and JS. PS does not mention the term *arcā* but adds a section on Kṣetras and Lords of Kṣetras, which includes several pilgrim places like the temple of Simhācala with their deities (PS 36, 17-28). The Lakṣmī Tantra (LT 2, 59) mentions the term *arcā* and includes it in the pure creation. But, when giving a detailed enumeration of all divine manifestations, LT and AS, both late texts, stick to the traditional account of the pure creation consisting of only three categories (LT 11; AS 5).

2.4

Impure creation consists of the conscious individuals (*jīva*) and the material world. JS (3, 1-9) describes it as the creation of *prakṛti*; that is, primordial matter. The conscious subject experiences this diverse world of *prakṛti* on the base of the *vedya-vedaka* dichotomy, which he takes to be real. Being of impure intelligence, he does not realize that all his cognitions and their contents are integrally identified within himself, as the gods of pure creation do (LT 6, 12-13). The conscious subject is endowed with discursive intelligence, egohood, thought that is actively engaged in bringing in information about the external world and carrying out the subject's reactions to that information. These components constitute the subject's inner or subtle personality and are counted as ontological categories (i.e., the microcosm). Out of these components, the first, intelligence, is the primary factor to endow the individual with a personality, because it contains one's store of *karma*, one's conceptual language, and one's store of experience, resulting in one's faculty of judgment. All these make up one's world-view and notion of oneself. Thus, intelligence (*buddhi*) is the agent that delimits the conscious entity into the *jīva*.

2.5

The first category of impure creation is *prakṛti*, a material emanation from *śakti* with three cosmic aspects: *sattva*, *rajas*, and *tamas*. As mentioned before, god Padmanābha presides over this creation as its Lord (*Īśvara*). He replaces the Sāṃkhya category of the conscious *puruṣa*. He is associated with primordial water, the first concrete manifestation of the material *śakti* and with Brahmā, the creator of the traditional mythology. The symbolism of the Lord's navel lotus on which Brahmā sits is important for the *sādhaka* because it symbolizes both eternal time and the basis of the world (Lt 5, 22-23; 6, 21-22; JS 2, 37).

The individual's physical body as well as all other physical phenomena are created from the five element-essences (*tanmātra*) and the five great elements (*mahābhūta*). Corresponding to the five elements are the five sense organs and five motor organs. These four groups of five—*tanmātras*, elements, sense organs, and motor organs—constitute the last stage of impure creation. All impure categories are produced from *prakṛti* and possess its three ingredients: *sattva*, *rajas*, and *tamas*.

2.6

Each object of the external world has its indicator or designation (*vācaka*), and each individual possesses a conceptual language that consists of all these designations and evaluates them. In an ordinary empirical situation, each person uses language to designate his or her experiences, evaluate them, and react accordingly. The residual impressions of these experiences are stored in one's intelligence in a linguistic form known as subtle speech. Thus on the empirical level, the original speech; that is, God's experience congeals into the individual's conceptual speech (i.e., knowledge and its external manifestations in the form of uttered speech). We must realize, however, that the transcendent divine *śakti* inheres in every phenomenon as its essence. Subtle speech, which essentially is the same as divine transcendent knowledge, guides the individual's mental activities of experiencing, relating, and reacting. Finally comes articulated speech, which is considered gross like the gross bodies and objects that constitute the pragmatic world. This world is impure because, as stated before, its experiencing subject, the individual, is deluded and thinks that the contents of his varied experiences are extraneously existing realities and wrongly desires or hates them. The *sādhaka* aspires to overcome this delusion. His sādhanā is to reduce the countless experiences and their content into one divine plenum of existence in which his own individuality also is dissolved, bringing his release from delusion and integral experience of bliss (JS 4, 30-71; PS 33, 89-122).

2.7

We have seen that the pure and impure creations along with speech (which is the same as knowledge in Indian philosophy) are divided in three levels: transcendent, subtle, and gross. We can discern the same division in the individual. Individuals are differentiated from each other by their subtle and gross bodies, and they differentiate themselves from God by identifying with their intelligence and thence with the rest of their psychophysical existence. Consciousness is the divine essence abiding in all individuals as their transcendent cores. It is obscured, first by the psychological components: intelligence with its knowledge born of experiences and its burden of *karma*, the ego, and the active mind (PS 33, 138-139). This is further compounded by the acts of sense and motor organs and the physical body. However, every day, one experiences one's three states; viz., gross, subtle, and transcendental. When awake, one functions through the exercise of one's body and organs, interacting with external entities. When one dreams, one still continues one's experiential activity. Presumably here only one's subtle or inner person is the subject of those experiences. Finally, one falls deeply asleep and when awake remembers that even in deep sleep one was conscious of being happy. There have been long and complicated discussions in various Indian philosophical texts about the nature of this experience in deep sleep. Following the Māṇḍūkya Upaniṣad and the Yoga system, the Āgamas claim this to be the experience of the person's transcendent state (see SS 3, 15).

These three states of the individual play a great role in the Yogic *sādhanā* of all Tantric systems. In Pāñcarātra theology the Vyūhas and the Vibhavas are arranged in the same paradigm of three states (*pada*). The Vibhavas represent the waking state of differentiated existence and limited divine sovereignty. Among the Vyūhas, Aniruddha is the aggregate of the Vibhavas; Pradyumna and Saṃkarṣaṇa represent the states of dream and deep sleep respectively.

2.8

The three states of the individual represent only empirical existence. For soteriology it is imperative to realize that beyond these three exists the transcendent state that is the person's real identity, where one abides alone beyond all differentiated experience. In the Māṇḍūkya Upaniṣad these states or levels of consciousness are aligned with the spiritual development of a *yogin*. As the yogin progressively withdraws his awareness from external phenomena by mental reflection, analysis, and concentration (consisting of *dhyāna, dhāraṇā,* and *samādhi*), he approaches the state of realization of the highest reality. When finally achieving this state, the *yogin* is released from the bondage of the cycle of birth and death and *karma*. The consciousness is free from any experience of the subject-object dichotomy as there exists no subject to have experience and nothing to form the content of experience. This state is called the *fourth* or *turya state,* the real state of consciousness.

2.9

For the theistic systems this fourth state cannot be the final state of the unique conscious entity, because the godhead must possess divine power and splendor as well as omniscience, even beyond the point of the disappearance of the diversity of the physical world and empirical existence. Therefore, for the supreme divine there exists a state of consciousness prior to the aforesaid fourth state signifying the cosmic moment prior to creation. This is known as the *turyātīta* state. The Vyūha Vāsudeva represents the *turya* state and Nityodita Vāsudeva the *turyātīta*. For a theistic *yogin,* the goal is to refine his spirituality to be able to reach the awareness of this fifth state. Of course, theists acknowledge a state of conscious existence of ultimate reality even beyond the Nityodita state, where divine sovereignty and splendor remain unmanifest in the plenum (*brahman*) of pure consciousness that is conscious of nothing, not even itself. But the theist conceives of two points of a swinging pendulum: on the one hand, the unpolarized Brahman and, on the other, the polarized God (Para Vāsudeva) and His *śakti*. Sādhanā concentrates on this *śakti* in the form of speech. One should further remember that the Vyūha Vāsudeva and the transcendent Vāsudeva basically are the same divinity and the awareness of the one leads automatically to the other. We shall soon see how this occurs.

3.1

Before starting yoga, the aspiring novice must understand one more philosophical concept that is worked into the fabric of his yogic system. This is the concept of the six ways (*adhvan*) or graduated stages in which God has manifested Himself, through the medium of His *śakti*, as the differentiated creation. These are known as the *varṇa, kalā, tattva, mantra, pada,* and *bhuvana*. The first four are considered pure (*sita*) ways, the last two are impure (*asita*). These two groups remain parallel, and the first thing the *sādhaka* learns is to distinguish the pure from the impure. In his *sādhanā,* he occupies himself only with the pure and gradually reaches the highest spiritual plane and then *mukti*. In the pure realm, each previous way is the source of its immediate follower. The first one is the same as unmanifest sound or speech, as well as manifest speech appearing as letters (*varṇa*).

3.2

The next development of divine speech, that is, divine knowledge, is the manifestation of all divine qualities. These are called *kalā* because here divine power is manifest in six parts or aspects. These I already have described as the qualities of the transcendent Vāsudeva, the fully manifest godhead. Although at this point the dichotomy is conceptually present as the indicator, that is, the transcendent mantra of Vāsudeva and its referent, the manifest godhead, yet these are not differentiated. Therefore in the *dhyāna* on this form no anthropomorphic iconography is given. Instead, the practitioner imagines a mass of light surrounded by eight rays representing the Vyūha gods in their descending and ascending orders (PS 33, 29; SS 2, 70-73). The first order represents creation, the second resorption. Alternatively, Vāsudeva alone is envisaged (see the commentary of Alaśiṃga Bhaṭṭa on SS 2, 30-73).

3.3

From the *kalās* emerge the four Vyūha gods: Vāsudeva, Saṃkarṣaṇa, Pradyumna, and Aniruddha. They are called the *way of the tattvas* or cosmic realities and represent the degrees of differentiation. Vāsudeva represents the evolving divine omnipotence in the dormant state. At this stage there is no diversity, and thus, strictly speaking, there exists no real *vyūha* (diversification) at the Vyūha Vāsudeva stage. Then the *śakti* gradually manifests herself as the three successive stages of her really differentiated states of Saṃkarṣaṇa and so on, representing, for the *yogin*, the states of deep sleep, dream, and waking. Each of these predominantly manifests two of the six *kalās* or parts of the transcendent *śakti.* Thus, Aniruddha represents the fully differentiated state at the cosmic level, and Saṃkarṣaṇa stands for the initial stage of creation when *śakti* first starts pulsating and still is totally blissful.[3]

In fact, each of these three Vyūha gods is a quadruple god incorporating all four forms. The transcendent Vāsudeva and His *śakti,* speech, pervade all four stages of the development of the *tattva* way as their essence; that is, the divine omniscient self. This is visualized as a shaft of light penetrating through the middle of the four quadruple gods (SS 4, 6-7; 9, 47-51; see my article, "The Caturvyūha and the Viśākha-yūpa in the Pāñcarātra," *Adyar Library Bulletin,* 35: 189-204.). The iconography of each of these four Vyūha gods shows their progression from the very subtle state to relatively less subtle ones. Aniruddha represents the dawn of gross creation contained in his form as the cosmic aggregate of all empirical phenomena. The Ṛgvedic concept of the cosmic man (*Virāṭ-puruṣa*) has been exploited in the concept of the *vyūha tattvas.* Moreover, the active *vyūhas* starting from Saṃkarṣaṇa's *suṣupti* state are really twelve. As the pulsation of *śakti* indicates the beginning of a time cycle, one may equate these with the twelve *vyūhāntara* gods of the solar cycle of twelve months. But the Āgamas are silent on this.

3.4

From Aniruddha emerges the fourth way of the divine manifestation, the mantras and the deities to which they refer (*mantrādhvan*). The mantras are endowed with a minute portion of the six divine qualities. Therefore they have the power to bestow on their *sādhakas* the spiritual excellence that may give them miraculous power, wisdom, and other religious objectives. The mantras and their deities are the support for the *sādhaka's* meditation (*dhāraṇī*) and hence are instrumental to his spiritual journey toward the liberating realization of the true nature of God and self (SS 19, 68-149; LT 22, 17-22).

3.5

The last two "ways" of divine manifestation are the individual, that is, the cognizer, and the contents of the cognition, the empirical world. The first is called *pada* with reference to the four states of cognition (*jāgrat* etc.). The second is called the *way of the worlds* (*bhuvana*). Of the six ways, these last two are deemed impure.

At the time of initiation, the aspirant's guru teaches him the concept of these six *adhvans* to explain how the unique and contentless divine knowledge (*cit*), that is, *śakti*, manifests itself as the differentiated creation and the experiences that grasp all created phenomena. At the empirical level stand the two last *adhvans*, *bhuvana* and the individual. The experiencing individual feels that the content of each specific experience is different from both oneself and the experience. The guru advises the *sādhaka* to transcend this notion. The mantra received by the latter is not an empirical entity separate from him. It is only a convenient medium through which to understand the ultimate unity of experience, its subject and its content, on the one hand, and the godhead, on the other. To realize this truth the *sādhaka* must follow the steps of these *adhvans* in the reverse order. One must begin with meditation on the identity of oneself and one's mantra. One must reflect on this identity constantly and at the same time must propitiate God by regularly worshipping the mantra, which is how God appears to one at that time. If and when one succeeds in pleasing God one receives His grace. This is the first step forward to salvation. Without grace one is doomed to be bound to the cycle of death and birth for eternity (SS 19, 142-146).

3.6

Through divine grace, the *sādhaka* becomes able to rise to the fourth state of awareness through constant practice of his religious duties and meditation on God. As I have mentioned the program of worship includes the method of musing and reflecting as well as meditating with deep concentration on the unity of the universe in God. The first two components of the worship program are purification of one's mortal self together with its apotheosis and mental worship. Besides, the *sādhaka* every day must perform deep meditation on the mantra through its repetition (*japa*) and yoga-meditation. As the sādhaka progresses spiritually toward understanding divine unity, he gets promoted by means of a special initiation to the higher levels of mantra and deities; viz., the *tattva* level, the subtle and more united level of the creation. After crossing the level of Aniruddha the *sādhaka* no longer needs to perform the external worship of God. The SS, my main source of description of Vyūha worship, does not describe the external worship of Pradyumna, Saṃkarṣaṇa, or Vāsudeva.

3.7

After reaching the stage of worshipping Vyūha Vāsudeva, the sādhaka automatically passes into the stage of Nityodita Vāsudeva and attains *mukti.* SS asserts total identity between these two phases of Vāsudeva; it gives only one mantra for both and calls it the *mantra of the single formed deity* (Vāsudeva). This is correct as even in Vyūha Vāsudeva the three other gods remain in conceptual form only. This mantra is prescribed for both the renouncer-worshipper and the nonrenouncer-devotee of the system (SS 2, 13-42). Thus even though all Āgamas make a distinction between the very advanced *sādhaka,* the *yogin* renouncer, and the fairly advanced householder brahmin *sādhaka,* the first qualified for *nirbīja* initiation, the last for *sabīja vyūha* initiation, the distinction vanishes when one has passed beyond Aniruddha's *jāgrat* state.

3.8

The first divine manifestation, that is, *varṇa,* speech, is explained to the *sādhaka* as the circuit of divine manifestation and resorption through the medium of speech-power. This consists of forty-nine letters (*varṇa cakra*) starting from the first letter of the Sanskrit alphabet, *a,* and ending with the last letter, *ha.* The *sādhaka* sees it as a closed circuit, manifestation starting from *a* and stopping at *sa* and resorption starting at *ha* and stopping at *ā.* Thus there are forty-eight letters in both the descending (creative) and ascending (resorptive) orders. These series are divided into groups of four standing for the quadruple deity, repeated twelve times in both orders. The quiescent Vāsudeva corresponds to the forty-ninth letters (*a* and *ha*) falling beyond the quadruple groups and is referred to as the *dvādaśānta* (beyond the twelve).

We must remember that the quadruple state really starts from the *Saṃkarṣaṇa* stage and therefore the total number of these deities in the states of deep sleep, dream, and waking is three times four; that is, twelve (see Illustations 1 and 2). This number is crucial and recurs repeatedly. Thus, the general scheme of arrangement of the Vibhava gods follows that of the Vyūhas and one finds there a division of three times twelve. The first two Vibhava deities correspond to the quiescent Vāsudeva and the Virāṭ-*puruṣa,* respectively, in the gross level of creation. Moreover, the twelfth god in each of the three groups repeats the image of Padmanābha floating on the primordial water (see Illustration 3; SS 9, 98-109).

Illustration 1. *Vyūhas.*

Vyūhātīta: transcendent (*Nityodita*) Vāsudeva with six *kalās: jñāna, śakti, aiśvarya, bala, vīrya,* and *tejas*. Fully manifest form of speech-*śakti*.

Vyūha:

(*turya*)	Vāsudeva, *viśrānti*	= dormant state of transcendent (*para*) speech
(*suṣupti*)	Saṃkarṣaṇa, *udaya*	= *paśyantī* state of speech; *jñāna* and *bala*.
(*svapna*)	Pradyumna, *vyāpti*	= *madhyamā* state of speech; *aiśvarya* and *vīrya*.
(*jāgrat*)	Aniruddha, *vyakti*	= *vaikharī* state of speech; *śakti* and *tejas*.

Illustration 2. Beginning of Diversity

Saṃkarṣaṇa	=	Vāsudeva, the state of *viśrānti udaya,*	1
		Saṃkarṣaṇa, the state of *udaya udaya,*	2
		Pradyumna, the state of *vyāpti udaya,*	3
		Aniruddha, the state of *vyakti udaya,*	4
Pradyumna	=	Vāsudeva, the state of *viśrānti vyāpti,*	5
		Saṃkarṣaṇa, the state of *udaya vyāpti,*	6
		Pradyumna, the state of *vyāpti vyāpti,*	7
		Aniruddha, the state of *vyakti vyāpti,*	8
Aniruddha	=	Vāsudeva, the state of *viśrānti vyakti,*	9
		Saṃkarṣaṇa, the state of *udaya vyakti,*	10
		Pradyumna, the state of *vyāpti vyakti,*	11
		Aniruddha, the state of *vyakti vyakti,*	12

Illustration 3. Vibhava Deities.

0. Viśākhayūpa

1. Padmanābha
2. Dhruva
3. Ananta (the first circle of twelve, 3-14)
4. Śaktīśa
5. Madhusūdana
6. Vidyādhideva
7. Kapila
8. Viśvarūpa
9. Vihaṃgama (Haṃsa)
10. Kroḍātman
11. Vaḍavāvaktra
12. Dharma
13. Vāgīśvara
14. Ekārṇavaśaya (this form is the same as Padmanābha)
15. Kūrma (the second circle of twelve, 15-26)
16. Varāha
17. Narasiṃha
18. Amṛtāharaṇa
19. Śrīpati
20. Kāntātman
21. Rāhujit
22. Kālanemighna
23. Pārijātahara
24. Lokanātha
25. Dattātreya
26. Nyagrodhaśāyin (child Viṣṇu lying on a banyan leaf floating on the primordial water)
27. Ekaśṛṅgatanu (Matsya) (the third circle of twelve, 27-38)
28. Vāmana
29. Trivikrama
30. Nara
31. Nārāyaṇa
32. Hari
33. Kṛṣṇa
34. Rāma carrying the war axe
35. Rāma carrying bow and arrows
36. Vyāsa, the sage
37. Kalkin
38. Pātālaśāyin (this form, too, is the same as Padmanābha)

3.9

The homology of the four Vyūha states with the four states of a yogin's awareness, in the description of the *adhvans*, is replaced by the image of the progressive congealment of the evolving divine *śakti*-speech into creation. From the point of view of the primal divine *śakti*, that is defined as (1) inertia (*viśrāma*); (2) awakening (*udaya*); (3) pervasion (*vyāpti*); and (4) manifestation (*vyakti*). The first state is that of the quiescent Vyūha Vāsudeva, who is represented by the first and last letters of the alphabet to emphasize being the starting as well as the finishing point of the cycle of creation and resorption.

These letters of the *varṇādhvan*, grouped in twelves following the patterns of the Vyūha gods, are used as props (*dhāraṇī*) for meditation (SS 19, 151-159; LT 20, 9-25). The four Vyūha gods appearing in vertical progression represent the four stages of gradual appearance and congealment of speech (*parā, paśyantī, madhyamā,* and *vaikharī*), corresponding to the four states of *viśrāma* and so on (see Illustration 2). The letters are identified with these forms. There seems to be some unclarity about how the twelve letters are distributed in each of the four states *viśrāma* and so on, and Alaśiṃga Bhaṭṭa, the commentator on the SS, is not sure which explanation to accept. However, the main point here is that the advanced *sādhaka* engaged in the worship of the Vyūha deities uses these *dhāraṇīs* while meditating on these gods and directly realizes the identity of seminal speech and the Vyūha forms and their mantras (i.e., the *vācya-vācaka* units). The letters of the *varṇādhvan* are used as rungs of a ladder to progress upward to the highest spiritual state, until the *sādhaka* reaches the *dvādaśānta* where there is no dichotomy. As he attains, in meditation, the end of all six *adhvans* he comes close to the experience of bliss (SS 19, 158-159; LT 20, 12-23).

4.1

Pāñcarātra *mantra-sādhanā* demands that its sādhaka must first understand the true nature of his mantra as a manifestation of God's omnipotent *śakti*, and its deity as a conceptual concretization of that power. Having realized that, one daily should worship it and offer fire oblation to it after having mentally visualized its form and fixed one's mind on it in meditation (*dhyāna*). The sādhaka also should perform repetition (*japa*) of the mantra for a fixed number of times while continuing *dhyāna* and ultimately identifying with the mantra in deep meditation.

The JS and PS enumerate eight parts (*aṣṭāṅga*) of the Pāñcarātra system of worship: (1) meditative worship (*mānasa yāga*), (2) ritual worship with material offerings, (3) fire sacrifice, (4) *bali* offerings to the spirits, (5) feeding brahmin guests, (6) *tarpaṇa* offered to the fire, (7) ancestor worship, and (8) partaking of the offered food that has been left over. But before even starting on any ritual program, the *sādhaka* has to purify himself both physically and psychologically (*bhūtaśuddhi*; that is, purification of the elements that go to form one's individuality), and then ritually achieve his own apotheosis. I have used the term *psychologically* to indicate the method of performance that is nothing but psychological activity. The same goes for the method of the *sādhaka's* apotheosis. These and the first part of the worship program all are psychological activities done in meditative concentration aided by a powerful mental act of visualizing the theories described earlier.

4.2

To start with the *bhūtaśuddhi*, the *sādhaka* takes a ritual bath and then, wearing clean clothes and with hair dressed, enters the enclosure of worship. After some preliminary rites to purify the enclosure and his seat, and so forth, the *sādhaka* sits down and ritually renders the place safe for worship (SS 17, 16-21). Next one starts renovating one's personality, *tattvaśuddhi* (PS 33). The procedure is threefold: (1) the present body is destroyed by merging it step by step into its cause; (2) when it reaches its primary state of evolution, it is burnt to ashes by the cataclystic fire (*dāhana*); (3) finally, it is revived by divine nectar (*āpyāyana*) and once again, following the steps of evolution, restored to its original form, now purged of any empirical impurity. We shall describe these three parts in some detail.

(1) One begins by withdrawing all sense organs including one's mind from contact with external objects. In yogic terms, this withdrawal is known as *pratyāhāra*. One's sense organs and organs of action thus are neutralized. This process also includes one's gross body. Then one concentrates on the cosmic elements that went into making one's body. One identifies one's causal cosmic categories with the aforesaid *adhvans* of manifestation of the divine power. Thus the element earth equates with the *bhuvana* way, the element water with *pada*, the element fire with *mantra*, the element

air with *tattva*, the element void with *kalā*, and manas with *varṇa*. At last, one identifies one's consciousness with the category of *buddhi*. This is the seat of the impure conscious entity, the *jīva* (SS 18, 127-195; JS 10, 22-69).

The empiricity of each category is withdrawn by using the category's special mantra to identify it with its deity. Thus each category has three identities: empirical (*ādhibhautika*), divine (*ādhidaivika*), and mantric (*ādhyātmika*). According to JS (10, 22) Aniruddha, Pradyumna, Saṃkarṣaṇa, Vāsudeva, and Satya, respectively, are the deities of the elements earth, water, fire, air, and void. Their mantras are ŚLĀṂ, ṢVĀṂ, SRĀṂ, HYĀṂ, and KṢMĀṂ. The SS, on the other hand, names the Vibhava deities, Padmanābha to Varāha, as the *bhūtādhideva*; that is, the presiding deities of the elements. The mantras are given there to be the first letter of the name of the relevant element added by "Ṃ" (see Illustration 4).

Illustration 4. The Seven *Tattvas* and Their Deities and Mantras Used for *Bhūtaśuddhi*.

adhyātman (mantra)	*bhūtādhideva* (god)	*adhibhūta*
Vyāhṛti mantra: HSṢMLRAṂ		
BAṂ	Padmanābha	*buddhitattva*
MAṂ	Viśvarūpa	*manastattva*
KHAṂ (ŚLĀṂ), formless	Vāgīśa (Satya)	*ākāśatattva*
VAṂ (ṢVĀṂ), circle	Khagāsana (Vāsudeva)	*vāyutattva*
TAṂ (SRĀṂ), triangle + svastika	Narasiṃha (Saṃkarṣaṇa)	*tejastattva*
AṂ (HYĀṂ), halfmoon + lotus	Sarasśāyin (Pradyumna)	*aptattva*
KṢĀṂ (KṢĀṂ) square + *vajra*	Varāha (Aniruddha)	*bhūtattva*

tanmātras

kṣmātattva	= element essence of earth	= *gandha*	= *bhuvanādhvan*
aptattva	= element essence of water	= *rasa*	= *padādhvan*
tejastattva	= element essence of fire	= *rūpa*	= *mantrādhvan*
vāyutattva	= element essence of air	= *sparśa*	= *tattvādhvan*
ākāśatattva	= element essence of ether	= *śabda*	= *kalādhvan*
manastattva	= element essence of mind		= *varṇādhvan*

Source of *vyāhṛti* mantras: SS 18, 127-195; within parentheses: JS 10, 22-69.

The *sādhaka*, by means of yogic breathing technique (*prāṇāyāma*) envisages his essential self going out of his body through the yogic channel situated on the right of the central yogic channel (*suṣumnā*) and merged with the self of the deity of his mantra who is seated inside a brilliant halo above the supreme divine abode (*dvādaśānta*). Just under Him are the deities of the elements in their quiescent state.

One now starts imagining the construction of one's microcosmic body made of elements, beginning with the earth. This element is seen as a square, marked by a thunderbolt, possessing trees, hills and so forth. It has all five subtle elemental essences. One visualizes the earth-square entering one's body as one inhales and settling down in the lowest part inside the body upto one's knees. Next one utters the mantra of the earth, visualizing it as having the form of god Varāha. One then imagines the square of earth dissolving in Varāha's form and the subtle element of smell. Next one exhales to throw the essence of smell out of one's body and merges it with the element water and its deity. One follows the same method for the element of water, visualizing it as a half moon marked by a lotus and in possession of all objects peculiar to water. The half-moon form enters one's body and settles in the region just above his knees and under the groin. One uses the element's mantra as a *dhāraṇī* to keep one's concentration fixed on its form and concretely imagine its dissolution in its essence (*tanmātra*), and then both the essence and the element merge in the element of fire that is their source. The elements of fire, air, and ether occupy, respectively, the space between the groin and the navel, from navel to the throat, and from throat to the crown. As one utters a specific mantra, for instance the mantra of earth, one visualizes its divine form, the mantra-deity, in this case Varāha or Aniruddha, the referent of the mantra. In this way one can visualize the gross element and its essence as a manifestation of *śakti*; that is, speech in the form of its mantra. This system of mental concretization of abstract ideas enables the *sādhaka* mentally to picture the process of annihilation of his impure microcosmic body. This is achieved by merging, one by one, all five cosmic elements into their respective sources, each time respectfully bowing down to their deities. In the course, one's sense organs and organs of action related to the elements and their *tanmātras* also are eliminated.

Finally, with the sixth *dhāraṇī* of *manas* one envisages the mantra of *manas* with which one identifies oneself, rising to the state of the transcendent *kalādhvan* and becoming immersed in the transcendent *śakti*. At this last phase, the *sādhaka*, his self now free from the five material elements that encaged him, via the quiescent state of Vāsudeva Vyūha, and the transcendent *kalās*, attains to the *śabdabrahman* state of *varṇādhvan*. Here he visualizes his *jīva*-self (ego, *asmitā*, SS 18, 152) identified with the *buddhitattva*. As stated before, this *tattva* is the seat of the *jīva* who is fettered with *karman* (SS 18, 168-169). Visualizing the deity of this *tattva* (Padmanābha), the *sādhaka*, uttering the *vyāhṛti* mantra, HSṢMLRAṂ (JS 6, 213-214), which pervades all seven *tattvas*, dissolves all *tattvas* in Padmanābha. There he becomes immersed in the primordial blissful *śakti*.

(2) From that primordial position, the *sādhaka* then by means of the appropriate mantra burns his elemental body, which has been emptied of its mantra essence. Next he visualizes flooding the ashes of the burnt impure material body with celestial water while he utters the appropriate mantra (SS 17, 23 and 18, 125-150; JS 10, 15-58 and 71-76).

(3) The third phase of *bhūtaśuddhi* starts with the *sādhaka*'s envisaging the transcendent mantra power as the source of all creation. From that he re-creates his pure elemental body, following the steps of *ṣaḍadhvan*. He now becomes consubstantial with the transcendent deity (JS 10; SS 17, 16-26; 19, 112-114). This finally completes the *sādhaka's* deification, without which he is not entitled to worship the deity.

The entire process, described as briefly as possible, is done in deep meditation known as *jñāna samādhi* and has its roots in the penultimate part of Patañjali's yoga method; that is, *samprajñāta samādhi*. The efficacy of this method is upheld in the Āgamas; the JS even says that through the mere practice of this *bhūtaśuddhi* the *sādhaka* can reach the transcendent (10, 102).

4.3

After the *bhūtaśuddhi*, the *sādhaka* invests his main mantra and its various limbs on specific parts of his body, conjuring up in meditation both the sound and the iconographic forms of these mantras and envisaging the transformation of his own personality into the mantra personality. This whole process is known as *mantra-nyāsa*. To personify the mantra, he has to divide it into six limbs (*aṅga*), each of which possesses one of the six *kalās* that together form the god's transcendental body. Hence each mantra possesses six *aṅga* mantras. Only now can the real worship start.

5.1

The LT describes mental worship (*antaryāga*) in the following way. The deity existing in transcendental blissful form in the *sādhaka's* heart is propitiated with offerings made of transcendental matter (LT 36, 1; SS 17, 42; *bhāvanājātair bhogaiḥ*). Mental worship is a service of contemplation, in which the worshipper follows in imagination the entire ritual procedure from the evocation of the deity to the final leave-taking. As Beyer observed, the main objective of this ritual is one-pointed meditation on the deity. He quite rightly points out that the "living soul" of this contemplation is the worshipper's capacity for concrete visualization.[4] This ability to vividly conjure up his deity is the basis for the *sādhaka*'s actually relating (*yoga*) to the power of his mantra and its deity, and it is that connection which enables him to harness this power as a means to his goal. This capactiy of concentrating on so detailed a mental image needs long practice in meditation and indicates great spiritual advancement; it is rated much higher than the ordinary rite of servicing god with concrete materials (LT 34, 137-141).

5.2

First of all, the *sādhaka* must envisage in himself the divine throne, to which he must invoke the deity. For gods of the *mantrādhvan* level, this throne is constituted by a fixed sequence of deities and phenomena (SG trans. LT 212-215). In case of the transcendent Vāsudeva one should first envisage one's psychophysical system as the temple of God. Inside that, at the end of the vocal chord, is the first heart lotus, facing downward with its petals unopened; inside its pericarp is the second heart lotus, facing upward. The first lotus is the moon lotus full of nectar and the second is the sun lotus. The first represents the eclipse (*nimeṣa*) of Śabdabrahman and the second its awakening (*unmeṣa*). Resting on the pericarp of the second lotus, the middle channel (*madhya nāḍī*, more commonly *suṣumnā*, vide Kurt F. Leidecker's note on Kṣemarāja's Pratyabhijñā-hṛdayam, 146) rises, containing the orbs of sun, moon, and fire. This middle channel represents manifest sound or speech, whereas unmanifest speech remains above it. Manifest speech, which is transcendent knowledge (*cit*), keeps contact with transcendent reality by flying to it along with the breath as the *sādhaka* performs *prāṇāyāma*. Usually cosmic *cit-śakti*, manifest as the cosmic movement, *spanda* or *prāṇa*, enters the *jīva* through the moon channel and pervades him from top to bottom, after which it returns to its cosmic position by way of the sun channel. This happens with the regular breathing process of all *jīvas*. By the technique of *prāṇāyāma*, the *sādhaka* can suspend the *prāṇaśakti* from returning to its cosmic stance. Instead, he forces it into his *suṣumnā* channel, where the transcendent manifest speech resides. The *prāṇaśakti* merges into the speech and in this way brings the *sādhaka* in direct contact with *cit-śakti*. The central channel containing manifest speech (i.e., divine omniscience) with all its individual contents is conceived to be the center of the universe. The divine omniscience is the second state of Śabdabrahman; viz. *paśyantī*. The *sādhaka* envisages manifest speech that is Vāsudeva's *śakti* as a resonance, like the humming of a bee that pours forth the (Sanskrit) letters from *a* to *ha*. The *sādhaka* must now visualize the void beyond this manifest speech. This void signifies the divine *śakti* in an unmanifest state. There the worshipper now envisages the supreme God existing together with god Ananta, the deity of *buddhitattva* (SS 9, 98-102). Here Vāsudeva, who is unmanifest, appears in a transcendental form of exquisite beauty. He appears to the *sādhaka* only out of his immense compassion for his devotees.

Iconography

Vāsudeva here is two-armed, his hands held in the gesture of granting boons and protection, and they are marked with a shell and a wheel. He is surrounded by the still unmanifest quadruple form of himself, known in the unmanifest state as Vāsudeva, Acyuta, Satya, and Puruṣa. These appear like rays surrounding the God's brilliant form. Sometimes, anthropomorphy is altogether absent at this stage of *sādhanā*, and the *sādhaka* only envisages a luminous disc surrounded by rays. The latter represents the Nityodita Vāsudeva and the former Śāntodita Vāsudeva. The mantra mentioned in SS (2, 26-32) actually refers to the Śāntodita.

Mantra

"OṂ I salute the Śāntodita, who is knowledge and vital air, who is omniscient and the supreme consciousness." The commentator seems to think that the mantra refers to both forms of Vāsudeva jointly (SS 2, 33-34). However, the total identity of these two forms is established in the text (5, 81) by an analogy with the seed of the banyan tree, which contains the future tree in all phases of development in a dormant form. The *aṅga* mantras are formed by dividing the mantra into six consecutive words, then adding the six *kalās* (*jñāna, aiśvarya, śakti, bala, vīrya, tejas*) and the six limbs (*hṛt, śiras, śikhā, kavaca, astra, dṛk*), respectively, to each of them, while adding OṂ at the beginning of the mantras, and dative case endings to all the words. The resulting mantras are finished, respectively, with NAMAS, SVĀHĀ, VAUṢAṬ, HUṂ, PHAṬ and VAUṢAṬ. As remarked earlier, these limb mantras are needed to give the mantra-deity a concrete form (*sakalī-karaṇa*) that can be visualized.

Next the worshipper envisages the celestial river Gaṅgā flowing down the moon lotus onto the deity's head. One then visualizes the five objects of offering: water for washing God's feet (*pādya*) and so on and purifies these with the water of Gaṅgā. Then, mentally announcing the intention to worship the deity with these objects, one imagines oneself holding each item and declaring that one is offering it, concluding with the words: "Let the deity be pleased and show grace to me." After this, the *sādhaka* in the same contemplative way performs fire oblation to God and the rite of *japa*, and finally offers himself unreservedly to God. He then performs the *visarjana* rite, again through vivid contemplation; he envisages the deity becoming *niṣkala*, integral and immutable, and returning to the void.

5.3

It was explained earlier that Vāsudeva, even in his primary *vyūha* state, is equated with the fourth plane of awareness, which is totally free from differentiation. Therefore He is worshipped alone as the Śāntodita. In the third or *suṣupti* plane, the quadruple god is in the primary phase of differentiation, the first descending step of the divine for his creative activity. The *sādhaka* is to envisage how the single transcendent deity acquires a dichotomy inside his heart lotus. In the case of the former image the deity as manifest speech appeared as the cycle of letters. Now He is conjured up as a lotus floating on the ocean represented by the letter *kṣa*. *A* is its core, *ā* its stalk, and *ha* its pericarp. Inside the last, divine transcendent speech exists like a square pillar and becomes the indicator or the concept (*vācaka*). The referent (*vācya*) of that concept is the quadruple god discernible on that pillar on its cardinal sides: Vāsudeva possessing all six *kalās* on the east; Saṃkarṣaṇa, characterized by divine knowledge and force, on the south; Pradyumna, possessing sovereignty and valor, on the west; and Aniruddha, possessing power and energy, on the north.

Iconography

The deities are of the same form, excepting the marks on their palms. Saṃkarṣaṇa's right and left hands are marked with a shell and a plough. Pradyumna's right hand bears the mark of arrows and his left that of a bow. Aniruddha holds the marks of sword and shield in his right and left hands. The similarity of their forms indicates that they have advanced but little into differentiatedness. They seem all to possess the six divine attributes, though each of them, other than Vāsudeva, shows predominance of some qualities. Finally, their lack of activity is indicated by the mere symbolical presence of their weapons and so forth. The hands of the quadruple gods are turned downward and their faces upward. One may speculate here on the significance of the fact that the quadruple gods in the *suṣupti* stage differ in posture from Vāsudeva in the *turya* stage of awareness. Perhaps the down-facing hands indicate their inaction and signify that their only characteristic is knowledge of their own selves differentiated from the Vyūha Vāsudeva; hence also the upturned position of their faces.

The *sādhaka* is to regard this state as the primary creative state of flux (*spanda* or *prāṇaśakti*). At this stage the omnipotent cosmic power manifests as cosmic vibration. At the microcosmic level the same power pervades the individual as vital breath. Although being in continual movement, the power never loses its static and immutable center. Like a swiftly turning wheel, *śakti* is ever active but its center is still. But the *sādhaka* also realizes the *śakti*'s identity with God by being blissful (*svānandā*) and quiescent (*śāntā*); that is, inactive (SS 5, 15-16). This indeed is her Vyūha Vāsudeva state. As stated earlier, the *vācya-vācaka* dichotomy is but two aspects of the same *śakti* and so is her active-inactive dichotomy. In deep sleep, the quadruple deity holds all differentiated phenomena in dormant and conceptual state (SS 5, 52-53).

Mantras

There are four separate mantras for the four *vyūha* deities: (1) "OṂ I salute the Supreme Lord, the agent, who is irresistible and incessant movement" (Vāsudeva), (2) "OṂ I repeatedly bow down to Thee who art the infallible omnipotent reality" (Saṃkarṣaṇa); (3) "OṂ I salute the supreme irresistible movement, the vital air—*prāṇa, apāna, samāna, udāna,* and *vyāna*" (Pradyumna); and (4) "OṂ I bow down to the manifest Lord, the immutable changeless eternal one" (Aniruddha). The *sādhaka* again worships these mantras and their deities with offerings mentally conjured up, envisaging them to be consubstantial with the nectar in the moon lotus inside his heart. Each of these mantras again is divided into six *aṅga* mantras, following the same method as was used in the first mantra.

5.4

In the dream state of awareness, the quadruple deities become more clearly visible in their differentiated forms. Their abiding central unity, formerly conceptualized as a central pillar, becomes more illuminated. The *sādhaka* conceives the Supreme Self manifesting Himself identified with the *sādhaka's* own self, stationed on the aforesaid lotus of letters, that is, manifest speech, inside his heart lotus. The Supreme God is conceived as a luminous form made of His six divine *kalās*, resplendent with the unrefracted colors of the rainbow. Having visualized this brilliant form, the *sādhaka* then envisages the four *vyūha* forms corresponding to their mantras as standing on the tips, the filaments, of the speech lotus. Next he visualizes the divine power, which extends beyond the reach of time, absorbing these *vyūha* deities within itself and appearing, as described, as a luminous pillar that extends through the center of the speech lotus. On this central brilliant column, the quadruple gods are envisaged, appearing gradually on the surfaces facing the cardinal directions, east and so on, like the sprouting of stems from the central trunk.

Iconography

Vāsudeva appears first, on the east side of the pillar, bright white in color. Next appears Saṃkarṣaṇa on the south, red and luminous. Pradyumna of golden hue then appears on the west; and finally Aniruddha manifests himself, blue as the sky, on the north of the column. Physically they resemble the primal Vāsudeva form, but their expression no longer is absorbed nor their gaze fixed upward. Instead they wear a deeply compassionate expression as if eager to help their devotees, which signifies that they are now aware of the creation besides themselves. Each is encircled by his own brilliant aura and holds his special insignia. All the detailed marks on their bodies are visible; this underscores their further distance from the transcendental primordial unity.

The *sādhaka* then performs his contemplative worship as described earlier, taking each deity singly in the order of creation, starting from Vāsudeva. Immediately afterward, he worships them in the same way, following the order of resorption, starting from Aniruddha. But the luminous pillar, the abiding *śakti*, and the essence of these gods is worshipped first, before the meditative worship of the quadruple deity is started. This is to enable the ritualist to grasp the unity of the four differentiated gods, as well as to conceptualize the *vācaka-vācya* duality, the pillar as speech and instrument of cognition being the former, and the four deities the latter.

Mantras

The pillar (*yūpa*) mantra: "OṂ I salute the supreme, the manifest divine energy, who is independent of the supreme (i.e., *svātantrya śakti*) and whom the supreme reality does not depend on." This mantra identifies the pillar with *śakti*, which in its turn is identified with Śabdabrahman. Next come the Vyūha mantras: (1) "OṂ AṂ salute to Bhagavān Vāsudeva"; (2) "OṂ ĀṂ I salute Bhagavān Saṃkarṣaṇa"; (3) "OṂ AṂ (i.e., AṂ + Ṃ) I salute Bhagavān Pradyumna"; (4) "OṂ AḤ I salute Bhagavān Aniruddha."

Two points should be observed here. First, at this stage we get the *bīja* mantra for the first time because at the dream stage of the Vyūha manifestation the mantras also show a further stage of differentiation: a dichotomy between soul and body (SS 9, 13-32). As the central pillar, that is, the *śakti*, is clearly distinguished from the four Vyūha deities as their essence, so too the mantras of the quadruple deities are divided into two units: the *bīja* and the rest of the mantra. *Bīja* indicates the essence or soul of a mantra. But even in the dream state the gods are not fully differentiated and hence not concrete or empirical. Therefore, even now the quadruple gods cannot and should not be worshipped with any empirical object; only contemplative worship is recommended (SS 4, 46).

Second, for the first time the deities are mentioned by name. These names signify for the *sādhaka* the differentiated states of the deities. The dichotomy of *vācya* and *vācaka*, here the dichotomy consisting of the mantras and their *dhyāna* forms, is complete, yet they are still in a conceptual or "subtle" state. To penetrate the mystical cosmogony and theology, the *sādhaka* must totally immerse himself in contemplation on each stage, worship the deities in the creative, evolutionary steps, and again retrace those steps to witness their merging by involution into the divine source. The SS states that the transcendental primary god Vāsudeva also is all-pervasive and exists in all states of awareness of the Vyūha manifestations. All the mantras manifest in the Vyūha states are refractions of His own divine form made of the six qualities. As He (the Nityodita Vāsudeva) projects Himself gradually as the Vyūha gods, He appears in each stage of awareness as the deity appearing on the east side of the pillar, predominating over the other three. The diversity of the primal Vāsudeva should be understood as a reflection like that of the sun in various containers of water. Thus all Vyūhas (mantras and gods) possess all six divine qualities, only Vāsudeva possesses them all in equal force whereas the other three mantras and their gods each possess two that preponderate over the other four (SS 4, 31-34).

5.5

In the next ritual stage, the worshipper moves to the plane of concrete or empirical existence (*jāgrat*), the domain of Aniruddha, who is the supreme authority (Adhyakṣa) of this plane. This is the concluding stage of the primal god's self-projection through the *tattva* trajectory. At this stage, all conceptions of spatial and temporal differentiation are clearly discernible on the persons of the quadruple divinity.

Iconography

The *sādhaka* first envisages the aforesaid speech lotus containing the letters. On the *jāgrat* level, the four forms of the quadruple gods are envisaged in the cardinal points as before, but they now rest on the petals of the speech lotus. For the ritualist, this not only indicates that this stage is the most external one, but also that this is the lowest level (with the *śānta* level as the highest). This is emphasized by the vertical pillar, which at this stage is not only luminous but also clearly shows the four Vyūha figures branching out of it. Hence the pillar now no longer is called the *brahma* ('essential) *pillar* but the *pillar that is branching out* (*viśākha-yūpa*). This emphasizes the presence of two dimensions of space; namely, vertical as well as horizontal (SS 5, 4; 9, 49-50).

The *sādhaka* envisages the transcendent Vāsudeva as a luminous plenum identified with the mantra OṂ, pervading the space from the pericarp of the speech lotus to the tips of its stamens. Next one witnesses the rise of the four supreme *bījas*: AṂ, ĀṂ, AṂ (i.e., AṂ + Ṃ), and AḤ, each preceded by OṂ, in the four cardinal directions. Each of these *bījas* appears like a brilliant orb surrounded by countless rays. Out of each orb appears in the appropriate direction a Vyūha god bearing distinct, personal characteristics. The SS compares these advents to the separation of sparks from a fire. Each *bīja* is the referring semantic unit (*vācaka*) indicating its referent, a Vyūha god (SS 5, 8). This emphasizes the causal connection between *vācaka* and *vācya*, the former being the source of the latter.

Vāsudeva, the primary Vyūha god, appears now as pure white in color and wearing a peaceful expression. He has large lotus-shaped eyes, four arms, and yellow silk clothes. His banner is an eagle. He is holding his primary right hand in the gesture of protection and his primary left hand bears a conch shell. In his secondary right hand he holds a wheel and in his secondary left hand a club, its tip resting on the ground.

Saṃkarṣaṇa is red and also possesses four arms. The primary hands are similar to Vāsudeva's, but in his secondary right hand he holds a ploughshare and in his left hand a pestle. His clothes are dark blue, and his banner is a palm tree.

Pradyumna is a brilliant yellow. He wears red silk clothes and also has four arms of which the primary two are like Vāsudeva's. In his secondary left hand he holds a bow, and his same right hand holds five arrows (Pradyumna is equated with the god of love who wields a bow made of flowers and bees and has five arrows made of five spring flowers). He has a *makara* (dophin or aquatic animal) on his banner.

Aniruddha is very dark in color and wears pure white clothes. Of his four hands, the primary two are like Vāsudeva's. He holds in his secondary right hand a sword and in the secondary left a shield. His banner bears the sign of a fawn. All four gods wear garlands made of wild flowers and bear on their chest the *śrīvatsa* mark. Each has a *kaustubha* jewel on his breast. All are similarly ornamented, crowned like kings, and suitably besmeared with fragrant paste.

Thus the *sādhaka* envisages the appearance of the four Vyūha deities in the cardinal directions, indicating the process of creation. Next he envisages them on the petals of the same speech lotus but now appearing in the intermediate directions, indicating the order of resorption. At this stage each god becomes bicolored. The order of envisaging the gods also is reversed. Thus one first envisages Aniruddha on the northeast corner, half dark and half white. Then one sees Pradyumna on the northwest corner, half dark and half yellow. Next one visualizes Saṃkarṣaṇa in the southwest, half yellow and half red. Finally one envisages Vāsudeva in the southeast, half white and half red. The *sādhaka* envisages these forms only when dwelling on the process of dissolution of the four Vyūha gods, toward the end of his contemplative worship of these gods.

The active deity of the *jāgrat* state of the Vyūha gods is Aniruddha, who is the sovereign Lord of the empirical creation and oversees its smooth functioning. This creation functions under the rule of time and its various divisions: into the four eons (*yuga*), and further into years, days, and full and half watches. This last system of time division is evidently solar, and the *sādhaka* takes it into account when worshipping the solar manifestations of the Vyūha gods, the twelve Vyūhāntara gods: Keśava, Nārāyaṇa, Mādhava; Govinda, Viṣṇu, Madhusūdana; Trivikrama, Vāmana, Śrīdhara; Hṛṣīkeśa, Padmanābha, Dāmodara. Each group of three emanates from one of the Vyūha gods.

The *sādhaka*, performing the contemplative worship of the quadruple gods in the *jāgrat* state, takes into account only the cosmic time division of the *yugas* and their twilight periods. The gods change their color in each of these periods. The color scheme of Vāsudeva, Saṃkarṣaṇa, Pradyumna, and Aniruddha as described, that is, white, red, yellow, and black, respectively, is true for the first *yuga*; viz., Kṛta. In Tretā it is red, yellow, black, and white; in Dvāpara, yellow, black, white, and red; and finally in Kali it is black, white, red, and yellow, respectively. In each twilight period all four gods wear the same pair of colors: after the end of Kṛta and before the beginning of Tretā, red + white; after Tretā and before Dvāpara, red + yellow; after Dvāpara and before Kali, yellow + black; and after Kali, black + white. The *sādhaka* installs these quadruple gods on his own body during the *nyāsa* rites in the following manner. One who aims at acquiring power installs the gods at Kṛta on his head, at Tretā on his heart, at Dvāpara on his navel, and at Kali on his body below the navel, going from the head downward. But one who is after salvation starts from low on his body and arrives at the head. The twilight manifestations are installed respectively on the neck, shoulders, knees, and ankles. One meditates on the gradual advent of these four *yuga* variations and the four twilight variations and again envisages their gradual resorption into their source.

But only are the quadruple deities recalled in full detail at the *jāgrat* state, but also their subsidiary mantras (*aṅga mantra*), *śaktis* and attendant gods are envisaged installed on the filaments and petals of the speech lotus.

Mantras

Vāsudeva: "OṂ AṂ I salute you who are without any division, who are marvelous, Lord of the yogins, possessor of the wheel, eagle-bannered, the yellow-clothed Vāsudeva." Saṃkarṣaṇa: "OṂ ĀṂ I salute Saṃkarṣaṇa [Bala-]rāma, the carrier of the pestle called *Saunanda*, who is destruction (*pralaya*) itself, whose banner is marked by the palm tree, who wears blue clothes and is called *Kāmapāla*." Pradyumna: "OṂ AṂ I bow down to Pradyumna, the carrier of the bow, the *makara*-bannered god who wears red clothes, who is called *Sanatkumāra* and is beloved of all." Aniruddha: "OṂ AḤ I bow down to Aniruddha who holds in his hand the pleasant [sword] Nandaka, whose banner is marked by a fawn, who wears black (?) clothes, and whose army covers the universe (*viṣvaksena*)." The *aṅga* or *pada* mantras are constructed in the usual manner by dividing each mantra into six units.

The order of mantras is reversed for the dissolution and starts from the fourth god Puruṣa: "OṂ I salute Puruṣa"; Satya: "OṂ I salute Satya"; Acyuta: "OṂ I salute Acyuta"; Vāsudeva: "OṂ I salute Vāsudeva." As these gods represent the unmanifest quadruple gods inherent in transcendent Vāsudeva, they possess no differentiating name or description, nor a special *bīja* mantra or *aṅga* mantra.

6

The preceding account describes the contemplative worship of the single transcendent Vāsudeva, the quadruple god Vāsudeva and his differentiated forms in three successive stages that include the Vibhava gods and the *yūpa*. The *sādhaka* must envisage at length each deity appearing out of its immediate source and descending into his own heart, which contains the two lotuses described earlier. Inside these two lotuses is the place of the principle of speech, which in the last two stages of the quadruple deities' descent from transcendence to gross creation appears in the form of the speech lotus. Each mantra emerges out of the speech-principle and is the designating (*vācaka*) entity referring to a divine form that is its referent (*vācya*). Thus we see how designation (*nāma*) is equated with the principle of speech. It also is equated with cognition. The terms *vācaka* and *vācya* also mean cognition and its content. As long as the thinking-cognizing entity, the individual, is aware of the dichotomy between *vācaka* and *vācya*, his spiritual state remains imperfect. Only when dissolving all differentiated experiences into the unity of a single consciousness, Vāsudeva who is conscious of nothing as there is nothing, does the sādhaka achieve release from transient existence.

The SS briefly describes contemplative worship (*antaryāga*), in which after the primary *prāṇāyāma, bhūtaśuddhi,* and *nyāsa,* the *sādhaka* must envisage the descent of each mantra from its source, contemplate the appearance of the deity designated by the mantra, first in general and then for each part of the deity by means of its *pada* mantra, and identify through *nyāsa* with that deity's personality. Then he must offer Him one by one the basic items of offerings, also in meditative imagination, each time pronouncing the item's name and asking the god to favor him by accepting the offering. At the end of this rite he performs the *japa* of the deity, offers himself in humility, and finally visualizes the deity returning to his source. The whole procedure is performed in *samādhi,* which the *sādhaka* must not interrupt. The ritually and spiritually advanced can perform the contemplative worship in a single *samādhi,* in which one takes into account all stages of God's descent in the pure creation, beginning with the single or Nityodita Vāsudeva through all the stages of development and diversification of the Vyūha Vāsudeva, and finishing with the Vibhava manifestation. By Vibhava, in this context, I guess, the text means the Viśākha *yūpa* (SS 5, 94-95).

Every *sādhaka* is free to choose any of the divine forms for worship; but must keep in mind a difference between the two forms of Vāsudeva, the primal God and the undifferentiated Vyūha god, on the one hand, and the three differentiated Vyūha deities, on the other. The latter are evolutions of God's active *śakti* whereas in the former case this *śakti* is totally inactive; in that sense the two Vāsudevas are one and the same. In the case of the Vibhava deities, the same *śakti* actively manifests them using only a fraction of her full potency. The choice of the deity depends on the nature of one's initiation, and that again depends on the aspirant's spiritual and intellectual development.

7.1

There are three hierarchically arranged forms of initiation: *vaibhava, vyūha,* and *brahma* initiation, the last being the most significant one (SS 19, 169-179). The *sādhaka* receives from his preceptor a prolonged and detailed training in the ritual acts, but also is initiated into the technique of yogic meditation and the method of *prāṇāyāma* with the central *nāḍī*. At one's initiation one's *tattvaśuddhi* is thorough. The disciple receives practical instruction as the ritual of initiation proceeds, and the guru performs the purification of his psychophysical system, treating it as a microcosm; this is called the *purification* of the initiant's six *adhvans*. This ritual then is followed by the disciple every time he ritually worships his god, in the rite of *bhūtaśuddhi* (SS 18, 113-171, 185-196, 201-210; 19, 48-56, 69, 81, 94-125). After that, the guru carefully teaches the disciple the concepts underlying the system of the *adhvans* and how to distribute the basic dichotomy of cognition and its content over them. The guru also teaches the disciple their relative value: which are pure and hence to be accepted and which impure and so to be shunned (SS 19, 126-149). The guru further teaches him the mystery of God and His *śakti* and his own relationship with both.

7.2

When the disciple by long and intelligent practice acquires perfection both in performing the rites and understanding the ideology behind them, the guru performs the consecration ceremony to impart complete authority to perform rituals with all sectarian mantras. I have used the term *sādhaka* in a general meaning. In the Tantras it bears a narrower technical meaning. A *sādhaka* is the practitioner who follows the ritual duties and sādhanā for his own perfection only (SS 22, 42-46). Others possessing the same qualifications but having a more compassionate disposition are trained by the guru to become religious teachers (*ācārya*).[5]

Notes

1. Every mantra has a mantra form (*mūrti*), which generally is anthropomorphic. As said earlier, each mantra emanating from the category speech (*vāc*) has a referent form; the primary mantra is that of the *para* (transcendent) Vāsudeva and refers to His form that is made of *śakti*'s six *kalās*. The essence of this mantra form is the transcendent consciousness (*cit* or *jñāna*), whereas other parts are constituted by other *kalās*. For the ritual of *nyāsa*, the mantra needs to be concretized by means of a series of five or six mantras known as *pada* or *aṅga* mantras, depicting various parts or limbs of the mantra deity's body. These are *hṛdaya* ('heart, essence'), *śiras* ('head'), *śikhā* ('topknot'), *kavaca* ('armor, torso'), and *netra* ('eyes').

These then are equated with the six *kalās: jñāna, aiśvarya,* etc. The subsidiary mantras are constructed by breaking the main mantra into six parts (*pada*) and adding to each part one *aṅga* and one *kalā.* In this way a concrete mantra body is imagined. The process is known as *sakalīkaraṇa,* or making a composite mantra body.

2. A Pāñcarātra sādhaka divides his ritual day into five parts: *abhigamana* (early morning rites), *upādāna* (acquiring and making ready all the ingredients for the ritual worship of his mantra deity), *ijyā* (ritual worship, in eight parts), *svādhyāya* (often means just singing *stotra* etc.), and finally *yoga.* JS 22, 68-74.

3. *Sthitiṃ brāhmīṃ svānandāṃ spandalakṣaṇām,* SS 3, 15. The PS introduces four *śaktis, prāṇa, icchā, śabda,* and *kalā,* belonging to the Vyūhas. In another place, PS calls them *jñāna, kriyā, icchā,* and *prāṇa.* It is possible that PS equates *jñāna* with *śabda* and *kriyā* with *kāla.* But PS also mentions a list of five śaktis: *kāla, jñāna, kriyā, icchā,* and *prāṇa,* which God used as medium of His creation (33, verse 19, 117, 140).

4. His description and analysis of the worship of Tārā are very useful for a general understanding of ritual worship of Indian deities (S. Beyer, *The Cult of Tārā, Magic and Ritual in Tibet,* Berkeley, 1973).

5. I have used three Pāñcarātra texts quite extensively. These are the SS, JS, and PS. I am fully aware that they represent three different traditions within the system. I needed to consult all three of them alongside some late texts to get a systematic picture of the general ritual and conceptual tenets of the sect. These are quite constant in all separate traditions within the Pāñcarātra.

Chapter Seven

Pāśupata Studies (1)

Minoru Hara

Those who read the Pañcārthabhāṣya, which was written by Kauṇḍinya as a commentary to the Pāśupata-sūtra, may soon be aware that the text is replete with the concepts and terminology peculiar to the Sāṃkhya school of philosophy. Because the Pāśupata-sūtra was primarily a manual of the rituals peculiar to Pāśupata Śaivism, it was the task of Kauṇḍinya to reinforce the sūtras philosophically as well as theologically, so that the Pāśupata school of Śaivism might be well furnished with philosophical foundations. Although the date of Kauṇḍinya is still uncertain, the main source he used for the philosophical foundation obviously was from the Sāṃkhya school of thought, though we meet occasionally the concepts of Nyāya as well as Vaiśeṣika.

However, it is not an easy task to determine the date of Kauṇḍinya on the basis of his reference to the Sāṃkhya ideology. This is because the Sāṃkhya philosophy itself had a long history before it took the final form in the Sāṃkhya-kārikā of Īśvarakṛṣṇa, as has been elucidated by E. Frauwallner.[1] Again, as is clearly outlined by M. Hulin,[2] some Sāṃkhya terminology even is traced back to the Vedic literature, especially Upaniṣadic texts such as Kāṭhaka, Śvetāśvatara, and Praśna. The doctrines are further formulated in the Mokṣadharma-parvan of the Mahābhārata and systematized by such philosophers as Pañcaśikha and Vṛṣagaṇa. Again, in the Purāṇic and Tantric literature we often come across amorphic doctrines tinged with the Sāṃkhya philosophy in its vulgar form.

Under such circumstances, it would be mere nonsense if one were to pick up some Sāṃkhyaic elements from a particular text like the Pañcārthabhāṣya, and compare them with those found in the Sāṃkhya-kārikā to determine the historical priority and posteriority of the texts concerned. One should be always aware of the fact that many of the Sāṃkhya concepts and terminology have their own history with regard to their origin and development.

Yet, it is a stimulating task for a Pāśupata student to bring to light some Sāṃkhyaic elements that are scattered throughout the Pañcārthabhāṣya[3] and present them along with an English translation to the attention of the specialists of Indian philosophy for further comparative study.

Without entering into detailed discussion, in the following pages we shall elucidate several points from Kauṇḍinya's commentary on the first sūtra of the Pāśupata-sūtra. First, we shall discuss a verse quoted therein, which describes the qualifications of the Pāśupata novice to be initiated, and try to trace it in the Sāṃkhya treatises. Second, we shall investigate the idea of the Pāśupata yoga and compare the concept of *saṃyoga* therein expounded by Kauṇḍinya, with that illustrated in the Sāṃkhya and Vaiśeṣika treatises. And finally, we shall elucidate the Pāśupata theory of cognition (*pramāṇa*), especially the threefold inference (*anumāna*), and compare it with those mentioned in the philosophical treatises.

1

The Pāśupata-sūtra begins with the word *athātaḥ* ('now, therefore')[4] as is the case with the Brahma-sūtra,[5] Mīmāṃsā-sūtra,[6] and Vaiśeṣika-sūtra.[7] According to Kauṇḍinya, the second word, *ataḥ*, presupposes the presence of a pupil (*śiṣya*) to be initiated by the teacher (*ācārya*).[8] Though there remains a problem of attribution with regard to the first four sūtras of Kaṇāda,[9] this interpretation of Kauṇḍinya finds its parallel in the commentary on the Vaiśeṣika-sūtra 1.1.1 by Candrānanda who, unlike Śaṅkara and Śabarasvāmin, understood the word *ataḥ* as indicating the presence of a pupil.[10] Then, Kauṇḍinya proceeds to define the Pāśupata *śiṣya* (pupils) as well as the Pāśupata *ācārya* (teachers), the foremost among whom, of course, is the god Śiva himself. Now, in the enumeration of the qualifications of the pupil to be initiated to the Pāśupata order, Kauṇḍinya quotes a verse, the identification of which will constitute the main discussion of this section. We shall present here the relevant passages with an English translation.

tathā brāhmaṇa-grahaṇāt, strī-pratiṣedhād, indriya-jayopadeśāc ca uktaṃ hi,

> *bādhiryam āndhyam aghratvaṃ mūkatā jaḍatā tathā /*
> *unmādaḥ kauṇyaṃ kuṣṭhitvaṃ klaibyaṃ gudāvarta-paṅgutā //*

[*evam-*]*ādi-rahitaḥ paṭv-indriyo brāhmaṇaḥ śiṣyaḥ* (p. 3, lines 4-8)

> In like wise, the pupil [is established here in the Pāśupata scripture], because of the scriptural statement that [he must be] a Brahmin (PS.4.20), the prohibition [for him to address himself to] women (PS.1.13) and the specific mention of victory over the bodily organs (PS. 5.7.). For it is said, "Deafness, blindness, inability to smell, dumbness, numbness, madness, malformation of the arm, leprosy, impotence, obstruction of the bowls and lameness.' The pupil [to be initiated to the Pāśupata order] must be free from such defects as enumerated above and must be a Brahmin possessed of keen senses.

The first three compounded expressions (*brāhmaṇa,*[11] *strī-pratiṣedha,*[12] *indriya-jaya*)[13] are quotations from the Pāśupata-sūtra. It is a common practice of Kauṇḍinya throughout the whole of the Pañcārthabhāṣya, to quote passages from the Pāśupata-sūtra with the intention of authorizing his own statement. Apart from this, the portion that remains presents no difficulty.

The verse quoted here by Kauṇḍinya that enumerates the eleven types of physical deficiencies reminds us of the *ekādaśendriya-vadha* as mentioned in Sāṃkhya-kārikā 49. We shall see later how the commentators of Kārikā 49 define the eleven types of *indriya-vadha* and ascertain whether there is quoted a verse comparable to ours.

First, we shall examine Gauḍapāda and Māṭhara who explain the eleven *indriya-vadha* in prose form. As the meaning is clear enough, we quote here only the Sanskrit texts.

1 *tatraikādeśendriya-vadhā bādhiryam andhatā prasuptir upajihvikā ghrāṇapāko mūkatā kuṇitvaṃ khāñjyaṃ gudāvartaḥ klaibyam unmāda iti.*
(Gauḍapāda-bhāṣya p. 60, lines 17-20)

2 *ekādaśendriya-vadhāḥ āndhya-bādhirya-ghrāṇapāka-jaḍatva-kuṣṭhatva-mūkatva-kuṇitva-paṅgutva-gudāvarta-klaibyonmāda ity . . .*
(Māṭhara-vṛtti p. 65, lines 14-15)

Among the remaining several commentaries, only the following three quote the verse. We shall list them one after the other.

3 *ekādaśendriya-vadhā* iti . . .
bādhiryam āndhyam ajighratvaṃ mūkatā jaḍatā tathā /
unmāda-kauṇya-kuṣṭhitva-klaivyodāvarta-paṅgutāḥ //

evam ekādaśānām indriyāṇām ekādaśendriya-vadhāḥ
(Sāṃkhya-saptati-vṛtti, p. 63, lines 5-10)

4 *ekādaśendriya-vadhā:*

> *bādhiryaṃ kuṣṭitāndhatvaṃ jaḍatājighratā tathā /*
> *mūkatā kauṇya-paṅgutvaṃ klaibyodāvartamandatāḥ //*

yathā-saṃkhyam indriyāṇāṃ śrotrādīnām
(Tattvakaumudī p. 154, lines 27-30)

5 *tad yathā,*

> *bādhiryam āndhyam aghratvaṃ mūkatā jaḍatā ca yā /*
> *unmāda-kauṣṭhya-kauṇyāni klaivyodāvarta-paṅgutāḥ //*

tatra bādhiryaṃ śrotrasya, āndhyaṃ cakṣuṣaḥ . . .
(Yuktidīpikā p. 129, lines 14-17)[14]

In addition to the difference in the manner of presentation, that is, either in prose or in verse from, we notice here also divergences in the appellation of particular diseases. Gauḍapāda, for example, has *upajihvikā* (inability to taste) for *jaḍatā, khañjya* (lameness) for *paṅgutā,* and a peculiar word, namely, *prasupti,* which apparently corresponds to *kuṣṭhitva* (leprosy, the defect in *sparśa* or *tvac*).[15] Furthermore, the order of enumerating these eleven diseases varies from one text to the other. Among all these, we may say, the verse that is closest to our verse given by Kauṇḍinya is that of the Sāṃkhya-saptati-vṛtti and the Yuktidīpikā.

Though the context is quite different, that is to say, the one in describing the qualifications of the pupil (*śiṣya*) to be initiated and the other in enumerating the kinds of physical deficiencies (*indriya-vadha*), all the same it is obvious that these verses derive from the same origin, not to speak of the borrowing from each other.

2

Unlike the ordinary definitions given in the other systems of thought, Kauṇḍinya understands by the technical term *yoga* the contact (*saṃyoga*) between the individual soul (*ātman*) and God (*īśvara*).[16] But, it is in his explanation of *yoga* that we have some parallels of the Pāśupata concept of *saṃyoga* with that expounded in the Sāṃkhya commentaries. For the sake of comparison, let us see first Kauṇḍinya's statement.

> *atrātmeśvara-saṃyogo yogaḥ / sa punaḥ puruṣasyādhyayanādi-naimittikatvād anyatara-karmajaḥ sthāṇu-śyenavat/ codanādhyaya-nādi-vacanād meṣavad ubhaya-karmajaḥ.* (p. 6, lines 8-10)

> Here *yoga* means contact of the individual soul and God. This contact, again, inasmuch as it may be due to a man's repetition of the scripture[17] etc., may be born of the action of only one of the two [uniting factors], like the contact of a hawk with his perch.[18] Or, because [we have scriptural authority] of God's propulsion[19] [as well as of] man's repetition[21] etc., it may be born of the action of both, like the contact of two [fighting] rams.

In the Sāṃkhya-kārikā the word *saṃyoga* appears in connection with the well-known contact between *puruṣa* and *prakṛti* (20 and 21). In commenting on the Kārikā, the commentators expatiate the concept of *saṃyoga*, while differentiating it into several categories like *saṃyogaja*, *svābhāvika*, *śaktihetuka*, and *yādṛcchika* in addition to the previously mentioned two. We need not dwell on the details, but shall examine how these Sāṃkhya commentators understood the *anyatara-karmaja-* and *ubhaya-karmaja* types of *saṃyoga*. Among the commentaries on the Kārikā, only the Māṭhara-vṛtti, Yuktidīpikā, and the Sāṃkhya-saptati-vṛtti are to be considered here for comparison.[21]

> *anyatara-karmajo yathā sthāṇu-śyenayoḥ.* (Māṭhara-vṛtti, p. 34, lines 15-16)

> *puruṣasya hi guṇānāṃ ca saṃyogaḥ parikalpyamāno 'nyatara-karmajo vā parikalpyate yathā sthāṇu-śyenayoḥ, ubhaya-karmajo vā yathā meṣayoḥ.* (Yuktidīpikā, p. 88, lines 3-5)

> *kasmād yathā (anyatara-karmataḥ) śyena-sthāṇvoḥ / ubhaya-karmato yathā śyenayoḥ.* (Sāṃkhya-saptati-vṛtti, p. 35, lines 25-27)

In these three quotations we notice that the Māṭhara-vṛtti gives only the example of the *anyatara-karmaja* (hawk and perch), whereas the other two have both the *anyatara-karmaja* and the *ubhaya-karmaja*. In the illustration of the *ubhaya-karmaja*, the Yuktidīpikā has *meṣa* (fighting rams), but the Sāṃkhya-saptati-vṛtti has *śyena*. From the viewpoint of Kauṇḍinya's illustration, we may say that the examples given in the Yuktidīpikā are closest to that of Kauṇḍinya.

It was due to F. A. Schultz's service that the concept of Pāśupata *saṃyoga* was first brought to the attention of scholars of Indian philosophy. He compared our passage with Praśastapāda's definition of *saṃyoga*, which is classified as one of the Vaiśeṣika *guṇas*.[22] As has been shown by him, Praśastapāda divided *saṃyoga* into the following three categories, *anyatara-karmaja*, *ubhaya-karmaja*, and *saṃyogaja*, and illustrated the first two as follows: *tatrānyatara-karmajaḥ kriyāvatā niṣkriyasya, yathā sthāṇoḥ śyenena, vibhūnāṃ ca mūrtaiḥ / ubhaya-karmajo viruddha-dik-kriyayoḥ saṃnipātaḥ, yathā mallayor meṣayor vā* (Praśastapādabhāṣya pp. 348-350).

We have here the example of hawk and perch (*sthāṇu* and *śyena*) as the illustration of *anyatara-karmaja* and that of (fighting) rams (*meṣa*) for the illustration of *ubhaya-karmaja*. Because Candrānanda's commentary on the Vaiśeṣika-sūtra appeared after the contribution of F. A. Schultz, it would be worth while to quote here its relevant portions: *anyatara-karmajaḥ saṃyogaḥ śyenasyopasarpaṇa-karmaṇā sthāṇunā / mallayor upasarpaṇād ubhayajaḥ* (Candrānanda on Vaiśeṣika-sūtra 7.2.10) and *anyatara-karmajo vibhāgaḥ śyenasyāpasarpaṇāt / ubhaya-karmajo meṣayor apasarpaṇāt* (7.2.11). Here we notice that Candrānanda uses for the illustration of *ubhaya-karmaja* two wrestlers (*malla*) in place of rams (*meṣa*, Kauṇḍinya and Yuktidīpikā) and hawks (*śyena*, Sāṃkhya-saptati-vṛtti), but he uses rams (*meṣa*) in the illustration of *vibhāga* in place of *saṃyoga*.

3.1

Next, we shall discuss the section in the Pañcārthabhāṣya dealing with the theory of cognition (*pramāṇa*). In the Pañcārthabhāṣya the *pramāṇa* theory is expounded in connection with the explanation of the prefix *vi-* of the word *vy-ā-khyā-syā-maḥ*, which appears in the first sūtra of the Pāśupata-sūtra. The texts reads as follows,

> *atra viḥ vistare vibhāge viśeṣe ca bhavati / tatra vistara iti pratyakṣānumānāptavacanānīti pramāṇāny abhidhīyante.*
> (p. 6, line 24-p. 7, line 1)

> Here the prefix *vi-* is used in the sense of prolixity, separation, and distinction.[23] Under *prolixity* are included the valid instruments of knowledge (*pramāṇa*); that is, perception, inference, and authoritative statement.

Among these three *pramāṇa*s, the second, that is, *anumāna*, is further subdivided into two categories, (*viśeṣato?*) *dṛṣṭa* and *sāmānyato dṛṣṭa*, and the former again is subdivided into two categories, *pūrvavat* and *śeṣavat*. The defnitions are given in the text as follows,

> *tac ca dvividham, dṛṣṭaṃ sāmānyatodṛṣṭaṃ ca / tatra dṛṣṭam api dvividham, pūrvavac cheṣavac ca / tatra pūrva-dṛṣṭo 'yaṃ ṣaḍ-aṅgulīyakaḥ sa eveti pūrvavat / viṣāṇādi-mātra-darśanād gaur iti śeṣavat / sāmānyato-dṛṣṭaṃ apīha gati-pūrvikāṃ deśāntara-prāptiṃ dṛṣṭvā candrādityādi-*[24] *gati-prasiddhiḥ* (p. 7, lines 11-12)

> That [inference] is further of two sorts: *dṛṣṭa* (inference from what one has seen) and *sāmānyato-dṛṣṭa* (inference from similarity), of which *dṛṣṭa* again is of two sorts: *pūrvavat* (inference from what one has seen in the past) and *śeṣavat* (inference of the whole from a part). Of these the *pūrvavat* inference is such as "this man with six fingers has been seen [by me] before, [so] this is the same man." The *śeṣavat* inference is such as the knowledge "this is a cow" from the sight of only its horns. The *sāmānyato-dṛṣṭa* inference is such as after observing the fact in this world that the attaining of a new position is preceded by motion, one concludes that the moon and the sun are in motion.

This threefold inference, *pūrvavat, śeṣavat, sāmānyato-dṛṣṭa*, is familiar to specialists of Indian philosophy.[25] It is referred to without specification in Sāṃkhya-kārikā 4[26] and mentioned as such in Nyāya-sūtra 1.1.5[27] and others.[28] But the definitions and illustrations of these three kinds of inference given by the commentators of Sāṃkhya-kārikā 4 and Nyāya-sūtra 1.1.5 differ considerably from one to the other as has been fully illustrated recently by B. K. Matilal.[29] This is mainly because we have two ways of interpreting the suffix *-vat* in case of *pūrvavat* and *śeṣavat* according to Pāṇini 5.1.115 (*tena tulyam*) and 5.2.49 (*tad asya asti* and *tad asminn asti*). Thus, *pūrvavat* can be taken either in the sense of *pūrveṇa tulyam* or *pūrvam asya asti* and likewise *śeṣavat* either *śeṣeṇa tulyam* or *śeṣam asya asti*. The most common illustration of *pūrvavat* given by commentators is to infer rain (in the future as the effect) from the advent of a rain cloud (in the present as the cause).[30] The illustration given by Kauṇḍinya, then, is based on *pūrvavat* interpreted by Pāṇini 5.1.115 (*pūrveṇa tulyam*). It was A. Wezler, however, who brought this point to clarity, and in this connection he quotes an illustration of *pūrvavat* as found in the Upāya-hṛdaya (= Prayoga-sāra),[31] which can be compared to that of Kauṇḍinya as given in our translation.[32] The unique example of a man with six fingers is met with here in the Upāya-hṛdaya, which is preserved only in Chinese, although the wording is not exactly the same. A Sanskrit text reconstructed by G. Tucci reads as follows,

> *yathā ṣaḍ-aṅguliṃ sapiḍaka-mūrdhānaṃ bālaṃ dṛṣṭvā paścād vṛddhaṃ bahuśrutaṃ devadattaṃ dṛṣṭvā ṣaḍ-aṅguli-smaraṇāt so 'yam iti pūrvavat* (Upāya-hṛdaya, p. 13, lines 21-23).[33]

Previously one saw a boy with six fingers and pustulous head and later he saw Devadatta full grown and learned.

> With these sights [in past and present] and from the remembrance of six fingers, he infers the man being the same. Such is the *pūrvavat* type of inference.

To the best of my knowledge, we find no other example of the man with six fingers for the illustration of *pūrvavat* beside these two.[34] Yet, if we compare them, we notice that the explanation of Kauṇḍinya is much simpler than that of the Upāya-hṛdaya, which has *sapiḍaka-mūrdhan* in addition to the *ṣaḍ-aṅguli.* If the simplicity indicates a historical priority, we may say that Kauṇḍinya is prior historically to the author of the Upāya-hṛdaya (Prayoga-sāra), who knew this older type of *pūrvavat* inference.[35]

The illustration of Kauṇḍinya concerning *śeṣavat* also is unique. The most common definition of the *śeṣavat* type of inference is to infer the cause from the effect. Thus, the Caraka-saṃhitā[36] and the Yuktidīpikā[37] give an example of the parents' copulation (the cause) from the birth of a body (the effect), and we have in the Nyāya-bhāṣya an example of inferring the rainfall up the river (the cause) from the sight of abundant water (the effect).[38] As regards an example based on the interpretation of *śeṣeṇa tulyam,* we come across it in the Upāya-hṛdaya[39] and in the Māṭharavṛtti,[40] which present an example of inferring the saltiness of the ocean from tasting a drop of its water. A similar example is given by Gauḍapāda,[41] but Piṅgalākṣa presents an example of a different sort.[42] All these examples, however, agree in illustrating an inference from the part (drop) of the remaining whole (the ocean), which is comparable to Kauṇḍinya's example of inferring the cow (the whole) from its part (the horn). This example of Kauṇḍinya, however, has no parallel in Buddhist, Sāṃkhya, and Nyāya treatises, but rather reminds us of a passage of the Mahābhāṣya, which deals with a definition of cow.[43] In reality, however, an example of *śeṣavat,* which is comparable to that of our author, is found in the Praśastapāda-bhāṣya, the relevant portion of which reads as follows: *tatra dṛṣṭaṃ prasiddha-sādhyayor atyanta-jāty-abhede 'numānam / yathā gavy eva sāsna-mātram upalabhya deśāntare 'pi sāsna-mātra-darśanāt gavi pratipattiḥ.*[44] The terms indicative of cow's parts are known to the Vaiśeṣika-sūtras themselves,[45] but here again we notice that Kauṇḍinya's explanation is much simplier than that of Praśastapāda. Again, if the solar movement is a naive example of reasoning as we have in Kauṇḍinya's illustration of *sāmānyato dṛṣṭa,*[46] this simplicity and naiveté also may indicate the historical priority of Kauṇḍinya to the philosophical writers, at least to Praśastapāda, as has been pointed out by other scholars of Indian philosophy.[47]

3.2

The reader of the Pañcārthabhāṣya is puzzled by Kauṇḍinya's abrupt reference to *prastha* in the midst of his explanation of *ātma-pratyakṣa*. The relevant portion of the text reads as follows,

> *ātma-pratyakṣaṃ tad-upahāra-kṛtsnatapo-duḥkhāntādi-vacanāt siddham / yathā prasthena mito vrīhiḥ prasthaḥ*
> (p. 7, lines 4-6)

> Self-perception is proved by [the scriptural reference to] the offering of oneself (PS.1.8), the [aspirant] full of asceticism (PS. 3.19), and the end of suffering (PS. 5.40), and so forth, just as rice that is measured by bushel measure is called a *bushel.*

One may suspect that here the text is corrupt, for the phrase led by *yathā* does not fit in the context and may be better placed a few lines earlier, where *pramāṇa, pramāpayitṛ, pramātṛ, prameya,* and *pramiti* are successively expounded (p. 7, lines 19-21). However, those who are familiar with Sāṃkhya treatises may soon be reminded by this example of *prastha* of the statements of commentators on the Sāṃkhya-kārikā 4 (*prameya-siddhiḥ pramāṇād dhi*). Yuktidīpikā, for example, reads as follows:

> *etasmāt prameya-siddhir ity avagantavyam / kasmāt? / vrīhy-ādivat / yathā vrīhy-ādi-prameyaṃ prasthādinā pramāṇena paricchidyate evam ihāpi vyaktādi-prameyaṃ pratyakṣādi-pramāṇena paricchidyata iti.*
> (Yuktidīpikā p. 29, line 31-p. 30, line 1)

> From this one should understand the words *prameya-siddhi* [of the Kārikā]. How? As in the case of rice and so forth. Just as the object of measurement such as rice is fixed accurately by such measurement as *prastha*, so too here the object of measurement [the valid means of cognition] such as the manifested is defined accurately by such measurement as direct perception.

Gauḍapāda and Māṭhara also speak of the same purport. Here only the text is given *iha loke prameya-vastu pramāṇena sādhyate / yathā prasthādibhir vrīhayas tulayā candanādi* (Gauḍapāda-bhāṣya p. 7, lines 6-8) and *tena pramāṇena kiṃ sādhyam ity āha—prameya-siddhiḥ pramāṇād dhi / yasmāt prameyaṃ sakalaṃ pramāṇena pramīyate, yathā tulayā candanādi, karṣādinā ghṛtādi, prasthādinā vā vrīhya-ādity-ādivat* (Māṭharavṛtti p. 12, lines 1-4). Here are illustrated the unit of volume or weight (*prastha, karṣa, tulā*) as the standard for the objects to be measured (*vrīhi, ghṛta, candana*), as *pramāṇa* for *prameya*. Here, again, Kauṇḍinya's statement is much simpler than those of the Sāṃkhya commentators.[48]

3.3

As we have seen, the number of the *pramāṇas* approved in the Pañcārthabhāṣya is three; viz., *pratyakṣa* (direct perception), *anumāna* (inference), and *āpta-vacana* (authoritative statement), which also is called *āgama*.[49] The triple division of *pramāṇa* is the same as that given in the Sāṃkhya-kārikā 4 (*trividhaṃ pramāṇam iṣṭam*). The commentators on the Kārikā expounded these three *pramāṇas* and rejected at the same time the *pramāṇas* other than these three, which were approved in the other systems of philosophy. These *pramāṇas*, disapproved here by the Sāṃkhya writers, often are said to be six in number, but sometimes four, seven, eight, or even ten.

Here in our Pañcārthabhāṣya the six *pramāṇas* other than the three (*pramāṇa-traya*) also are referred to, and Kauṇḍinya includes these six under the approved three.[50] The passage under question reads as follows:

> *eṣv evopamānārthāpatti-saṃbhavābhāvaitihya-pratibhādīnāṃ vyākhyāyamānānām antarbhāvaḥ / evam etāni trīṇi pramāṇāni.* (p. 7, lines 18-19)

> Other means of knowledge described [in other systems] such as identification (*upamāṇa*), implication (*arthāpatti*), possibility (*saṃbhava*), absence (*abhāva*), traditional history (*aitihya*), and intuition (*pratibhā*) are included in these [three valid means of cognition]. Thus, these three are the valid means of cognition (*pramāṇa*).

Among these six *pramāṇas*, the following five, *upamāna, aitihya, arthāpatti, saṃbhava*, and *abhāva*, are mentioned in the Nyāya-sūtras 1.1.3, 6 and 2.2.1, where *upamāna* is approved as a valid means of cognition (1.1.3 and 6), and the remaining four are rejected (2.2.1ff.). The last, that is, *pratibhā*, does not appear in the philosophical sūtras.[51] We have its negative form *apratibhā* only in Nyāya-sūtra 5.2.1 and 18.

Yet, we come across these six in the commentaries on the Sāṃkhya-kārikā. Not only the enumeration of these six *pramāṇas*, but also the inclusion of these into the orthodox three (*pramāṇa-traya*) is discussed in full detail especially in the Yuktidīpikā.[52] However, here for brevity's sake, we shall quote the passages from the Māṭharavṛtti and the Gauḍapāda-bhāṣya: *nanv arthāpattiḥ saṃbhavo 'bhāvaḥ pratibhā aitihyam upamānaṃ ceti prabhṛtīni santi bahūni pramāṇāntarāṇi katham atra trividhaṃ pramāṇam iti saṃgatiḥ / . . . / sarvāṇi hi pramāṇāni pramāṇa-traye 'viruddhāni* (Māṭharavṛtti, p. 11, lines 6-9). Although the order of enumeration is different, *upamāna* being enumerated last here, the names of the six *pramāṇas* are exactly the same as those in the Pañcārthabhāṣya. Similarly, Gauḍapāda enumerates these six and attributes them to Jaimini: *eteṣu pramāṇeṣu sarva-pramāṇāni siddhāni bhavanti / ṣaṭ pramāṇāni jaiminiḥ / atha kāni tāni pramāṇāni / arthāpattiḥ saṃbhavo 'bhāvaḥ pratibhaitihyam upamānaṃ ceti ṣaṭ pramāṇāni* (Gauḍapāda-bhāṣya p. 8, lines 3-8).

As mentioned earlier, the Yuktidīpikā refers to those who hold four, six, and nine *pramāṇas*[53] and Sāṃkhya-vṛtti speaks of a group of people who advocate seven *pramāṇas.*[54] In the Sāṃkhya-saptati-vṛtti we also have four, six, eight, and ten *pramāṇas.*[55] All these Sāṃkhya commentators are busily engaged in the discussion, thereby revealing the reasons why the number of their *pramāṇas* is no more than three.

Compared with the exposition of these Sāṃkhya commentators, Kauṇḍinya's account is very simple, because he says only that these six are included in the approved three without further discussion, regarding details. The simplicity here again would indicate the historical priority of Kauṇḍinya to these Sāṃkhya commentators. But a more important question would be, Since when are these six mentioned together? If this question could be answered satisfactorily, then we would be in a better position to speak of the date of Kauṇḍinya. But at the present stage of our research, we cannot say anything definite concerning this problem.

4

All the problems discussed here bring to light the following points. The Pañcārthabhāṣya of Kauṇḍinya being replete with the concepts and terminology peculiar to the Sāṃkhya philosophy, Pāśupata Śaivism then would owe its philosophical foundation to some variety of Sāṃkhya philosophy, not to speak of the orthodox Sāṃkhya school of thought.

Yet, when we compare the parallels found both in Sāṃkhya treatises and the Pañcārthabhāṣya, we receive the impression that the latter is simpler and more primitive in shape than the former. We come across the case where the same concepts are simply referred to by Kauṇḍinya, whereas they are discussed fully in detail by the authors of the Sāṃkhya treatises. Sometimes the parallels are found in completely different contexts. The eleven defects of sense organs (*indriya-vadha*) enumerated in Sāṃkhya-kārikā 49 are dealt with by Kauṇḍinya in the context of enumerating the qualifications of pupils to be initiated to the Pāśupata order. Kauṇḍinya's treatment and illustration of the three kinds of inference (*anumāna*) also are different from those of Sāṃkhya authors. The examples given there seem to indicate an early stage of the philosophical speculation, as represented by the Upāyahṛdaya (Prayogasāra) and others.[56] It is hardly possible to imagine that Kauṇḍinya borrowed his statements from the Sāṃkhya or Nyāya-Vaiśeṣika treatises that we possess now. Possibly, we may postulate some sources that now are lost, from which Kauṇḍinya as well as the authors of these philosophical treatises may have derived their material. Presumably, Kauṇḍinya and these authors used these common sources and developed their discussion independent of each other. In the future, we hope, we shall be able to elucidate some additional points to substantiate this hypothesis.

Notes

1. Frauwallner (1953), pp. 275ff.

2. Hulin (1978), pp. 128ff.

3. See Hara (1973).

4. *Athātaḥ paśupateḥ pāśupataṃ yoga-vidhiṃ vyākhyāsyāmaḥ* (PS.1.1).

5. *Athāto brahma-jijñāsā* (Brahma-sūtra 1.1.1.).

6. *Athāto dharma-jijñāsā* (Mīmāṃsā-sūtra 1.1.1.).

7. *Athāto dharmaṃ vyākhyāsyāmaḥ* (Vaiśeṣika-sūtra 1.1.1). We have a similar opening in Mahābhāṣya (*atha śabdānuśāsanam*) and in Yoga-sūtra (*atha yogānuśāsanam*), but these lack the word *ataḥ*.

8. *Atha-śabdātaḥ-śabda-vyākhyāna-vacana-snānaśayanādy-upadeśāc ca śiṣyācāryayoḥ prasiddhiḥ* (p. 2, lines 18-20). *Atra ataḥ-śabdaḥ śiṣya-guṇa-vacane / . . . / pūrvaṃ cātrārthato 'taḥ-śabdo draṣṭavyaḥ* (p. 4, lines 15-19). *Yāvad ayam ācāryo gṛhasthādibhyo 'bhyāgataṃ pūrvam ataḥ-śabdāt parīkṣitam brāhmaṇam* . . . (p. 8, lines 5ff.). As regards the problem of the Pāśupata novice to be initiated being necessarily of Brahmin caste, see Hara (1964).

9. Cf. Frauwallner (1984), pp. 35-41. For a further discussion, one must refer to Wezler (1982), pp. 669ff.

10. *Ataḥ-śabdo 'pi vairāgya-prajñā-kathā-paripākādikaṃ śiṣya-guṇa-saṃpadaṃ hetutvenāpadiśati, yasmād ayaṃ śiṣyo guṇa-saṃpadā yuktas tato 'smai praśnebhyo 'nantaraṃ dharmaṃ vyākhyāsyāmaḥ* (Candrānanda on Vaiśeṣika sūtra 1.1.1 (p. 1, lines 8-10). It should be noted here also that Candrānanda has an explanation comparable to that of Kauṇḍinya in their first sūtras.

11. PS. 4.20: na kaś cid brāhmaṇaḥ punar āvartate.

12. PS. 1.13: strī-śūdraṃ nābhibhāṣet.

13. PS. 5. 7: indriyāṇām abhijayāt.

14. The original Sanskrit text of Svarṇa-saptati apparently has no verse. Cf. Taisho 54, p. 1257a, and Takakusu (1904), pp. 1035-36.

15. Cf. Esnoul (1964), p. 103.

16. *Atrātmeśvara-saṃyogo yogaḥ* (p. 6, lines 8-9). See also p. 41, line 13 (*atrātmeśvara-saṃyogo yogaḥ pratyetavyaḥ*); p. 110, line 19 (*atra yogo nāma—ātmeśvara-saṃyogo yogaḥ pratyetavyaḥ*); p. 118, line 2 (*ātmeśvara-saṃyogo yogaḥ*); p. 122, line 1 (*atra yogo nāmātmeśvarayor yogaḥ*); p. 124, lines 9-10 (*ātmeśvara-saṃyogo yoga iti mantavyaḥ*).

17. PS. 5.12 (*ṛcam iṣṭām adhīyīta gāyatrīm ātma-yantritaḥ*).

18. See also PABh. p. 111, line 8 (*vṛkṣa-śakunivat*).

19. PS. 4.24 (*tan no rudraḥ pracodayāt*).

20. See above note 17.

21. We have no explanation comparable to that of Kauṇḍinya in Gauḍapāda-bhāṣya, Tattvakaumudī, and Sāṃkhya-vṛtti. Nor have we a detailed discussion on *saṃyoga* in the Chinese version of the Svarṇa-saptati (Takakusu 1904, pp. 1005-7).

22. Schultz (1958), pp. 138-140.

23. Here *viśeṣa* is one of the viewpoints for explication that Kauṇḍinya often refers to together with *samāsa, vistara, vibhāga, upasaṃhāra,* and *nigamana.*

24. The printed edition reads here *cāsyādityādi,* but the text should be emended as we read here (p. 7, line 19).

25. For detailed discussion see Oberhammer (1965), Wezler

(1969a), Schuster (1972), Hara (1974), p. 60, and Matilal (1985), pp. 29-42.

26. *Trividhaṃ pramāṇam iṣṭam* (Sāṃkhya-kārikā 4 c).

27. *Atha tat pūrvakaṃ trividham anumānaṃ pūrvavac cheṣavat sāmānyato dṛṣṭaṃ ca* (Nyāya-sūtra 1.1.5).

28. See also Nyāya-sūtra 2.1.37 and 38.

29. Matilal (1985) pp. 29-42. I owe this reference to M. Hattori.

30. *Pūrvavat iti / yatra kāraṇena kāryam anumīyate yathā meghonnatyā bhaviṣyati vṛṣṭir iti* (ASS. 91, p. 20, lines 3-4).

31. Wezler (1969b), pp. 837 ff.

32. See Schuster (1972) p. 380.

33. See also *Taisho*, vol. 32, p. 25.

34. Those scholars who noticed this illustration in the past are Ui (1925) (pp. 519-524), Tucci (1929), Dasgupta (1955), p. 133, Oberhammer (1963), p. 98, Wezler (1969a), p. 199, Schuster (1972), p. 380, Matilal (1985), p. 30. Cf. Hara (1974), p. 60.

35. See Wezler (1969b), pp. 840 ff.

36. *Pratyakṣa-pūrvaṃ trividhaṃ trikālaṃ cānumīyate /*
vahnir nigūḍho dhūmena maithunaṃ garbha-darśanāt //
(Carakasaṃhitā 1.11.21).

37. *Tad yathā kumārakaṃ dṛṣṭvā dvaya-samāpattim* (Yuktidīpikā p. 38, line 15).

38. *Śeṣavat tat, yatra kāryeṇa kāraṇam anumīyate / pūrvodaka-viparītam udakaṃ nadyāḥ pūrṇatvaṃ śīghratvaṃ ca dṛṣṭvā srotaso 'numīyate bhūtā vṛṣṭir iti,* Nyāya-bhāṣya 1.1.5 (ASS. 91, p. 20, lines 4-6).

39. *Śeṣavat yathā, sāgara-salilaṃ pītvā tal-lavaṇa-rasam anubhūya śeṣam api salilaṃ tulyam eva lavaṇam iti* (Upāya-hṛdaya pp. 13-14).

40. *Śeṣavad yathā, samudrodaka-binduṃ prāśya śeṣasya lavaṇa-bhāvo 'numīyate iti śeṣavat* (Māṭharavṛtti, p. 13, lines 5-6).

41. *Śeṣavad yathā / samudrād ekaṃ jalapalaṃ lavaṇam āsādya śeṣasyāpy asti lavaṇa-bhāva iti* (Gauḍapādabhāṣya p. 10, lines 11-12).

42. See Wezler (1969b), pp. 840-841.

43. *Atha gaur ity atra kaḥ śabdaḥ / kiṃ yat tat sāsnā-lāṅgūla-kakuda-khura-viṣāṇy-artha-rūpaṃ sa śabdaḥ* . . . (Mahābhāṣya, ed. F. Kielhorn, p. 1 lines 6-7).

44. Praśastapādabhāṣya, pp. 507-508. Cf. Schuster (1972), p. 373.

45. See Vaiśeṣika-sūtra 2.1.8 (*viṣāṇī kakudmān prāntevalādhiḥ sāsnāvān iti gotve dṛṣṭaṃ liṅgam*) and 3.1.12 (*viṣāṇī tasmād aśvo viṣāṇī tasmād gaur iti ca*).

46. See Schuster (1972), p. 362.

47. See G. Chemparathy (1965).

48. The same weight unit of *prastha* appears again in the discussion of *saṃbhava*, one of the six *pramāṇas* proposed by the other schools of philosophy, as is revealed in the commentaries on the Sāṃkhya-kārikā 4. Māṭhara, for example, says: "*prastha ity ukte catvāraḥ kuḍavā iti bodhaḥ saṃbhavaḥ*" (p. 11, line 11).

49. *Āgamo nāma ā maheśvarād guru-pāraṃparyāgataṃ śāstram / āgamo 'laukidādi-vyavahāra-hetur ācakṣitaḥ smṛtaḥ* (?) / *rudraḥ provāca-vacanāt siddhiḥ* (p. 7, lines 15-18).

50. See Schultz (1958), p. 16.

51. I refer to Honda (1954), p. 282. As regards *pratibhā* as *pramāṇa*, one may refer to Vākyapadīya 2.147 (ed. W. Rau, Wiesbaden 1977) and for *pratibhā* in general; cf. M. Hattori "Apoha and Pratibhā," *Sanskrit and Indian Studies* (D. H. H. Ingalls Festschrift, Dordrecht 1979): 71, note 9.

52. See Wezler (1974), p. 444.

53. Yuktidīpikā p. 31, line 23: (*tantrāntarīyāḥ kecit catvāri pramāṇānīcchanti*); line 23: (*tathā ṣaḍ ity anye*); line 27: (*etāni saṃbhavaitihya-ceṣṭa-sahitāni navety apare*).

54. Sāṃkhya-vṛtti p. 9, lines 7-9 (*evam etāni sapta pramāṇāni* . . .).

55. Sāṃkhya-saptati-vṛtti p. 11, lines 21-22 (*catvāri ṣaḍ aṣṭau daśa ca pramāṇānīcchanti*).

56. Cf. Frauwallner (1957), p. 5 (Das Upāyahṛdayam, einer der ältesten Versuche, die Dialektik auf buddhistischen Boden zu übertragen . . .) (= *Kleine Schriften* p. 719). Cf. also Wezler (1969b), p. 840.

Abbreviations

ASS	*Ānandāśrama Sanskrit Series* [Poona]
BEFEO	*Bulletin de l'école française d'extrême-orient* [Hanoi]
GOS	*Gaekwad's Oriental Series* [Baroda]
IIJ	*Indo-Iranian Journal* [The Hague and Dordrecht]
JIPh	*Journal of Indian Philosophy* [Dordrecht]
PS and *PABh*	*Pasupata Sutras with Pancharthabhashya of Kaundinya*, ed. R. A. Sastri, Trivandrum Sanskrit Series 143 (Trivandrum, 1940)
Taisho	*Taisho Shinshu Daizokyo* [Tokyo]
WZKS (O)	*Wiener Zeitschrift für die Kunde Süd[-und Ost]Asiens* [Wien]

Bibliography

Sanskrit Texts

Caraka-saṃhitā: *The Carakasaṃhitā by Agniveśa* (Nirnaya Sagar Press, 1941).

Gauḍapāda-bhāṣya: *Les strophes de Sāṃkhya (Sāmkhya-kārikā) avec le commentaire de Gauḍapāda, texte sanskrit et traduction annotée par A. M. Esnoul* (Paris, 1964).

Mahābhāṣya: *The Vyākaraṇa-Mahābhāṣya of Patañjali*, 3rd ed., ed. F. Kielhorn vol. 1 (Poona, 1962).

Māṭhara-vṛtti: *Māṭharavṛtti*, Chowkhamba Sanskrit Series 296 (Benares, 1922).

Nyāya-sūtra: *Śrī-gautama-muni-praṇīta-nyāya-sūtrāṇi*, ASS 91 (Poona, 1922).

Praśastāpadabhāṣya: *Praśastapādabhāṣyam*, Gangānāthajhā-Granthamālā 1 (Varanasi, 1977).

Sāṃkhya-saptati-vṛtti: *Sāṃkhya-saptati-vṛtti* (V), ed. E. Solomon (Ahmedabad, 1973).

Sāṃkhya-vṛtti: *Sāṃkhya-Vṛtti* (V), ed. E. Solomon (Ahmedabad, 1973).

Tattvakaumudī: *Vācaspatimiśras Tattvakaumudī, Ein Beitrag zur Text kritik bei kontaminierter Überlieferung von S. A. Srinivasan* (Hamburg, 1967).

Vaiśeṣikasūtra: *Vaiśeṣikasūtra of Kaṇāda with the Commentary of Candrānanda*, 2d ed., GOS. 136 (Baroda, 1982).

Yuktidīpikā: *Yuktidīpikā, An Ancient Commentary on the Sāmkhya-Kārikā of Īśvarakṛṣṇa*, ed. R. C. Pandeya (Delhi, 1967).

Studies

Chemparathy, G. 1965. "The Testimony of the Yuktidīpikā Concerning the Īśvara Doctrine of the Pāśupatas and Vaiśeṣikas," *WZKSO* 9: 119-146.

Dasgupta, S. 1955. *A History of Indian Philosophy*, vol. 5 (Cambridge).

Esnoul (1964): See Sanskrit texts, Gauḍapāda-bhāṣya.

Frauwallner, E. 1953. *Geschichte der indischen Philosophie*, 1 (Salzburg).

———. 1957. "Vasubandhu's Vādavidhiḥ," *WZKSO* 1: 104-146 (= *Kleine Schriften*, pp. 716-758).

———. 1984. "Der ursprüngliche Anfang der Vaiśeṣika Sūtren," *Nachgelassene Werke* 1, ed. E. Steinkellner (Wien), pp. 35-41.

Hara, M. 1964. "Pāśupata Kenkyū I," *Journal of Indian and Buddhist Studies* 12: 414-398 [in Japanese].

———. 1973. "Pāśupata and Sāṃkhya-Yoga," *Journal of Oriental Research* [Madras] 34-35: 76-87.

———. 1974. Review, *Pāśupata Sūtram with Pañcārtha-Bhāṣya of Kauṇḍinya*, trans. H. Chakroborti (1970), *IIJ* 16: 57-80.

Honda, M. 1954. "An Index to the Philosophical Sūtras," *Proceedings of the Okurayama Oriental Research Institute* 1: 306-344.

Hulin, M. 1978. *Sāṃkhya Literature*, A History of Indian Literature, vol. 6, Fasc. 3 (Wiesbaden).

Matilal, B. K. 1985. *Logic, Language and Reality* (Delhi).

Oberhammer, G. 1963. "Ein Beitrag zu den Vāda-traditionen Indiens," *WZKSO* 7: 63-103.

———. 1965. "Zur Deutung von Nyāyasūtram 1.1.5," *WZKSO* 10: 66-72.

Schultz, F. A. 1958. *Die philosophisch-theologischen Lehren des Pāśupata-Systems* (Walldorf-Hessen).

Schuster, N. 1972. "Inference in the Vaiśeṣikasūtras," *JIPh* 1: 341-395.

Takakusu, J. 1904. "La Sāṃkhyakārikā, étudiée à la lumière de sa version chinoise (II)," *BEFEO* 4: 978-1064.

Tucci, G. 1929. *Pre-Diṅnāga Buddhist Texts on Logic from Chinese Sources*, GOS 44 (Baroda).

Ui, H. 1925. *Indo Tetsugaku Kenkyū II* (Tokyo).

Wezler, A. 1969a. "Die 'dreifache' Schlussfolgerung im Nyāyasūtra 1.1.5," *IIJ* 11: 190-211.

———. 1969b. "Dignāga's Kritik an der Schlusslehre des Nyāya und die Deutung von Nyāyasūtra 1.1.5," *Zeitschrift der deutschen morgenländischen Gesellschaft* Supplementa I (Wiesbaden): 836-842.

———. 1974. "Some Observations on the Yuktidīpikā," *Zeitschrift der deutschen morgenländischen Gesellschaft*, Supplement II (Wiesbaden): 434-455.

———. 1982. "Remarks on the Definition of 'yoga' in the Vaiśeṣikasūtra," *Indological and Buddhist Studies* (Festschrift J. W. de Jong) (Canberra), pp. 643-686.

Chapter Eight

Tantric Meditation: Vocalic Beginnings

Paul E. Muller-Ortega

Introduction

This essay represents an attempt toward interpretation of one aspect of the world-view of the non-dual Śaivism of Kashmir.[1] It will approach notions of meditation on the continuous cosmogony as narrated by the sequence of sixteen Sanskrit vowels. By examining the profound symbolism inherent in this sequence, we gain access to a deep framework structure of the tantric meditational method as described by the tenth century Kashmiri master of Śaivism, Abhinavagupta.

Indological scholarship is often quite content to stay within the important but narrow boundaries of translation, description, and organization of knowledge. Yet it is clear that even within these activities, an implicit interpretive pattern is operative. It is not truly possible to be purely descriptive and postpone interpretation until a second moment. In this chapter a series of terms derived from a short work by quantum physicist David Bohm, *Wholeness and the Implicate Order,* will be juxtaposed with the fundamental cosmogonic myth of the non-dual Śaivism of Abhinavagupta.[2] Not only does Bohm's work detail a theory that displays an intriguing congruence with that of the non-dual Kashmiri Śaivites, but perhaps more important it opens up useful interpretive approaches to these matters. Bohm's terminology has been drawn into this analysis not because it is deemed that his scientific myth grants authenticity to the Śaivite myth nor because it is thought that Bohm and Abhinavagupta are saying the same thing. Bohm will be employed as an interpretive matrix that clarifies the understanding of Abhinavagupta. Nevertheless, it is not simply a question of importing Bohm's categories wholesale, but rather of allowing them to "relevate" certain aspects of the tantric world-view that would otherwise remain obscure.

In his book, Bohm makes a number of intriguing statements that will prove useful in our interpretation of Abhinavagupta. Bohm coins the neologism *holomovement* and describes it as follows:

> The new form of insight can perhaps best be called Undivided Wholeness in Flowing Movement. This view implies that flow is, in some sense, prior to that of 'things' that can be seen to form and dissolve in this flow. There is a universal flux that cannot be defined explicitly but which can be known only implicitly, as indicated by the explicitly definable forms and shapes, some stable and some unstable, that can be abstracted from the universal flux. In this flow, mind and matter are not separate substances. Rather, they are different aspects of one whole and unbroken movement.[3]

> To generalize so as to emphasize undivided wholeness, we shall say that what "carries" an implicate order is the holomovement, which is an unbroken and undivided totality. . . . Thus in its totality, the holomovement is not limited in any specifiable way at all. It is not required to conform to any particular order, or to be bounded by any particular measure. Thus, the holomovement is undefinable and immeasurable.[4]

Growing out these notions, Bohm proposes the terms *explicate* and *implicate* as useful in managing the unwieldy notion of the holomovement. He says:

> We propose that a new notion of order is involved here, which we call the implicate order (from a Latin root meaning 'to enfold' or to 'fold inward'). In terms of the implicate order one may say that everything is enfolded into everything. This contrasts with the explicate order now dominant in physics in which things are unfolded in the sense that each thing lies only in its own particular region of space (and time) and outside the regions belonging to other things.[5]

> Our basic proposal is then that what is is the holomovement and that everything is to be explained in terms of forms derived from this holomovement.[6]

Without entering into a detailed description of Bohm's theories, let us maintain these statements in the background as we turn to an examination of Abhinavagupta. In his magnum opus, *Light on the Tantra* (*Tantrāloka*), Abhinavagupta describes the nature of Śiva in the following terms:

> The Śiva which they imagine, completely pacified, differentiated from all other things, transcendent to all other paths, similar therefore to something insentient or inert like glass, does not exist anywhere at all. Śiva in effect is nothing more than this consciousness, which unfolds itself everywhere in the form of a great light. Its very condition as Śiva indeed consists in the fact that all the varied forms of the universe appear. This process of manifestation into all the forms of the universe produces itself completely freely within him.[7]

In another of Abhinavagupta's texts, a very complex work, *Longer Commentary on the Thirty Verses* (*Parātriṃśikā-vivaraṇa, PTv*), Abhinavagupta expands on the notion of Śiva:

> Everything that exists resides within the blessed Lord Bhairava. Whatever, appears within our Heart or leaves the point of our tongue resides, I say, in Parameśvara, who is not limited by time, is one with consciousness, and is perpetually united with all the powers. He constitutes a unity which coexists without contradiction with the hundreds of creations and dissolutions which are manifested by his contraction and expansion, and it is by means of these that he expresses his freedom. This reality of Śiva, therefore, has neither beginning nor end and is luminous with its own light. Its essence is a complete freedom which consists of perfect independence determined by the fullness of all things. Within itself it embraces all principles, which are in effect identical with it.[8]

The concern in this essay will be to narrate interpretively the fundamental cosmogonic myth of the non-dual Kashmir Śaivism of Abhinavagupta. The account of the cosmogonic myth presented here is derived from a conflation of various versions to be found in Abhinavagupta's tantric works, the previously mentioned *Tantrāloka*; the shorter *Tantrasāra*, the *Essence of Tantra*; the *Parātriṃśikā-vivaraṇa* and the *Parātrīśikā-laghuvṛtti*, that is, the *Longer and Shorter Commentaries on the Thirty Verses.*[9]

Although traces of traditional and ancient Indic cosmogonic themes are to be found throughout Abhinavagupta's works, the focus on sādhanā that forms the overwhelming preoccupation of these texts dictates a conceptualization of what might be called the *continuous* or *instantaneous cosmogony.*[10] This cosmogony literally is spelled out in terms of a vibratory, periodic table of elements known as the *mātṛkā,* the fifty phonemes of Sanskrit.[11] It seems clear that the notion of the continuous cosmogony expressed by the concept of the *visarga-śakti,* the Emissional Power, underlies all later cosmogonic formulations found in the Hindu Tantra.[12]

It is important to note that Abhinavagupta details this cosmogony in the third chapter of the *TĀ,* which is given over to an exposition of the highest meditational method of the non-dual Kashmir Śaivas known as the *Śāmbhavopāya,* and that, along with the so-called secret ritual—the *kula-yāga* (taught in Chapter 29)—is thought to belong to the Kaula lineage.[13] In fact, all of the previously mentioned texts betray a powerful Kaula orientation, so that the continuous cosmogony may be thought of as a particularly Kaula formulation. It is in the context of elaborating this cosmogony—narrated entirely in terms of consciousness and its nonduality—that Abhinavagupta is able to expound a spiritual perspective in which the usual notions of the person, of time, of language, of sexuality—in fact of all aspects of reality—are reversed. This reversal contributes directly to the transgressive posture taken by the realized individual toward the Embodied Cosmos (*kula*).

The sequence of the unfolding vocalic *śaktis* portrays a symbolic representation of the unrepresentable implicate order of Śiva. It displays the play of forces embedded within the supreme level of reality. The sādhaka capable of attuning to this level of reality uses these energies as a meditational vehicle. Balancing delicately at the paradoxical junction point between the unbounded reality of Śiva and the manifestational energies of the *śaktis,* the sādhaka inhabits a primeval zone of existential power. This is the expanding and contracting Heart of Śiva, wherein resides the Emissional Power, the Rudra-dyad, the continuous and unceasing fundamental act of disclosing the contents of the visible reality and enclosing them in a liberating and surpassing movement of transcendence back into the Supreme. For this reason the connection between these apparently grammatical discourses and the fundamentals of tantric meditation, not entirely obvious at first glance, are of the utmost importance. The examination of the myth of the continuous cosmogony, filtered through and unpacked by Bohmian categories, makes some of the most abstruse and rarefied meditational ideas of the Tantra understandable.

Bhairava and the Emission of the Cosmos

This version of the myth begins with Bhairava dallying with the Goddess. The Goddess, here glossed by Abhinavagupta as the Self in the process of awakening, takes the occasion to inquire of Bhairava as follows: "O Powerful Lord, My very Self, Tell me that mysterious secret, great, unconcealed. Reveal to me the power, which abides in the Heart, known as the *kaulinī*. Reveal to me the way to fulfilment (*tṛpti*), to the perfect egoity, *AHAM*. How can the Ultimate (*anuttara*) of its own accord grant the *kaulika* perfection?"[14] That is to say, in what way does the condition of embodied enlightenment (*jīvanmukti*) come about?

Bhairava, well pleased by the inquiry of his consort, answers: "Hear O Goddess, O One of Great fortune, about the higher than the highest. I will describe to you the Ultimate . . . which grants the *kaulika* perfection. That *kaulika* function, O Goddess, abides in the great space of my Heart."[15] He then proceeds to instruct the Goddess. The Supreme Word (*parā-vāk*) is the Power (*śakti*) and the unitive vision of totality (*paśyantī*), and She is perpetually conjoined with Lord Śiva, the Supreme (*anuttara: A*), from whom She is nondifferent. From their blissful embrace in the secret Heart of the Center arises the illuminating light of consciousness (*prakāśa*), and the perpetual self-referentiality (*vimarśa*) of that light, the self-awareness that animates the light and makes it into the vibrating, pulsating life (*spanda*) in all beings.[16] Time itself resides in this pulsating light of consciousness as the goddess Kālī, so the actuality of this eternal reality of Śiva and Śakti is without beginning and without end.[17] When does the cosmos emerge? To relegate its inception to some long-distant moment is to misunderstand the contemporaneous and perpetual actuality of the event. The fruitful embrace of the dyad occurs continuously as the source point (*bindu*) of all that is, occurs, that is to say, outside of the sphere of manifestation of time and space. It is beyond beginnings and endings.

Therefore, to begin again, before the beginning is the Word that is the Supreme (*anuttara*), Śiva as the supreme transcendent, joined with his Power, but beyond himself as Power and Power holder, the unmanifest ocean of silence, waveless and still, the Sky of consciousness of Bhairava, the full moon of enlightenment. Or rather, it is not silence, but a perfectly coherent and self-contained vibration (*spanda*), one in which the various waves coherently and implicately cancel each other out, as the Supreme Self overflows within itself, and the overflowing is contained as the universal vibration (*sāmānya-spanda*). To speak of existence or nonexistence, death or immortality, night or day, darkness or light is fundamentally to distort the unbounded and unconditioned nature of that primordial One, who is, simultaneously, Two.[18]

The Word is emitted (*visṛṣṭi*) within Śiva, and it is *A*. In the self-contained and implicate overflowing within the Universal Self, *A* joins with *A*, and there results *Ā*, the power of Bliss (*ānanda-śakti*), whose nature is Śiva's total freedom (*svātantrya*) within himself. This is the perpetually expanding and contracting Heart of reality, the mouth of the *yoginī*, the Rudra-dyad, the Emission (*visarga*) present at the beginning and the end of the process of manifestation. Out of his sheer unimpeded freedom Śiva undertakes the paradoxical act of self-concealment, the uninhibited dance that will sunder the totality and bring about the finite realities. Simultaneously, there is the power of Śiva's Will (*icchā-śakti: I*), and the Will amasses itself within itself and becomes the power of Domination or Lordship (*īśanā: Ī*) and its nature is Śiva's astonishment (*camatkāra*). Present also at the beginning is the Opening (*unmeṣa: U*), and the opening expands and becomes Decrease (*ūnatā: Ū*). These three, *A, I, U*, are praised as the Supreme Power of Bhairava.[19]

Bhairava continues his narration to the Goddess. When in Śiva's Will (*I*) there appear objects, at first vaguely and then more clearly, the four seeds of immortality (*amṛta-bījas*) arise (*Ṛ, Ṝ, Ḷ, Ḹ*). Then, when the Supreme (*A*) and the Bliss (*Ā*) join with Śiva's Will (*I*) and his Lordship (*Ī*), there arises first the *yoni-bīja*, the vagina vowel *E*, the *trikoṇa*, the triadic, and then *AI*, the six cornered or hexagrammatic. Similarly, when the Supreme (*A*), and the Bliss (*Ā*) join with the Opening (*U*) and Decrease (*Ū*), there result, first the phoneme *O*, and then *AU*, the tridentine, (*triśūla*). Finally, this process of Emission within Śiva terminates when the bindu (*Ṃ*), the infinite knowing subject, is manifested. This completes the perfect Emission that occurs at the highest plane of reality. The supreme Bhairava couple then releases the Emissional Power (*Ḥ*), the *visarga*, which is said to reside generically within each of these fifteen vowels, collectively known as the lunar stations (*tithi*). This forms the perfect egoity, the primordial consciousness known as the *AHAM*.[20]

Actually, the process of manifestation is much more complicated as, after these sixteen vowels, there still remain to be manifested the five classes of phonemes from *K* to *M*, each of which is linked to a particular *tattva* or principle, ranging from earth to the *puruṣa*. Beyond that are the four supports, the semivowels *Y, R, L, V*, linked to the sheaths (*kañcukas*) that keep the transmigrating soul stuck in the middle of things like Triśanku, neither descending to the inertness of a rock nor ascending to the sublime elevation of Bhairava. Finally, there occurs the pentad of *brahman*, *Ś*, *Ṣ*, *S*, *H*, *KṢ*, which corresponds to the highest and most elevated principles that merge blissfully back into the reality of Śiva.

To complicate matters even further, the whole process of manifestation occurs in four steps, the four levels of the Word, the supreme (*parā*), which we have just described; *paśyantī*, the holistic visioning of the entire range of manifestation about to occur, in which the link of phoneme to *tattva* is reversed; *madhyamā*, the intermediate, in which the phonemes appear in a peculiar order known as the *garlanded* (*mālinī*). Finally, this entire process spills out onto the plane of ordinary embodied language (*vaikharī*) within the context of the fully manifested universe[21] (see Figure 1).

Figure 1.

Matrix of Seed-Vowels

Anuttara		***Ānanda-śakti***	=	***svātantrya***
supreme		bliss		freedom
A + A	=	Ā		
• + •	=	:		
Bindu		***Visarga***		
primordial point		emissional power		
Icchā-śakti		***Īśanā***	=	***camatkāra***
will		lordship		astonishment
I + I	=	Ī		
Unmeṣa				
unfolding				
U + U	=	Ū		***Ūnatā***
				decrease
Ṛ Ṝ Ḷ Ḹ				***Amṛta-bīja-s***
				immortality
A or Ā + I or Ī	=	E		***Trikoṇa***
				triangle
A or Ā + E	=	AI		
A or Ā + U or Ū	=	O		
A or Ā + O	=	AU		***Triśūla***
				trident
Ṃ ***Bindu***				
Ḥ ***Visarga***				

Continuous Cosmogony and the Enfolding-Unfolding Universe

The Goddess asks Bhairava to reveal to her the mysterious secret of reality. Promising to do so, he apparently launches into a discussion of the fundamentals of Sanskrit grammar. The *PT* verses, in which this sacred dialogue is recorded, form one of the most compressed statements about the nature of Tantric meditation to be found in the revealed literature of Śaivism. The text itself betrays no self-consciousness about the perplexity of modern readers attempting to fathom the connection between the references to Sanskrit grammar and the process of Tantric meditation. Nor does Abhinavagupta reflect on this apparent topical disjunction in his two commentaries on these verses. He devotes long passages in both of them to the cosmogonic process as symbolized by the unfolding of the phonemic orders of Sanskrit, especially the play of Sanskrit vocalic *saṃdhi.* These are followed, both in text and commentary, with a description of the experiential transformation undergone by the Tantric meditator who properly employs the empowered and secret mantra concealed in code in PT verse 9.[22]

The entire sequence of Sanskrit phonemes manifested by this cosmogonic process is known as the *mātṛkā,* which may be conveniently rendered as matrix. The *mātṛkā* is the matrix of sounds, of vibratory resonances, of powers set up to vibrate within the nonvibratory or metavibratory Heart of Śiva. The field of vibration (*spanda*) arises within the abyss of the heart of reality. As the pure illumination, *prakāśa,* Śiva continuously illuminates himself, reflects back on himself and thus there is always the *vimarśa,* the synchronous self-referentiality of the field of light and consciousness. The primary feature of consciousness is that it is self-consciousness; that is, that it always is doubled back on itself in bliss ($A + A = \bar{A}$). The Supreme blissfully impinges upon itself. The Ultimate reality is shot through with the blissful motion of a peculiar kind known as *vibration.* This is the undivided self-referential consciousness (*avibhāga-parāmarśa*), the unbroken plenum that precedes all manifestation, but that also is asynchronously present within the manifestation.[23]

If we were to adopt Bohm's vocabulary at this point, we might say that Śiva is the holomovement, the undefinable and immeasurable universal flux. The Heart is the implicate order in which everything is enfolded into everything. Present within the Heart is the *visarga-śakti,* the continuous urge toward manifestation, toward the unfolding or explication of the infinite potentialities harbored within Śiva. This gives rise to a series of explicate orders known as *kulas,* Embodied Cosmos, relatively autonomous structures that nevertheless are "marked" or "sealed" by the implicate order within them. Importantly, the Emissional Power also is the continuous movement by which all of the *kulas* are continuously subsumed back into Śiva.

The mystery of the cosmogony, as symbolically narrated by Abhinavagupta, revolves around the freedom of Śiva that underlies the power of his Will and eventually results in the fifty self-divided cognitions (*vibhāga-parāmarśa*) that represent the thirty-six *tattvas* of the objective order and simultaneously the fifty phonemes of the cognitive order. These fields of resonance are likened to the arising of waves on the waveless ocean and begin with the injection of a disruptive pattern of vibration, the Will (*I*), that causes the unbroken plenum enfolded within itself to unfold into the variety of manifestation. Like grains of sand around which pearls will form, the emanation of the vocalic phonemes within Śiva sets up the finest traces of disruption and shadowing (*pracchādana*). It is around these phonemes that the interference patterns or cognitions (*parāmarśa*) that will form both the subjective and objective orders of things eventually will coalesce.[24]

Thus, Śiva's Will (*I*) amassed within itself gives rise to the Rulership of the universe (*Ī*), and those two, joined to the Supreme (*A*) and the Bliss (*Ā*) result in the *yoni-bīja,* the womb vowel, the triangular, the concatenation of the three Powers of Will, Knowledge, and Action. These three are conjoined in the triangle with the Emissional Power at its center and form the male-female, vagina-seed, Śiva-Śakti, Rudra-dyad, the activated source place of manifestation that results in the display of all finite realities.

The process of *parāmarśa,* of setting up separate cognitions that will give rise to the phenomenal universe of everyday experience, is spelled out in terms of the coagulation or thickening (*ghanatā, śyānatā*) of realities around interference patterns set up in the fundamentally unbroken and waveless Śiva. The vocalic order of phonemes represents this order of powers that arise as two masses or currents of consciousness collide (*A* or *Ā* + *I* or *Ī* = *E*). In this way disturbances in the perfect synchrony of the undivided self-referential consciousness arise and interference patterns occur. These disturbances are areas of patterned vibratory activity that result from the merging of the *śaktis.* They could be understood to constitute the generative matrices that give rise to finite objects and may be seen as discrete event areas. At first exceedingly subtle, these event areas increase in solidity or density as they cast a shadow downward through the various levels of the process of manifestation. Thus, the different powers of the Self, of the Lord, symbolically ordered by the vowels, intermingling with each other in various ways, create the patterns that result in the specific cognitions of apparently separate and finite objects.[25]

Objects are indeed finally cognitions (*parāmarśa*) because they are nothing more than cognitions within the Supreme. Perception is thus a process in which the infinite consciousness encounters its own interference patterns and takes cognizance of them. Furthermore, just as in the Sāṃkhya, it might be noted that the word *objects* (rendering *tattva*) includes all the psychological structures of awareness of the individual. Thus, knowable objects in essence are nothing more than the absolute consciousness, but with the difference that objects, which appear to be solid and separate, in reality are discrete areas of patterning set up by the internal interferences of the *śaktis.* By contrast absolute consciousness is just that—unbounded and unconstrained by pattern of any sort.

Visarga and Meditation

The language of manifestation and of cosmogony might lead one to conceptualize the process of *sṛṣṭi* as an emergence out of Śiva, as a separation. Consequently, it also leads one to think of the process of return as a reentrance into Śiva. This is the viewpoint of the ordinary individual, sunk in the ocean of transmigration and subject to what Abhinavagupta conventionally calls the *Veda,* the construction of a social reality on the background of a world-maintaining sacrifice and ordained in terms of the limitations of the *varṇāśrama-dharma,* the conventional morality of the righteous.

However, from the supreme Kaula point of view, the claim is made by the tradition that nothing really emerges from Śiva. The entire *sṛṣṭi* takes place neatly ensconced within the all-pervasive and untranscendable reality of Śiva. Thus, the practitioner of the Tantra, the *vīra,* the *kaula,* the sādhaka, seeks to reverse the ordinary conventional point of view, which s/he identifies with spiritual ignorance. The Tantric hero knows that the cosmogony has never taken place, that no separation is possible from the Ultimate, that all things are bathed in the purity of consciousness, and that one of the methods for the realization of this truth lies precisely in the transgression of all of the ordinary boundaries of conventional morality and sacrificial pattern that claim to maintain the world in being.

Thus, Tantric sādhanā attempts a reversal of the initial cosmogonic act. The transgressive character of its secret ritual, and the "destructive" character of its central God stem from this desire for reversal. The Tantric secret ritual coheres around reversal. It conspires to go against the grain of the ordinary, to reverse the movement toward dispersion and contraction. It seeks to awaken the fundamentally lawless and nonordinary power of Śiva. It is this power—which is the same *visarga-śakti* that "manifests" to begin with—that will finally prove destructive of spiritual ignorance. It will break down the chafing restrictions of caste purity. It will annihilate the social ego that arises in the context of *varṇāśrama-dharma*. Finally, it will implode the awareness of the sādhaka and the yoginī, into the all-encompassing globe of the universal sky of Bhairava, the moon of awakened consciousness, the cave of the Heart-Goddess.[26]

The narration of the continuous cosmogony has at its center a reduplicative fractionation literally spelled out in terms of a kind of vibratory periodic chart. The phonemic structure of Sanskrit represents the process by means of which the explicate, unfolded order displays itself when it is impelled by the Emissional Power. This explicate order always is the unfolding of Śiva; that is to say, of the implicate order of the Supreme wholeness. The potentialities harbored within Śiva manifest as the infinitely nested and interpenetrated *kulas*, the self-sufficient and relatively autonomous structures of reality each of which is a part, and yet, each of which contains the whole. The *kulas*—universe, clan, family, body—are the structures enfolded within Śiva. Each of the *kulas*, each explicate reality, contains the entire implicate order, and thus all of the other *kulas* as well. Each *tattva*, Abhinavagupta tells us, is itself, while at the same time containing all other *tattvas*. Each area of patterned disturbance, of cognition, is itself, while at the same time containing all other areas of patterned disturbance, that occur in the matrix. Each phoneme contains by implication the Supreme *A*, and thus all other phonemes.[27]

Moreover, the paradox of the *visarga* that unfolds the implicate order of Śiva, that explicates the infinite meanings contained in Śiva, revolves around the simultaneous manifestation and reabsorption, the twin oscillatory wave nature of the *visarga-śakti*. It is simultaneously expansive and contractive, emissional and reabsorptive. That is, the matrix of all simultaneously is emitted into the structure of time, space, and causality, and it is reabsorbed. The progressive-contractive *visarga* oversees the display of the enormous variety of *kulas*. These groups or sets of relative reality always replicate the non-dual yet dyadic nature of the reality of Śiva. As *kulas,* they are finite structures with a coherent autonomy and necessary adherence to the lawful patterns of order of which they are systematic reflections. Yet, they always are undercut by the absolute order, the holonomic structure of Śiva. Śiva thus appears to be destructive with respect to the autonomy of the *kulas.* The regressive-expansive *visarga* always appears to dissolve and sublimate the areas of coagulation and condensation that have gathered around the interference patterns.[28]

Thus, the *visarga,* which is lauded as the supreme secret of the Kaulas, constitutes the essence of the *Śāmbhavopāya,* which is the effortless meditation technique of simply observing the continuous cosmogony at play.[29] At the center of the *kula,* lies the energy of the *kula,* the *kaulikī-śakti.* The *kula*—in this case the body—has its center esoterically in the Heart and exoterically in the sexual organ. The advanced sādhaka is overtaken by the *kaulikī-śakti,* by the descent of the Power, by the activation of the implicate order within the explicate structure of the body. This activation often is mediated by an empowered mantra containing one of the vocalic resonances we have just analyzed at its core and ending in the *visarga.* The tradition, for example, praises the liberating power of the Heart-mantra, SAUḤ.[30] The *bīja*-mantra functions as the specific vibratory key, as the powerful resonant software that drives the neuronal circuitry of the *cakras* and catalyzes the unfurling of the coiled energy of the *kuṇḍalinī.*[31] As the *kuṇḍalinī* activates the hidden meta-programs of wholeness within the body, the consciousness of the sādhaka merges with the holomovement, becomes that which moves in the Heart (*hṛdayaṅgamībhūta*); that is, experientially replicates the implicate order.[32] At this point, the sādhaka is able to observe in awe as the matrix of time and space dissolves into the *bindu,* the infinite point of the Heart. The experience of the *visarga* in the center of the Heart provides the framework for the dissolution of all that exists. As the sādhaka progresses in this highest of methods, s/he is able to observe the oscillatory manifestation and dissolution of the universe occurring as the *visarga* moves in two directions at once. In this way, the practitioner replicates the experience of the guru, achieves identity with the whole, with Bhairava, and is able to utter the ecstatic cry "*Śivo'ham*—I am Śiva."[33]

The Śaiva traditions categorize the movement of reality in terms of an initially dyadic pattern, the *visarga,* which modulates into a triadic interaction between three powers, the three initial vowels *A, I, U,* representing the Will, Knowledge, and Action powers of Śiva, and finally into a pentadic classification that stands for the five divine actions of Śiva (*pañca-kṛtya*), his capacity to manifest (*sṛṣṭi*), maintain (*sthiti*), and reabsorb (*saṃhāra*), linked to his capacity to conceal (*vilaya*) and gracefully reveal (*anugraha*).[34] This final classification itself reduplicates the previous two and details the activities of Śiva in which he is simultaneously (1) manifestational: continuously cosmogonic, always giving rise to the unfolding of the explicate order of finite patterns overseen by the progressive-contractive *visarga*; (2) maintaining: continuously unfolding the explicate order, which is accomplished by the vibratory polarity of the *visarga* merging back and reemerging out of Śiva with infinite speed, that is to say, with a cycle whose duration is zero; (3) destructive: reenfolding the explicate into the implicate overseen by the regressive-expansive *visarga*, the power in the Heart, the *kaulikī* function, which is the essential impeller of the Tantric sādhanā. As we can see, this triadic division essentially is the expansion of the dual nature of the *visarga* that also may be expressed in terms of the powers of Śiva to conceal and reveal.

Our ordinary hylotropic awareness in linear, sequential, and temporal fashion continuously parses the wavelike nature of space and time to us as it conceals the instantaneous nature of nonsequentiality, nonlocality, noncontinuity, and nonextensional interpenetration of wholeness. The extraordinary, yogic, holotropic consciousness pursued by the Tantric sādhaka through the various levels of yoga—which the Śiva-sūtra labels *astonishment* or *wonder* (*vismaya*)[35]—consists in finally coming to see that the narration of coming into being, of the cosmogony, of the manifestation of the *kula* essentially is false—it never emerges from the total immersion in the oceanic wholeness of Śiva. Therefore, all structures of lawfulness and adherence to patterns of relative order dissolve enfolded in lawlessness, the totally free structure of holonomic integration.[36] We can conclude in the words of Abhinavagupta:

> The light is one, and it cannot ever be divided, and for this reason there is no possible division capable of sundering the non-duality, the Lord, beautiful with light and bliss. But [someone might object] space, time, forms, knowledge, qualities, attributes, distance, and so on are usually considered to be diversifying elements. Not so [we reply], because that which so appears is nothing but light. If the light were not such, then non-duality would be useless. Difference then is only a word devoid of reality. But even if we admit a portion of reality to differences, then according to what we have said, it will have its basis

only in non-duality. This is a pot, this is a cloth, the two are different one from the other. The two are different from other cognizing subjects, the two are different even from me. All these are nothing but the one light, which by its own intrinsic nature displays itself in this way.[37]

Notes

1. The primary textual sources for this article are the following Sanskrit texts by Abhinavagupta published in the Kashmir Series of Texts and Studies: *Parātrīśikā-laghuvṛtti* (*PTlv*), *Parātriṃśikā-vivaraṇa* (*PTv*), *Tantrāloka* (*TĀ*), *Tantrasāra* (*TS*), and *Mālinīvijaya-vārtika* (*MVv*). The interested reader should see the fairly complete bibliography on the non-dual Śaivism of Kashmir in my book, *The Triadic Heart of Shiva*, which also contains an English translation of the *Parātrīśikā-laghuvṛtti* in an appendix. For a recent English translation of the *Parātriṃśikā-vivaraṇa*, see Singh's *A Trident of Wisdom*. The *Tantrāloka, Tantrasāra*, and *Mālinīvijaya-vārtika* still await translation into English. Raniero Gnoli has published translations into Italian of the *Tantrāloka* (1972), *Tantrasāra* (1960), *PTlv* (1978), and *PTv* (1985). Readers also may consult Padoux's translation into French of the *PTlv* (1975). My own interest in this tradition and in the specific sequence of vocalic unfolding described in this chapter was first awakened by André Padoux's masterful treatment of this topic in his *Recherches*, first published in 1963 and revised in 1975. The importance and profundity of Padoux's ground-breaking and pioneering contributions to the study of this tradition cannot be overemphasized. My investigations as presented in this chapter, although based on a detailed reading of the Sanskrit texts, have received continuous orientation and guidance from Padoux's work. It is heartening to see that Padoux's *Recherches*, a work of the utmost importance in the understanding of the Hindu Tantra, has become available to a much wider audience in an English translation, *Vāc: The Concept of the Word in Selected Hindu Tantras.*

2. David Bohm, *Wholeness and the Implicate Order.*

3. Ibid., 11.

4. Ibid., 150.

5. Ibid., 177.

6. Ibid., 178.

7. Abhinavagupta, TĀ 15.264b-266.

8. Abhinavagupta, PTv, comment on verses 5-8, pp. 142-143.

9. Although I would argue that this myth functions as an omnipresent deep structure implicit in all of Abhinavagupta's writings, for specifics on the emergence of the sequence of vowels the interested reader may consult the following important passages: *PTv*, pp. 97-216; *TĀ* 3.66-293; *PTlv*, pp. 5-9; and *MVv* 1.884-904.

10. See for example Abhinavagupta, *PTlv*, comment on 33-34, where he talks about the incessant or unceasing (*anavaratam*) expansion of the Heart.

11. Technically, the term *mātṛkā* is the name given to the collection of phonemes on the *paśyantī* level of emanation. See Padoux, *Recherches*, pp. 183-190 for more details.

12. On the notion of the *visarga-śakti*, see Muller-Ortega, *Triadic Heart*, pp. 118-141.

13. On the Kaula lineage as well as the notion of the *kula*, see Muller-Ortega, *Triadic Heart*, pp. 25-63, 100-117. The most profound investigator at present of the historical problems involved in sorting out the relationships between the many preceptorial lineages referred to in these texts is Alexis Sanderson. See for example Sanderson, "Śaivism and the Tantric Traditions," for a detailed rehearsal of the place of the Kaulas within the larger context of Śaivism. Another very useful exploration of the Kaula lineage is Dyczkowski, *The Canon of the Śaivāgama.*

14. Abhinavagupta, *PTlv*, verses 2-4. My rendering of these verses is slightly condensed.

15. Abhinavagupta, *PTlv*, verses 3b-4.

16. See Abhinavagupta, *PTv*, commentary on verse 1.

17. On the relationship of Kālī to notions of time and the continuous cosmogony, see Abhinavagupta, *TĀ* 4.148-173 as well as 6.7-215.

18. On the notion of *spanda*, see Muller-Ortega, *Triadic Heart*, pp. 118-124. An important passage on the *spanda* is Abhinavagupta, *TĀ* 4.181b-186.

19. For a compact statement on the unfolding of the phonemes, see Abhinavagupta, *PTlv*, commentary on 5-9a. See also Muller-Ortega, *Triadic Heart*, pp. 113-117. On the Supreme Power of

Bhairava, see Abhinavagupta, *TĀ* 3.192b-193a. The most detailed and masterful rendering of this unfolding remains Padoux *Recherches*, especially Chapter 5.

20. The citations given in note 17 remain important here. On the notion of the *AHAM*, a remarkable passage is Abhinavagupta, *PTv*, pp. 84-88.

21. See Singh, *A Trident of Wisdom*, pp. 106-165 for translation of and commentary on Abhinavagupta's rendition of this process. Of course, Padoux, *Recherches* remains the most complete descriptive statement.

22. For an English rendering of both the *PT* verses and Abhinavagupta's short commentary on them, see Muller-Ortega, *Triadic Heart*, pp. 203-232. The *PT* verses, in slightly variant form and with Abhinavagupta's longer commentary, are translated in Singh, *A Trident of Wisdom.*

23. See Abhinavagupta, *PTlv*, comment on 5-9a for a compact description of the unfolding of the *parāmarśas.*

24. Abhinavagupta, *PTlv*, commentary on 5-9a.

25. See Padoux's treatment of this in *Recherches*, pp. 236-238. An important reference to the concept of coagulation (*śyānatā*) is Abhinavagupta, *PTv*, p. 33. The narration of the myth continues to follow most closely Abhinavagupta's exposition in *PTlv*, commentary on 5-9a. See also Muller-Ortega, *Triadic Heart*, pp. 146-151, on the concepts of the undivided and self-divided self-referential consciousness, *avibhāga* and *vibhāga parāmarśa.*

26 On the ritual implications of the *visarga-śakti*, see Muller-Ortega, "The Power of the Secret Ritual: Theoretical Formulations from the Tantra," *Journal of Ritual Studies*, volume 4, number 2, Summer 1990, pp. 41-59. Sanderson's masterful article "Purity and Power among the Brahmans of Kashmir" should be consulted for its deep insight into notions of personhood in these texts.

27. See Abhinavagupta, *PTv*, pp. 45-51 and 133-143 for interesting statements of this idea.

28. See notes 11 and 24 on the *visarga-śakti*. The terms *progressive-contractive* and *regressive-expansive* are my own coinage, but are based on Sanskrit pairs *pravṛtti-nivṛtti* and *saṃkoca-vikāsa.*

29. Abhinavagupta, *TĀ* 29.115b-117a. See Muller-Ortega, *Triadic Heart*, p. 140.

30. See Muller-Ortega, *Triadic Heart*, pp. 162-181. On mantra generally and the Heart-mantra specifically, Chapter 7 of Padoux's *Recherches* remains the most detailed study.

31. For a powerful description of this process, see Abhinavagupta, *TĀ* 23.33-39. See also Muller-Ortega, ibid., pp. 167-168.

32. On the notion of experiential replication, see ibid., pp. 182-201.

33. See for example Abhinavagupta, *TĀ*, 5.27b-53 for an example of a powerful passage that details this form of meditation.

34. Abhinavagupta refers to three powers in *PTlv*, commentary on 5-9a. See Muller-Ortega, *Triadic Heart*, pp. 114-117. Abhinavagupta begins the *PTv* with a reference to the fivefold divine actions of Śiva. See Singh, *A Trident of Wisdom*, pp. 4-10.

35. Śiva-Sūtras 1.12: *Vismayo yogabhūmikāḥ*.

36. On the distinction between hylotropic and holotropic consciousness, see Stanislav Grof, *Beyond the Brain*, pp. 344-347.

37. Abhinavagupta, *MVv* 1.620b-630.

References

The following Sanskrit editions and translations are of texts by Abhinavagupta.

Primary Sources: Sanskrit Editions

Mālinīvijaya-vārtika, ed. Madhusūdan Kaul, Kashmir Series of Texts and Studies, no. 31. Srinagar: Research Department, Jammu and Kashmir Government, 1921.

Parātrīśikā-laghuvṛtti, ed. Jagaddhara Zādoo, Kashmir Series of Texts and Studies, no. 68. Srinagar: Research Department, Jammu and Kashmir Government, 1947.

Parātriṃśikā-vivaraṇa, ed. Mukunda Rāma, Kashmir Series of Texts and Studies, no. 18. Srinagar: Research Department, Jammu and Kashmir Government, 1918.

Tantrāloka, ed. Mukunda Rāma and Madhusūdan Kaul, Kashmir Series of Texts and Studies, nos. 23, 28, 30, 35, 36, 29, 41, 47, 59, 52, 57, 58. Srinagar: Research Department, Jammu and

Kashmir Government, 1918-1938.

Tantrasāra, ed. Mukunda Rāma, Kashmir Series of Texts and Studies, no. 17. Srinagar: Research Department, Jammu and Kashmir Government, 1918.

Primary Sources: Translations

Gnoli, Raniero, trans. *Essenza dei Tantra*. Turin: Boringhieri, 1960.

———. *Il Commento di Abhinavagupta alla Parātriṃśikā*. Roma: Instituto Italiano per il Medio ed Estremo Oriente, 1985.

———. *La Trentina della Suprema*. Turin: Boringhieri, 1978.

———. *Luce Delle Sacre Scritture*. Turin: Unione Tipografico-Editrice Torinese, 1972.

Padoux, André, trans. *La "Parātrīśikālaghuvṛitti" de Abhinavagupta*. Publications de l'Institut de Civilisation Indienne, Fasc. 38. Paris: Editions E. de Boccard, 1975.

Singh, Jaideva, trans. *A Trident of Wisdom*. Albany: State University of New York Press, 1989.

Secondary Sources

Bohm, David. *Wholeness and the Implicate Order*. London: Ark Paperbacks, 1983.

Dyczkowski, Mark. *The Doctrine of Vibration: An Analysis of the Doctrines and Practices of Kashmir Shaivism*. Albany: State University of New York Press, 1987.

———. *The Canon of the Śaivāgama and the Kubjikā Tantras of the Western Kaula Tradition*. Albany: State University of New York Press, 1988.

Goudriaan, Teun, and Sanjukta Gupta. *Hindu Tantric and Śākta Literature*. In Jan Gonda, *A History of Indian Literature*. vol. 2, Fasc. 2. Wiesbaden: Otto Harrassowitz, 1981.

Grof, Stanislav. *Beyond the Brain*. Albany: State University of New York Press, 1985.

Gupta, Sanjukta, Dirk Jan Hoens, and Teun Goudriaan. *Hindu Tantrism*. Leiden: E. J. Brill, 1979.

Muller-Ortega, Paul E. *The Triadic Heart of Shiva: Kaula Tantricism of Abhinavagupta in the Non-Dual Shaivism of Kashmir*. Albany: State

University of New York Press, 1989.

———. "The Power of the Secret Ritual: Theoretical Formulations from the Tantra," *Journal of Ritual Studies*, volume 4, number 2, Summer 1990, pp. 41-59.

Padoux, André. *Recherches sur la Symbolique et l'Énergie de la Parole*, 2d ed. Publications de l'Institut de Civilisation Indienne, fasc. 21. Paris: Éditions E. de Boccard, 1975.

———. "Tantrism." *The Encyclopedia of Religion*, ed. Mircea Eliade. New York: Macmillan, 1987.

Pandey, Kanti Chandra. *Abhinavagupta: An Historical and Philosophical Study*. Chowkhamba Sanskrit Studies, vol. 1. Varanasi: Chowkhamba Sanskrit Series Office, 1963.

Sanderson, Alexis. "Purity and Power among the Brahmans of Kashmir." In *The Category of the Person: Anthropology, Philosophy, History*, ed. Michael Carrithers, Steven Collins, and Steven Lukes, pp. 190-216. Cambridge: Cambridge University Press, 1986.

———. "Śaivism and the Tantric Traditions." In *The World's Religions*, ed. Stewart Sutherland, Leslie Houlden, Peter Clarke, and Friedhelm Hardy, pp. 660-704. London: Routledge, 1988.

Silburn, Lilian, trans. *Śivasūtra et Vimarśinī de Kṣemarāja*, Institut de Civilisation Indienne, Fasc. 47. Paris: Diffusion E. de Boccard, 1980.

———. *Kundalini, the Energy of the Depths*. Albany: State University of New York Press, 1988.

Singh, Jaideva, trans. and ed. *The Doctrine of Recognition*. Albany: State University of New York Press, 1990.

Chapter Nine

The Yogic Disciplines in the Monistic Śaiva Tantric Traditions of Kashmir:

Threefold, Fourfold, and Six-Limbed

Navjivan Rastogi

1

This chapter aims at enquiring into the standard form of yoga in the monistic Śaiva traditions of Kashmir. The genesis of this enquiry lies in the very statements one finds in the systemic literature on yoga. Over the span of four hundred years, from the ninth to the thirteenth centuries, no one can miss an overt tendency to posit the Tantric yoga as six-limbed (*ṣaḍaṅga*), distinguished from the eight-limbed (*aṣṭāṅga*) yoga of Patañjali. In practice, however, this stand is countered by several parallel techniques laying a similar claim, necessitating a deeper perspectival look into the whole problem.

A student of Indian philosophy and cultural traditions does not require an additional proof to believe the authenticity of Mircea Eliade's statement that yoga is a characteristic dimension of the Indian mind.[1] This observation is particularly relevant in the context of the Tantric schools in general and the Tantric Śaiva schools of Kashmir in particular. In the Āgama literature basic to the Tantric traditions, the fourfold division of the Āgamic subject matter into doctrine (*jñāna*), *yoga*, ritual (*kriyā*), and conduct (*caryā*) points to the essentiality of yoga in the Tantric scheme. Some Āgamas do follow this line of classification, but the majority, though subscribing to this division in principle, often fail to stick to it in practice. Sometimes there is overlapping among the four, or an attempt—with or without conscious effort—is made, especially in the monistic Śaiva Tantras, to find out an equation or a mutual parallel. This tendency is at its peak in the Tantrāloka (TA) as well as its source Tantra, the Mālinīvijayottara (MVT). The tendency sharpens the doubt with which we began our quest as to what is the intrinsic nature of yoga accepted in Kashmir Śaivism (KS). Is it simple, complex, or an aggregate of several models? At this point, the observation by Mircea Eliade that yoga represents a "pan-Indian corpus of spiritual techniques"[2] acquires more relevance. It appears that several techniques of yoga have earned acceptance in the Tantric Śaiva monism and that, despite their outward formal divergences, there is a close internal agreement. One of the important factors contributing to this agreement is a sort of genetic relationship with the fundamental spirit of the original yoga of Patañjali.

2

For an adequate understanding of yoga in KS, it will be helpful to concentrate on the role of a *yogin.* The analogy of a yogin has been employed as an argument toward establishing the godhead or supreme lordliness (*māheśvarya*). This illustration functions particularly well as an unexceptionable, universally acceptable, and ultimate proof, accounting for agency inherent in ultimate reality or freedom inherent in being. Not only in the Āgamas, but in the later scholastic literature as well, this argument has been resorted to consistently. That is, a *yogin* offers a model, seen and met with in this world, embodying transworldly autonomy and agenthood. The implication is that the supreme agency is not just an imaginary ideal but a state attainable in this very life. From this, we arrive at a conclusion that has a direct bearing on the fundamentals of Indian thought. To know reality or an object means to "realize" it. This synonymity between knowledge and attainment shows itself strongly in the field of yoga. Among the meanings of the term *yoga,* current in the tradition, one is "achievement."[3] The element of "attainment" pervades all other accepted meanings of yoga in one way or other. Kṣemarāja (KR) considers yoga to be the realization of identity with ultimate reality.[4] Even before him, the MVT, the basic scripture of Trika, posits yoga as the realization of identity between two objects.[5] There are several technical and conventional senses of yoga, such as the union of empirical self with supreme self, the union of inward and outward breaths.[6] Gopinath Kaviraja adds one more to them: unity or harmony between Śiva and Śakti.[7] The notion of attainment underlies all of them. In the Lakulīśa Pāśupata system, one of the two basic streams (the other emanates from Śrīkaṇṭha) presented in the TA,[8] the definition of yoga in terms of "linking the self with God through mind"[9] unmistakably carries the imprint of "attainment." This touch of agency or doership seems to have been a part of the original concept of yoga. In the Mahābhārata (Aśva. 43, 25), yoga is described to be of the nature of conduct or activity (*pravṛttilakṣaṇo yogaḥ*). This sense has found currency in Vedic as well as Pāli religious texts. The gloss of Śaṅkara on Vedānta-Sūtra 2, 1, 3 also assigns this meaning. In the Gītā, where the two paths (*niṣṭhā*) of knowledge and action are discussed (3, 3), yoga is associated with both, but the author leaves us in little doubt as to the real relation of yoga with the path of *karma-yogins*. Rāmakaṇṭha, a monist, presents the basic thrust of the monistic yoga as lying in action-performance.[10] This leads one to believe that the activistic notion of yoga has a hoary antiquity and obtains a full-fledged logical development in the monistic traditions of Kashmir Śaivism.

3

Pāṇini derives the word *yogin* from the root *yuj-* with suffix *-in* (*dhinuṇ*) in the sense of 'being in the habit of' (*tācchīlye*). The root *yuj-* in the *rudhādi* class denotes 'to join, to unite.' On this basis, yoga is 'being together.' The means, vehicle, technique, or action instrumental to the achievement of such a state also goes by the name of *yoga*. The depiction of yoga as *saṃhananopāya* 'means of togetherness'[11] is intelligible only from this point of view.

But the usual meaning in which *yoga* is employed deviates slightly from this. The commonly accepted meaning happens to be *samādhi*. According to the author of the Kāśikā, the root *yuj-* figures in the *divādi* class also in the sense of *samādhi*. In fact, the Kāśikā assigns equal weight to both significations;[12] but in Patañjali's school, which in Indian parlance has become synonymous with yoga, *samādhi* appears to be its usual purport. Vyāsa, the celebrated commentator of the Yogasūtras (YS), explicitly identifies yoga with *samādhi*.[13] It is remarkable that the Śaiva author RK also employs *yoga* in this sense.[14] There is no denying the fact that the preceptors do differ on the precise meaning of *samādhi*. Patañjali's "suppression/annihilation of mental states,"[15] offered as the definition of yoga, actually is the definition of *samādhi*. This is endorsed by Hariharānanda Āraṇya: "yoga must be understood to stand for *samādhi* in the system."[16] Likewise, in KS *samādhi* is believed to be the yoga having for its content recognitive realization of the nondual self that is pure awareness. Focusing on this notion of *samādhi*, RK underscores the divergence between the Sāṃkhya and Śaiva approaches.[17]

Hence, the conclusion will not be totally unfounded that *yoga*, both etymologically and semantically, is neither a negative proposition nor an affirmative one. The notions of negativity or affirmativity stem from our appraisal of *samādhi*. To a student of Pātañjala Yoga, the negativity involved in the annihilation of the mental states is just metaphoric. If one were to confide in Āraṇya, the ultimate goal of yoga is absolute tranquility in the form of "isolation" (*kaivalya*).[18] Yoga, that is *samādhi*, is not a totally inactive or negative, but a self-dependent fully conscious state. Mere paralyzing of mind, whether self-induced or unoccasioned by will, is not yoga. Yoga consists in the annihilation of only those mental states that follow in the wake of willed fixation or concentration of the mind on any of the knower, knowing, and knowable.[19] If this interpretation is right, the activity-orientation found in the Mahābhārata permeates even the so-called negativity of the Sāṃkhyan Yoga.

This contention gets strengthened from a different direction as well. The formal structure of Trika Yoga evinces a deep-rooted imprint of Patañjali's notion of yoga. On close analysis one notices that KS knows of two yogic methods for reaching the godhead: one is the technique of refinement of logical constructs (*vikalpa-saṃskāra*), which alternatively may be called *refinement of mental states;* the other is the technique of the loss or destruction of mental states (*vṛtti-kṣaya*). A comparison of the two methods will occupy our attention a little later. What should be kept in mind right now is that the technique of "loss of mental states" is championed more ardently by the Spanda wing of KS. Interestingly, both the rival camps of Spanda—disciples of Kallaṭa and adherents of Vasugupta—agree on this issue. RK, a follower of Kallaṭa, propounds the entering of all mental states into the fourth state.[20] KR, the disciple of Vasugupta, views the suppression-cessation of all "other" mental states as the most conducive element of yoga.[21] In fact Spanda, by definition, entails *vṛttikṣaya*. *Yogins* are always prepared to analyze this principle of vibration. Whether they speak of "loss of state(s)" or "suppression of state(s)," they denote the same meaning in the system.[22] The characteristic of a *yogin*, according to Abhinavagupta (AG), is the inner blissful experience arising from the loss of states.[23] The terminal stage of the second technique described earlier, that is, refinement of mental constructs, is considered indeterminate. This means the loss of mental constructions, which is identical with the loss or rejection of mental states.[24] This is the state of revelation of awareness.

Both these methods are considered as one from the point of view of the outcome. Hence, reconciling traditional undertones of yoga with the systemic approaches, yoga comes to embody such a *samādhi* as is constantly marked by subjective ideality or supreme subjectivity resulting from the cessation of all mental states.[25] In systemic parlance, it represents the state of self-ascertainment originating from pure gnosis (*śuddhavidyā*).

Samādhi is the fruition of life-long *sādhanā*. The whole process of *sādhanā* too therefore is called *yoga*. In fact, Indian philosophy is marked by an integral tendency toward *sādhanā* that draws its sustenance from its yoga centricity. According to P. V. Kane, there are two main currents of yoga. One, propagated by Pātañjala Yoga, is related to disciplining the mind; the other, developed in the Gorakṣaśataka, Haṭhayogapradīpikā, and so on, to disciplining the body.[26] These are known as Rājayoga and Haṭhayoga, respectively. Patañjali's yoga does not deal with plexuses, arteries, and veins; whereas in Haṭhayoga the modes of sitting, breath control, physical postures, and other practices seek to push forward the coiled energy (*kuṇḍalinī*) to the cranial aperture via the plexuses and central canal (*suṣumṇā nāḍī*). The description of yoga generally found in the Tantras represents the combination of the two in many respects. But, because the Haṭhayogic process can be enacted entirely mentally in the monistic Śaiva Tantras, it emerges there as a mere variant of Rājayoga. In our view, there is a third current, too, which may be termed the *supramental current* concerned with revealing the identity of the individual as pure ideality. The yoga of KS is linked with the growth of this third brand.

4

Let us go back to our initial premise. To decide on a standard form of Trika Yoga, cast in a precise mold, is a difficult exercise. On closer analysis, we encounter three basic patterns of yoga. Two of them are threefold and one six limbed. The first triple yoga is found in the MVT; it acquires, however, a fourfold format with AG and others, which accounts for our designating it as *fourfold*. The second triple yoga is found in the Netra Tantra (NT) and duly nurtured later by KR. Important in this connection is that KR subjects this yoga to a detailed treatment from the points of view of both *kulaprakriyā* and *tantraprakriyā*.[27] The third or *ṣaḍaṅga* yoga, seeds of which are indirectly traceable in the MVT, is endowed with a relatively tangible shape by Jayaratha (J). The available material on the subject, however, is, quite meager.

We propose to start with the pattern of yoga propounded by

the MVT, because this text constitutes the earliest source material on Trika. The student of Tantric yoga may find it fascinating to mark that the MVT is admittedly dedicated to expounding yoga—real yoga for that matter,[28] as against the NT, which deals with yoga as an auxiliary subject. As already observed, yoga in the MVT means realization of identity.[29] On the lines of three possessions-penetrations (*samāveśa*), yoga is constructed as threefold,[30] though the respective designations are missing. These *samāveśas*, called *Āṇava*, *Śākta*, and *Śāmbhava*, figure in the second chapter.[31] One naturally infers that these three yogas must be called *āṇava yoga*, *śākta yoga*, and *śāmbhava yoga*. However, we do not come across any outright statement as to the nature or technique of these yogas. But if we go somewhat deeper into the treatment of the triple possessions, allusion to their respective means becomes discernible. In the given circumstances, these means are but to be viewed as yogas. Thus the techniques such as concentration on the source of breath (*uccāra*), the external and internal postures or conscious practices (*karaṇa*), contemplative envisioning (*dhyāna*), movement of phonemes in the breath (*varṇa*), and mental projection of the support of the ritual (*sthānaprakalpa*) will come under *Āṇava yoga*. At this plane, the notions of mantra, *mudrā*, diagrams, and mental installation (*nyāsa*) assume implicit importance. Meditation on an object through thought alone without recourse to *prāṇic* movement is *śākta yoga*. Inner awakening or awakening by a teacher, marked by freedom from all (discursive) thoughts is *śāmbhava yoga*. Thus in the MVT, yoga basically is viewed as a means, and the threefold yoga has been expounded by way of elucidating the three distinct instruments to the goal; that is, possession.[32] No more material is available in the MVT with regard to the pattern of yoga.

The yoga of the MVT assumes two forms in later literature: on the one hand, as modes of instrumental, that is, redemptive, cognition; on the other, as distinct stairs of yogic structure. Of course, the first current displays the impact cast by the Vijñāna-bhairava (Vbh) as well, in addition to the MVT, in projecting the three means as the three modes-states of single cognition marked by duality, duality-cum-nonduality, and nonduality. The second line of thought treats them as three different planes of Trika Yoga. Later on, taking cue from the fourth chapter of the MVT, an attempt has been made to synthesize the two developments into one. AG himself does the same in the TA, yet this equation is not immediately relevant despite its tremendous significance. In the two books (*kāṇḍas*) of the Mālinīvijayottaravārttika (MVV), the successive stress on knowledge and yoga is clearly perceptible.[33]

In the subsequent literature, our attention is arrested by one more development; that is, the devising of a fourth mode in the form of nonmeans (*anupāya*). The characterization of this yoga as fourfold reflects this author's implied intention of including this later dimension as well. In the view of AG, this fourfold yoga represents a unique feature of the Trika path.[34] It is described by AG as the instrumental technique marked by the heart's vibration.[35] AG falls back on this method especially to accomplish what may be termed *ānanda yoga*[36] (bliss yoga), a basic theme to which the MVT commits itself. There is a hierarchy of six stages of bliss, beginning with "personal bliss" (*nijānanda*) and culminating into universal bliss (*jagadānanda*), wherein the joy of the ultimate unitary state is overbrimming.[37] Toward attaining this state, the immediate step of the heart's vibration is *śāmbhava*, which consists in the total I-hood. The next is *śāktopāya*,[38] and the third is "movement of heart" (*hṛdayoccāra*),[39] which may be identified with *āṇavopāya*. This is the realm of the movement of breath constituting the ladder for our final ascension to the plane of awareness. It aims at climbing the absolutic plane (*bhairavabhūmi*) through the series of stairs consisting of *bhrūkuṭi* ('frown'), *bindu* ('point'), *nādānta* (indicative of the eighth *mātrā* or state of Sadāśiva), and *śakti* ('power') together with categorial creation and linguistic activity on the way. At this point the *yogin*, completely established within the own self, whether resting in the realm of the vibration of Śiva-consciousness or in the particularized vibration in the form of external object, continues to be enshrined in this absolutic plane[40] of universal vibration defined by universal bliss.[41] The ultimate plane that is the destination of the three means integrated in a hierarchical order is the state of dissolution of all mental states.[42] A point worth noting is that AG connects it again[43] with *śāmbhava yoga*[44] and also that the original definition of yoga (i.e., annihilation of *vṛttis*) is extended right up to this point. When AG presents this plane as *anupāya*, his sole intention is to integrate the means (*upāya*) with the goal (*upeya*). In this sense alone *anupāya* is mentioned independently, otherwise it represents the final phase of *śāmbhava*.[45] The dissolution of all the states simply means emergence of the state of pure awareness in which the universe is ever shining in its totality. Emancipation within life (*jīvanmukti*) is nothing but one's establishment in such a trance on a permanent basis technically described as "ever-awake" (*nityodita*) *samādhi*. This is what we understand by Trika- or anuttara-yoga.[46]

5

We do not intend to dwell upon the subsequent ramifications of this *upāya-yoga.* Three points, however, merit attention. First, *āṇava yoga* is associated with body and vital breath, *śākta yoga* with mind and meditation and *śāmbhava* with pure consciousness. Second, these three types are prescribed by AG in the context of *kuṇḍalinīyoga* as well. In tune with the three divisions of yoga, *kuṇḍalinī* happens also to be of three types: *prāṇa-*, *nāda-*, and *bodha-kuṇḍalinī* (i.e., coiled energy at the levels of vital breath, resonance and knowledge, or consciousness, respectively). The first is awakened by recourse to physical yoga corresponding to *āṇavopāya* and consisting in breath control and so forth. *Nādakuṇḍalinī* is awakened by recourse to mental yoga corresponding to *śāktopāya* and consisting in concentration on the plexuses and so forth. *Bodhakuṇḍalinī* is awakened by recourse to spiritual yoga corresponding to *śāmbhavopāya* consisting in the discovery of pure I-ness.[47] The whole process is somewhat like this. Owing to the complete surrender or merger of ego in self or transcendental subjectivity, a deepening of consciousness takes place that results in its vertical expansion. Side by side, this resting within self leads to a widening of consciousness reflected in its horizontal expansion. This is what essentially is meant by the perpetual rise (or experience) of universal I-ness.

The third point is that triple yoga also has a mind-centric dimension. Viewed from the perspective of mind (*citta*) alone, the triplicity of yoga may be reduced to the three final phases of mind centricity; viz., (1) complete repose of mind (i.e., individual consciousness) or *cittaviśrānti* in self-awareness; (2) thorough grasp of such repose of mind (*cittasaṃbodha*); and (3) withdrawal or dissolution of mind (*cittapralaya*).[48] They correspond directly to the states of dichotomy of thought, rescinding of dichotomic thought, and immediacy of plenary thought.

KR's contribution to the subject is significant. On the one hand, in his Spanda Nirṇaya (SpN) and Śivasūtravimarśinī (SSV), he reconciles MVT, SVT, Vbh, and NT and so on with Spanda theories and, on the other hand, places the yogic process on a more solid footing by setting it against the backdrop of Patañjali's yoga. According to KR, the term *dhyāna* (visualization) in the MVT's definition of *āṇava* includes breath control (*prāṇāyāma*), abstraction (*pratyāhāra*), retentive concentration (*dhāraṇā*), meditation, and *samādhi* all together.[49] His subsequent treatment shows that the physical and elemental purifications (*deha-*, *bhūtaśuddhi*) are also included. In other words, Patañjali's technique is subsumed under *āṇava yoga*. As its operation is confined to the realm of ignorance, all the fulfilments turn out to be in the form of categorial enjoyments.[50] The suppression of ignorance (*moha*) leads to the rise of spontaneous knowledge. This is the plane of *śākta yoga*. The rise of spontaneous gnosis is instrumental to the realization of self replete with the supernatural ambrosia. This is the plane of *śāmbhava yoga*.[51] In KR's view, *āṇavopāya* represents the gross form of yoga whereas *śākta* and *śāmbhava* are its subtle forms.[51] The gross method fails to become a direct vehicle for the experience of supreme awareness.

In the MVT, too, there are two axiological divisions of yoga; that is, artificial and natural or spontaneous. Yoga effected with the aid of *prāṇāyāma* and so forth is considered artificial. Hence, the chance of liberation is here almost nil.[53] The characteristic feature of spontaneous yoga; that is, Trika Yoga lies in the fact that right logic (*tarka*) constitutes its best or direct part.[54] Pure gnosis taking on the form of discrimination between the valuable and the spurious also is designated by the synonym *bhāvanā*.[55] Its rise instantly brings about *samādhi*.[56] The utility of *prāṇāyāma* is only through the medium of *tarka*.[57] There has been a lot of discussion on the nature of this right logic in the TA and the TS (Tantrasāra), and its close link with pure gnosis (*śuddhavidyā*) and descent of grace (*śaktipāta*) particularly has been asserted.[58] Such descriptions of *tarka* as being pure gnostical and intuitive imply an effort to retract yoga from the planes of mind and to found it on the base of pure gnosis. This positing of yoga on the plane of pure wisdom (*prajñā*) transcending body and mind clearly points to the third current of yoga. These twin ideas—rejection of *prāṇāyāma* and assertion of *sattarka*—are extremely important from the point of view of the historical evolution of Trika yoga, because to J such an analysis is seminal to the emergence of a new model or pattern of yoga.

6

According to J, Trika yoga is six-limbed (*ṣaḍaṅga*) yoga as distinguished from the eight-limbed (*aṣṭāṅga*) yoga of Patañjali. AG finds an echo of the original spirit of Patañjali's yoga in the twofold division of artificial and spontaneous types propounded by the MVT together with another Āgama, the Vīrāvali. Restraint, observance, sitting posture, breath regulation, and abstraction are the five external *aṅgas* whereas retentive concentration, meditation, and trance are considered the inner aspects (*aṅgas*) in Patañjali's yoga.[59] Even this inner triad is viewed as external from the point of view of *nirbīja samādhi.*[60] In this *samādhi,* the innermost elements are steadiness (*abhyāsa*) and absolute nonattachment (i.e., absolute independence: *para-vairāgya*).[61] The triple instrumental scheme of Pātañjala yoga may be presented in tabular form in the following manner:

1. Innermost—steadiness and absolute nonattachment;
2. Internal—meditation, retentive concentration, and trance;
3. External—five *aṅgas* from restraint to abstraction.

AG seeks to introduce a modification in the traditional scheme inasmuch as the eight limbs or parts of yoga (which are interknitted in a linear sequence where each succeeding element serves as an instrument of the preceding) are conducive to the rise of *tarka.* They have no immediate bearing on awareness.[61] From this it follows that even *samādhi,* the final component of yoga, is an aide of or a tool for *tarka,* which acquires finality and supremacy in the hierarchy of *yogāṅgas.*

J tries to rationalize AG's allusion to Patañjali's eight limbs at the expense of the six limbs of his own *tantrayoga* on the grounds that nowhere *yogāṅgas* exceeding eight are spoken of and that all of them are conducive to *tarka* and not to the perceptual experience of consciousness. This vision of awareness is realizable through *tarka* alone.[63] The Trika Yoga is distinguished from Patañjali's Yoga on these grounds.[64]

J's reticence as to the identity of these six parts, however, is intriguing. While explaining the word *tarka* in his Viveka on TA 1, 15, he cites a verse from an unnamed source[65] that reproduces verbatim five parts of Pātañjala yoga from *prāṇāyāma* to *samādhi* placing a sixth, *tarka,* in between *dhāraṇā* and *samādhi.* We actually encounter this verse in Bhaṭṭa Bhāskara's commentary on the Gītā, dated long before J.[66] But there, too, it is extracted from some other source.[67] The earliest reference on *ṣaḍaṅga* is traceable to the Maitrāyaṇī Upaniṣad[68] (MaiUp), whose six parts tally with J's, but appear in a different sequence. Similar enumerations with minor alterations in order are found in the Viṣṇu Saṃhitā (30, 61-72), one of the Pāñcarātra Āgamas. On the other side, a closer perusal reveals that the citation of J and Bhaṭṭa Bhāskara is traceable to the Guhyasamājatantra[69] with a single variation: substitution of *tarkaś caiva* with *anusmṛtiḥ.*[70] The term *anusmṛti* stands for remembrance of realization(s) in the previous birth, a meaning radically different from the concept of *tarka* in the Tantric traditions. One point is crystal clear, however: that the doctrine of *ṣaḍaṅga* yoga is a more or less common trait of the Tantra-yoga traditions and that it has fairly early roots in history. There must have been a fair amount of interaction among the several Tantric traditions as well as between the Vedic and Tantric cultures. It is difficult, indeed, to hypothesize on who exactly was the borrower or lender. The rationale behind the frequent rejection of *yama, niyama,* and *āsana* from the scheme of *yogāṅgas* seems to lay in the belief that Tantra yoga is a convenient method as compared to the non-Tantric yogas, which are painfully cumbersome because of their insistence on torturing the body;[71] and also that the main occupation of yoga is to discipline the mind, thereby reducing *yama* and so on, which obviously are body based, to superfluity.[72] Thus the class of yogas characterized by *prāṇāyāma* and so forth and described as "artificial" by the MVT (18, 19) not only covers Patañjali's yoga, it also includes other Tantric traditions that do not subscribe to the notion of *tarka*.

7

The problem, however, remains unresolved as to whether Trika yoga is six limbed. Both the MVT and the Vīrāvali Tantra are silent on the issue. They classify the *yogāṅgas* into two types: ordinary (*sādhāraṇa*) and excellent (*utkṛṣṭa*). Whereas all other *yogāṅgas* are ordinary, *tarka* is extraordinary or excellent. *Tarka* reflects that state of mind which is temperamentally disposed to discriminate between what to accept and what to discard (*upādeya* and *heya*) and is endowed with the capacity to redirect the mind set on an undesirable path toward the immaculate plane. Drawing on an anonymous source, J projects it as a synonym of *ūha* (reasoning, examining).[73] The Mṛgendrāgama mentions *vīkṣaṇa* or *abhivīkṣaṇa* (literally, perception) as a part of yoga.[74] The same is equated with *ūha*.[75] The commentator, Nārāyaṇakaṇṭha, quotes the Svāyambhuvāgama to endorse *ūha*.[76] Another citation by J defines *sattarka* as *tarka* (logic) in harmony with the scriptures.[77] This citation then is a reiteration of Manu's statement.[78] In Indian tradition, the idea of *tarka* has enjoyed enviable prestige right from the date of the Nirukta. After the lineage of seers came to its end, people enquired of the gods as to who was now to discharge a seer's function from their midst. The gods in answer granted the faculty of *tarka* to humankind announcing that this faculty henceforth would be a substitute for seership among them.[79] From the preceding discussion it is amply evident that the evolution of the theme of *sattarka* offers a lively record of fertile exchange between the Vedic and Tantric cultures. But it hardly goes to strengthen the six-limbed character of Trika yoga.

Besides J, KR is the only person in the monistic tradition of KS who mentions *ṣaḍaṅga* yoga. For him the term *yogin* in the NT 1, 8 stands for the worshipper of God through *ṣaḍaṅga* yoga.[80] KR does not go beyond this. The NT itself refers to the *aṣṭāṅga* (eight-limbed) yoga.[81] At a proper occasion we propose to look into the mutual divergences of the two—the NT's and Patañjali's—*aṣṭāṅga* yogas. Just before we found the Mṛgendrāgama to adhere to the eight-limbed yogic modality,[82] though it is substantially different from that of Patañjali. Until later, even through the eighteenth century, this predilection for the *aṣṭāṅga* continues. Bhāskarakaṇṭha, the commentator of AG's Vimarśinī, interprets *yogī* to mean *aṣṭāṅga yogī*.[83] Moreover, not only is the order of *ṣaḍaṅga* yoga as adopted by J totally absent in MVT (except that *samādhi* is retained after *tarka*), it also is not endorsed by the order upheld by AG in the TA. According to J, *tarka* precedes *samādhi* whereas for AG it succeeds *samādhi* and thereby retains its position as the most exalted and ultimate part of yoga.

On the strength of the preceding discussion perhaps it might not sound premature to suggest that under the spell of the tendency to *ṣaḍaṅga* in the Tantra yoga repeated efforts were made to rechannel the original current of Trika yoga into that of the *ṣaḍaṅga* yoga right from the start. But they failed because of the totalistic (*aṣṭāṅga* tendency) and nondualistic (only *sattarka*) orientations of Trika yoga.

8

Let us now move over to the third model of Tantra yoga. The entire approach of the NT seems to be triadic. For the realization of the absolute, technically called *Mṛtyujit* ('Conqueror of Death') or *Amṛteśa* ('Lord of Ambrosia') or *Netra* ('Eye-Vision'), three means are envisaged here; viz., mantra, yoga, and *jñāna*. Amongst these, yoga, too, is threefold on the basis of its division into the gross, the subtle, and the ultimate (*sthūla, sūkṣma,* and *para*). *Homa* ('fire rite'), *japa* ('muttering'), *mudrā* ('posture'), *dhyāna* ('meditation'), *yantra* ('diagram'), and a variety of mantras are subsumed under *sthūla* yoga. *Sūkṣma* yoga is accomplished through the rise of the arteries (*nāḍīs*) led by *kalā* and through the vehicle of the six plexuses (*ṣaṭcakra*) and sixteen bases (*ādhāra*). *Para* yoga consists in envisioning the universal plenary essence of Amṛteśa. *Sthūla* yoga secures the attainment of higher worlds or entrance into the realm of *śuddha-vidyā*. *Sūkṣma* divinizes the body, paving the way for reaching the absolute. And, through *para* yoga, the *yogin* achieves total liberation and supreme subjectivity.[84] KR attempts a double interpretation of *sūkṣma* yoga on the basis of *kula*- and *tantra-prakriyās*.[85] According to *kulaprakriyā*, in brief, the *yogin* elevates the power of consciousness identical with the absolute through the path of *udāna* (upward vital breath), which is located in the central artery (*suṣumṇā*). Having secured a foothold in the genetic region (*janmādhāra*) due to the force of the virility of the mantra, the *yogin* reaches the *dvādaśānta* (a point twelve finger spaces above the crown of the head) by piercing the sixteen bases and twelve knots with the needle of resonance (*nāda*) via the route of the central artery. Here the *yogin* tastes the wondrous elixir of life through the envisioning the everpresent Parama Śiva and Parā Śakti in his heart lotus. The *yogin* then visualizes that this elixir has filled every part of the body, flowing through the innumerable arteries. Thus conquering age and death, the *yogin* becomes the Lord Mṛtyujit himself.

Under *tantraprakriyā*, *sūkṣma* yoga seeks to integrate the *yogin's* individual consciousness (*citta*) with the vital energy vibrating in the genetic region (*kandabhūmi*). The yogin established in the *khecarī* state enters the *dvādaśānta* by piercing six plexuses, sixteen bases, and twelve knots. Having directly perceived Parama Śiva he or she makes Him descend to the mental plane (*samanāpada*) and inclines Him toward creation. Having brought down the inward power through the central artery, the *yogin* sprinkles all the plexuses and bases with the ambrosia obtained from the moon on its rise at the emergence of the outgoing or downward vital breath (*apāna*). This ambrosia purifies the body of the *yogin* who then gets united with Śiva having will, knowledge, and action as His powers. Toward the twentieth chapter of the NT, KR in his commentary identifies subtle yoga under *tantraprakriyā* with *śāktopāya*. According to him the power of knowledge reflecting spontaneous resonance (which is the crux of *śāktopāya*) is very well suited to become the vehicle of this kind of spiritual realization.[86]

Aṣṭāṅga yoga itself is recognized as *para* yoga in the NT,[87] but it is quite different from its namesake propagated by Patañjali. Even though all the terms are derived from Patañjali's, they carry gnostical definitions. Thus, restraint (*yama*) consists of constant detachment from the world. Observance (*niyama*) is the continued visualization of the ultimate principle. Sitting posture (*āsana*) consists of staying in the power of knowledge with the assistance of the middle, that is, ascending, vital breath (*udāna*). Regulation of breath consists of the experience of vibration of consciousness, which is one with the suprasubtle state of vital energy, far beyond its gross and subtle states. Abstraction (*pratyāhāra*) consists of entering into the ultimate abode through the vehicle of one's mind, retracting it from experiences of determinate objective states such as sound and touch. Retentive concentration (*dhāraṇā*) is that by which the ultimate reality is held within. Meditation (*dhyāna*) is the envisioning of the self-experiential transcendental reality by going beyond the operation of intellect. As to *samādhi*, the NT resorts to four definitions.[88] According to KR, these four are assertions of *samādhis* attainable through four *upāyas*; namely, *āṇava*, *śākta*, *śāmbhava*, and *anupāya*. Equanimity with regard to all creatures constitutes the first kind. The feeling "I am verily Śiva and there is nothing beyond me" ensuing from the synthesis of I-ness and thisness constitutes the *śākta samādhi*.[89] According to KR, it also represents the standard notion of *samādhi* in the Śaiva traditions.[90] The spontaneous manifestation of self-experiential plenary consciousness constitutes *samādhi* of the third type, which is homologous with the ever-awake transphenomenal (*avyutthāna*) *samādhi* attainable through *anupāya*. Similarly, the figuring of the eternal and permanent principle of consciousness permeating the entire sentient and insentient creation constitutes indeterminate *samādhi* of the *śāmbhava* type.

The triplicity in the triple yoga—*para*, *sūkṣma*, and *sthūla*—set forth by the NT may be accounted for in terms of its primary dependence on *jñāna*, yoga, and mantra, respectively.[91] On this count, there is a semblance of similarity between these three and the four *upāyas*. *Sthūla* yoga (primarily of the nature of gross meditation) may be identified with *āṇava upāya*; *sūkṣma yoga* (primarily of the nature of subtle meditation) with *śākta* and *śāmbhava upāyas* in accordance with its adherence to the *tantra*- and *kulaprakriyās*; and *para* yoga[92] (primarily of the nature of transcendental meditation) with *anupāya* characterized by immediacy of knowledge. This is the only valid upshot that ensues from the thesis of fourfold *samādhi* resulting from *para* yoga. By extending the idea one may also contend that though a direct parallelism between the triple yoga of the NT and the threefold/fourfold yoga of the MVT may not be apparent, the possibility of synthesizing the fourfold yoga, developed subsequently, with the present four *samādhis* cannot be ruled out.

The main contrast between the *aṣṭāṅga* yoga of the NT and that of Patañjali is that the latter is action oriented and the former knowledge oriented. KR, however, has a different perception. To him the *aṣṭāṅga* yoga in the NT is actuated by transmundane considerations, and that of Patañjali by mundane ones.[93] But such contentions are acceptable only to a certain point. It is like this: there is no generally accepted relationship between the *upāya* and *aṣṭāṅga* schemes, yet by positing four classes of *samādhi* on the basis of the four *upāyas* and by assigning their accomplishment to the instrumentality of these *upāyas*, an effort is definitely under way to forge unity between the yogic process of the *aṣṭāṅga* and the Tantric process of the fourfold *upāya*. It is possible that the *aṣṭāṅga* process inheres evenly in all the four *upāyas-yogas* and emerges as the background mechanism for effecting these *upāyas*. In a nutshell, the yogic scheme of the NT as interpreted by KR may be presented in a tabular form as shown in Figure 1.

Figure 1.

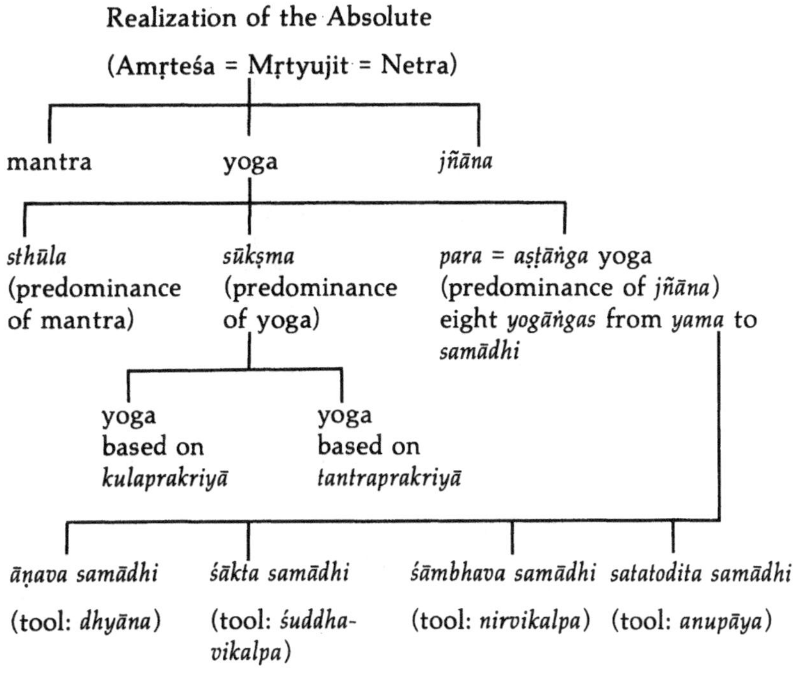

Two conclusions clearly emerge from the foregoing discussion. In the first place, Pātañjala yoga has substantially influenced the evolution of Trika yoga with regard to both inner structure and formal growth. This has led to two obvious consequences. One is the continued fidelity to *aṣṭāṅga* yoga despite the occasional leanings toward *ṣaḍaṅga* yoga; the other is that *aṣṭāṅga* yoga has gained acceptance only after undergoing a transformation of its original stance. The second conclusion is that the intrinsic characteristics of the Tantric current have lent a new framework, shape, and thrust due to which Trika yoga represents a mixed form of Pātañjala and Haṭha yoga, acquiring along the way a transcendental disposition. This is because of its sole occupation with the immersion in or the rise of plenary awareness, which is nothing but the synthesis of knowledge and action.

9

Interestingly, there is a dearth of systematic presentation of the linear structure of these *yogāṅgas*, notwithstanding the reverential attitude toward them in the Śaiva tradition. Barring the definitions in the NT, duly endorsed by the SVT 7, 252-253, the treatment of *yama* and *niyama* largely is conspicuous by its absence.[94]

SS 3, 16 and KR[95] come quite close to Patañjali in their presentation of *āsana*. But KR's interpretation of SS 3, 16 reverses the trend and echoes the position taken by the NT that replaces its substrate *jñānaśakti* with *śāktabala* (autonomous force).[96] *Prāṇāyāma*, however, has elicited relatively solid analysis. After having secured stability in *āsana*, effecting cessation of either motions—that is, inhalation and exhalation (*gati-viccheda*)—is *prāṇāyāma* in Patañjali.[97] This cessation of motion offers the real ground for the cessation of mental states (*nirodha* = *gativiccheda*). *Dhāraṇā* (retentive concentration) and *dhyāna* (meditation) in fact are gradual extensions of this process. Through the process of increasing attenuation, inhalation and exhalation cease completely in *samādhi*. From this we may take it that the notions of *recaka* ('exhaler'), *pūraka* ('inhaler'), and *kumbhaka* ('holder or retainer'), and so on, frequently figuring in Tantra yoga, are different from the *prāṇāyāma* of Pātañjala yoga.[98] Nonetheless, the concept of *prāṇāyāma* that one gets in the MVT is couched in terms of "break in motion" (*gatibhaṅga*) reminiscent of the yogic phraseology. But here it has five varieties: *pūraka*, *recaka*, *kumbhaka*, *apakarṣaka* (going back or reverting), and *utkarṣaka* (reaching out).[99] Another mode of *prāṇāyāma*, already noticed in the NT, ipso facto is different from the yogic *prāṇāyāma*, because of their conflicting emphases on the experience of supreme vibration and the absence thereof respectively. The third interpretation presents *prāṇāyāma* in terms of subjecting the vital breath to one's will by conquering, that is, consummating, its spontaneous flow. This is KR's definition in SVTU.[100] But the SVT itself does not offer any definition of *prāṇāyāma*, though it does talk of *recaka, pūraka,* and *kumbhaka*. Each of them has two forms: external and internal. The external represents the form in which we ordinarily understand them. In their internal form, *recana* exists in the *dvādaśānta, pūraṇa* in the heart and *kumbhaka* in the state of motionlessness. This is an important idea, because it strengthens the foundation of the upward movement of the vital breath, a highly valued theme in the Tantras, or that of the subtle yoga propounded in the NT. Besides these six, there is a seventh mode of *prāṇāyāma*, also called *praśānta-kumbhaka* (literally, motionless holding of breath).[101] This is its effortless state. Together with *pratyāhāra, dhāraṇā,* and *dhyāna*, it accounts for the "tenfold yogic path"[102] alluded to in the SVT.

Elaboration on *pratyāhāra* is difficult to come by in Tantra yoga. In Patañjali, abstraction is that by which the senses, without coming in contact with their objects, imitate the mind as if it were the vacant state of mind.[103] According to KR, the phrase *bhūtakaivalya* in SS 3, 5 (freedom from elements) denotes the stage of abstraction.[104] Isolation from the five elements leads to the abstraction of mind. KR provides a Haṭhayogic dimension to it by pointing to the correspondence of *suśāntaprāṇāyāma* (literally, 'extremely motionless state of breath holding'), which succeeds *praśāntakumbhaka*, with *pratyāhāra*. To install both the vital breath (by slowly bringing it down from the heart) and the mind (by distracting it from objects) in the navel is *pratyāhāra*. The MVT, too, dwells briefly on *pratyāhāra*. By steadily concentrating on any external object such as sound, the mind becomes one with the object during the course of grasping it. After having attained unity with it, the mind again becomes vacant to the extent that it remains totally unattached from other objective activity notwithstanding vigorous efforts to the contrary. The yoga is consummated through the regulation of breath accompanied by repeated mental abstraction. The MVT here squares with Patañjali's teaching on *pratyāhāra* except that the senses are replaced here by mind.[105] As cautioned earlier, these presentations suffer from the lack of tidy consecutiveness of Patañjali's yogic scheme. The elucidation of *pratyāhāra* in the MVT only comes as a sequel to *tarka* and *samādhi* and not before.

Dhāraṇā ranks first among the internal *yogāṅgas* in Patañjali's scheme. According to Vyāsa, *dhāraṇā* is the experiential steadfastness of mind in (spiritual) centers such as the plexus of the navel, the lotus of the heart, the cerebral light, the nasal forepart, and the forepart of the tongue. The sensory steadfastness of mind in the external objects also is *dhāraṇā*.[106] Āraṇya talks of a twofold division of *dhāraṇā*: metaphysical and objective.[107] Even though the first type depends on the spiritual centers located within the senses, metaphysical knowledge remains its primary support. Among the objective *dhāraṇās* those of light and sound happen to be the frontal ones. The notion of *dhāraṇā* draws widespread acclaim in the Tantras, as the idea of plexuses or cycles obtains enormous significance in them in connection with the ascent of coiled energy (*kuṇḍalinī*). Though *dhāraṇā* and so forth in the MVT are called *external yogāṅgas* and considered inconsequential for the realization of pure awareness, it merits special notice that its Chapters 12 to 18[108] are focused on the theme of *dhāraṇās*.

There is no apparent attempt to define *dhāraṇā* in the MVT, yet some traces come to notice that throw light on the interaction between yoga and Tantra. *Dhāraṇās* are subjected to division either on the basis of their objects (*lakṣyabheda*) or focused mental state (*cittabheda*). Six types of objects are taken note of: ether (*vyoma*), body (*vigraha*), point (*bindu*), syllable (*arṇa*), region (*bhuvana*), and sound (*dhvani*).[109] The variety of objects leads to a variety of fruitions. But the difference in mental states or in the *dhāraṇās* based on them does not cause any difference in fruition.[110] Four *dhāraṇās* figure mainly in this context: *śikhi, ambvi, īśānī*, and *amṛtā*. Their spiritual spheres are navel, heart, palate, and throat. The uniform characteristic of these *dhāraṇās* lies in the grasp of the focused object in its universality.[111] The other feature consists in the *yogin's* attainment of the excellent abode preceded by relinquishing the undesirable. What is most striking to note is that a vigorous attempt is afoot to tune in the yogic *dhāraṇās* with the Trika concept of yoga. The intimate proximity of the division of mental states and that of objects with the yogic attempt to differentiate between the metaphysical and the objective *dhāraṇās* is quite obvious; similar is the case of the regions of navel and heart and their yogic counterpart, that is, plexus of navel and so forth. KR connects the "conquest of the elements" (*bhūtajaya*) in SS 3, 5 with *dhāraṇā*. The conquest over the earth and other elements implies their submission to the *yogin's* control wrought by *dhāraṇās*.[112] KR refers to SVT 7, 299-300, where the four *dhāraṇās*—windy, fiery, earthy, and watery—are stated to lead to all sorts of fulfillment on their ascension from the big toe to the *dvādaśānta* by concentrating upon navel, throat, heart, and uvula (*ghaṇṭikā*). This description of *dhāraṇā* seems to deviate somewhat from the yogic notion. KR admits that the fulfillments (*siddhi*) arising from *dhāraṇās* belong to the orbit of delusion (*moha*) and not to the realm of metaphysical knowledge.[113] For a *yogin* who has transcended the realm of *moha*, the connotations of *dhāraṇā*, *dhyāna*, and so on are completely transformed into the interpretations accorded by the NT, as already seen by us.

There is hardly any pronouncement on *dhyāna* as a *yogāṅga* in the Trika texts. At a couple of places where it is mentioned (e.g., TA 1, 89), it represents transcendental meditation or *japa*. Apart from the NT, which interprets *dhyāna* in purely metacognitive terms, RK resorts to the terminology of *prāṇic* movement to define *dhyāna* in the SB. As a *yogāṅga*, *dhyāna* is that singly focused intellect by which both the inward and outward vital breaths (*prāṇa* and *apāna*), having a simultaneous even flow, are transfigured into the mode called *samāna* (i.e., 'even').[114]

10

We have made some observations with regard to *samādhi* at the outset of this chapter as well as during our treatment of *para* yoga in the NT. At this point, only two issues merit attention. In the first place, *samādhi* in Pātañjala yoga is essentially the self-repose (*svarūpa-pratiṣṭhā*) of the consciousness (*citiśakti*) or *puruṣa*; that is, it is a state of absolute isolation entirely devoid of any contact with matter (*prakṛti*). In Trika yoga it is the spontaneous condition of awareness characterized by integral dynamism. *Samādhi* thus is the realization of or the reflection on the *yogin's* autonomous essence subsuming even the unconscious (*acit*), its own offshoot, within itself.[115] Unlike the state of absolute motionlessness or that of the cessation of mental states as propounded in yoga, it is the recognition and reaffirmation of self-being. Whereas *kaivalya* underscores the exclusion of consciousness from unconsciousness, Trika *samādhi* reflects the emphasis on the progressive sublimation of unconsciousness and consequent synthesis of it with consciousness.

In the second place, the opposition between the two *samādhis* issues forth from the fundamental attitudes of the two philosophical systems toward reality and life best illustrated by their aesthetic propositions. In *sāṃkhya* (that is, *yoga*), the *yogin* or the emancipated being observes the operation of Prakṛti like an uninvolved spectator of a dramatic performance.[116] But in KS, the senses of the *yogin* by turning inward directly apprehend their essential nature exclusively centered on enjoyment arising from the projection of this worldly drama. Having dissolved their dichotomic existence they bring to fulfillment the rapture of self-relish in its totality because of the consummation of the dramatic performance.[117]

But it is also true, and noteworthy too, that the compact structure of *samādhi* that has evolved with time in the Yoga system is not easily to be seen in Trika yoga. Whatever structure one gets at is quite loose and scattered. We therefore shall endeavor to see if there is a possibility of a coherent structure emerging on the basis of a comparative estimate of various levels and types attributed to yoga as well as to the *yogin.*

At one place, the MVT mentions seeded (*sabīja*) yoga. This implies that there must be some trace of the seedless (*nirbīja*) yoga in the mind of the proclaimer of the MVT. These two terms remind us of their Pātañjala counterparts, which encompass all the varieties of *samprajñāta-* and *asamprajñāta-samādhi,* respectively. However, the MVT does not offer any definition of *sabīja* yoga except laying down the efficacy of mantra knowledge for crystallization of *sabīja* (i.e., determinate) yoga.[118] It appears that the notion of Śaiva yoga must be a relatively broad one; because Śaiva initiation, identical with knowledge and action, is held to be indispensable for earning eligibility for Śaiva yoga. Now this *śivadīkṣā* grants eligibility not for yoga alone, but for mantra too. If the knowledge of mantra is a tool for the fulfillment of *sabīja* yoga, the conclusion could be drawn that the term *yoga* in the phrase *eligibility for yoga* (*yogādhikāritva*) stands for *nirbīja* yoga. The term *śivadīkṣā* (or *śāṃkarī dīkṣā*) in the MVT has occurred before. Differentiating Śiva initiation from yoga initiation, its author asserts that the former leads to liberation instantly, or at the fall of the body after the fruition of deeds. Yoga initiation (which relates to gradual yoga) leads to yogic perfection and, in the end, to the eternal abode; that is, ultimate self.[119] On the strength of the available material we might perhaps contend that both knowledge and mantra, or Śiva initiation and yoga initiation, fall within the wide orbit of Śiva initiation, and that both initiations make one attain the ultimate fulfillment of yoga through recourse to knowledge and mantra, respectively. This appears to be the only intelligible implication of the "conduciveness" (*upakāritā*) of mantra knowledge for the consummation of the seeded yoga.

KR, in the SpN,[120] refers to two types of *samādhi*; viz., *nimīlana* ('enfolding') and *unmīlana* ('unfolding'). In *nimīlana samādhi,* the enfolding consists in turning in toward the self, by the process of involution or retrogression, of that consciousness which is expanding externally through the senses. Similarly, the expansion of *śakti* consists of the outward growth and expansion of the internally hidden *śakti* through the simultaneous opening of all the sense organs in the course of evolution. KR considers this process as particularly Tantric and takes credit for its propagation even though it is omitted by the Pratyabhijñā texts.[121] The Śaivāṣṭaka Kośa equates the enfolding *samādhi* with the absolutic state accessible through *śāmbhavopāya* and unfolding *samādhi* with the experience of the universal I-ness attainable through *śāktopāya*.[122] But KR's treatment makes it abundantly clear that he relates it with all the *upāyas*. To Maheśvarānanda it represents the pinnacle of Trika yoga marked by synthesis of the two *samādhis*.[123] The impact of the phenomenal (*vyutthāna* = literally rise) and transphenomenal (*nirvyutthāna*, literally, absence of rise), or the seeded and seedless (*sabīja* and *nirbīja*) *samādhis* propounded by Patañjali, is quite evident here—with regard to both content as well as formal structure—because *nityodita* (ever-awake) *samādhi* is recognized here as the transphenomenal (*nirvyutthāna*) *samādhi*. In the Yoga system, the phenomenal *samādhi* is considered determinate and the transphenomenal indeterminate. All the *siddhis* and fruitions, technically styled as *vibhūtis*, pertain to the ordinary worldly mind (*vyutthita citta*). Otherwise, they are deemed to be obstacles for the mind permanently stabilized in *samādhi* (*samāhitacitta* or *nirvyutthāna*). In Trika yoga, the synthesis of these two states has been brought about in two ways: one, characteristic of Trika yoga itself, by asserting the continuity and interaction between the two, as we saw in the enfolding-unfolding *samādhi*; and two, characteristic of Patañjali's yoga, by distinguishing between the finite and the great or supreme yogin (*mitayogin* and *mahā-* or *paramayogin*, respectively) and, by implication, between the ordinary or finite yoga and the supreme yoga.[124] One who is steady in the practice of the vertical path of yogic progression is called *mitayogin*, and one who is effortlessly established in one's intrinsic essence is *mahāyogin*. All the *siddhis* relate to the finite yoga, whereas the ultimate fulfillment, that is, manifestation of one's essence, is intimately linked with the supreme yoga.[125] The NT places the issue in clearer focus by its division of *yogins* into two types: reflexive (*sābhāsa*) and nonreflexive (*nirābhāsa*). A reflexive *yogin* is endowed with qualities such as omniscience, envisioning their reflexiveness. Similarly, the *yogin* who concentrates exclusively on the reflective awareness transcending the object-referential and subject-referential awareness is called *nonreflexive*.[126]

The apparent contradiction between these two states is sought to be reconciled in Trika yoga by splitting them into a stage of processing (*sādhanāvasthā*) and a stage of accomplishment (*siddhāvasthā*). This technique of reconciliation has won support from almost all the quarters of Trika yoga. All other stages fall between these two extremes, creating a semblance of their organisation into a progressive hierarchical structure. Inspired by SpK, KR conceives three stages of a finite-adept *yogin*: the dull, the awake, and the thoroughly awake (*mūḍha, prabuddha,* and *suprabuddha*), respectively.[127] The dull is one whose essential nature is not adequately manifested. Despite having realized the quietive essence of all objects, one continues to slumber in the state of deep sleep or zero subjectivity (*śūnyapramātṛtā*). The awake one constantly exerts oneself to regain one's essential being. In the Spanda branch, one's being is said to consist in its vibrational essence. The *yogin* is ceaselessly making efforts to imbibe this essence. The effort (*udyama*) consists in the employment of the following two techniques:[128]

> 1. By the method of contraction of limbs like a tortoise, one stills or causes to subside the negative states such as doubt, anger, or frustration (*kūrmāṅgasaṃkocayukti*);
>
> 2. By the method of great expansion one causes the positive states such as joy, rapid movement, and so forth to vibrate and bloom (*mahāvikāsayukti*).

Having reflected on the power of vibration in such a state of spiritual readiness brought about by these techniques, the *yogin* is liberated.

The third kind of *yogin*, the thoroughly awake, dwells in the state of constant immersion styled as "ever-awake" (*nityodita*). Yet there is a stage beyond all of them, the stage of the *mahāyogin*. The thoroughly awake revels in eternal spiritual presence, but the *mahāyogin* is endowed with infinite agency and subjectivity (*kartṛtva* and *jñātṛtva*) as well. In the words of SpK, one remains constantly immersed in oneself viewing the whole universe as one's play and sporting its projection and withdrawal by unfolding and enfolding of his awareness.[129] Such a *yogin* liberated within lifetime (*jīvanmukta*) becomes verily the godhead on the fall of the body. KR authenticates this state from SS also[130] and, seeking correspondence with the phases of experience displayed by RK, he identifies the thoroughly awake with the fourth state and the great *yogin* with the "beyond fourth" state.[131]

For the original inspiration behind such a classification, resorted to by KR and subsequently by Maheśvarānanda and others, one may look in the MVT itself. The success of yoga lies in its consummation, hence the four types of *yogin* are thought of by the MVT in keeping with the stages of fulfillment reached.[132] These four are (1) the recipient (*saṃprāpta*), (2) the practicing (*ghaṭamāna*), (3) the accomplished (*siddha*), and (4) the supremely accomplished (*susiddha* or *siddhatama*). The recipient inherits the teaching through the established tradition that is threefold due to the three types of yoga; *śāmbhava*, *śākta*, and *āṇava*. The practicing is one who assiduously reverts one's mind, staying away from the continually focused reality. The accomplished is one whose mind is riveted on only one object to the exclusion of others. And the supremely accomplished is established unflinchingly in enjoying the object of contemplation. This one is likened to Sadāśiva in the system.[133] But the *mahāyogin* is above all, actually constituting the plane of the absolute; that is, Śiva. At this stage, whatever flavor one tastes becomes an offering to the divine; whatever syllable one utters becomes *japa*; whatever form one sees becomes meditation.[134] In fact, the whole life of a great *yogin* is metamorphosed into sublime yoga.

11

On the basis of what already has been said we may certainly assert that yoga constitutes the basic paradigm of Trika thought. We also may say that even though Trika yoga displays deep receptivity toward the far-reaching influences of Patañjali's yoga in format, framework, and structure of argumentation, it exploits these influences as the raw material for evolving its exclusive personality. The meaning, therefore, of the terms *vṛttiśama* and *nirvikalpa* undergoes a transformation. They do not mean "cessation or absence of the mental states," but instead represent the reveling of the self in its innate condition. This emphasis on spontaneity and effortlessness is not only natural but also logical for Trika yoga. The precise connotation of the effortless state consists in the repose of self within the self as such and at the same time in symbolizing its potential for autonomous expression. This is because the self is not simply a pure witness or observer, but also the autonomous agent. The autonomy of action or agency consists of its spontaneous overflow without being occasioned by any cause or purpose. The aim of Trika yoga, therefore, lies not in attaining one's inactive witnessing state, but in realizing one's essence defined by intrinsic freedom of action and cognition. In other words, even though Patañjali's yoga begins with activity, it rejects that by the time it reaches its finale. On the other hand, Trika yoga, and for that matter Tantric yoga as such, starts with activity and culminates in activity. As a logical corollary, the yogin falls back on the process of sublimation or upliftment in place of cessation or suppression (*nirodha*). Such a course accounts for the continuity of awareness as well as its perfection. In the annals of Trika yoga, the supreme *yogin* has earned a specific designation, namely, *sāṃsiddhika* (one having instinctive realization), in whom *sattarka* rises on its own, instantaneously.[135] Such a person is the great being alluded to in the system as *yogin*[136] or *mahāyogin*[137] to illustrate and symbolize the supreme agency or the ultimate lordliness.

Notes

1. Mircea Eliade, *Yoga: Immortality and Freedom.* trans. Williard R. Trask (Princeton, N.J.: Princeton University Press, 1970), p. 359.

2. *Yoga: Immortality and Freedom*, p. 359.

3. *Yogakṣemaṃ vahāmy aham*, Bhagavad-gītā (BhG) 9, 22. Yoga is achieving something unattained hitherto: *aprāptasya prāpaṇam.*

4. *Jñānaṃ tattajjñeyatattvānubhavaṃ yogaṃ tadaikātmyaprāptim*, Uddyota on Svacchanda Tantra (SVTU) by Kṣemarāja (KR), published with the Svacchanda Tantra (SVT), in the Kashmir Series of Texts and Studies (KSTS), 1926, vol. 3, p. 141.

5. *Yogam ekatvam icchanti vastuno 'nyena vastunā*, Mālinīvijayottara Tantra (MVT), KSTS, 1922, vol. 4, p. 4.

6. *Pātañjala yogadarśanam* (PYD), Hariharānanda Āraṇya, Hindi translation from Bengali original, ed. R. S. Bhattacharya (Delhi: Motilal Banarsidass [MLBD], 1974), p. 3, note 1 (4).

7. Gopinath Kaviraja, *Bhāratīya Saṃskṛti aura Sādhanā* [in Hindi] (Patna: Bihar Rashtrabhasha Parishad, 1963), Pt. II, p. 381.

8. *Tantrāloka* (TA) by Abhinavagupta (AG), ed. R. C. Dwivedi and Navjivan Rastogi (MLBD, 1987), vol. 8, Āhn. 37, 14-15.

9. *Cittadvāreṇa ātmeśvarasaṃbandho yogaḥ*, Pāśupata-Sūtra 5, 2, as quoted in *Sarvadarśanasaṃgraha* (SDS), translated into Hindi by Umashankara Rishi, (Varanasi: Chowkhamba Vidyabhavana, 1964), p. 310.

10. *Tathā iha upadiṣṭasya ātmādvayajñānasya karmānuṣṭhānasamādhau niṣṭhā*, Sarvatobhadra commentary on the BhG (SB) by Rājānaka Rāmakaṇṭha (RK) (KSTS, 1943), p. 46.

11. *Yogaḥ saṃhananopāyadhyānasaṃgatiyuktiṣu*, Amarakośa by Amarasiṃha, (Varanasi: Haridas Sanskrit Series, 1949), 3, 3, 22.

12. *Yuj samādhau divādiḥ / yujir yoge rudhādiḥ / dvayor api grahaṇam*, Kāśikā on Aṣṭādhyāyī 3, 2, 142, by Vāmana and Jayāditya (Kashi Sanskrit Granthamālā, 1952).

13. *Yogaḥ samādhiḥ*, Bhāṣya on Yoga Sūtra (YS) 1, 1, by Vyāsa (YSB), incorporated in PYD, p. 1.

14. *Samādhir yoga ucyate*, SB, p. 46; *yogaḥ samādhiḥ*, SB, p. 62.

15. *Yogaś cittavṛttinirodhaḥ*, YS 1, 2.

16. See PYD, p. 3 (translation from Hindi mine).

17. SB, p. 62.

18. See PYD, Introduction, p. 28.

19. For detailed discussion, see PYD, Introduction, pp. 25-28.

20. *Samastavṛttipratyastamaye sati saṃvitturīyāṃ daśām avaśyam evāviśati, tatpratyavamarśābhyāsāt paratattvopalabdhiḥ*, Spanda Kārikā Vivṛti (SpKV), KR, (KSTS, 1969), p. 78.

21. *Sarvatra tāvad upāyamārge samastetaravṛttipraśamapūrvam ekāgrībhavanti yoginaḥ*, Nirṇaya on Spanda Kārikā (SpN) by KR (KSTS, 1925), p. 39.

22. TA 3, 260-261.

23. *Anāviśanto 'pi nimagnacittā jānanti vṛttikṣayasaukhyam antaḥ*, Mālinīvijayavārttika (MVV) by AG (KSTS, 1921), 2, 114.

24. Vikalpasya ca nirhrāso nirvikalpopalakṣaṇam / . . .
vikalpaviśrāntibalāt taṃ vṛttiṃ nābhimanvate /
vikalpanirhrāsavaśena yāti vikalpavandhyā paramārthasatyā, (MVV 1, 988-990).

25. *Sarvāvasthāsu aviluptabhairavasamāpattiḥ / eṣaiva ca nirvyutthānasamādhyātmā mahārahasyabhūḥ / yogināṃ tu tatra ādyantamadhyadaśāvagāhipramātṛsvarūpāvismaraṇarūpā samādhānateti / śuddhavidyotthānādhyavasāyarūpā samādhiḥ* (note 140 on Śivasūtravimarśinī (SSV), 1, 15, KR, KSTS).

26. See P. V. Kane, *History of Dharmaśāstra* (Kane), vol. 5, Pt. II, 1962, p. 1427.

27. KR is perhaps the first author in the history of KS, much before Jayaratha (J), who directly mentions both liturgies; i.e. *kula-* and *tantraprakriyā.*

28. Sā ca yogaṃ vinā yasmān na bhavet tam ato vada /
ṛṣibhir yogam icchadbhiḥ sa tair evam udāhṛtaḥ //
(MVT 1, 10).
Yogamārgas tvayā proktaḥ suvistīrṇo maheśvara
(ibid., 1, 10).

29. See note 5.

30. *Samāveśoktivad yogas trividhaḥ samudāhṛtaḥ,* MVT 4, 34.

31. See MVT 2, 21-23. For a detailed discussion, see my upcoming work, "*The Malinīvijayottara Tantra*" to be published by the Rudra Press, Cambridge, Mass.

32. The word *samāveśa* is generally rendered as "immersion." But this is a meaning acquired in the course of time. The rendering "possession" adopted here is close both to its original sense and the sense in which it figures in the MVT.

33. Evaṃ maheśvaro devo viśvātmatvena saṃsthitaḥ /
kramikajñānayogābhyāṃ dhāraṇābhir upāsyate //
(MVV 2, 1).

34. Ibid., 2, 32-33.

35. Ibid., 2, 19.

36. *Yatraivānandayogaḥ kvacana nanu bhavet tatra pūrṇaḥ svabhāvaḥ* (MVV 2, 118).

37. Ibid., 2, 34.

38. Ibid., 2, 26.

39. Ibid., 2, 41.

40. Ibid., 2, 83.

41. Ibid., 2, 20/77.

42. *Mahāsāhasasaṃyogavilīnākhilavṛttikaḥ,* ibid., 2, 86.

43. Ibid., 2, 87.

44. Ibid., 1, 23.

45. Ibid., 2, 120-121.

46. Ibid., 2, 140-141.

47. See also *The Significance of Tantric Tradition* by Kamalakara Misra, (Varanasi: Ardhanārīśvara Publications, 1981), pp. 144-145. I consider Misra's treatment excellent and agree on most points.

48. *Tantrasāra* (TS) by Abhinavagupta (KSTS, 1918), p. 17; TA 3, 211-213. See also my projected second volume of *The Krama Tantricism of Kashmir* (KT) (Delhi: MLBD, forthcoming), Chapter 1.

49. SSV, p. 39.

50. Ibid., p. 40.

51. *Tad evaṃ nāḍisaṃhārādyāṇavopāyakramāsāditamohajayonmajjacchud-dhavidyātmakaśāktabalāsādanaprakarṣād ātmīkṛtaparāmṛtahṛdātmakaśāmbhava-pado yogī* . . . (SSV, p. 46).

52. Ibid., pp. 38, 50.

53. Na ca kṛtrimayogeṣu sa muktaḥ sarvabandhanaiḥ //
prāṇāyāmādikair liṅgair yogāḥ syuḥ kṛtrimā matāḥ /
tena te 'kṛtakasyāsya kalāṃ nārhanti ṣoḍaśīm //
(MVT 18, 18-19).

54. Yogāṅgatve samāne 'pi tarko yogāṅgam uttamam /
heyādyālocanā tasmāt tatra yatnaḥ praśasyate //
(MVT 17, 18).

55. *Tad eva paramaṃ jñānaṃ bhāvanāmayam iṣyate* (ibid., 17, 20).

56. *Muhūrtād eva tatrasthaḥ samādhiṃ pratipadyate* (ibid., 17, 21).

57. Ityanena vidhānena pratyāhṛtya mano muhuḥ /
prāṇāyāmādikaṃ sarvaṃ kuryād yogaprasiddhaye //
(ibid., 17, 24).

58. TA 4, 34-37.

59. *Trayam antaraṅgaṃ pūrvebhyaḥ* (YS 3, 7).

60. *Tad api bahiraṅgaṃ nirbījasya* (YS, 3, 8).

61. *Abhyāsavairāgyābhyāṃ tannirodhaḥ* (YS 1, 12).

62. Yogāṅgatā yamādes tu samādhyantasya varṇyate /
svapūrvapūrvopāyatvād antyatarkopayogataḥ //
(TA 4, 96).

63. *Yannāmātra yogasya svadarśanoktāni ṣaḍaṅgāny apahāya Pātañjalīyaṃ*

yamādyaṅgāṣṭakam uktaṃ, tatrāyam āśayo—yat kvacid apy etadaṅgāṣṭakātiriktam anyadaṅgāntaraṃ nāsti, iti sarvatra tarkasyaivāṅgāntarāṇy upāyaḥ, sa ca svasaṃvitsākṣātkārasyeti (Tantrālokaviveka [TAV] by J, published with TA, vol. 3, pp. 718-719).

64. *Svarasasiddhasaṃvidadvayātmano yogasya svalpenāpy aṃśena darśanāntarīyā yogāḥ sāmyamātram apy adhigantuṃ notsahante* (TAV, vol. 3, p. 729).

65. Prāṇāyāmas tathā dhyānaṃ pratyāhāro 'tha dhāraṇā /
tarkaś caiva samādhiś ca ṣaḍaṅgo yoga ucyate //
(TAV, vol. 3, p. 631).

66. *BhG-bhāṣya* by Bhaṭṭa Bhāskara (Varanasi: Sarasvati Bhavan Granthamālā, 1965), p. 127. The identity of Bhaṭṭa Bhāskara is not beyond controversy. But the Kashmir commentaries on the BhG reflect clear signs of his impact on them. The Gītārthasaṃgraha by AG (ed. Laksmana Brahmachari, Srinagar, 1933, p. 170) indicates AG's familiarity with him. One Bhāskara figures among AG's teachers as well. If he is the same, we are richer by one more information on the history of the Kashmir Śaiva tradition on Ṣaḍaṅga Yoga.

67. A variant of *ṣaḍaṅga* yoga (though not called this) is found in RK's SB, which enumerates six limbs of the traditional yoga from *āsana* to *samādhi*. There is no reference, even oblique, to *tarka* or *sattarka*. RK's treatment reminds one of the Dhyānabindu Upaniṣad:

Āsanaṃ prāṇasaṃrodhaḥ pratyāhāraś ca dhāraṇā /
dhyānaṃ samādhir etāni yogāṅgāni bhavanti ṣaṭ //

Verse 41, quoted by P. V. Kane.

68. *Tathā tatprayogakalpaḥ / prāṇāyāmaḥ pratyāhāro dhyānaṃ dhāraṇā tarkaḥ samādhiḥ ṣaḍaṅga ity ucyate yogaḥ* (MaiUp. 2, 18 quoted by Kane, p. 1419). Kane draws our attention to a similar enumeration by Aparārka (on Yājñavalkya Smṛti 3, 110) from an earlier Smṛti source, and also to the Dakṣa Smṛti (7, 3).

69. *Guhyasamājatantra*, ed. Benoytosh Bhattacharya (Baroda: Oriental Institute, 1967), p. 163.

70. For a fuller treatment of Buddhist *ṣaḍaṅga* yoga, see the Introduction by Gopinath Kavirāja to the *Tāntrika Bauddha Sādhanā aura Sāhitya* [in Hindi] (Varanasi: Kashi Nagari Pracarini Sabha), Sam. 2015; S. B. Das Gupta, *An Introduction to Tantric Buddhism* (Calcutta: University of Calcutta, 1958), pp. 164-173.

71. Pūrvair nirodhaḥ kathito vairāgyābhyāsayogataḥ /

asmābhis tu nirodho 'yam ayatnenopadiśyate //
(quoted in TAV, vol. 3, p. 905).

72. Unfortunately, this rejection led to an unintended adverse outcome by which the whole of Tantric conduct lost its credibility. Scholars like Kane (quoted in the Introduction of the *Vijñānabhairava*, ed. Vrajavallabha Dwivedi [Vbh(D)] [MLBD, 1978], p. 36) had to conclude that *yama* and *niyama* were dismissed because they were directly opposed to the unscrupulous practice of the five M's (*pañcamakāra*).

73. TAV, vol. 3, p. 631.

74. Prāṇāyāmaḥ pratyāhāro dhāraṇā dhyānavīkṣaṇe /
japaḥ samādhir ity aṅgāny aṅgī yogo 'ṣṭamaḥ svayam //
(Mṛgendrāgama [MA], Yogapāda 3, quoted in Vbh(D), Introduction, p. 37).

75. Ūho 'bhivīkṣaṇaṃ vastuvikalpānantaroditaḥ /
yadā vetti padaṃ heyam upādeyaṃ ca tatsthiteḥ //
(MA, Yogapāda, 8-9).

J gives a long citation from an unidentified Tantric source that proves the equation of *īkṣaṇa* (*vīkṣaṇa*), *ūha*, and *tarka*. We quote:

Labdhabhūmer viraktasya tajjayopāyapeśalaḥ /
ūho nāma vitarkoktiḥ pravicārekṣaṇātmakaḥ // . . .
śakyante muniśārdūla tasmāt tarko 'pi yujyate /
(TAV, vol. 3, pp. 709-710).

76. See Vbh(D), Introduction, p. 38.

77. TAV, vol. 3, p. 632.

78. Ārṣaṃ dharmopadeśaṃ ca vedaśāstrāvirodhinā
yas tarkeṇānusandhatte sa dharmaṃ veda netaraḥ
(Manusmṛti 12, 106, quoted in the Introduction of Vbh(D), p. 37).

79. *Manuṣyā vā ṛṣīṣūtkrāmatsu devān abruvan ko na ṛṣibhir bhaviṣyatīti / tebhya etaṃ tarkam ṛṣiṃ prāyacchan* (Nirukta 13, 12, quoted in Vbh(D), Introduction, p. 37).

80. *Yoginaḥ ṣaḍaṅgādiyogeneśvarārādhakāḥ* (Netratantra Uddyota [NTU] by KR, published with NT, KSTS, Pt. 1, pp. 9-10).

81. NT 8, 9; 21.

82. See note 74.

83. *Bhāskarī* by Bhāskara Kaṇṭha, ed. K. A. S. Iyer and K. C. Pandey, (Allahabad, 1938), vol. 1, p. 227.

84. In the course of his elaboration, KR introduces several auxiliary techniques (see, e.g., NTU 20, 38-39) that are skipped here.

85. For details of *kula-* and *tantra-prakriyās,* see KT, vol. 1, pp. 32-34, and so on.

86. In this context, KR alludes to a *golakavidhi* (literally 'circular technique') that, according to Dwivedi, is intended to incorporate *kuṇḍalinīyoga.* Cf. NT edited by Vrajavallabha Dwivedi (NT[D]) (Delhi: Parimal Publications, 1985), Introduction, p. 39, note 2.

87. NT 8, 9-16.

88. NT 8, 17-20.

89. Svaparastheṣu bhūteṣu jagaty asmin samānadhīḥ /
śivo 'ham advitīyo 'haṃ samādhiḥ sa paraḥ smṛtaḥ //
(NT 8, 18).

KR views it as transcendental judgment (*adhyavasāya*) originating from pure gnosis. If KR's interpretation is correct, we cannot miss an interesting similarity between AG's view of *sattarka* as pure gnosis (thereby holding it as a tool for perception of integral awareness), and *samādhi* of the second kind.

90. From here, the order is reversed in NT. *Anupāya* comes before *śāmbhavopāya.*

91. Yena yena prakāreṇa jñānayogena mantrataḥ /
yad yat paśyasi deveśa tad upāyaṃ vadasva me //
(NT 2, 7-8).

See also 2, 11 and NTU, vol. 1, p. 45.

92. Obviously the basis of the equation lies more in the primacy of power (*śakti*) than in that of thought.

93. NTU, vol. 1, p. 185.

94. Such a lack may be viewed as supportive of the *ṣaḍaṅga* thesis.

95. Uddyota on SVT 7, 290.

96. *Āsyate nityam aikātmyena sthīyate asminn ity āsanaṃ paraṃ śāktaṃ balam* (SSV, p. 46).

97. *Tasmin sati śvāsapraśvāsayor gativicchedaḥ prāṇāyāmaḥ* (YS 2, 49).

98. Cf. PYD, p. 241.

99. Gatibhaṅgaṃ tatas tasya prāṇāyāmena kārayet /
sa ca pañcavidhaḥ proktaḥ pūrakādiprabhedataḥ //
(MVT 17, 2).

100. *Prāṇasyāyamanaṃ yathāsthitavāhavijayena svāyattatānayanam* (Uddyota).

101. Cf. SVT 7, 296-297.

102. *Daśadhā yogamārgeṇa* (SVT 7, 293); also see SVTU on it. The "tenfold yogic path" is not a new technique or model, but constitutes the metaphorical presentation of the existing pattern.

103. *Svaviṣayāsamprayoge cittasya svarūpānukāra evendriyāṇāṃ pratyāhāraḥ* (YS 2, 54).

104. SSV on SS 3, 5, pp. 39-40; SVT 7, 297-298 with Uddyota.

105. Yat kiṃcic cintayed vastu nānyatvaṃ pratipadyate /
tena tanmayatām āpya bhavet paścād abhāvavat //
pañcatām iva samprāptas tīvrair api na cālyate /
tataḥ śabdādibhir yogī yoginīkulanandanaḥ //
ityanena vidhānena pratyāhṛtya mano muhuḥ /
prāṇāyāmādikaṃ sarvaṃ kuryād yogaprasiddhaye //
(MVT 17, 22-24).

106. YSB 3, 1. See also PYD, p. 259.

107. Cf. PYD, p. 260.

108. Tāny evoddiśya tat sarvaṃ pūraṇāya dharāditaḥ //
śivāntaṃ bahudhā bhedair dhāraṇāgrantha ucyate /
(MVV 1, 1133-34).

109. MVT 12, 8-9. There is no need to recount their numerous subtypes.

110. MVT, 12, 14.

111. Ibid., 17, 13-15.

112. *Bhūtānāṃ pṛthivyādīnāṃ jayo dhāraṇābhir vaśīkāraḥ* (SSV, p. 39).

113. *Evaṃ dehaśuddhi-bhūtaśuddhi-prāṇāyāma-pratyāhāra-dhāraṇā-dhyāna-samādhibhir yā tattattvarūpā siddhir bhavati sā mohāvaraṇāt, na tu tattvajñānāt . . . vigalitamohasya tu . . . śrīmanmṛtyujidbhaṭṭārakanirūpitanītyā dhāraṇādibhir api paratattvasamāveśa eva bhavati, na tu mitasiddhiḥ* (SSV, pp. 40-41).

114. In this connection, a reference to RK's approach on the *yogāṅgas* may be in order. Although KR occasionally offers interpretations of *yogāṅgas*, we have seldom singled out his definitions unless it was necessary, because in most cases he accords or reiterates Patañjali's definitions. As he himself admits (see SpKV, pp. 22-23), his mission is to look for correspondences between the Trika-congruent states of our experience and the various stages of yoga. Thus, he identifies the waking state with yogic *dhāraṇā*, dreaming with *dhyāna*, sleep (*savedya suṣupta*) with cognitive (*samprajñāta*) *samādhi*. In the last case, RK's definition of *samprajñāta* really covers only a subtype, *savicārā samāpatti*, but he extends it to include all states of cognitive trance (SpKV, p. 23). He identifies deep sleep (*apavedya suṣupta*) with ultracognitive (*asamprajñāta*) *samādhi* (loc. cit.). In our view, such equations touch on only superficial similarity and originate from a sort of philosophical superiority complex. They hardly succeed in honestly projecting the inner spirit of the opposite number.

115. Cf. TAV, vol. 2, p. 517.

116. *Prakṛtiṃ paśyati puruṣaḥ prekṣakavat sthitaḥ svasthaḥ* (Sāṃkhya Kārikā, verse 65).

117. *Yoginaś cakṣurādīny indriyāṇi hi saṃsāranāṭyaprakaṭanapramoda-nirbharaṃ svasvarūpam antarmukhatayā sākṣātkurvanti, tatprayogaprarūḍhyā vigalitavibhāgāś camatkārarasasampūrṇatām āpādayanti* (SSV, p. 44).

118. Sabījayogasaṃsiddhyai mantralakṣaṇam apy alam /
na cādhikāritā dīkṣāṃ vinā yoge 'sti śāṅkare //
kriyājñānavibhedena sā ca dvedhā nigadyate /
dvividhā sā prakartavyā tena caitad udāhṛtam //
na ca yogādhikāritvam ekam evānayā bhavet /
api mantrādhikāritvaṃ muktiś ca śivadīkṣayā //
(MVT 4, 6-8).

119. Tam ārādhya tataṣ tuṣṭād dīkṣām āsādya śāṅkarīm /
tatkṣaṇād vopabhogād vā dehapātāc chivaṃ vrajet //
yogadīkṣāṃ samāsādya jñātvā yogaṃ samabhyaset /
yogasiddhim avāpnoti tadante śāśvataṃ padam //
(MVT 1, 45-46).

AG connects these verses with the instantaneous initiation (*sadyonirvāṇadīkṣa*) as well. Cf. TA 19, 1c. This is not of relevance in the present context.

120. SpN, pp. 25. 49.

121. *Śaktisaṃkocādayas tu yady api pratyabhijñāyāṃ na pratipāditāḥ, tathāpy āmnāyikatvād asmābhiḥ prasaṅgāt pradarśyante* (Pratyabhijñāhṛdaya [PrH], trans. Jaideva Singh [MLBD, 1973], p. 85).

122. *Nimīlanasamādhiḥ paramaśivāvasthā śāmbhavopāyaḥ / unmīlanasamādhir manmayam evedaṃ sarvam ityuktayukti samyakpariśīlanaśaktidaśārūḍhiḥ śāktopāya iti* (Śaivāṣṭaka kośa [MS], word no. 65).

123. *Iyaṃ ca nimīlanonmīlanasamādhidvayasāmarasyaucityād atyantam upalālyate* (Mahārthamañjarī by Maheśvarānanda, ed. B. V. Dwivedi, [Varanasi: Yogatantra Granthamālā, 1972]), p. 90. In KS literature, this state is described variously as Bhairavī Mudrā and Krama Mudrā, etc.

124. *Iti śrīmanmṛtyujidbhaṭṭārakanirūpitanītyā dhāraṇādibhir api paratattvasamāveśa eva bhavati, na tu mitasiddhiḥ* (SSV, p. 41).

125. *Prāṇarūpaḥ parasyāḥ śakteḥ . . . paraśaktipadānupraveśāvaṣṭambhapūrvam eva svacchandabhairavatā avāpyate mahāyogibhiḥ / mitayogibhiś ca tattadāntarakālāṃśaviśrāntipūrvaṃ vidhim anutiṣṭhadbhiḥ sā siddhir avighnenāsādyate* (SVTU, vol. 3, pp. 173-174).

126. NT 8, 32-34.

127. SpKN, pp. 42-43.

128. SpKN, p. 40.

129. Iti vā yasya saṃvittiḥ krīḍātvenākhilaṃ jagat /
sa paśyan satataṃ yukto jīvanmukto na saṃśayaḥ //
(SpK, [KSTS, 1969], 3, 3).

130. Cf. SS 3, 25.

131. *Turyapariśīlanaprakarṣāt prāptaturyātītapadaḥ paripūrṇasvacchasvacchandacidānandaghanena śivena bhagavatā tulyo, dehakalāyā avigalanāt tatsamo jāyate / tadvigalanena sākṣāc Chiva evāsau* (SSV, p. 53).

132. Samprāpto ghaṭamānaś ca siddhaḥ siddhatamo 'nyathā /
yogī caturvidho devi yathāvat pratipadyate //
(MVT 4, 33).

133. MVT 4, 34-38.

134. Ibid., 18, 45-47.

135. Sa tāvat kasyacit tarkaḥ svata eva pravartate /
sa ca sāṃsiddhikaḥ śāstre proktaḥ svapratyayātmakaḥ //
(TA 4, 40-41).

136. Yogīva nirupādānam arthajātaṃ prakāśayet (Īśvarapratyabhijñākārikā by Utpaladeva, KSTS, 1, 5, 7).

137. Bījasyāntar ivāṅkuro jagad idaṃ prāṅ nirvikalpaṃ punaḥ
māyākalpitadeśakālakalanāvaicitryacitrīkṛtam /
māyāvīva vijṛmbhayaty api mahāyogīva yaḥ svecchayā
tasmai śrīgurumūrtaye nama idaṃ śrīdakṣiṇāmūrtaye //
(Śrīdakṣiṇāmūrtistotram by Śaṅkarācārya, 1972: Prācyavidyāsaṃśodhanālayagranthamālā, verse 2).

Chapter Ten

The Doctrine of the Mālinīvijayottaratantra

Alexis Sanderson

The most fundamental feature of the corpus of the Tantric Śaiva scriptures is its division into two orders of texts: those teaching the cult of Śiva—these are the works known collectively as the *Siddhānta*[1] or *Siddhāntaśāstra*[2] and individually as the *Siddhāntas*,[3] *Siddhāntaśāstras*,[4] or *Siddhāntatantras*[5]—and those teaching the cults of Tumburu, Bhairava, and various manifestations of the Goddess (Devī).[6] Texts of the second kind claim superiority over those of the first. They see the Siddhānta as a general and exoteric revelation (*sāmānyaśāstram*), which they transcend as special or esoteric teachings (*viśeṣaśāstram, rahasyaśāstram*).

For Abhinavagupta and related authorities who followed these traditions in Kashmir and the Tamil region since the late tenth century A.D. the inferiority of the Siddhāntas was proved not only by the less esoteric nature of their practice but also, less ambiguously, by the fact that they taught a nonultimate view of reality. They maintained that, while the Siddhāntas propagated a dualistic view of the relations between the basic entities or categories of their

---

1. See, e.g., RatnTrU, 10-12: *siddhāntaśabdaḥ paṅkajādiśabdavad yogarūḍhyā śiva-praṇīteṣu kāmikādiṣu daśāṣṭādaśasu tantreṣu prasiddhaḥ* 'The term *Siddhānta* is established in common usage to denote the ten and eighteen Śiva-authored Tantras beginning with the *Kāmika* through specialization of its general, literal meaning, just as the word *paṅkaja* [literally] 'mud born' [is used to mean 'lotus']'; TĀ 15.319; 37.27.
2. See, e.g., BhogKāVṛ p. 2^{15}: *śrīmadrauravatantropalakṣitasiddhāntaśāstre*; SvTU 6 (11)55^{6-7}: *kairaṇādi siddhāntaśāstram.*
3. See, e.g., BhogKā 2: *rurusiddhānta-*; HarCarCint 31.162-172: *analasiddhāntaḥ*; NeTU 1 (8) 191^{12}: *siddhāntānām*; SvTU 1 (2) 15^{4}: *siddhānteṣu.*
4. See, e.g., TĀV 3 (4) 280^{12-13}: *anantavijayāt siddhāntaśāstrāt.*
5. See, e.g., BṛhKāl fol. 38, verse 2: *tantre siddhānte lalitāhvaye.*
6. See Sanderson 1988 for an account of the various divisions of the Śaiva Tantras.

ontology, the esoteric Tantras formulated these same relations in the terms of an absolute nondualism. If these Tantras were indeed nondualistic, then they could convincingly be presented as a revelation intended by Śiva to go beyond the Siddhāntas; for nondualism, being the transcendence of dualism, can accommodate the latter as a lower or provisional view, whereas dualism can only exclude nondualism as its antithesis.

The purpose of this chapter, which I offer with respect and affection to my distinguished colleague André Padoux, is to begin to test this claim that the "special teachings" are nondualistic. I shall do so by examining the doctrine of the Mālinīvijayottaratantra. This is the scripture that Abhinavagupta expounded as the core-text of the Trika Tantras.[7] He considered the latter to be the highest division of the esoteric teachings and therefore saw the Mālinīvijayottara as embodying the very essence of the nondualistic tradition.[8]

Dualism (*īśvaradvaitam*[9])

The dualism attributed to the first division of the canon by the nondualists—and also by the Saiddhāntikas themselves; that is, by those who followed the Siddhāntas alone—is the doctrine that (1) Śiva, (2) souls, and (3) the rest of reality, mental and material, are essentially and eternally distinct from each other.[10] According to this view Śiva is only the efficient cause (*nimittakāraṇam*) of the universe. Its material cause (*upādānakāraṇam*), that out of which it is fashioned, of which it consists, and into which it dissolves, is not Śiva but *māyā*.[11] The latter is the single, eternal, and unconscious

7. In his *Mālinīvijayavārtika, Tantrāloka,* and *Tantrasāra,* all of which are exegesis of this text.

8. On the privileged position assigned by Abhinavagupta to the *Mālinīvijayottaratantra,* see later, pp. 291-92.

9. For this term see ParMokṣaNirKāVṛ p. 38^{4-5}. Cf. the term *bhedeśvaravādaḥ* in TĀV 3 (4) 81 (glossing *bhede* in TĀ 4.74c).

10. For the term *Saiddhāntika* denoting an (exclusive) follower of the Siddhāntas, see, e.g., TĀV 10(22)256^{15}: *adharadarśanasaṃstheneti yathā saiddhāntikena* 'by a [guru] in a system lower [than the Trika], by a Saiddhāntika, for example'; ibid., 3(4)295^{1}: *saiddhāntikasya sādhakasya* 'of a Saiddhāntika mantramasterer.' The term also may be used to refer to whatever is proper to the Siddhāntas; see, e.g., NeTU 2(18)124^{5}: *saiddhāntikaśrāddhavidhiḥ,* 'the Saiddhāntika *śrāddha* ritual'.

11. MṛgVṛ VP p. 189^{14-15}: *upādānakāraṇasya māyākhyasya* 'the material cause [of the universe] which we call *māyā*'; Mṛg VP 9.1-4.

source of the worlds and everything in them, including the bodies and faculties of each soul.[12] To initiate a period of cosmic emanation (*sṛṣṭiḥ*) Śiva relies on a vicegerent, the Lord Ananta (Ananta-bhaṭṭāraka, Ananteśa), to irradiate *māyā* with his powers and so cause it to give birth to these forms.[13] Śiva causes Ananta to activate

12. See Mṛg VP 9.2: *tad ekam aśivaṃ bījaṃ jagataś citraśaktimat / sahakāryadhi-kārāntasaṃrodhi vyāpy anaśvaram //* 'That [*granthitattvam*, i.e., *māyā*] is the unconscious material cause of the universe, one but many-powered, holding [the soul in bondage] until there is nothing further for [the past acts that are] the concomitant cause [of bondage] to accomplish, all-pervading, eternal'; TattvSaṃ 26: *vikṛteḥ parato māyā nityā vibhvī hy acetanā caikā / sargasthitivilayānām ādhāraḥ kāraṇaṃ ca sā jagataḥ //* 'Beyond the process of transformation is *māyā*, eternal, pervasive, unconscious and one, the basis of emission, preservation and resorption, the [material] cause of the universe.'; MṛgVṛ VP p. 195[16-19]: *yat tu māyākhyaṃ kāraṇam upapāditaṃ tadāśrayāṇi tanukaraṇabhuvanādīni saṃhāra-kāle śaktirūpāṇy avatiṣṭhante / sṛṣṭau tu vyaktirūpāṇi svasvaprayojananiṣpattaye savyāpārāṇi bhavantīti . . .* 'During the period of resorption the bodies, faculties, worlds and the rest which are dependent on that which the text has taught to be the material cause, namely *māyā*, remain in a state of potentiality. But when there is emission they become manifest and active, so that each accomplishes its specific purpose'; *Saurabheya* quoted in ibid. p. 58[6-7]: *śaktirūpāṇi kāryāṇi tallīnāni mahākṣaye / vikṛtau vyaktim āyānti . . .* 'The effects [of *māyā*] remain dissolved within it as potencies during the period of a Great Resorption and become manifest again when that period comes to an end'; MatPār VP 8.(2-)4(-5): *sūkṣmaṃ sarvagataṃ nityam atyadbhutaguṇāvaham / caitanyanilayaṃ viśvam acetanam arūpakam //* 'Subtle, all-pervading, eternal, bearer of the most astonishing properties, locus of the consciousness [of the unliberated at the time of resorption], the [stuff of the] universe, unconscious and formless'; *Pauṣkara* quoted in ŚaivParibh, p. 88[7]: *nityaikā vyāpinī vasturūpā karmāśrayāśivā /* 'Eternal, one, pervasive, objectively existent, the receptacle of acts [during periods of nonemission], non-*śiva*.'; TattvPrak 38b-39: *. . . māyopādānam iṣyate sūkṣmā / ekā nityā vyāpiny anādinidhanā śivāsaktā // sādhāraṇī narāṇāṃ kāraṇam api ceyam akhilabhuvanānām / nikhilajanakarmakhacitā svabhāvato mohasaṃjananī //* 'We hold *māyā* to be the material cause. She is subtle (i.e. imperceptible), one, eternal, pervasive, without beginning or end, not inherent in Śiva (*śivāsaktā*, i.e. non-Śiva). It is this that is the common cause for [all] creatures of all the worlds. [in periods of nonemission] she holds the variegated pattern of the acts of all [unliberated] souls. By her very nature she causes delusion.'

13. MatPār 9.1: *kṣobhito 'nantanāthena granthir māyātmako yadā / tadā svena vikāreṇa karoti vipulaṃ jagat //* 'When the Knot (*granthiḥ*) which is *māyā* is stimulated by Anantanātha it creates the vast universe as its own transformation.'; MatPār VP 8.53cd: *jagac carācaraṃ saiva vidhātrā kṣobhitā satī //* 'When stimulated by the Creator that same [*māyā*] becomes the universe moving and unmoving.'; RatnTr 40: *māyā . . . kṣobhitānantatejasā . . . tattvajātam asūta sā //* 'When *māyā* was stimulated by the radiance of Ananta she procreated all the *tattvas*.'

māyā in this way in order that souls which have not yet been released may have the means of experiencing the fruits of their past actions and the possibility of working toward their eventual salvation.[14]

When Śiva judges a soul to be ready for release he liberates it into a state of omniscience and omnipotence in which it is his equal (*śivasamānaḥ, śivatulyaḥ*).[15] Even in this state of enlightenment and liberation each soul remains distinct from every other and from Śiva himself. There is no question of the soul's surrendering its separate identity by dissolution (*layaḥ*) into some form of trans-individual consciousness.[16]

Śiva alone liberates.[17] In the case of souls that are incarnate as humans Śiva accomplishes this liberation through a ritual of initiation (*dīkṣā*)[18] performed by a human officiant (*ācāryaḥ*). The

14. See, e.g., BhogKā 114(p. 60): *jagadbījaṃ mahāmāyā janyaśaktir acetanā / tasyāḥ kalādisaṃbhūtir bhogināṃ bhogasiddhaye //* 'Great *māyā* is the seed of the universe, unconscious, its power requiring to be activated. [The *tattvas*] beginning with *kalā* arise from it in order that those still subject to the experience of the effects of actions may have [the means and locus of] such experience'; ibid., 4-7; *Para* (*Saurabheya*) quoted in SiddhSūVṛ, pp. 33^{26}-27^{2}; MṛgVṛVP, p. 173^{16}-175^{12}.

15. NarParīkṣ 3.145c: *muktiḥ pareśatulyatvam* 'Final liberation is a state of equality with the Lord'; 3.162b (*śivatulyatā*); TattvSaṃ 51d: *pareha śivasamatā*, 'Final [liberation] is equality with Śiva'; TattvPrak 36 (*śivasamānatā*). Final liberation is distinguished in these passages from a lesser liberation (*aparā muktiḥ*), which is to attain the rank of a Vidyeśvara. See also TĀV 3(4) 81^{3-10} for the Saiddhāntika distinction between the Original Śiva (*anādisiddhaḥ śivaḥ*) and *Liberated Śivas* (*muktaśivāḥ*); cf. NarParīkṣ 3.140ab and commentary.

16. MṛgVṛ VP, p. 68^{12-16}: *yata eva saṃsāritāyāḥ prabhavas tatraiva niraṃśe paramātmani yadi layo mokṣas tat punar api tata eva prādurbhāvaḥ punaś ca mokṣa iti seyaṃ gatānugatikā na tu mokṣaḥ* 'If to be liberated were to be dissolved into the same partless super-soul from which one's original state as a transmigrating, embodied soul had arisen, then one would re-emerge from it [at the next creation] and be liberated again [in due course, and so on ad infinitum]. This would be not liberation but circulation.'

17. NarParīkṣ 3.150cd: *īśān mokṣo 'nyathā naiva puṃsām etan nirūpitam* 'The liberation of souls is the work of Śiva and can come about in no other way. This has been taught [in the scriptures]'; commentary ad loc.: *tathā ca śrīpauṣkare "na mokṣaṃ yāti puruṣaḥ svasāmarthyāt kadācana" iti / śrīmaddīkṣottare 'pi "śivād evātmanāṃ mokṣaḥ " iti /* 'And this is so in the *Pauṣkara[pārameśvara]*, which reads "The soul never attains liberation by its own power [but only by the favor of Lord Śiva remover of *māyā* (*muktvā prasādaṃ devasya śivasyāśivahāriṇaḥ* [quoted in MṛgVṛ VP, p. 95^{10-13}]))]," and in the *Dīkṣottara* [section of the *Niśvāsakārikā*], which reads "The liberation of souls is brought about by Śiva alone."' See the whole passage, NarParīkṣ 3.144c-150.

18. NarParīkṣP, p. 256^{12}: *dīkṣaiva mocayaty ūrdhvaṃ śaivaṃ dhāma nayaty asau*

officiant, who must himself have received both this initiation and the higher consecration (*ācāryābhiṣekaḥ*) that qualifies him for this office, is simply the medium through whom Śiva acts. When he prepares himself to perform the ritual he must surrender all sense of individual agency. He must see his person as the locus and instrument of the action of Śiva himself.[19]

Liberation cannot by achieved through mere knowledge of reality without recourse to ritual. This is because the state of bondage, in which the soul fails to realize its innate omniscience and omnipotence, is not caused by mere ignorance. The ignorance that characterizes the unliberated is the effect of an imperceptible Impurity (*malam*) that acts on the soul from outside; and this Impurity, though it is imperceptible, is a material substance (*dravyam*). Because it is a substance, only action (*vyāpāraḥ*) can remove it; and the only action capable of removing it is that of the rituals of initiation and their sequel taught by Śiva in his Tantric scriptures.[20]

Under the influence of Impurity the soul continues to be subject to the products of *māyā*. It is bound by incarnation in a particular world, with a particular body, mental, and physical faculties. It has limited powers of knowledge (*vidyā*) and action (*kalā*). It is bound to experience the effects of its past acts (*niyatiḥ*). It is subject to time (*kālaḥ*); and it is driven by a nonspecific craving for worldly experience (*rāgaḥ*).[21] While it is caught by these products of *māyā* it acts and experiences the fruits of its actions in birth after birth. The unliberated soul (*paśuḥ, aṇuḥ*) is therefore said to be constrained in its condition by four fetters (*pāśāḥ*): (1) Impurity (*malam*), (2) *māyā*, (3) its past actions (*karma*), and (4) the power of Śiva's will that holds it subject to these three (*rodhaśaktiḥ*).[22] In later texts the term *Impurity* is extended from the first fetter to the second and third. The first is then termed the *Impurity associated with* [all] *the Unliberated* (*āṇavaṃ*

(quoting the *Svāyambhuva*) 'Initiation alone liberates. It is that which leads one up to the Śiva state.'

19. MṛgVṛKP, p. 112[16]: *ācāryādhikaraṇasya parameśvarasyānugrāhyān anugṛhṇataḥ karaṇaṃ mantrāḥ* 'When the Supreme Lord shows his favor to those worthy of it he acts in the person of the officiant and the mantras are his instruments'; MokṣKā 91: *deśikasthena śambhunā* 'By Śiva in the officiant.' For references to the officiant's self-perception, see note 69.

20. MokṣKā 47c-68; MatPārVṛKP, p. 2[10-19]; ibid., VP, p. 27[19]-28[8]; NarParīkṣP, pp. 254[11]-55[2]; MokṣKā 25c-32b; SvTU 3 (5)84[10]-86[2]; TĀ 13.41c-52.

21. See, e.g., Mṛg VP 10.1-30 (on the evolution of the *tattvas* out of *māyā*).

22. For the four fetters (*pāśāḥ*) see, e.g., Mṛg VP 2.7abc and commentary (*prāvṛtiḥ / malam, īśabalam / rodhaśaktiḥ, karma, māyā*). They are treated one by one in Mṛg VP 7.1-10 (*malam*), 11-23 (*rodhaśaktiḥ*), 8.1-6 (*karmapāśaḥ*), 9.1-21 (*granthipāśaḥ / māyāpāśaḥ*).

[< *aṇuḥ*] *malam*), whereas the second and third become the *Impurities of Māyā* (*māyīyaṃ malam*) and *Karma* (*kārmaṃ malam*).[23]

When Śiva is ready to liberate an individual from beginningless bondage he weakens the power of Impurity over him to the extent that he experiences the desire to be liberated, is disinclined to continue worldly existence, feels devotion (*bhaktiḥ*) to the devotees of Śiva, and conceives faith in the Śaiva doctrines. He therefore seeks out an officiant for initiation. Recognizing these attitudes and commitments as evidence of "the descent of Śiva's power" (*śaktipātaḥ*),[24] the officiant proceeds to perform the liberating ritual of initiation (*dīkṣā*). Unless the candidate opts for that form of this procedure which guarantees a period in a paradise before final release (*bhogadīkṣā, sādhakadīkṣā*), he will never be reborn.[25] In this sense initiation liberates; but it does not liberate immediately. Actual liberation occurs only at the time of death. Initiation cannot be said to have destroyed all the individual's fetters when the individual is seen to live on in the embodied state, particularly when initiation is seen to bring about no marked change of personality in the majority of those who receive it. Thus it is that the mantras, which are the immediate agents by which the fetters are destroyed during the ritual, are formulated to spare that portion of the person's past actions (*karma*) that is already bearing fruit (*prārabdham*) as current physical and mental life. This explains to the followers of

23. Sadyojyoti, Nārāyaṇakaṇṭha, Rāmakaṇṭha, Aghoraśiva, and other adherents of the Kashmirian dualistic school stick to the original terms. The use of the terms *āṇavaṃ malam, māyīyaṃ malam*, and *kārmaṃ malam* ("the three *Impurities*" [*malatrayam*]) is seen in some south Indian Saiddhāntika sources such as the *Suprabheda* (quoted in ŚaivāgParibhMañj 3.21-23b), Aj KP 2.6d (*māyeyam āṇavaṃ karma*)—on the nonoriginality of these Tantras, see later, p. 291 and note 42—ŚaivParibh (p. 62[19]: *malatrayanivṛttyā*; p. 73[3]: *āṇavamalasya*) of the Tamil Śivāgrayogīndrajñānaśivācārya (fl. c. A.D. 1550-1600) and SiddhSūVṛ (p. 50[7]: *āṇavamala-*). These are all texts influenced by the nondualism of the Tamil Śaiva Siddhānta.

24. See Mṛg VP 5.4-5: *yeṣāṃ śarīriṇāṃ śaktiḥ pataty api nivṛttaye / teṣāṃ talliṅgam autsukyaṃ muktau dveṣo bhavasthitau // 4 // bhaktiś ca śivabhakteṣu śraddhā tacchāsake vidhau / anenānumitiḥ śiṣṭahetoḥ sthūladhiyām api //* 'Those embodied souls on whom [Śiva's] Power descends in order that [their transmigration] may cease, show as the sign of that [descent = *śaktipātaḥ*] a longing to be liberated, hate for the fact that they remain in the world [of bondage], devotion to the devotees of Śiva, and faith in his Scriptures. By this [sign] even those of gross intelligence can infer that there is some cause of bondage still remaining'; MatPār CP 4.10cd: *nipātād yat sphuṭaṃ cihnaṃ bhaktir avyabhicāriṇī //* 'Unswerving devotion is the sure sign of the descent [of power].'

25. All this applies equally to women.

the system why individuals continue to live after initiation and indeed why the survivors generally appear no wiser or better for having gone through it. According to the semantic analysis (*nirvacanam*) traditional in the Śaiva literature the word *dīkṣā* ('initiation') is appropriate to the rite (*anvartha-*) because it means 'that which bestows (√ *dā*) knowledge and destroys (√ *kṣi*) the fetters.' But the bestowing of knowledge (*jñānadānam*), which is said to account for the first syllable of the word, is not the imparting of a conscious knowledge or enlightenment (*bauddhaṃ jñānam*), because such knowledge would surely transform the individual beyond recognition. The knowledge claimed is one that is said to have been received on a deeper, subconscious level within the individual (*pauruṣaṃ jñānam*), where it can lie latent until the moment of death when the remnant of the fetters that has obscured it disappears and the Śiva state (*śivatā*, *śivāvasthā*) becomes manifest.[26] The complicated issue of how the attainment of this goal is affected by the regular rituals that competent initiates are obliged to perform throughout their lives has been discussed elsewhere.[27]

Nondualism (*īśvarādvaitam*, *saṃvidadvaitam*[28])

The nondualistic doctrine attributed to the second division of the canon contains all the categories of this dualistic system; but

---

26. See Kir 6.19: *anekabhavikaṃ karma dagdhaṃ bījam ivāṇubhiḥ / bhaviṣyad api saṃruddhaṃ yenedaṃ tad dhi bhogataḥ //* 'The *mantras* burn the *karma* of one's many former lives and prevent any future *karma*. [But] that [*karma*] by means of which [one lives] this [present life is destroyed only] by [its fruition into] experience.' This is the *locus classicus*; see, e.g., RatnTrU, pp. 59^{6-8}, 106^{5-7}; TattvPrakVṛ, p. 56^{6-7}; MatPārVṛKP, p. 150^{17}; SārdhTriśKālVṛ, pp. 27^{14}, 74^{3}; SvTU 4.141/TĀ 15.27. On the fact that the initiate's personality generally is unaffected by *dīkṣā*, see SvTU 2(4)96^{3-4}; 3(5)77^{15}-78^{5}; TĀ 1.36-51; TĀV 1(1)57^{6-10}; MatPārVṛVP, pp. 27^{19}-28^{8}.
27. See Sanderson 1991.
28. For this term see, e.g. GurNP 40 (*īśvarādvaitam*); ŚivDṛVṛ, p. 36^{1}, TĀV 1 (1) 109^{8} and 195^{15} (*īśvarādvayavādaḥ*); ĪśvPraVivVim, vol. 1, p. 2^{4} (*īśvarādvayakathā*), ibid., vol. 2, p. 114^{20} (*īśvarādvayavādī*); ŚivDṛVṛ, p. 142^{6}, PraHṛ, p. 22^{14} (*īśvarādvayadarśanam*); TĀV 12(37)429^{22} (*īśvarādvaitavādaḥ*); GurNP 14b (*śivādvaitam*); ŚivDṛVṛ, p. 88^{7} (*śivādvaitapakṣaḥ*); ibid., p. 89^{2} (*śivādvayam*); ĪśvPraVivVim, vol. 3, p. 406^{2} (*śivādvayavādaḥ*); ParamSViv, pp. 1^{7} and 196^{9} (*śivādvayaśāsanam*). Kṣemarāja in SpSaṃd, p. 10^{7} and Rājānaka Ānanda in ṢaṭtrTSaṃdViv, p. 1^{1} refer to the doctrine more specifically as *svatantraśivādvayavādaḥ* 'the doctrine of the nonduality of autonomous Śiva'. In TĀV 9(15)96^{5} Jayaratha applies the term *saṃvidadvayavādaḥ* 'the doctrine of the nonduality

it denies that they are ultimately distinct. It holds that it is Śiva alone, as a single autonomous and omnipotent consciousness, who is manifest in the form of individual souls,[29] *māyā*,[30] and its products;[31] so that none of these is other than an aspect of the power of self-representation (*vimarśaśaktiḥ*) that constitutes his nature.[32] To be fettered in embodiment is therefore to be Śiva himself in a state of voluntarily assumed contraction (*saṃkocaḥ*).[33]

The three Impurities, *āṇava, māyīya,* and *kārma*—only this terminology is used in the nondualistic system—remain but are radically redefined. The Impurity associated with [all] the Unliberated (*āṇavam malam*), which for the dualists was a material substance

---

of consciousness.' Maheśvarānanda names the doctrine *svatantrādvaitasaṃvitsamayaḥ* 'the doctrine of the consciousness of autonomous nonduality' (MahārthMañjP, p. 71[25]) and *anuttarasaṃvidadvaitasiddhāntaḥ* 'the doctrine of the nonduality of absolute (i.e. all-inclusive) consciousness' (p. 129[22]).

29. See, e.g., ĪśvPraKā 4.1ab: *svātmaiva sarvajantūnām eka eva maheśvaraḥ* 'It is Śiva who is the one identity of all souls.'; TĀ 9.144c-45b: *aṇavo nāma naivānyat prakāśātmā maheśvaraḥ // cidacidrūpatābhāsī pudgalaḥ kṣetravit paśuḥ /* 'Indeed individual souls are nothing other [than him]. What we call the "individual," the "knower of the field', and the "bound [soul]" is Śiva himself, the Light manifesting itself as an entity whose nature is part consciousness and part unconsciousness.'

30. TĀ 9.149c-150a: *māyā ca nāma devasya śaktir avyatirekiṇī // bhedāvabhāsasvātantryaṃ* '*Māyā* is in fact the faculty (*śaktiḥ*) of the Lord himself and [therefore] not other than him. It is his quality as autonomous agent (*svātantryam*) when his action is the manifestation of duality [in consciousness].'

31. ĪśvPraKā 1.38: *cidātmaiva hi devo 'ntaḥsthitam icchāvaśād bahiḥ / yogīva nirupādānam arthajātaṃ prakāśayet //* 'For it is God, i.e., Consciousness, who causes all phenomena, though grounded within him, to appear [as though they were] external to him, ['creating' them] without [extrinsic] material, as a yogin [creates], by the force of his will [alone].'

32. ĪśvPraKā 1.42: *svabhāvam avabhāsasya vimarśaṃ vidur anyathā / prakāśo 'rthoparakto 'pi sphaṭikādijaḍopamaḥ //* [Our masters] hold that the essence of Manifestation (*prakāśaḥ*) is Representation (*vimarśaḥ*). If it were not, then Manifestation, even if affected by an object, would be no different from an unconscious [reflector of images] such as a crystal.' This representation (*vimarśaḥ*) is always self-representation, because its agent is always the self; namely, Śiva as manifestation (*prakāśātmā maheśvaraḥ*). However, as it appears as subject ("I," self) or object ("this," not-self), the Pratyabhijñāśāstra refers to it simply as *Representation* (*vimarśaḥ, parāmarśaḥ, āmarśaḥ, pratyavamarśaḥ*) and differentiates within this between "I"-representation (*ahaṃvimarśaḥ*) and "this"-representation (*idaṃvimarśaḥ*).

33. PraHṛ, sūtra 9: *cidvattacchaktisaṃkocān malāvṛtaḥ saṃsārī // 9 //* 'Through the contraction of the Conscious and his powers there arises the transmigrating soul enclosed by the [three] Impurities.'

impeding the soul's powers of cognition and action from the outside, is now simply the unknowing or contracted consciousness that constitutes the appearance of individual selfhood: it is consciousness believing that it is contracted (*apūrṇaṃmanyatā*).[34] The Impurity of *māyā* (*māyīyaṃ malam*) becomes the manifestation in consciousness of differentiated objects of awareness (*bhinnavedyaprathā*),[35] of objects, that is, which are differentiated from each other and from the contracted subjects that perceive them: for *māyā* is no longer an entity outside Śiva and souls, but simply Śiva's miraculous power to project himself within himself as subjects at various levels of contraction and as the object-worlds appropriate to each. The Impurity of *karma* (*kārmaṃ malam*) is equally subjectivized: it becomes the *belief* that one is affected for good or bad by one's actions (*śubhāśubhavāsanā*). It is said that it is this belief that causes consciousness to project the experience of retribution and reward in various worlds and successive births.[36]

Just as the nondualists' bondage is said to be incomplete awareness of Śivahood (*apūrṇakhyātiḥ*)[37] so their liberation is defined as the unconditional realization that one's true identity is this one autonomous light of consciousness (*prakāśaḥ*) eternally immersed in the macro- and microcosmic activity of self-representation (*vimarśaḥ*).

---

34. ĪśvPraKā 3.15: *svātantryahānir bodhasya svātantryasyāpy abodhatā / dvidhāṇavaṃ malam idaṃ svasvarūpāpahānitaḥ //* 'This *āṇavam malam* which comes about from the loss of [awareness of] the self's real nature is of two kinds. It is lack of autonomy in consciousness and unawareness of autonomy.' TĀ 9.65a: *apūrṇaṃmanyatā ceyaṃ*; commentary ad loc.: *apūrṇaṃmanyatāṇavamalalakṣaṇā* 'The state of believing oneself to be incomplete, i.e. *āṇavaṃ malam*'; PraHṛ p. 21[7]: *apūrṇaṃmanyatārūpam āṇavaṃ malam.*

35. ĪśvPraKā 3.16ab[1]: *bhinnavedyaprathātraiva māyākhyaṃ* '[The Impurity] termed *māyā* is the manifestation of the object as other which presupposes that [(ĪśvPraVim ad loc.:) twofold contraction of the self's nature which is *āṇavaṃ malaṃ*].'

36. ĪśvPraKā 3.16b[2]c: *janmabhogadaṃ kartary abodhe kārmaṃ tu* 'As for *kārmaṃ malam*, it is that in the unenlightened agent which gives rise to rebirth and the experience of reward and retribution'; ŚivSūVim, p. 16[10]: *-śubhāśubhavāsanātmakam*; TĀV 1(1)61[5–6]: *-śubhāśubhavāsanā-*. See also the passage from the *Kālikākrama* quoted by Kṣemarāja in SivSūVim, p. 132[1–8].

37. See ŚivDṛVṛ, p. 13[7]: *māyāśaktikṛtapūrṇasvarūpākhyātimayacitrakāryatāpanna-* 'Having taken on that state of diverse effects which is the nonmanifestation of the uncontracted nature of the self brought about by the power of *māyā*'; ibid., p. 25[2]: *ātmapracchādanātmakābhedākhyātimayīṃ saṃsārarūpāṃ bhrāntiṃ krīḍāṃ* 'the "game", the error, whose form is transmigratory existence and which consists of that nonmanifestation of nonduality which is [Śiva's] self-concealment.'

One is therefore not merely Śiva's equal—the liberation (*mokṣaḥ*) of the dualists—but aware that one is and always has been Śiva himself, the efficient and material cause of everything. This liberating expansion of consciousness into its Śiva state is held to be the certain reward of all who receive Śaiva initiation (*dīkṣā*) and observe an initiate's obligations. It is accepted that for most it will occur only at death.[38] In this at least the nondualists claim no advantage over the dualists. They appear after all to have been directing their theory to much the same constituency: those for whom Śaiva *dīkṣā* must have been more a matter of family tradition than the expression of an intense personal religiosity. However, they part from the dualists in that they insist that complete enlightenment and liberation are also possible before death (*jīvanmuktiḥ*), and that this higher goal and the special means of realizing it distinguish their own branch of the Śaiva tradition from the Saiddhāntika.[39]

Naturally, because Impurity is no longer a substance but merely the unawareness of a self-contracted consciousness, then the nondualists must see the function of ritual quite differently: if initiation liberates then it must do so not as action, but as a kind of knowledge coded in action and experienced by the initiator.[40]

Moreover, if ritual is believed to work only because it is a mode of knowledge, then, as it is not the only mode of knowledge, it need not be the only means of liberation. Knowledge alone, immediately intuitive or initially discursive, may liberate without relying on the symbolic activities of ritual. Ritual has been validated; but it has

---

38. See TĀ 1.43: *tatra dīkṣādinā pauṃsnam ajñānaṃ dhvaṃsi yady api / tathāpi taccharīrānte taj jñānaṃ vyajyate sphuṭam //* 'Although the ignorance constitutive of individual consciousness is destroyed by initiation and its sequel, the knowledge [of the self, which is simply the absence of that ignorance (commentary)] is made manifest explicitly only with the cessation of the [current] body.'

39. TĀ 1.44: *bauddhajñānena tu yadā bauddham ajñānajṛmbhitam / vilīyate tadā jīvanmuktiḥ karatale sthitā //* 'But if the manifestations of ignorance on the level of the conscious mind cease through conscious [self-]realization, then liberation before death rests in the palm of one's hand.'; MālVijVārt 1.193-196b (194c-195b: *kevalaṃ kvāpy anāyāsā jīvanmuktikrameṇa ca // śīghram eva parā siddhir yathāsmaddarśaneṣv iti /*, 'It is just that in some cases, such as the systems of our [Trika Tantras], the ultimate perfection is achieved quickly, without great exertion, and in such a way that one may be liberated before death').

40. See TĀ 1.149-155 (155: *tasmāt kriyāpi yā nāma jñānam eva hi sā tataḥ / jñānam eva vimokṣāya yuktaṃ caitad udāhṛtam //* 'Therefore ritual action too is nothing but a [kind of] knowing. So this claim that knowledge alone causes liberation is sound'). For a detailed treatment of the nondualist Śaivas' semanticization of ritual, see Sanderson 1991.

been demoted to admit the authenticity of purely gnostic gurus (*jñāninaḥ*) who have achieved liberation and deserved authority without being processed by ritual and who are capable of perpetuating their spiritual lineages by liberating others through oral instruction or inspiration alone. Because initiation and consecration are the indispensable means of liberating oneself and others in the common Śaiva system of the Saiddhāntikas, to deny that such individuals need these means would be to contradict a fundamental principle and so invite condemnation for heresy. They are said therefore to have received initiation and consecration, but in a higher form, an invisible ritual performed not by a common officiant but by the Powers of Śiva embodied in their consciousness.[41]

The *Mālinīvijayottaratantra*

It is generally true that the Tantras of the Siddhānta follow the dualistic doctrine, seeing Śiva, souls and *māyā* as coeternal essences. Such deviations as there are from this norm occur, with one notable exception, in texts that bear the names of listed Siddhāntatantras, but have certainly been redacted, if not entirely composed, at a much later period, and in the Tamil-speaking region of the South: the nondualism of these texts reveals the influence of the South Indian Vedāntic currents that affected the Tamil Śaiva Siddhānta.[42] The one evident exception is the Sarvajñānottara. This work is cited frequently by South Indian neo-Saiddhāntikas in support of their unscriptural nondualism; but temptation to assume that it too is a late South Indian addition is prevented by the existence of an early Nepalese manuscript of the text.[43]

---

41. See TĀ 4.40c-50; 13.131c-142b.

42. See, e.g., Aj KP 2.1-27, where Śiva is the supreme soul whose form is being, consciousness, and bliss [1bc: *paramātmā maheśvaraḥ / saccidānandarūpī*], who is the identity of everything including the individual soul (6a: *bhoktā*), Impurity (6c: *āṇavam*), and *māyā* (16a: *rāgo māyā*) with its products (6b: *bhojyaṃ ca bhogakam* [Ed. *bhojyakam* against manuscripts E and F]); *Vātula-śuddhākhya* 9.81cd (quoted in the critical apparatus in Aj, loc. cit.), where Śiva is everything and nothing but him exists (*sarvam etac ca deveśas tasmād anyan na vidyate*). See also Brunner 1967, pp. 52-53 on the *Suprabheda's* nondualistic doctrine that the soul comes from Śiva and p. 54 on its nondualistic definition of Śiva as the source (the material cause) of everything.

43. The manuscript (NAK MS 1/1692) is from the ninth or tenth century; see Goudriaan in Goudriaan and Gupta 1981, p. 38, note 28. The unambiguously nondualistic passages of the *Sarvajñānottara* known to the southern

It is generally true, then, that the Saiddhāntika Tantras are dualistic. It is not equally true, however, that the non-Saiddhāntika Tantras are nondualistic. If there is one text in which one might be predisposed to expect the nondualism of the Kashmirian commentators it is surely the Mālinīvijayottaratantra. For this is the Tantra that Abhinavagupta takes as the basis of his presentation of the Trika in the Tantrāloka, his most comprehensive work of Tantric exegesis.[44] The Tantras of the Trika (*trikaśāstram*), he tells us, are the very essence of the nondualistic corpus, and among them the Mālinīvijayottara teaches the doctrine in its purest form:[45]

> Above the [common] scripture in ten and eighteen Tantras that is [the product of the diverse combinations of] the five streams, there is the Bhairava[-śāstra] comprising sixty-four Tantras. . . . [Therein] are four Collections (*pīṭham*[46]) in the following order of ascending importance: the Maṇḍalapīṭha, the Mudrāpīṭha, the Mantrapīṭha, and the Vidyāpīṭha. The most important scripture of the Vidyāpīṭha is the Siddhayogeśvarīmata. Beyond even that, as its ultimate essence, is the Mālinīvijayottara.

Śaivas (such as the verses quoted in ŚaivParibh, pp. 159^{11}-160^{15}) occur in the Nepalese manuscript, which also contains the various *Sarvajñānottara* quotations that occur in the Kashmirian literature. The dualists, of course, refused to take the nondualism literally; see ŚaivParibh, p. 160^{16-18}: *eteṣāṃ vacanānāṃ gauṇārthatām avalambya mahatā prayāsena dvaitaparatayā racitāny ekadeśināṃ vyākhyānāntarāṇi na samañjasānīti sarvajñānottaravyākhyāne 'smābhiḥ pratipāditam* 'Some dissenting Śaivas (*ekadeśināṃ*) have gone to great lengths to offer alternative, dualistic interpretations of these statements, claiming that they are not meant to be taken literally. I have refuted these in my commentary on the *Sarvajñānottara*.'

44. TĀ 1.17-18: *na tad astīha yan na śrīmālinīvijayottare / devadevena nirdiṣṭaṃ svaśabdenātha liṅgataḥ //* 'There is nothing in this [*Tantrāloka*] which has not been taught by the God of gods in the *Mālinīvijayottara*, either explicitly or by implication.'

45. TĀ 37.13c-25b: . . . *daśāṣṭādaśadhā srotaḥpañcakaṃ yat tato 'py alam / utkṛṣṭaṃ bhairavābhikhyaṃ catuḥṣaṣṭivibheditam // 17 // . . . maṇḍalaṃ mudrikā tathā // 23 // mantro vidyeti ca pīṭham utkṛṣṭaṃ cottarottaram / vidyāpīṭhapradhānaṃ ca siddhayogeśvarī (īśvarī)matam // tasyāpi paramaṃ sāraṃ mālinīvijayottaram /*. See also TĀ 1.18: *daśāṣṭādaśavasvaṣṭabhinnaṃ yac chāsanaṃ vibhoḥ / tatsāraṃ trikaśāstraṃ hi tatsāraṃ mālinīmatam //* 'The core of Lord's teaching in its divisions of ten, eighteen and sixty-four [Tantras] is the Trika; and the core of that is the *Mālinīvijayottara*.' For the doctrine that the Bhairavatantras, of which this Tantra is the core, are nondualistic, see MālVijVārt 1.391c-392b and TĀV $1(1)45^{1-3}$.

46. See TĀ 37.18 for *pīṭham* in this sense.

However, I propose that the text reveals no certain evidence of this doctrine and that on the contrary it contains certain clear indications that it followed the dualism of the mainstream Śaivism of the Siddhāntas. I shall consider first the evidence for nondualism in the text and then that for dualism.

Nonduality (*advaitam*) is taught in 18.4 and 18.44-48, but it is very doubtful that the nondualism of a monistic ontology is intended in either case.

In 18.4b the initiate is exhorted to adopt "the highest nonduality" (*paramādvaitam*); but the context is praise of the worship of an internal, spiritual "idol" (*liṅgam*) in preference to a blind cult of external images:[47] "One should worship the internal idol (*liṅgam*) in which [the universe of] the moving and the unmoving is dissolved, not one [made] from clay, stone, metal, crystal or any other [inert matter]; for an external idol deserves its name only because it is empowered by that [within]. It is therefore the latter that one should worship, adopting the highest nonduality."

The duality to be transcended here therefore may be no more than that which arises between outward worship and internal awareness when the former is done without the latter. As Abhinavagupta says (MVV 2.66), paraphrasing the Mālinīvijayottara itself:[48] "It is in vain that men resort to the worship of external idols, if their awareness lacks the knowledge of this [internal] idol. Their action is nothing more than physical exertion. It can have no effect."

This sort of nonduality, that of resorting to the inner (signified) alone or of resorting to the external only as the sign of the inner, does not entail ontological nondualism. A Śaiva can believe that one's ritual will be efficacious only if one performs the mental action of identifying the internal and the external without having to believe that the internal and the external actually are identical.

It is equally true, of course, that this sort of nonduality is not inconsistent with the ontological nondualism that Abhinavagupta sees in the text. However, if the Mālinīvijayottara intended such nondualism, it is striking that it is absent from its account of the

---

47. MālVij 18.2b-4b: *mṛcchailadhāturatnādibhavaṃ liṅgaṃ na pūjayet // yajed ādhyātmikaṃ liṅgaṃ yatra līnaṃ carācaram / bahirliṅgasya liṅgatvam anenādhiṣṭhitaṃ yataḥ // ataḥ prapūjayed etat paramādvaitam āśritaḥ /*.

48. MālVijVārt 2.66: *etalliṅgapraviyuktahṛdo* (? Ed. *-hṛdā*) *vṛthaiva hi bhajante / bāhyasthaliṅgapūjāṃ prayāsamātraṃ phalāya na hi tat syāt*. Paraphrasing MālVij 18.9c-10b: *etal liṅgam avijñāya yo liṅgī liṅgam āśrayet / vṛthā pariśramas tasya na liṅgaphalam aśnute* / 'That ascetic (*liṅgī*) who resorts to an idol (*liṅgam*) without knowing this 'idol' exerts himself in vain. He does not get the reward of idol-[worship].'

meditation itself. That account runs as follows:[49]

> If he concentrates his awareness on the subtle movement (*spandanam*) which we perceive in the heart, [he will experience] Trembling and Ascent. When after a month [of practice] that [state] has been stilled the master of yoga [sees], O goddess, that the idol has risen from his heart to the aperture of Brahmā [at the top of his cranium], illuminating with spotless radiance all [the space between this aperture and] the point beyond his body [twelve finger breadths above his head (*dvādaśāntam*)]. If he concentrates upon [the idol in the aperture of Brahmā] for a month, he will rise above it and behold within it the entire cycle of the *mantras*. When after six months that [stage] is perfected [he will attain] all the *siddhis*. . . . This, the great Śiva-idol, is accomplished by means of the self-idol (*ātmaliṅgena*).

Abhinavagupta gives a nondualistic interpretation of this passage in *Tantrāloka* 5.112c-20, but it is obviously forced.[50] First of all the "subtle movement which we perceive in the heart" (*spandanaṃ hṛdaye*), with which the Mālinīvijayottara's meditation begins, is equated with the metaphysical *spandaḥ* of his lineage's nondualistic idealism.[51] *Spandaḥ* in this special sense, as he explains elsewhere, is that *appearance of movement in the motionless*[52] that constitutes the dynamic

49. MālVij 18.5c-9b, 10cd [for 9c-10b see the preceding note]: *yad etat spandanaṃ nāma hṛdaye samavasthitam // 5 // tatra cittaṃ samādhāya kampa udbhava eva ca / tatra praśāntim āpanne māsenaikena yogavit // 6 // hṛdayād utthitaṃ liṅgaṃ brahmarandhrāntam īśvari / svaprabhoddyotitāśeṣadehāntam amaladyuti // 7 // tatraiva paśyate sarvaṃ mantrajālaṃ mahāmatiḥ / tanmastakaṃ samāruhya māsamātram ananyadhīḥ // 8 // tatas tatra suniṣpanne ṣaṇmāsāt sarvasiddhayaḥ / . . . śaivam etan mahāliṅgam ātmaliṅgena siddhyati // 10 //*.

50. See also MālVijVārt 2.61-69b, which covers the same ground.

51. I say that the concept of *spandaḥ* is proper to Abhinavagupta's lineage because in TĀ 28.3 38cd he speaks of Kallaṭa, the ninth century author of SpKā, as *asmatsaṃtānaguruḥ*, 'guru in my lineage.' *Lineage* (*saṃtānaḥ, saṃtatiḥ*) is synonymous with *maṭhikā* ('lodge') in the use of our authors. Abhinavagupta probably is referring therefore to the nondualistic Traiyambikā *maṭhikā* (Terambā, Tairimbhā, etc.).

52. ĪśvPraVim, vol. 1, pp. 208⁹-209³: *spandanaṃ ca kiṃciccalanam* (Ed. *kiṃcit calanam*) *eṣaiva ca kiṃcidrūpatā yad acalam api calam ābhāsata iti / prakāśasvarūpaṃ hi manāg api nātiricyate 'tiricyata ivety acalam evābhāsabhedayuktam eva ca bhātīti //* 'Moreover [the verb √*spad* means 'to move slightly' (see Dhātupāṭha 1.14: *spadi kiṃciccalane*). Thus] *spandanam* means 'slight movement.' Now slightness of movement [here] is this, that something which is actually unmoving

core (*śāktaṃ tattvam*[53]) of the light of consciousness (*prakāśaḥ*), the power of representation (*vimarśaḥ*) by virtue of which this light appears as coordinated subjects and objects. According to Abhinavagupta the Mālinīvijayottara is teaching that by meditating on this *spandaḥ* as it is manifest in the individual (*viśeṣaspandaḥ*) one is to penetrate through the Power state to the nondual ground in which the Individual (*naraḥ*), Power (*śaktiḥ*), and Śiva, the triad that the Trika considers its hallmark, coincide in an undifferentiated unity. The individual (*naraḥ*) is consciousness in which object representation (*idaṃ-vimarśaḥ*[54]), and therefore duality, predominate. One is to transform this state into Power consciousness by dissolving all object cognitions into the self. One does this by establishing the following awareness: "Whatever exists is nothing but myself" (*yad idaṃ tad aham eva*[55]). The result is said to be the state of duality within nonduality (*dvaitādvaitam, bhedābhedaḥ*). Śiva consciousness arises when the objective universe, collocated (*samānādhikaraṇa-*) with the subject in Power consciousness, dissolves entirely into nondualistic self-representation (*ahaṃ-vimarśaḥ*[56]). Here everything is experienced as the self and not, as in the preceding phase, simply equated with it.

According to Abhinavagupta, it is these three states of *spandaḥ* that are taught in the Mālinīvijayottara as the three stages through which the internal idol passes. These are the Idol of the Individual (*naraliṅgam*), the Idol of Power (*śaktiliṅgam*), and the Idol of Śiva (*śivaliṅgam*), or, as he also terms them, the Manifest (*vyaktam*), the Manifest cum unmanifest (*vyaktāvyaktam*), and the Unmanifest (*avyaktam*) Idols.[57] The last is obviously the Mālinīvijayottara's

appears to be in motion; for the essential nature [of consciousness] as Manifestation is never compromised even to the smallest extent and yet it appears to be: though actually unchanging it appears to have the [changing] plurality of its individual manifestions (*ābhāsa-*).' Abhinavagupta then shows that this analysis is to be applied to the *spandaḥ* / *spandatattvam* of SpKā by quoting from that work.

53. SpKāViv, p. 1, verse 1d: *paraṃ śāktaṃ tattvaṃ jagati jayati spanda iti tat //.*

54. TĀV 3(5) 427[6] (on TĀ 5.118): *ātmākhyam idaṃvimarśāspadaṃ vyaktaṃ liṅgaṃ . . .*

55. Ibid., continuing: *tatra* (Ed. *tantra*) *ātmākhye liṅge yad idaṃ tad aham eva ityevaṃrūpatayā viśvaṃ vilāpayato yogino 'haṃtedaṃtayoḥ sāmānādhikaraṇyena sphuraṇād vyaktāvyaktaṃ liṅgaṃ . . .*

56. Ibid., continuing: *tasmād vyaktāvyaktād api liṅgāt tasmin viśvasmin galite 'haṃparāmarśaśeṣatām āpanne tad avyaktaṃ liṅgaṃ bhaved ity arthaḥ //.*

57. TĀ 5.116c-117b, 118-120b: *yan nyakkṛtaśivāhaṃtāsamāveśaṃ vibhedavat // 116 // viśeṣaspandarūpaṃ tad vyaktaṃ liṅgaṃ cidātmakam / . . . ātmākhyaṃ yad vyaktaṃ naraliṅgaṃ tatra viśvam arpayataḥ / vyaktāvyaktaṃ tasmād galite tasmiṃs tad avyaktam //*

"great idol of Śiva."[58] The other two are not mentioned in the Tantra; but he tells us that his "idol of the individual" is what it calls the self-idol (*ātmaliṅgam*) in 18.10d.[59] As for his intermediate idol, the idol of Power, that is evidently his reading of the Mālinīvijayottara's state of the internal idol when it has risen to the aperture of Brahmā. This is indicated by the fact that he defines it not only as "that in which objectivity is active yet overshadowed by subjectivity" but also as "the power of the mantras" (*mantravīryam*).[60] This connects his definition with the Mālinīvijayottara, which says that the characteristic of the yogin's perception when

---

118 // tenātmaliṅgam etat parame śivaśaktyaṇusvabhāvamaye / avyakte viśrāmyati nānuttaradhāmagā tv iyaṃ carcā // 119 // ekasya spandanasyaiṣā traidhaṃ bhedavyavasthitiḥ / 'The "manifest" (*vyaktam*) idol is that which, [though] its nature is consciousness, appears to be outside [consciousness]. Its nature is individualized *spandaḥ* (*viśeṣaspandaḥ*). For in it has been suppressed [the innate state of] immersion in the awareness that one's identity is Śiva' (116c-117b). . . . Injecting the universe into the "manifest" idol, i.e. into the idol which is individualized consciousness, the "self-idol" [of the *Mālinīvijayottara*], [the meditator experiences] the manifest-unmanifest [idol] (*vyaktāvyaktam*). When the [universe] is dissolved [within that intermediate state and so is absent] from it, [he experiences] the unmanifest [idol]. Thus this self-idol [= *naraḥ*] is [withdrawn into the intermediate idol which fuses the individual (*naraḥ*) and Power (*śaktiḥ*) and thence] comes to rest in the supreme, unmanifest idol which embodies the individual (*aṇuḥ* [= *naraḥ*]), Power and Śiva. [This is the end.] The process is not continued [with the dissolution of the unmanifest idol] into an absolute ground [beneath the three. For the absolute ground is precisely that manifestation of consciousness as the unity of these three which is already accomplished in the third stage].'

58. MālVij 18.10c: *śaivam etan mahāliṅgam*.

59. TĀ 5.118ab[1]: *ātmākhyaṃ yad vyaktaṃ naraliṅgam*. This evidently interprets *ātmaliṅgena* in MālVij 18.10d.

60. TĀ 5.114c-116b: *dehagādhvasamunmeṣe samāveśas tu yaḥ sphuṭaḥ // ahaṃtācchāditonmeṣibhāvedaṃbhāvayuk sa ca / vyaktāvyaktam idaṃ liṅgaṃ mantravīryaṃ parāparam // naraśaktisamunmeṣi śivarūpād vibheditam /* 'This is the manifest-unmanifest idol, namely vivid immersion [in the trance of transcendence] while the universe is [still] manifest [, because one remains] in the [state in which the self identifies with a] body, [an immersion therefore] in which objectivity (*idaṃbhāvaḥ*) is active (*unmeṣi-*) but enveloped in subjectivity (*ahaṃtācchādita-*). It is the intermediate [stage], distinct from that which embodies Śiva, [being that] which emerges through individualized consciousness (*nara-*) and Power (*śakti-*) alone. It [therefore] is the power of [all] Mantras (*mantravīryam*).' Jayaratha ad loc. explains that no mantra can bestow its effect unless immersed in this intermediate state (*etaddaśām adhiśayāno hi mantraḥ svocitaphaladānasāmarthyabhāg bhavatīti bhāvaḥ /*).

the internal idol has reached this point in the yogic microcosm is that he sees all the mantras arrayed within it.

It is possible, even probable that the Mālinīvijayottara did intend the stages of its internal idol to be associated with the three components of the Trika triad, namely, the Individual (*naraḥ*), Power (*śaktiḥ*), and Śiva; for, though this triad is not taught explicitly anywhere in the text,[61] it is implicit in the meditation taught in 18.32-40 shortly after our passage. But even if it did intend this equation, there is no indication that it meant these categories to be understood in any but dualistic terms. In the Mālinīvijayottara's meditation on the internal idol there certainly is no trace of the idealistic nondualism that Abhinavagupta discovers in it. For it is the object of awareness that changes as the *yogin* perfects his practice; there is no transformation, as there is in Abhinavagupta's tendentious interpretation, of the nature of the subject-object relation itself such that the meditator is thought to be passing from a dualistic to a nondualistic state of cognition.

In the Mālinīvijayottara's second reference to nonduality, in 18.44c–48b, the yogin—and it is to him rather than to the common ritualist (*karmī*) that this chapter is addressed—is enjoined to practice what the text calls *nondualistic worship* (*advaitayajanam*). The passage runs as follows:[62]

> He has only to touch some liquid substance to accomplish his [preliminary] ritual bath (*snānam*). He has only to inhale the fragrant powder, flowers and the like to accomplish his presentation of offerings to the deities (*yajanam*). Simply relishing food of the six flavours serves as the offering of nourishment to the deities (*naivedyam*). To accomplish his recitation of mantras (*japaḥ*) he may utter any sound he chooses. His sacrifice in the fire (*homaḥ*) endures for as long as his awareness is immersed while focused on that [sound] in the contemplation of the flames of anything burning. As for the divine image to be visualized in his worship (*dhyānam*), this may be anything on which he chooses to rest his gaze. I have

61. See TĀV 7 [10] 124^{7-10}: Jayaratha finds Abhinavagupta explaining how the triad is implicit in MālVij (even though not explicit).

62. MālVim 18.44c-48b: *dravaddravyasamāyogāt snapanaṃ tasya jāyate // gandhapuṣpādigandhasya grahaṇaṃ yajanaṃ matam / ṣaḍrasāsvādanaṃ tasya naivedyāya prakalpate // yam evoccārayed varṇaṃ sa japaḥ parikīrtitaḥ / tatra cetaḥ samādhāya dahyamānasya vastunaḥ // jvālāntas tiṣṭhate yāvat tāvad dhomaḥ kṛto bhavet / yad eva paśyate rūpaṃ tad eva dhyānam iṣyate // prasaṅgād idam uddiṣṭam advaitayajanaṃ mahat /.*

taught this great nondualistic mode of worship following the implication of our present subject.

This passage is elaborated by Abhinavagupta with some modifications in his exposition of the means of attaining liberation through thought alone (*śāktopāyaḥ*), in the fourth chapter of his *Tantrāloka.* The rare person whom he considers capable of this method is said to have no need of the ordinary processes of ritual. He practices a higher, nondualistic cult of the deity (Bhairava)[63] in which, as I have shown elsewhere,[64] the phases of outer worship are effected metaphorically as modes of immersion in the reality of the self. The offerings are the objects of his senses; the recipient deity is his own consciousness; and the act of presentation is the fusion of the two through the contemplation that the reality of the perceived is entirely within that consciousness.[65] This fusion also includes the worshipper's individual identity: that too is resorbed in the contemplation of this higher self which is the ground of all that appears in awareness; for that contracted identity appears only in the dualistic structure of the state of consciousness which this contemplation uproots. According to this point of view, then, the *Mālinīvijayottara's* nondualistic worship (*advaitayajanam*) expresses, and therefore teaches as fact, the identity with Śiva/Bhairava of individual selves and the external world (the products of *māyā*).

However, there is no compelling reason to accept Abhinavagupta's interpretation. The fact that the performer of this nondualistic cult worships the deity by taking the offerings into himself does not imply idealism, nor does the fact that he may take anything he sees as the deity's icon (*dhyānam*). The first may imply only that the worshipper is to treat himself *as though* he were identical with or equivalent to the deity; and the second may express no more than the doctrine shared by the Saiddhāntika dualists that the deity is all-pervading and limited to no particular form.

We are then left with the worshipper's identifying himself with the deity. That this much is intended is confirmed by the immediate

---

63. TĀ 4.276: *ketakīkusumasaurabhe bhṛśaṃ bhṛṅga eva rasiko na makṣikā / bhairavīyaparamādvayārcane ko 'pi rajyati maheśacoditaḥ //* 'It is the bee not the fly that truly relishes the fragrance of the flowers of the Ketakī (Pandanus Odoratissimus). It is a rare person (*ko 'pi*) who is so inspired by Śiva that he is drawn to [this] supreme nondualistic cult of Bhairava.'

64. See Sanderson 1991.

65. TĀ 4.121c-122b: *pūjā nāma vibhinnasya bhāvaughasyāpi saṃgatiḥ // svatantravimalānantabhairavīyacidātmanā /* 'the presentation of offerings is the fusion of the [apparently] external mass of sense-objects with the autonomous, uncontaminated and non-finite self which is the consciousness of Bhairava.'

context. For the passage is preceded by a verse in which the meditator is instructed as follows:[66] "The yogin should constantly and fervently worship himself with fragrant powders, flowers and the like, [placing them as offerings on the top of his head,] at the aperture of Brahmā, [either actually] or in imagination."

But this injunction that the yogin should act out identity with the deity, though it is consistent with a philosophical doctrine that the individual actually is identical with the deity, does not entail it. Identification with the object of worship or meditation is fundamental to all Tantric practice and was accepted just as much by the dualists as by the nondualists. The initiate is to identify himself with the deity in order to assimilate his or her powers or nature; and this injunction, if it requires philosophical theory at all, is just as consistent with the Saiddhāntika doctrine that the soul's liberation is its attainment of simple equality with Śiva.[67]

Therefore, to determine a Tantra's metaphysical orientation, it is not enough to consider the implications of the forms of the rituals and meditations it enjoins. What one requires for that purpose are unambiguous statements of doctrine (*jñānam, vidyā*) outside the contexts of ritual (*kriyā*), observance (*caryā*), and meditation (*yogaḥ*).

Like many other Tantric texts the Mālinīvijayottara is inadequate in this respect. Nowhere does it assert openly that it is or is not dualistic. This, of course, is itself strong prima facie evidence of its being dualistic. For a nondualistic Śaiva text is one that must explicitly negate dualism, grounding the categories of the dualistic tradition (souls, *māyā*, and Śiva) in a higher unity.

Nonetheless one passage in the text, though it occurs in the context of ritual, may be taken as a serious statement of belief regarding the nature of the self. This is 9.52-53b. In it we are told what the officiant should think when about to commence a ceremony of initiation:[68] "[i] It is I that am the highest category (*tattvam*). [ii] In me this whole universe is located. [iii] I am the controller and author of all. [iv] It is when a creature has attained equality with me that he is said to be liberated (*muktaḥ*)."

Now this passage contains both views of the relation between

---

66. MālVij 18.43c-44b: *gandhapuṣpādibhir yogī nityam ātmānam ādarāt // brahmarandhrapradeśe tu pūjayed bhāvato 'pi vā /.*

67. See Sanderson 1991.

68. MālVij 9.52-53b: *aham eva paraṃ tattvaṃ mayi sarvam idaṃ jagat / adhiṣṭhātā ca kartā ca sarvasyāham avasthitaḥ // matsamatvaṃ* (Ed. *tatsamatvaṃ*) *gato jantur mukta ity abhidhīyate /.* My emendation of *tatsama-* to *matsama-* follows the testimony of sense and TĀ 16.93a.

the individual self and Śiva, the nondualistic and the dualistic. The nondualistic view is seen in the first three propositions. Here the officiant asserts that he *is* Śiva. The dualistic is expressed in the remaining proposition, which defines liberation as a state of mere equality with the deity (*matsamatvam*). This view, as we have seen, is a corollary of the doctrine that the plurality (*bhedaḥ*) of souls is absolute and eternal. Of these two views, the nondualistic and the dualistic, evidently the second represents the Mālinīvijayottara's true position. For if the text adhered to nondualism—and so was reacting against dualism—it would hardly have contradicted itself on so crucial a point of doctrine. The converse, however, is easily explained. The officiant is to assert that he *is* Śiva not because the text subscribes to nondualism but because he is to qualify himself for the ritual by believing fervently in the doctrine that it is not he that is about to liberate the soul of the initiand but Śiva residing in his person and working through him. This doctrine is attested by all the Tantric Śaivas without distinction; and all require this act of identification.[69]

The Mālinīvijayottara, then, is dualistic in its view of the relation between the individual soul and Śiva. The same conclusion is unavoidable on that other great point of dispute, the nature of *māyā*. The Mālinīvijayottara defines *māyā* as follows:[70] "[*Māyā*] is one (*ekā*), all-pervasive (*vyāpinī*), imperceptible (*sūkṣmā*),[71] partless (*niṣkalā*),

69. For the form of this "nondualistic" mediation, see the following strictly dualistic sources: MatPārVṛ KP, pp. 97[16]-98[7]: . . . *tan mama viśeṣānuṣṭhānaṃ bhagavān karotu yena tvayā sahaikakārakībhūyānugraham eṣāṃ saṃpādayāmi* . . . 'Therefore empower me intensely, O Lord, so that fused with you in the factors of my action (*kāraka-*) I may favor these [initiands]' (glossing MatPār KP 5.16cd: *śivavad bhāvayen nityam ātmānaṃ deśikottamaḥ*, 'The excellent officiant should always contemplate himself as though he were Śiva'); SārdhTriśKālVṛ, pp. 65[17]-66[15]: . . . *ya evāyaṃ parameśvaro . . . so 'ham iti tatkārakaikyāt* 'I am this Parameśvara who . . ., because of the unity of my action-factors with his.' See also the Saiddhāntika SomŚPaddh giving the officiant's preparations for the neophyte's initiation (SomŚPaddh, vol. 3, pp. 25-29, verses 23-28). It tells the officiant to think that he is Śiva and to make this identification before commencing the initiation: *śivo 'ham iti bhāvayet* (verse 23d) . . . *śivād abhinnam ātmānaṃ kartāraṃ bhāvayed* (26cd[1]) . . . *so 'ham eveti kurvīta bhāvaṃ sthirataraṃ guruḥ* (verse 28cd) 'He should meditate 'I am Śiva.' . . . He should meditate that he himself, the performer [of the ritual], is identical with Śiva. . . . The officiant should generate the firmest conviction that it is he himself that is Śiva.'

70. MālVij 1.26: *sā caikā vyāpinī sūkṣmā niṣkalā jagato nidhiḥ / anādyantāśiveśānī vyayahīnā ca kathyate //*.

71. I read *sūkṣmā* for the inappropriate *-rūpā* of the KSTS edition on the

the receptacle of the universe (*jagato nidhiḥ*), without beginning or end (*anādyantā*), indestructible (*vyayahīnā*), baneful/unconscious/Śivaless/non-Śiva (*aśivā*),[72] [but] able to act (*īśānī*)."[73]

This ability to act (*īśānatvam*) is realized when *māyā* is activated at the beginning of each period of cosmic activity (*sṛṣṭiḥ*) by the powers of Ananta, the Lord of Mantras (*mantrarāṭ*).[74] Ananta holds his office at the command of Śiva, who acts directly only in the Pure Universe (*śuddho 'dhvā*) above *māyā*.[75] When *māyā* has been

---

strength of the gloss on this verse at TĀ 9.152b and its quotation at TĀV 6(9)117[5-6].

72. I have analysed *pāda* 3 (*anādyantāśiveśānī*) to yield *aśivā* rather than *śivā* and interpreted the word to mean 'unconscious' (*jaḍā, acetanā*) following the same gloss (TĀ 9.152c). The *pāda* could be analyzed as *anādyantā śivā īśānī*. Abhinavagupta has chosen that analysis in MālVijVārt 1.174b (*māyātattvasvarūpe hi śiveśānīti vakṣyate*), but evidently to make the nondualist's point that *māyā* after all is Śiva's *śaktiḥ* (*śivā*) and therefore identical with him. *Aśiva-* rather than *śiva-* is supported by its occurrence in parallel verses in the Tantras; see, e.g., Mṛg VP 9.2: *tad ekam aśivaṃ bījaṃ jagataś;* and *Pauṣkara* quoted in ŚaivParibh, p. 88[7]: *nityaikā vyāpinī vasturūpā karmāśrayāśivā* [Ed. *-āśrayā śivā*]. Its meaning is not free from disagreement. Nārāyaṇakaṇṭha on the *Mṛgendra's* definition says simply that it is called *aśiva-* because it causes ignorance (MṛgVṛ VP, p. 187[13]: *aśivaṃ mohakatvāt*). The expression *avivekākulam* 'full of nondiscrimination' that occurs in the *Svāyambhuva's* definition of *māyā* quoted in SiddhSūVṛ, p. 18[5-7] may well have been intended as an explanatory synonym. Trilocanaśivācārya's definition of *māyā* in SiddhSārāv 8 includes the words *aśivakaraṃ mohakam* and appears, as this shows, to be based on that of Mṛg as explained by Nārāyaṇakaṇṭha. For him, then, *aśivam* in Mṛg means *aśivakaraṃ*, 'causing what is *aśiva*,' which his commentator Anantaśambhu explains as follows: *śivajñānavyatiriktatvād evājñānakaram* 'causing ignorance, because it is void of Śiva-knowledge.' These glosses can be taken as explanations in context of the word *aśiva-* in its common senses of 'inauspicious' or 'hostile.' But Bhojarāja seems to be taking it to mean 'Śivaless' when he includes *śivāsaktā* 'not attached to Śiva' in his definition of *māyā* in TattvPrak 38. Aghoraśiva ad loc. takes 'not attached' to mean 'not internally related to' or 'not inherent in' (*asamavetā*). Others took *aśiva-* to mean 'unconscious' (*jaḍa-, acetana-*). This is the sense recognized (but overcoded) by Abhinavagupta in TĀ 9.152b: *sā jaḍā bhedarūpatvāt*. Cf. the unknown source quoted ad loc. by Jayaratha: *aśivā bhedaprathāpradā*, '[*māyā* is] *aśiva-* [unconscious] in the sense that it is the cause of the manifestation of plurality.'

73. For my literal interpretation of *īśānī* as 'able to [act]'; i.e., 'possessing *kartṛśaktiḥ*,' see pp. 304-05.

74. MālVij 1.25b[2]cd: . . . *mantrarāṭ / jagad utpādayām āsa māyām āviśya śaktibhiḥ //* 'The Lord of Mantras caused the universe to be created by penetrating *māyā* with his Powers.'

75. The *locus classicus* for this delegation of power is Kir 3.27: *śuddhe 'dhvani*

activated by Ananta it emits (*sṛjati*) the thirty impure *tattvas* and the many submāyic worlds (*bhuvanam, puram*), so that souls once more may possess the means and locations of experience.[76]

This definition of *māyā* contains no trace of nondualism. Indeed, it agrees entirely with parallel passages in the dualistic scriptures and exegesis of the Saiddhāntikas.[77] And like them it upholds the doctrine that as Śiva is of the nature of consciousness he can be only the efficient cause (*nimittakāraṇam*) of the universe, and that the stuff of which the universe consists, its material cause (*upādāna-kāraṇam*), must be a source outside Śiva's nature.

For the nondualists, of course, there can be nothing outside Śiva's nature. They assert, as we have seen, that *māyā* is Śiva's Power (*śaktiḥ*). If it is his Power, then according to a principle accepted by both dualists and nondualists, it must be an aspect of his identity. Thus *māyā* ceases to be something outside the consciousness that constitutes the essence of Śiva and souls and becomes instead the power *of* consciousness to project plurality within itself so that it appears to be limited from the outside by something that it is not.[78]

śivaḥ kartā prokto 'nanto 'site prabhuḥ 'Śiva acts in the Pure Universe. In the Impure Ananta rules.'

76. See MālVij 1.27-35. The purpose of this emission is stated in 1.25a (*bhogasādhanasaṃsiddhyai* 'to bring about the means of experience') and 1.34b (*bhogināṃ bhogasiddhaye* 'to bring about the experience [of the fruition of their past acts] for those [still] subject to such experience').

77. See note 12 for parallel Saiddhāntika passages.

78. TĀ 9.149c-150a (after paraphrasing MālVij 1.24c-25 and before analyzing 1.26, the definition verse): *māyā ca nāma devasya śaktir avyatirekiṇī // bhedāvabhāsasvātantryaṃ tathā hi sa tayā kṛtaḥ* / '*Māyā* indeed is the inherent power of God himself, his capacity to manifest diversity'; TĀ 4.8-11: *nanu saṃvit parāmraṣṭrī parāmarśamayī svataḥ / parāmṛśyā kathaṃ tāthārūpyasṛṣṭau tu sā jaḍā // ucyate svātmasaṃvittiḥ svabhāvād eva nirbharā / nāsyām apāsyaṃ nādheyaṃ kiṃcid ity uditaṃ purā // kiṃ tu durghaṭakāritvāt svācchandyān nirmalād asau // svātmapracchādanakrīḍāpaṇḍitaḥ parameśvaraḥ // anāvṛte* (emending Ed.'s *anāvṛtte*) *svarūpe 'pi yad ātmācchādanaṃ vibhoḥ / saiva māyā yato bheda etāvān viśvavṛttikaḥ* 'Surely consciousness is in itself awareness of. It is that which carries out acts of representation. How, then, could it be itself the object of such representation. If it were to assume such a character it would no longer be consciousness. To this we answer as follows. The consciousness which is our identity is all-containing by its very nature. We have already said that nothing can be subtracted from it nor anything added to it. Yet by virtue of that absolute freedom which is his power to accomplish the impossible the supreme Lord is adept in the game of self-concealment. The actual nature of the all-pervading Lord is not concealed. Yet he seems

Of course, it was not beyond the ingenuity of Abhinavagupta and his commentator Jayaratha to subject this apparently dualistic definition of *māyā* to a nondualistic reading. Thus we are told that *māyā* is called *unconscious* (*jaḍā*, glossing *aśivā*) because it is manifest as a discrete phenomenon in consciousness, discreteness in consciousness being the nondualistic school's reformulation of what defines nonconsciousness (*jāḍyam*). *Yogins*, Jayaratha explains, are able to objectivate it through meditation.[79] It is unconscious, then, not because it is outside the nature of Śiva and souls, but in the sense that it is consciousness, the one, self-differentiating "soul," appearing to be nonconsciousness. Similarly, it is "eternal" (*anādyantā* and *vyayahīnā*) and "one" (*ekā*), not independently and in itself—as it is in the basic dualism—but because it is one with Śiva as his innate and inalienable power (*śaktiḥ*). Because of its oneness in this sense it is described as "partless" (*niṣkalā*). And it is described as "the receptacle of the universe" (*jagato nidhiḥ*) and as "able to act" because by virtue of his power, that is to say through *māyā*, Śiva can manifest the universe as outside himself even though its real existence is within his nature as consciousness.[80] In this reading *māyā* is described

---

to conceal himself. It is this self-concealment that is [meant by] *māyā*, the source of all this diversity which is active everywhere.' This echoes ŚivDṛ 1.32cd: *ātmapracchādanakrīḍāṃ kurvato vā kathaṃcana māyārūpam* '. . . miraculously accomplishing the game of self-concealment.'

79. TĀ 9.151c: *sā jaḍā bhedarūpatvāt* // 'It is[called *aśiva-*, i.e.] 'unconscious' because its form is differentiated.' Jayaratha ad loc.: *ayam eva hi jaḍasya svabhāvo yad idam atredānīṃ bhātīti paricchinnatayā prakāśyata iti / yad uktaṃ prāk "paricchinnaprakāśatvaṃ jaḍasya kila lakṣaṇam" / tataś ca mīyate paricchidyate yogibhir ity evam asyā abhidhānam / ata evāśivety abhidhānam / yad āhuḥ " . . . aśivā bhedaprathāpradā"* // 'For the essence of the unconscious is that it is manifested as something circumscribed, i.e. in the form 'This is manifest at this moment and in this place.' This is as Abhinavagupta has said above: 'The mark of the unconscious is evidently that its manifestation is circumscribed.' And so it owes its name to the fact that it is marked out (*mīyate [> māyā]*), i.e. discriminated by yogins as what is to be transcended. It is for this reason that it is called *aśivā* [i.e., unconscious]. This point has been made in the following: '. . . It is unconscious (*aśivā*) because it gives rise to discrete manifestation.'

80. TĀ 9.152cd^1: *śivaśaktyavinābhāvān nityaikā* 'It is [described as] eternal and one because of the inseparability of Śakti from Śiva.' Jayaratha ad loc: *śivas tāvan nityaḥ śaktiś ca tadavinābhūtatvāt taddharmadharmiṇīty uktaṃ nityeti / ata evānādyanteti vyayahīneti coktam / . . . / śivaś caika eva svatantraḥ padārthaḥ śaktiś cāsyātmabhūtety abhinnād abhinam abhinnam iti nyāyāt sāpy ekaivety uktam / ekety ata eva niraṃśatvān niṣkalety uktam / śivaś śaktivaśād evāntar evāvasthitam api viśvaṃ bahir avabhāsayed ity uktaṃ mūlakāraṇam iti / ata eva jagato nidhir itīśānīti coktam /*

as "the receptacle of the universe" (*jagato nidhiḥ*) because it is that power of Śiva within which all differentiated and objectifiable entities attain existence; and it is described as "able to act" (*īśānī*), that is, able to give birth to the universe of its transformations, not because it possesses this power in itself, needing only the stimulus of Ananta in order to be activated, but because it is the power of action (*kriyāśaktiḥ*) inherent in Śiva himself. This interpretation of *īśānī* is implicit in the Tantrāloka: Abhinavagupta gives 'the root cause' as a single gloss covering both "the receptacle of the universe" and "able to act"; and he evidently intends the word *cause* (*kāraṇam*) here to be analyzed both as 'that out of which things are made' and as 'that which makes things'; that is, as both 'material cause' and 'efficient cause.' For confirmation we have an earlier analysis of this passage in his Mālinīvijayavārtika:[81] "When [Śiva's] power of action reaches its most intense extroversion it becomes *māyā*; and the evidence for this is that it will be called *śiveśānī* in [the verse of the text which defines] the nature of *māyātattvam.*"

I understand Abhinavagupta to mean that the evidence for identifying *māyā* with Śiva's power of action (*kriyāśaktiḥ*) is that *śiveśānī* in the Mālinīvijayottara's definition of *māyā* is a synonym of *kriyāśaktiḥ*. He implies that he takes *śiveśānī* as "that power of Śiva (*śivā*) which has the capacity to act (*īśānī*)"; that is, as Śiva's power of action.[82]

'Śiva is eternal and his Power, since it is inseparable from him, shares his qualities. So it [too] is "eternal", i.e. that is why it is called "without beginning or end" and "without destruction" [in the *Mālinīvijayottara's* definition]. . . . Moreover, Śiva is one, the one [and] autonomous entity. His Power is his essence. Therefore, in accordance with the axiom that that which is not other than the undivided is itself undivided, *[māyā]* is described [there] as "one". And since she is one, and therefore partless, she is also termed *niṣkalā* [literally, "without division"]. Furthermore, it is by virtue of his Power that Śiva manifests the universe as outside himself, though in reality it exists in him alone. Hence *[māyā]* is termed the "root-cause" (*mūlakāraṇam*), i.e. [in the words of the *Mālinīvijayottara* itself] "the source of the world" and "able to act."

81. MālVijVārt 1.173c-174b: *kriyāśakteḥ sphuṭaḥ sphāro māyātvaṃ pratipadyate // māyātattvasvarūpe hi śiveśānīti vakṣyate /.*

82. Compare the dualistic formulation in TattvaTrNirṇ 3: *śambhuḥ puruṣo māyā nityaṃ vibhu kartṛśaktiyuktaṃ ca* 'Śiva, souls and *māyā* are each eternal, all-pervading and *endowed with capacity to act.*' See also the *Svāyambhuva's* definition of *māyātattvam* (quoted in SiddhSūVṛ, p. 18⁵⁻⁷): *māyātattvaṃ jagadbījam avināśy avyayātmakam / avivekākulaṃ sūkṣmam anādy avyayam īśvaram // 'Māyātattvam* is the seed of the universe, indestructible, eternal, pervaded by unknowing, imperceptible, without beginning, without end, *able to act*

In the Tantrāloka Abhinavagupta analyzes the syllables *anādyantā-śiveśānī* in the Mālinīvijayottara's definition as *anādyantā aśiveśānī*, with an initial privative *a-* in the second word (*aśivā*). In this passage of the Mālinīvijayavārtika, however, he has adopted the alternative analysis: *anādyantā śiveśānī*. *Māyā* ceases to be "baneful/unconscious/Śivaless/ non-Śiva" (*aśivā*) and becomes instead the "Power of Śiva" himself (*śivā*). In this way Abhinavagupta is able to squeeze an explicitly nondualistic (and therefore implicitly antidualistic) assertion from the text. But this reading, although it is grammatically possible, chooses to ignore both the occurrence of *aśiva-* or synonyms in verses defining *māyā* elsewhere in the Tantras themselves and in the traditional interpretation of this particular verse.[83]

To accept the nondualistic reading expounded by Abhinavagupta and Jayaratha therefore would be to reject the literal meaning of the verse as determined by its context in the canon; and we would be justified in doing so only if we were prevented from doing otherwise by some manifest incongruity. Abhinavagupta certainly sees such incongruity. But it follows only from metaphysical principles that are stated nowhere in the text.

For the followers of the nondualistic tradition this objection does not hold. Even if the incongruity does not follow from statements in the text itself, it follows from the truth of the doctrine that the Mālinīvijayottara belongs to a corpus of scriptures that is nondualistic. If there are valid scriptural statements that divide the Śaiva canon in this way then verses such as this definition of *māyā* in the Mālinīvijayottara must have been intended to be understood nondualistically, however dualistic they might appear at first sight. The close similarity of this verse to well-known Saiddhāntika definitions of *māyā* would therefore be seen as superficial. Indeed, a nondualist in this tradition might well have been inclined to argue that the similarity shows not that the Mālinīvijayottara is dualistic but that Śiva has left traces of nondualism even in the dualistic Tantras by using expressions that can be interpreted on both the dualistic and the nondualistic levels of his revelation. Claims that there is nondualistic meaning beneath the surface

---

(*īśvaram*).' The action of which *māyā* is the agent (*kartṛ-*) is that of giving birth (√*sū*), i.e., that of producing out of itself ('herself'), of procreating the lower *tattvas*; see, e.g., TattvaTrNirṇ 4cd: *ekaṃ prasāvitvayutaṃ māyātattvaṃ citivihīnaṃ ca*, '*Māyātattvam* is one, unconscious, [yet] endowed with the capacity to procreate'; MālVij 1.27a: *asūta sā kalātattvam* 'She gave birth to *kalātattvam*'; and RatnTr 40d: *tattvajātam asūta sā* 'She gave birth to the whole series of *tattvas*.'

83. See notes 12 and 72.

of the dualistic texts are not uncommon.[84]

Nonetheless it appears that there was a strong temptation to strengthen the case for nondualistic exegesis by tampering with the text itself. Of the four Kashmirian manuscripts that were used for the edition of the text in the Kashmir Series of Texts and Studies one (MS *ga*) omits the verse defining *māyā* altogether and the other two have strongly nondualistic variants.[85] In place of *niṣkalā jagato nidhiḥ* (1.26b), the reading guaranteed by Abhinavagupta and Jayaratha,[86] one (MS *ka*) has *niṣkalasya svabhāvajā* and the other (MS *kha*) has *niṣkalasya śivātmanaḥ*. This allows the verse to become unambiguously nondualistic by asserting that *māyā* is internal to Śiva: "[*Māyā*] is one (*ekā*), all-pervasive (*vyāpinī*), imperceptible (*sūkṣmā*), the innate [power] (*svabhāvajā*)[87] of partless [Śiva] (*niṣkalasya*) (MS *ka*)/ [the power] of the partless [being] who is Śiva [*niṣkalasya śivātmanaḥ*] (MS *kha*), without beginning or end (*anādyantā*), indestructible (*vyayahīnā*), [consciousness as the] unconscious (*aśivā* [i.e., *jaḍā*]), [his own] power of action (*īśānī*)."

Conclusion

It is evident, then, that Abhinavagupta has superimposed the nondualism of his school on to the Mālinīvijayottara. In a longer work in progress[88] I shall show that the claim that the non-Saiddhāntika Tantras are nondualistic is false as well for the Svacchandatantra and the Picumata-Brahmayāmala, the other major texts of that branch of the Śaiva canon.

84. See, e.g., MālVijVārt 1.196c-7b quoting the *Kālapāda* (i.e., *Kālottara*, = SārdhTriśKāl 8.7); ĪśvPraVivVim, vol. 3, p. 273^{12-20} quoting *Mataṅga* (= MatPār VP 10.21c-23); ibid., p. 278^{7-14} quoting *Rauravasūtra*; TĀ 1.66 quoting *Kāmika*; ŚivDṛVṛ, p. 31^{1-4} and ĪśvPraVivVim, vol. 2, p. 62^{2-9} analyzing nondualistically the definition of bound souls in the dualistic *Kiraṇatantra* (= Kir 1.15). See also NeTU 1 (8) 191^{5-14}.

85. In his Foreword, Madhusūdan Kaul mentions and describes only three manuscripts (*ka*, *kha*, and *ga*) as the basis of the edition, but in the notes on 1.26, and only there, he cites the reading of another (*gha*).

86. Quotation in TĀV 6(9) 117^{5-6}. Abhinavagupta overlooks *niṣkalā* (perhaps because after *ekā* it is pleonastic); but his *mūlakāraṇam* ($9.152d^{2}$) evidently glosses *jagato nidhiḥ*.

87. The adjective *svabhāvajā* echoes NeT 1.25cd-26ab: *sā mamecchā parā śaktiḥ śaktiyuktā svabhāvajā // vahner ūṣmeva vijñeyā raśmirūpā raver iva* / 'That supreme Power is my innate and omnipotent will, [one with me] as heat is one with fire or the sun's rays with the sun itself.'

88. Provisionally titled *Dualism and Nondualism in the Tantras.*

I shall show, however, that this nondualism did not originate entirely with the postscriptural interpretations and systematizations of Somānanda, Utpaladeva, and their successors in the Kashmirian lineage of the Trika. I shall argue that a nondualism of dynamic consciousness was already present in certain scriptures of the Trika and the Krama,[89] and that these texts were the authority for the intimate religious practice of our nondualistic exegetes, who accordingly have read the entire non-Saiddhāntika corpus in their light. To do so was easy enough. For nondualism was the prescription of a single view of the categories that both schools held in common. It was not a set of particular doctrines conflicting with the Siddhānta's in specific details at every turn. In principle it would be enough to insert into the corpus a single sentence expressing this view or metaview for the meaning of the whole to be transformed. If the texts to be interpreted had been conscious of this movement toward nondualism they might have protected themselves by asserting their dualism in terms that unambiguously excluded nondualism. In that case, our exegetes would have encountered a major obstacle to their project. But the texts seem not to have been conscious of any such fundamental challenge to their metaphysics. Nondualism or the one-soul doctrine (*ekātmavādaḥ*) is known and rejected in the Siddhāntas; but it is a Vedantic not a Śaiva nondualism.[90] It is only in the time of Abhinavagupta and Kṣemarāja themselves, around the turn of the tenth and eleventh centuries, that we see any reference to nondualism among other Śaivas in the writings of the Kashmirian dualists; and when we do, in Bhaṭṭa Rāmakaṇṭha's commentary on the Mataṅgapārameśvara, it is attacked not as the doctrine of the followers of the non-Saiddhāntika systems in general, the field of nondualism according to the nondualists themselves, but, much more narrowly, as the doctrine of the Kaula tradition within non-Saiddhāntika Śaivism,[91] the tradition, in fact, to which Somānanda, Utpaladeva, Abhinavagupta, and Kṣemarāja adhered.

---

89. Particularly the *Trikasāra* and *Triśirobhairava* in the Trika, and the *Kālikākrama*, *Kālīkulapañcaśatika*, *Kālīkulakramasadbhāva*, and *Jayadrathayāmala* (*Tantrarājabhaṭṭāraka*) in the Krama.

90. See, e.g., Mṛg VP 2.12: *vedānteṣv eka evātmā . . . pratijñāmātram evedaṃ . . . advaitahāniḥ . . .*

91. See Rāmakaṇṭha, MatPārVṛ VP, p. 41^{1-4}: *kiṃ ca niṣkampaḥ / na bindusadāśivātmanā bhedena nāpi mantramantreśvarāṇāṃ bhedena nāpi māyādipṛthivyantena bhedena sakampaḥ pariṇāmī / na tatprakṛtir upādānam ity arthaḥ / mṛdādivad acaitanyaprasaṅgād iti vakṣyāmaḥ / tataś ca yaiḥ kaulādiśāstravāsanayā vivartapariṇāmapakṣayor anyatarābhyupagamenātra patyur advaitavādaḥ samāropyate te pratikṣiptāḥ /* 'Moreover

If, then, any doctrine may be said to represent the mainstream of the Śaiva Tantras it is dualism. Nondualism takes over only at the Kaula fringe, to be superimposed by scholastic artifice on the rest of the non-Saiddhāntika literature. Certainly dualism is more natural to the Tantras considered in their primary character as a system of rites and meditations. Nondualism, I suggest, connotes, just as it does in orthodox Hindu thinking about the Vedic revelation, an undermining or subordination of the ritualism that inspired these systems. It is a metaview of a complex of practices that suggests their ultimate superfluity and therefore is hardly likely to have been the basic theoretical attitude of those who elaborated the mainstream tradition.

[Śiva] is unchanging. He does not change, undergo transformation, with the differentiation of *bindu* and Sadāśiva, nor that of the Mantras and Mantreśvaras, nor that of the *tattvas* from *māyā* down to earth. In other words, he is not their original substance, their material cause. I shall explain below that if he were then he would have to be unconscious, like the clay [out of which pots are formed]. This, moreover, answers those who, under the influence of Kaula and like doctrines, superimpose a theistic nondualism (*patyur advaitavādaḥ*) on this [verse], opting for one or other of the two [varieties of nondualism], that is, the view that [Śiva] undergoes merely transformation (*vivartapakṣaḥ*) or the view that this transformation is real (*pariṇāmapakṣaḥ*).'

Bibliography

Abbreviations Used in Citations

BGOML — *Bulletin of the Government Oriental Manuscripts Library*, Madras.

KSTS — Kashmir Series of Texts and Studies.

PIFI — Publications de l'Institut Français d'Indologie.

Primary Sources

Aj — *Ajitāgama*, ed. N. R. Bhatt, Pondicherry: Institut Français d'Indologie 24. Pondichéry: Institut Français d'Indologie, 1964 and 1967.

AṣṭPrak	*Aṣṭaprakaraṇa*, ed. Kṛṣṇaśāstrī. Devakoṭṭai: Śivāgamasiddhāntaparipālanasaṅgha, 1923 (TattvPrak, TattvSaṃ, TattvTrNirṇ) and 1925 (RatnTr, BhoKā, NādKā, MokṣK, ParMokṣNirKā).
ĪśvPraKā	*Īśvarapratyabhijñākārikā* of Rājānaka Utpaladeva with his autocommentary (*-vṛtti*) up to 3.20, ed. Madhusūdan Kaul Śāstrī, KSTS 34 [with *Siddhitrayī*]. Srinagar, 1921.
ĪśvPratVim	*Īśvarapratyabhijñāvimarśinī* of Abhinavagupta, ed. Mukund Rām Śāstrī, vol. 1, and Madhusūdan Kaul Śāstrī, vol. 2, KSTS 22 and 33. Bombay, 1918 and 1921.
ĪśvPratVivVim	*Īśvarapratyabhijñāvivṛtivimarśinī* of Abhinavagupta, ed. Madhusūdan Kaul Śāstrī, KSTS 60, 72, and 75. Bombay, 1938-43.
Kir	See Vivanti 1975.
GurNP	*Gurunāthaparāmarśa* of Madhurāja, ed. P. N. Pushp, KSTS 85. Srinagar, 1960.
TattvTrNirṇ	*Tattvatrayanirṇaya* of Sadyojyoti with commentary (*-vṛtti*) of Aghoraśivācārya. In AṣṭPrak.
TattvPrak, -Vṛ	*Tattvaprakāśikā* (/*Tattvaprakāśa*) of King Bhojarāja with commentary (*-vṛtti*) of Aghoraśivācārya. In AṣṭPrak.
TattvSaṃ	*Tattvasaṃgraha* of Sadyojyoti with commentary (*-ṭīkā*) of Aghoraśivācārya. In AṣṭPrak.
TĀ, -V	*Tantrāloka* of Abhinavagupta with commentary (*-viveka*) of Rājānaka Jayaratha, ed. Mukund Rām Śāstrī, KSTS 23, 28, 30, 35, 29, 41, 47, 59, 52, 57, and 58. Bombay and Srinagar, 1918-38.
NarParīkṣ, -P	*Nareśvaraparīkṣā* of Sadyojyoti with commentary (*-prakāśa*) of Bhaṭṭa Rāmakaṇṭha, ed. Madhusūdan Kaul Śāstrī, KSTS 45. Srinagar, 1926.
NeT, -U	*Netratantra* with commentary (*-uddyota*) of Rājānaka Kṣemarāja, ed. Madhusūdan Kaul Śāstrī, KSTS 46 and 61. Bombay, 1926 and 1939.
ParamSViv	*Paramārthasāra* of Abhinavagupta with commentary (*-vivṛti*) of Yogarāja, ed. J. C. Chatterji, KSTS 7. Srinagar, 1916.

ParMokṣNir-KāVṛ	*Paramokṣanirāsakārikā* of Sadyojyoti with commentary (*-vṛtti*) of Bhaṭṭa Rāmakaṇṭha. In AṣṭPrak.
PraHṛ	*Pratyabhijñāhṛdaya* of Rājānaka Kṣemarāja with autocommentary, ed. J. C. Chatterji, KSTS 3. Srinagar, 1911.
BṛhKāl	*Bṛhatkālottara:* Kathmandu, National Archives MS 5-778. Palm-leaf, 333 fols., Newari script, Nepālīyasaṃvat 538 [A.D. 1418/9].
BhogKā, -Vṛ	*Bhogakārikā* of Sadyojyoti with commentary (*-vṛtti*) of Aghoraśivācārya. In AṣṭPrak.
MatPār, -Vṛ VP	*Mataṅgapārameśvarāgama, Vidyāpāda,* with commentary (*-vṛtti*) of Bhaṭṭa Rāmakaṇṭha ed. N. R. Bhatt, Pondicherry: Institut Français d'Indologie 56. Pondichéry: Institut Français d'Indologie, 1977.
MatPār, -Vṛ KP, CP	*Mataṅgapārameśvara Kriyāpāda, Caryāpāda,* and *Yogapāda,* with commentary (*-vṛtti*) of Bhaṭṭa Rāmakaṇṭha up to KP 11. 12b, ed. N. R. Bhatt, Pondicherry: Institut Français d'Indologie 65. Pondichéry: Institut Français d'Indologie, 1982.
MahārthMañj, -P	*Mahārthamañjarī* of Maheśvarānanda (/Gorakṣa) [in Mahārāṣṭrī Prakrit] with [Sanskrit] autocommentary (*-parimala*), ed. Vrajavallabha Dviveda, Yogatantragranthamālā 5. Varanasi, 1972.
MālVij	*Mālinīvijayottaratantra,* ed. Madhusūdan Kaul Śāstrī, KSTS 37. Srinagar, 1922.
MālVijVārt	*Mālinīvijayavārttika* of Abhinavagupta, ed. Madhusūdan Kaul Śāstrī, KSTS 31. Srinagar, 1921.
Mṛg, -Vṛ VP	*Mṛgendratantra VP* and *YP,* with commentary (*-vṛtti*) of Bhaṭṭa Nārāyaṇakaṇṭha, ed. Madhusūdan Kaul Śāstrī, KSTS 50. Srinagar, 1930.
Mṛg, -Vṛ KP	*Mṛgendrāgama [= Mṛgendratantra] KP* and incomplete *CP,* with commentary (*-vṛtti*) of Bhaṭṭa Nārāyaṇakaṇṭha, ed. N. R. Bhatt, Pondicherry: Institut Français d'Indologie 23. Pondichéry: Institut Français d'Indologie, 1962.
MokṣKā	*Mokṣakārikā* of Sadyojyoti with commentary (*-vṛtti*) of Bhaṭṭa Rāmakaṇṭha. In AṣṭPrak.
RatnTr, -U	*Ratnatraya* of Bhaṭṭa Śrīkaṇṭha with commentary

(*-ullekhinī*) of Aghoraśivācārya. In AṣṭPrak.

ŚivDṛ, -Vṛ — *Śivadṛṣṭi* of Somānanda with commentary (*-vṛtti*) of Rājānaka Utpaladeva up to 4.74, ed. Madhusūdan Kaul Śāstrī, KSTS 54. Srinagar, 1934.

ŚivSū, -Vim — *Śivasūtra* with commentary (*-vimarśinī*) of Rājānaka Kṣemarāja, ed. J. C. Chatterji, KSTS 1. Srinagar, 1911.

ŚaivParibh — *Śaivaparibhāṣā* of Śivāgrayogīndrajñānaśivācārya, ed. H. R. Rangaswamy Iyengar and R. Ramasastri, Sanskrit Series 90. Mysore: Oriental Research Institute, 1950.

ŚaivāgParibh-Mañj — See Dagens 1979.

ṢaṭtrTSaṃdViv — *Ṣaṭtriṃśattattvasaṃdoha* with commentary (*-vivaraṇa*) of Rājānaka Ānanda, ed. Mukund Rām Śāstrī, KSTS 13. Srinagar, 1918.

SārdhTriśKāl, -Vṛ — *Sārdhatriśatikālottarāgama* with commentary (*-vṛtti*) of Bhaṭṭa Rāmakaṇṭha, ed. N. R. Bhatt, Pondicherry: Institut Français d'Indologie 61. Pondichéry: Institut Français d'Indologie, 1979.

SiddhSārāv, -Vyā — *Siddhāntasārāvali* of Trilocanaśivācārya with commentary (*-vyākhyā*) of Anantaśivācārya (/Anantaśambhu), ed. A. A. Ramanathan et al., *BGOML* 17, no. 1 (1965): 1-48 (verses 1-32); 18, no. 1 (1968): 1-68 (verses 33-59); 18, no. 2 (1968): 1-64 (verses 60-109); 19, no. 1 (1969): 53-84 (verses 110-130); 19, no. 2 (1972): 1-48 (verses 131-150); 20, no. 2 (1972): 49-71 (verses 151-169).

SiddhSūVṛ — *Siddhāntasūtra* (*Śivajñānabodha*) with commentary (*-vṛtti*) of Sadāśivaśivācārya, ed. A. A. Ramanathan, *BGOML* 16, no. 1 (1963): 1-56.

SomŚPaddh III — See Brunner (-Lachaux) 1977.

SpKā, -Viv — *Spandakārikā* with commentary (*-vivṛti*) of Rājānaka Rāmakaṇṭha, ed. J. C. Chatterji, KSTS 6. Srinagar, 1913.

SpSaṃd — *Spandakārikā* 1.1. with commentary (*Spandasaṃdoha*) by Rājānaka Kṣemarāja, ed. Mukund Rām Śāstrī, KSTS 16. Bombay, 1917.

SvTU *Svacchandatantra*, with commentary (*-uddyota*) of Rājānaka Kṣemarāja, ed. Madhusūdan Kaul, KSTS 31, 8, 44, 48, 51, 53, and 56. Bombay, 1921-35.

HarCarCint *Haracaritacintāmaṇi* of Rājānaka Jayadratha, ed. Paṇḍita Śivadatta and Kāśīnāth Pāṇḍurang Parab, Kāvyamālā 61. Bombay, 1897.

Secondary Sources

Brunner (-Lachaux), Hélène. 1967. "Analyse du Suprabhedāgama." *Journal Asiatique* 255: 31-60.

———. 1977. *Somaśambhupaddhati, Troisième Partie: Rituels occasionels dans la tradition śivaïte de l'Inde du Sud selon Somaśambhu II: dīkṣā, abhiṣeka, vratoddhāra, antyeṣṭi, śrāddha*. Pondicherry: Institut Français d'Indologie 25.III. Pondichéry: Institut Français d'Indologie.

Dagens, Bruno. 1979. *Le Florilège de la Doctrine Śivaïte: Śaivāgamaparibhāṣāmañjarī de Vedajñāna. Édition critique, traduction et notes*. Pondicherry: Institut Français d'Indologie 60. Pondichéry: Institut Français d'Indologie.

Goudriaan, Teun, and Sanjukta Gupta. 1981. *Hindu Tantric and Śākta Literature. History of Indian Literature Vol. II*, 2. Wiesbaden: Otto Harrassowitz.

Sanderson, Alexis. 1988. "Śaivism and the Tantric Traditions." In S. Sutherland, L. Houlden, P. Clarke, and F. Hardy, eds., *The World's Religions*. London: Routledge, pp. 660-704.

———. Forthcoming. "Meaning in Tantric Ritual." In A. M. Blondeau and K. Schipper, eds. *Essais sur le Rituel III: Colloque du Centenaire de la Section des Sciences religieuses de l'École Pratique des Hautes Études*. Bibliothèque de l'École des Hautes Études, Sciences Religieuses. Louvain and Paris: Peeters.

Vivanti, Maria Pia, ed. and trans. 1975. *Il "Kiraṇāgama": Tẹsto e traduzione del "Vidyāpāda."* Supplemento n. 3 agli ANNALI: vol. 35 (1975), fasc. 2. Napoli: Istituto Orientale di Napoli.

Chapter Eleven

The Kubjikā Upaniṣad and Its Atharvavedic Character

Jan A. Schoterman

Several Tantrically oriented schools and traditions have produced their own Upaniṣads, thus trying to gain more authority by linking their position with the hallowed *śruti.* This holds good as well for the sectarian worship of goddesses. We can point for instance to the Kālikā Upaniṣad, Durgā Up., and so forth. Generally speaking, these sectarian Upaniṣads are not very interesting; they tend to describe the mantra and ritual of the goddess in question in a conventional and more or less superficial way. Also the Kubjikāmata produced its own Upaniṣad, called *Kubjikā Upaniṣad* (henceforth, KuUp), and the goddess Kubjikā indeed is mentioned frequently in it. But on closer inspection this Upaniṣad is not what it might seem to be at first sight; on the contrary, the KuUp (which also, by the way, is much bigger than some other later Upaniṣads), turns out to contain, mixed up with the kind of material we might expect in a text of Kubjikā esoterism, a quite different original kernel. The purpose of this chapter is to show the hybrid character of the KuUp by means of a preliminary analytic survey of its contents.

The KuUp came to my attention in the course of the investigation of the literature of the Kubjikā school, a project that has been carried out over several years at the Indological Institute of Utrecht University. The Tantric school around Kubjikā produced a substantial number of texts, written down (as far as registered by us) in about 700 manuscripts that are preserved (with a very few exceptions) in the National Archives of Nepal at Kathmandu and subsequently filmed in the cadre of the Nepal-German Manuscripts Preservation Project. Among these sources figure three manuscripts of the KuUp. It is not necessary now to expatiate on the nature of these manuscripts; all three are undated, but rather recent, and written on paper in Newari script.[1] The Sanskrit is reasonable.

On its cover, one of them has a short notice in Sanskrit mixed with Newari: *śrīgaṇeśāya namaḥ vava nihma śrīvāgpatirājānandaśarmaṇaḥ* 'Hail to Gaṇeśa; [this book belongs] to these two, Vākpatirāja and Ānandaśarman.' On account of the script, as well as of the Newari in this notice (the demonstrative pronoun *vava* is an older form of the contemporary *o-o*) I propose a dating of these manuscripts in the eighteenth or early nineteenth century. The text itself of course could be much older. The text is handed down very uniformly in these manuscripts, so that in my opinion a correct insight about the contents of the KuUp can be obtained. There are only few interesting variants such as (to take an instance) in the second chapter, where *mahākubjikārdhāṅgadharam* (MS. A) contrasts with *mahakubjikārdhe giridharam* (MS C, without doubt wrongly suggesting a Vaiṣṇava connotation on this place; MS. B is defective).

The first question that should be posed with regard to the KuUp of course is: What has the text to do with the old Tantric school around Kubjikā as known to us from its basic literature, such as the Kulālikāmnāya or the Ṣaṭsāhasrasaṃhitā?[2] The answer can be short: very little. An external correspondence is the number of chapters. The KuUp contains twenty-five chapters; the same number is also found in the Kulālikāmnāya, which may be considered the *mūlatantra* of the school, and in the Śrīmatottara, another important text of the Kubjikāmata, whereas the Ṣaṭs. contains twice that number (fifty chapters). Kubjikā's name is repeated through the whole KuUp, but the ritualistic and mantric particulars described in connection with her and her male partner deviate greatly from the earlier tradition, although in many places we get the impression that the Goddess, so to say, has been dragged into the argument by the hair. In some cases we find the names of quite other goddesses, such as Śrīlakṣmī or Siddhilakṣmī, but with the mere name Kubjikā appended to their names like a determinant: Siddhilakṣmī-kubjikā, and so on. By this procedure, the author must have tried to establish the incorporation of existing goddesses within the Kubjikā tradition, at the cost of a serious alteration of that tradition, which on some places almost amounts to no more than mere lip service to the own *gurupaṅkti*. In other passages, such as the description of the Ten Mahāvidyās (see later), the author has not even gone to that trouble.

This lack of any direct relation between our text and the fundamental tenets of the Kubjikā school also appears from another notable feature. Although the KuUp bristles with mantras (or rather *vidyās*) and *bījas* or *kūṭas*, none of these corresponds to the *vidyās* and mantras we know from the old Kubjikā literature; this with the only exception of the Navātman, but this mantra is too generally known to allow any conclusions in this context. The KuUp, which consists partly of verse, partly of prose, contains not a single stanza or prose sentence from the three mentioned basic texts of the school. Another similar argument is formed by the way in which the KuUp presents its several *bījas* and *vidyās*. As is usually the case, this presentation is effected through a certain type of coding (which of course also has its own symbolic value), so as to protect these phonic expressions of the deity's secret nature from the uninitiated. To this end, the representants of the Kubjikā school developed a twofold system of their own: either the fifty letters of the Sanskrit alphabet are replaced by the names of fifty male or female deities, or one indicates the position of the respective letters within certain geometric figures (*prastāra* or *gahvara*) subdivided into fifty small compartments.[3] The remarkable fact is that the KuUp makes use of neither of these methods, although one without doubt would expect such a procedure in a text that claims adherence to the Kubjikā school. In the KuUp, the fifty letters indeed are replaced by the names of deities, but the respective codings differ from those prescribed by the authorities of the school. The system practiced in the KuUp is in accordance with the lists of code names provided by the (Prakārāntara)—Mantrābhidhāna, a text that (like many others) professes to be extracted from the Rudrayāmala.[4] I give one instance by way of illustration. In Chapter 4 of the KuUp we read: *kāmarūpaṃ vahnyārūḍhaṃ bindumālinībhūṣitaṃ, kālabindumilitam* 'Kāmarūpa, mounted by Fire, adorned by Bindumālinī and joined by Kālabindu.' This is said to be the *bīja* of Lakṣmī, and we find indeed her *bīja* ŚRĪṂ with the help of the mentioned Mantrābhidhāna, verse 153ab: *śaḥ savyaṃ ca kāmarūpī kāmarūpo mahāmatiḥ*, and 16ab: (ĪḤ) *śivottamaḥ śivā tuṣṭiś caturthī bindumālinī*; and so on.

Notwithstanding this negative evidence, there also—in addition to the occurrence of the name *Kubjikā*—are other traces of a relation of the KuUp with the Kubjikā school. For instance, the KuUp, just as the older texts of the school, associates the worship of Kubjikā with the Western Tradition (*paścimāmnāya*). Thus, we read in the tenth chapter that in preceding world periods people followed different *āmnāyas*, but that one should in the present Kaliyuga follow the Paścimāmnāya (*kalau paścimāmnāyopāsanaṃ kuryāt*).

Before making further statements about the nature and origin of the KuUp, the best thing to do is to give a short survey of its contents. As already has been said, there are twenty-five chapters. The first five chapters treat mantras and *Vidyās* of certain secondary forms of Kubjikā and her male partner, Śiva-Kubjeśvara. Chapter 1 begins with the coded description of two *bījas* or rather *kūṭas* (as they are called in the text): H-Ṣ-KṢ-MLVRYŪṂ and S-H-KṢ-MLVRYĪṂ. They represent respectively Kubjeśa and Kubjikā. Both are ninefold (*navātmaka*), and their fundamental unity is expressed in this way also, that the text consistently speaks of only one *mahākūṭa*. Besides the *h* and the *s*, which represent Śiva and Śakti, we find in this *kūṭa* constituents that represent the supreme element (*kṣ-m*) and those that stand for the four *tattvas*: earth to air (*l-v-r-y*). The subject is followed by an announcement of the different Kubjikās who will be treated in Chapters 2-5; only then comes an introduction of the usual Upaniṣadic type in which the speaker and interlocutor are mentioned by name. The passage is seemingly corrupt and purposely difficult to understand, but it seems that Pippalāda Aṅgiras poses questions to Sanatkumāra Ātharvaṇa[5] about mantra, *yantra*, worship, and so forth of Kubjikā, the Lady of the Western Tradition. Sanatkumāra first describes the *yantra* of the goddess (who in this connection is identified with Pratyaṅgirā); it consists of a *bindu*, triangle, hexagon, eight-petaled lotus, octagon, and square with four gates. The results of worshipping this *yantra* and wearing it on one's heart, crown, or arm while muttering the connected mantra lie in the sphere of supernatural powers, especially those that interest a ruler (annihilation of enemies, etc.); in a preceding passage the worshipper of Kubjikā's forms has already been equated to Viṣṇu. The end of Chapter 1 contains a thirteen-syllabled mantra of Kubjeśvara.

In the second to fifth chapters, we find the exposition of the *vidyās* of several forms of Kubjikā. Sanatkumāra, who studied all the nine schools of the Atharvaveda (see later), proceeds with the exposition of the *yantra* and the meditation of Mahākubjeśvara. The *yantra* is connected with the exegesis of the famous stanza *puṇḍarīkaṃ navadvāram* (AV 10, 8, 43). The god himself is identified with the Puruṣa, whereas Kubjikā is said to have Brahman as her nature (*brahmasvarūpā Kubjikā*). The next subject is the treatment of the *vidyās* of nine varieties (*bheda-*) of Kubjikā, as follows: Siddhikubjikā (seventeen syllables), Ugrakubjikā (sixteen), Vīrakubjikā (twenty-two), Jñānakubjikā (twelve), Bhīmakubjikā (seven), the important Siddhilakṣmīkubjikā (nine), Pracaṇḍakubjikā (six), Rudrakubjikā (five), and Śrīkubjikā (eighteen). The coded description of each *vidyā* is followed by an elaborate statement of rewards. This part of the text occupies the remainder of Chapter 2 and Chapters 3 to 5.

Chapter 6 and 7 seem to have developed around the morning ritual. The procedure starts with the worship of the guru lineage: Parameṣṭhiguru, Parāparaguru, Paramaguru, one's own guru. This is followed by worship of dawn and night with Atharvanic mantras, and meditation on the unity of one's self, the guru, and the Goddess. Without this Brahman wisdom revealed by Parāśara (the name is mentioned twice), the performance of the morning ritual is declared to be useless.

The long Chapter 7 begins with an expatiation on the mystical nature of the guru, who is to be meditated upon in the thousand-petaled lotus; he is inter alia identical with Brahman and with the union of Śiva and Śakti, and also with Siddhikubjikā (added secondarily?). After a bow to the Kula tree,[6] the officiant should practice the ascension of the *haṃsa* (ascending self) within his own mystic body. This is preceded by worship of Ajapā who is identified with Viṣṇu's Māyā, and again with Kubjikā. The following characterization of the *haṃsa* and its movements along the six *cakras* is greatly inspired by the Haṃsa Upaniṣad (see also later), the greater part of which is literally included. Also fragments from the Atharvaśira-Upaniṣad (on a Pāśupata-vrata of wearing ashes) and other texts figure in this chapter. A remarkable feature is the quotation of a stanza from Gauḍapāda's Māṇḍūkyakārikā's: *svapnamāyāsvarūpeṇa* and so on (I, 7c-8b).

In the supreme state of consciousness, the ascended *haṃsa* obtains its dissolution in the primeval sound (*nāda*). This supreme state is then equated with Mahākubjikā, also called *Siddhikubjikā*, who is seated on the Western throne on the five corpses (Brahmā, Viṣṇu, etc.). One should worship her in one's heart, after a renewed adoration of different gurus. There is also a Mahākujbikāgāyatrī: *OṂ Kubjikādevyai vidmahe kuladīpāyai dhīmahi HRĪṂ tan naḥ kubjiḥ pracodayāt.* On her throne in the heart, she is served by Kubjanātha or Kubjeśvara, who is equal to the eightfold form of Śiva and the thousand-eyed Puruṣa of the Vedic tradition. The practicer should also worship the earth and meditate on his or her identity with Kubjikā. The practicer then goes out for the daily bath. Throughout this chapter, Atharvanic mantras are quoted profusely.

In the eighth chapter, we find an exposition of the analysis of the syllable OṂ into three-and-a-half *mātrās*, said to be indispensable for a worshipper of Kubjikā. There are long quotations from the Gopatha-Brāhmaṇa (I, 24 and 25), and the Atharvaśira- and *Atharvaśikhā*-Upaniṣads. Kubjikā is mentioned only in the introductory part and in the very last line; the body of the text lacks even the slightest relation with her. The chapter is proclaimed by Prajāpati.

Chapter 9 is devoted to a magical ritual in true Atharvavedic fashion. In the middle of the night, on a cremation ground, the practicer should prepare with flour an image of a female deity, infuse it with life (*jīvanyāsaṃ kuryāt*) while reciting a series of Atharvavedic mantras, worship this deity and request her to destroy the enemy. He then commits this image limb by limb to a fire on that cremation ground; in the same way, the enemy's limbs should be burned. During the procedure, the perfomer should meditate on the identity of Ātman with Brahman. The ritual is concluded by a short worship of Yama.

In Chapter 10, we are informed a little more about the "Kubjikan" coloring of these magical rituals. The KuUp is eulogized, and its recitation recommended for a Brahmin of the Parāśara *gotra* who is (perhaps, "or") a teacher of the "*Pippalādaśaunakīśākhā*" and a worshipper of Kubjikā, after a fast of three nights (if the here rather corrupt text has been interpreted correctly). The performer should then ask for Kubjikā's gracious disposition before beginning (again at midnight on a cremation ground) the ritual of lighting a lamp in a Western direction. After repetition of the mantra "bring N.N. into my power, OṂ HSKHPHREṂ AṂ HRĪṂ KROṂ SHKHPHREṂ AṂ" (not one of the mantras mentioned in Chapters 2-5, but cf. the *kūṭas* at the beginning of Chapter 1)[7] for 108.000 times, the Goddess reveals herself and the ritual will be successful.

A quite different subject is described in Chapter 11: the worship of the ten Mahāvidyās, well known from Bengali Tantras. Their names are enumerated as Kālikā, Tārā, or Ugratārā, Ṣoḍaśī or Rājarājeśvarī, Bhuvaneśvarī, Bhairavī, or Caitanyabhairavī or Annapūrṇā, Chinnamastā or Pracaṇḍacaṇḍikā or Pracaṇḍogracaṇḍikā, Dhūmāvatī, Bagalāmukhī, Mātaṅgī, or Mātaṅginī, and Kamalā or Siddhilakṣmī.[8] This series of deities is then superimposed upon the Kubjikā tradition by being placed within the *yantra* of Kubjikā described in Chapter 1 (see earlier). To be precise, Siddhilakṣmī as supreme goddess on the central *bindu*; the first three, Kālikā and so on, on the triangle surrounding the *bindu*, and the numbers 4 to 9 on the hexagon surrounding the triangle. The deities are to be worshipped by means of a nocturnal Tantric ritual. Each of these ten deities is then the subject of a special chapter (Chapters 12 to 21). There are quotations from the Kālī Tantra and other texts; Chapter 14 contains the greater part of the Bhāvanā Upaniṣad (the last chapter of the Tantrarāja Tantra).

The last four chapters give more particulars on magical rituals: destroying an inimical army, creating delusion, liquidation, and subjugation. The exposition again is introduced by Prajāpati, who answers a question posed by Indra. The rituals are presided over by manifestations of Kubjikā such as Rudra- and Siddhikubjikā; to the latter, a Kubjikāsūkta should be recited (Chapter 25). Victory over the enemies can be effected by means of the sounding of a war drum (Chapter 22) after worship of Rudrakubjikā alias Pratyaṅgirā at midnight on a cremation ground. While the drum is being sounded, the Pratyaṅgirāgaṇa[9] should be recited. The goddess should receive a *bali* the nature of which is not clear,[10] while the Medhasūkta (?) is being recited.[11]

A short recapitulation of the contents of the KuUp leads to the following division:

1. Chapters 1-5: discussion of various mantras, *vidyās*, and *yantra* of Kubjikā and her various manifestations, and of her male partner Ku(b)jeśvara.

2. Chapters 6 and 7: on the philosophical and meditational background of the morning ritual.

3. Chapter 8: analysis of the syllable OṂ.

4. Chapters 9 and 10: description of magical ritual in Atharvanic style. The tenth chapter, especially the second part, is more "Kubjikan" in character.

5. Chapters 11-21: the worship of the ten Mahāvidyās presented with a "Kubjikan" veneer.

6. Chapters 22-25: further description of magical rituals, presided over by manifestations of Kubjikā, which may have been added secondarily.

This sixfold division again can be reduced to a threefold one. It is clear that the Chapters 1-5 and 11-21 treat of varieties of the Kubjikā pantheon (although in a way that differs strikingly from the older sources of the school). These two portions should be differentiated from the other chapters (6-10 and 22-25), which in essence have the character of a treatise in truly Atharvanic fashion and which we therefore might call the *kernel Upaniṣad.* That parts of these chapters have been substantially reworked or augmented in Kubjikan fashion, does not largely affect this picture. It is possible, however, that this Atharvanic part of the Upaniṣad did not originally form a unity but has been collected from different sources. The whole has then been welded together to the KuUp in a rather superficial way by a final redactor.

The succinct and superficial character of parts of the KuUp may be illustrated from the twentieth chapter, devoted to the ninth Mahāvidyā, Mātaṅginī. We give the essentials of the text: *Atha rājamātaṅginīṃ nīlotpalanibhāṃ nīlavastraparidhānāṃ nīlagandhānulepanāṃ nīlasaṃhāsanasthāṃ nīlaśukahastāṃ nīlābharaṇabhūṣitāṃ mahānīlāṃ sarvavidyārājñīṃ mahāmātaṅgīṃ vyākhyāsyāmaḥ* . . . [follows the coded exposition of the *vidyā*, which is OṂHRĪṂKLĪṂ*mātaṅginyai* PHAṬSVĀHĀ] . . . *mahāmātaṅgīṃ yo 'rcayati smarati dhārayati gurum upāste sa sarvasāmrājyavān bhavati sa caturvargaphalabhāg bhavati ya evaṃ veda. Pūjācakram: bindus trikoṇaṃ vasupattraṃ ṣoḍaśābjaṃ caturdvārahīnam* . . . [a second *phalaśruti*] . . . *Mahāniśārdhe mahāpañcamakāraiḥ sarvadā yajed iti vadanti brahmavādinaḥ śaunakāḥ.*

> *Meṣamārjāraraktena svayambhūkusumena ca /*
> *kuṇḍagolodbhavair māṃsair Mātaṅgīṃ sarvadā yajet //*

. . . [follows a third *phalaśruti*] . . . *mahākubjikopaniṣat.*

Translation:

> Now, we shall explain [the *vidyā* of] the Royal Mātaṅginī, the Great Mātaṅgī, the Blue One, who has the color of a blue lotus, who is clothed in a blue garment, scented with blue perfumes, seated upon a blue throne, with a blue parrot on her hand, adorned with blue ornaments, the Queen of *vidyās*; . . . he who, knowing thus, worships and meditates upon Mātaṅgī and wears [her *yantra* and *vidyā* on his body], and reveres his guru, such a one obtains complete lordship and enjoys the results [that realize] the four goals of human existence. The design of worship is as follows: a *bindu*, a triangle [around it], an octagon, a lotus of sixteen petals [and a square] without gates . . . [the Sādhaka] should sacrifice to her always at midnight with the Five M's; thus is the teaching of the Śaunakas, the specialists of Brahman [or, the Atharvanic teachers].
>
> With blood of ram and tomcat,
> with the red flower spontaneously grown;[12]
> with flesh from pit and bulb
> one should sacrifice to Mātaṅgī.

Although the preceding fragment contains a pretty complete enumeration of the constituents of worship (*dhyāna, vidyā, yantra, pūjā, dravya, phalaśruti*), little can be done with it in practice. Thus, for instance, the sixfold analysis of the *vidyā* that is indispensible for the ritual (*nyāsa*) is missing. Specialized texts such as the Mātaṅgī Tantra (Śāktapramoda, p. 333) do give this necessary information. It is true that a few other Mahāvidyās are treated by the KuUp with somewhat more elaboration. However, the incomplete treatment of Mātaṅginī contains at least this interesting feature: for her worship it refers to the authority of the Śaunakas with whom very probably the representants of the Atharvavedic school of that name are meant. We already have seen that the KuUp contains numerous other references to Atharvanic tradition.

In my opinion, the text that at present goes under the name of the Kubjikā Upaniṣad in its oldest part is a genuine Atharvaveda Upaniṣad. Of course, as is well known, many late and sectarian Upaniṣads claim a relation with the Atharvaveda; their status of a *śruti* text makes a connection with one of the four Vedas obligatory, and the Atharvaveda (AV) is best suited to this on account of its somewhat isolated and unorthodox position with respect to the other three Vedas.[13] Usually, this reference to the AV by these later Upaniṣads is a purely formal matter, and any internal relation to that text is absent. With our Upaniṣad, the situation is different; the relation with the AV cannot be denied, as is immediately clear from the fact that the Upaniṣad contains about 140 Atharvavedic stanzas—a really unique phenomenon in the Upaniṣadic corpus.[14] For the greater part, these Atharvanic stanzas are found in the Chapters 6 to 9, another reason why these chapters in any case should be considered as belonging to the oldest stratum.

The question should be asked, To which Atharvavedic school(s) may our Upaniṣad have belonged? There are different opinions on the number of Atharvanic schools, each of which have had its own version of the text. Most often, the number of the schools is given as nine.[15] Of these, the text of only two has been preserved: the Paippalāda and the Śaunakīya. Although there are hints that the former was the most popular in older times, the Śaunakīya text is the best known nowadays; and the Paippalāda text has been found only comparatively recently in a rather corrupted state in manuscripts of Kashmir and Orissa.[16] In our Upaniṣad, the nine schools are enumerated in the first part of Chapter 2, where Sanatkumāra Ātharvaṇa is said to be an expert in all (!) the nine schools: Pippalāda, Śaunaka, Dāmoda, Tottāyana, Jāpāla or Jābāla, Brahmapalāśa, Kunakhī, Devadṛśī, and Cāraṇavidya.[17] Because the Paippalāda school is mentioned first, and because Pippalāda also figures as the hearer in Chapter 1, one would expect that the "kernel Upaniṣad" is attached to this school. As we saw, the text also says (Chapter 10, beginning) that the officiant should be a teacher of the Pippalāda or the Śaunaka school, or even of both schools at the same time (*paippalādaśaunakīyaśākhādhyāpakaḥ*). It is known, by the way, that the Brahmans from Maharashtra who claim to be Atharvavedins consider themselves to be "Śaunakapaippalādins." The same passage from Chapter 10 mentions a preference for a Brahman of the Parāśara *gotra.* In this connection I would like to refer to a commentary on the Gopālatāpanī Upaniṣad where it is said that the Paippalāda Atharvaveda is handed down in Gurjara by Brahmans of this *gotra.*[18] As we already have noted, Parāśara also is mentioned as an authority elsewhere in the KuUp.

However, contrary to this expectation, all the Atharvavedic stanzas that occur in the KuUp have been quoted according to the Śaunaka version. It does not seem necessary to explicitize this point; the situation is directly clear after a comparison with the edited texts of both versions. As we saw in the text on Mātaṅginī (Chapter 20), the Śaunakas were mentioned there as the authority; whether this is done correctly or not does not seem to matter very much in this connection. We find the same situation on two other places in the Upaniṣad.

We shall not go into details concerning the nature, sequence, and textual form of the Atharvanic quotations in the KuUp. These questions seem to go beyond the scope of this chapter and must be reserved for a future publication.[19] In most cases, stanzas from different books or *sūktas* have been combined to form new litanies. A few times, there are deviating *pādas* (they deviate also from the Paippalāda text!). In addition, there are occasional instances of insertion of the names of Kubjikā or her partner. Thus, in Chapter 7, the stanza AV 19, 9, 3 *iyaṃ yā parameṣṭhinī,* which refers to goddess Speech, has been changed into *kubjikā parameṣṭhinī* (the stanza does not occur in the Paippalāda text). But, I repeat, this is an exception. An interesting detail is that the stanzas *eka eva rudro* (cf. TaiS 1, 8, 6, 1) and *asaṅkhyātā* (VājS 16, 54), found close together in Chapter 2, do not occur in the AV, but figure (also in close association) in Yāska's Nirukta, 1, 15.

Returning to the portions of the KuUp that have preliminarily been called the *kernel Upaniṣad,* we recall that these chapters contain large parts from other Atharvanic Upaniṣads such as the Haṃsa, Atharvaśira, and Atharvaśikhā. As to the Haṃsa Upaniṣad, although there also is a tradition that assigns it to the White Yajurveda, it usually is characterized as an Atharvanic Upaniṣad.[20] The same holds for the Mahā Upaniṣad, which is sometimes reckoned to the Sāmaveda. We might ask ourselves whether something can be said about the dating of this oldest portion of the KuUp. This is possible because, near the end of Chapter 7, as mentioned earlier, there is a stanza from the Gauḍapādakārikās (which associate themselves with the Māṇḍūkya, one of the most important Atharvanic Upaniṣads). These *kārikās,* each of whose four chapters sometimes is treated as an independent Atharvanic Upaniṣad,[21] must have been written in the first part of the second half of the first millennium A.D.[22] At least the seventh chapter of the KuUp therefore has to be placed after that date; but this does not help us very much due to the vagueness of the argument and the fragmentary nature of our text.

The most strikingly Upaniṣadic part of the KuUp is Chapter 8, which contains an exposition of the mystical meaning of the Praṇava (OṂ). It largely consists of a combination of passages from the first chapter of the (Atharvanic) Gopathabrāhmaṇa (which has a definitely Upaniṣadic character)[23] that also are partly found in the Atharvaśira- and -śikhā Upaniṣads, and from the Brahmavidyā Upaniṣad. Although no separate title is available, the title *Praṇava Upaniṣad* would be most suitable. A Praṇava Upaniṣad does not seem to occur in the traditional lists of Upaniṣads, and the contents of none of the Upaniṣads that are edited in the well-known collections is identical with those of our text (Chapter 8). Nevertheless, a text of this title does exist, although its Sanskrit text has long remained unnoticed. This text belonged to the collection of fifty Upaniṣads translated into Persian in 1656 on the initiative of Muhammad Dara Shikoh, eldest son of Shah Jahan, whose interest in Hindu philosophy and literature is well known.[24] From the Persian translation it appears that this Praṇava Upaniṣad consists of the literal text of Gopatha Brāhmaṇa I, 1, 16-30. Its Sanskrit text in the meantime has been published from Adyar in the collection strangely called *Unpublished Upaniṣads.*[25] In this latter collection are even two texts called *Praṇava Upaniṣad,* but the second one is identical with the mentioned Brahmavidyā Upaniṣad. We conclude that, from a rather early time, there must have circulated more than one Upaniṣadic text that dealt with the nature of OṂ (among them also the Māṇḍūkya Upaniṣad) and that therefore could be designated by the title *Praṇava Upaniṣad.* Our text (Chapter 8 of the KuUp) is one of these. It resembles a few others very much, but is not identical with them; and it also can rightly claim the title *Praṇava Upaniṣad.*

Other interesting aspects of the KuUp (e.g., parallels with still other Upaniṣads, the occurrence of the goddess Pratyaṅgirā or the magical application of the war drum) cannot be treated here. Our preliminary evaluation of this text can be that its oldest part, a genuine but somewhat heterogeneous Atharvavedic Upaniṣad (with an exposition of the Praṇava as its most characteristic element) was amalgamated with an evolved Kubjikā tradition by a group of Atharvaveda Brahmans who at a certain period had embraced her worship; the same persons also inserted a few more Atharvanic stanzas in the more typically Kubjikan passages. Another possibility would be that the goddess Kubjikā and her worship were conceived and developed as a whole within an Atharvanic milieu, but we cannot adduce any arguments for this supposition from the older Kubjikā literature. In any case, the KuUp should be considered a most welcome illustration of a process of mutual integration of Tantric and Vedic traditions.

Notes

Ed. Note: In the original planning of this book, a different chapter by Jan Schoterman was foreseen; viz., "Mahāyajña: The Great Ritual of the Ṣaṭsāhasrasaṃhitā." But the time to realize this project was not given to him. The present chapter is based on a lecture Jan held before a meeting of Dutch Indologists at Leiden in the spring of 1989. The Dutch text of the lecture has been translated into English and revised on a few points (mainly the inclusion of a more detailed survey of contents found in Jan's private notes and the addition of some technicalities).

1. MSS. 1-1696/929 (preliminarily called A; title *Kubjikopaniṣad*); no. 1871 of the collection M. M. Miśra (B); no. 7329 *Karmakāṇḍa* (C); in B and C, the title is *Kubjikopāsanāmṛtapūrṇopaniṣad.*

2. The *Ṣatsāhasrasaṃhitā*, Chapters 1-5, ed., trans., and annotated by J. A. Schoterman (Leiden: E. J. Brill, 1982) Orientalia Rheno-traiectina 27, thesis Utrecht; *The Kubjikāmatatantra*, Kulālikāmnāya Version, critical ed. T. Goudriaan and J. A. Schoterman (Leiden: E. J. Brill, 1988) Or.RhTr. 30.

3. See Ṣaṭs. 1-5 (see note 2), pp. 181f.

4. Ram Kumar Rai, ed. and trans., *Dictionaries of Tantra Śāstra or The Tantrābhidhāna* (Varanasi: Prachya Prakashan, 1978), pp. 28 and 10.

5. Or, as in the Atharvaśikhā Up.: Pippalāda, Aṅgiras, and Sanatkumāra (*nom. sg.* in our manuscripts) question Atharvan; but Sanatkumāra is definitely the speaker in Chapter 2 of the KuUp.

6. The Kulavṛkṣas are enumerated by L. Finn, *The Kulacūḍāmaṇi Tantra and the Vāmakeśvara Tantra* (Wiesbaden: Harrassowitz, 1986), p. 80, note 3.

7. For the *bīja* HSKHPHREṂ, see A. Sanderson in A. Padoux, ed., *Mantras et diagrammes rituels dans l'Hindouisme* (Paris: CNRS,

1986), p. 194.

8. On the ten Mahāvidyās, see Ch. Chakravarti, *The Tantras* (Calcutta, 1963), p. 85.

9. This *gaṇa* probably is identical with the Atharvanic *sūktas* given *pratīkena* at the beginning of Chapter 24.

10. MS. B: *Naranali*, thus suggesting, to say the least, ingredients of human provenance; an alternative is *navabali* ("ninefold *bali*"), which is explainable, because in this ritual eight Bhairavas figure beside Pratyaṅgirā.

11. Perhaps Aśvalāyana Gṛhyasūtra 1, 15, 2 *medhāṃ te devaḥ savitā*, but this is not found in the AV, only as an insertion between RV 10, 131 and 132, according to one manuscript (information in the Petersburg Dictionary). *Non liquet*.

12. That is, menstruate blood. It is not clear whether the usual meaning of *kuṇḍagola* (next line) is applicable here, and so a vague yet literal translation was preferred.

13. "Man zählte sie zum Atharvaveda, wiel dieser Veda schon von Anfang an kein kanonisches Ansehen genoss und es nahe lag, alles, was nicht orthodox-brahmanisch war, als zum AV gehörig zu bezeichnen" (M. Winternitz, *Geschichte der indischen Literatur*, Band I, 1908, reprinted Stuttgart 1968, p. 206).

14. Only the Cūlika or Mantrika Upaniṣad also contains quotations of Atharvanic stanzas, but much fewer.

15. Cf. A. Weber, *Caraṇavyūha, Uebersicht ueber die Schulen des Veda*, in *Indische Studien*, III, 1855, p. 247-283, on p. 277; *Atharvaveda-pariśiṣṭa*, ed. G. M. Bolling and J. von Negelein (Leipzig, 1909), p. 50 (II, 5, 2); *Devī Pur.* (corrupt), ed. Pushpendra Kumar Sharma (New Delhi, 1976), Chapter 107, 43 (ed., p. 391).

16. *Paippalāda Saṃhitā*, Devanāgarī transcription of the Kashmir ms., ed. Raghu Vira (Lahore, 1936-42, reprint n.d.); Orissan version, ed. Durgamohan Bhattacharyya (Calcutta 1964, 1970), Books 1-4 only.

14. The list should be corrected in some respects, see Weber's remarks, op. cit. (see note 15), p. 278.

18. D. Bhattacharyya, ed. of the Orissan Paippalāda Saṃhitā, vol. I, p. xiv.

19. Schoterman was planning a critical edition with an Intro-

duction and translation of the KuUp. (Editor).

20. The Haṃsa Upaniṣad is mentioned, for instance, as No. 24 in the list of twenty-eight Atharvaṇa Upaniṣads in the Caraṇavyūha (Atharvaveda Pariśiṣṭa, no. 49). Cf. also M. Bloomfield, *The Atharvaveda and the Gopathabrāhmaṇa,* (Strassburg, 1899; reprinted New Delhi, 1978), p. 18.

21. Bloomfield, ibid.

22. There is widespread uncertainty about Gauḍapāda's date, cf. Karl H. Potter, *Encyclopaedia of Indian Philosophies,* vol. 3: *Advaita Vedānta up to Śaṅkara and His Pupils,* (Delhi a.o.: Motilal Banarsidass, 1981), pp. 12f. According to S. N. Dasgupta, *A History of Indian Philosophy,* vol. 1 (Cambridge, 1922), p. 423, Gauḍapāda "was probably living when Śaṅkara was a student . . . in order to be able to teach Śaṅkara, G. must have been living till at least 800 A.D." Jadunath Sinha, *A History of Indian Philosophy,* vol. 2 (Calcutta: Central Book Agency, 1952), p. 444, places Gauḍapāda without comment at 600 A.D. Both Dasgupta and Sinha stick to Śaṅkara's traditional date of 788-820 A.D.

23. Bloomfield, op. cit., p. 107. Edition of the Gopathabr. by Dieuke Gaastra (Leiden, 1919).

24. P. Deussen, *Sechzig Upanishads des Veda* (Leipzig, ^{3}1921), p. 535. The Persian translation was further translated into Latin and French by Anquetil Duperron.

25. *Unpublished Upaniṣads (Aprakāśitā Upaniṣadaḥ),* ed. C. Kunhan Raja and the Pandits of the Adyar Library (Adyar, 1933), pp. 30f.

Chapter Twelve

The Pratyabhijñā and the Logical-Epistemological School of Buddhism

Raffaele Torella

Perhaps no other doctrines in the history of Indian thought have made such a general—overwhelming and subtle—impact on contemporary philosophical schools as those of Dignāga, Dharmakīrti, and continuers—at least one of whom, Dharmottara, deserves to be mentioned.[1] And this was not confined only to contemporary ones, as the work of these two masters compelled the opposing schools to carry out a general task of revision and rethinking, that was also to bear fruit much later—think for example of the development of the Navya Nyāya from the Nyāya, through Udayana.

None—Mīmāṃsakas, Naiyāyikas, Vedāntins, Jainas—could or wanted to avoid this challenge, for so it appears to be from Dharmakīrti's bitterly haughty tone.[2] The case of the Pratyabhijñā school, which constituted the highest point of philosophical self-awareness reached by nondualistic Kashmir Śaivism,[3] starting from Somānanda (c. 875-925 A.D.), then especially Utpaladeva (c. 900-950 A.D.), and later Abhinavagupta (c.950-1020 A.D.), is one of the most typical, though perhaps one of the least investigated.[4]

Somānanda definitely knew Dharmakīrti's works—at least one verse of the PV is clearly recognizable in the *Śivadṛṣṭi*[5]—but it is only from Utpaladeva onward that the masters of Buddhist logic rise to the role of principal interlocutors.[6] They are opponents, of course, but they are evoked so constantly and always with such profound respect, particularly Dharmakīrti,[7] that the nature of their relationship is not immediately evident. Moreover, it was inevitable that a school that first established itself in tenth-eleventh century Kashmir sooner or later should accept a confrontation with Buddhism, in a country where Śaivism was deeply rooted, but that also was impregnated with Buddhist culture. The Nīlamatapurāṇa and the Rājataraṅginī tell of Buddhism in Kashmir from very early times[8] and the Chinese pilgrims give us detailed information on the spread of the different Buddhist schools. In the commentaries on the Śivasūtra an echo remains of a certain aggressiveness that Buddhist proselytism, around the ninth century, must have assumed.[9] Furthermore, as the Rājataraṅginī (IV.5.498) informs us, one of the great names of Buddhist logic, Dharmottara (c. 750-810 A.D.), had settled in Kashmir at the invitation of the king, Jayāpīḍa (c. 775-806 A.D.);[10] Dharmottara's works in effect are well-known and frequently quoted and criticized by the Pratyabhijñā masters. Arcaṭa (c. 730-790 A.D.),[11] the author of the Hetubinduṭīkā and Ānandavardhana, besides the famous Dhvanyāloka, also the author of a vast commentary, now lost, on Dharmottara's Pramāṇaviniścayaṭīkā[12] were natives of Kashmir. Śaṅkarānanda or Śaṅkaranandana (ninth-tenth century), the Mahābrāhmaṇa of the Tibetans, deserves a special mention. He was an interesting and enigmatic figure halfway between the logical-epistemological Buddhist tradition, of which he is both an exponent and critic, and perhaps the emerging Śaiva gnoseology.[13]

The Buddhist logicians and Pratyabhijñā start from presuppositions that appear, and are, absolutely irreconcilable: an impersonal world of events, on the one hand, and, on the other, a world permeated and vivified even in its seemingly most inert crannies by the dynamism of the I (Śiva or Consciousness). Despite this, an undoubted fascination is exerted by the rigor of the Buddhist logicians' argumentation and their dauntless critical capacity that uses its sharp and original instruments on the doctrines of the most diverse opponents. The very air of superiority that sometimes may be glimpsed in their opposition to all others, though it does not fail occasionally to provoke a note of sarcasm in the Śaiva masters,[14] ends up by further enhancing their image. This contributes to causing them to be adopted by the Pratyabhijñā authors, partly, so to speak, as a touchstone to test the soundness of their theses and partly as a whetstone to sharpen their dialectic arms.

Buddhist logic, in its struggle against realism (particularly of the Nyāya) constantly is concerned with showing the fundamental importance of the mind in structuring reality, in contrast to those who, with the aim of underlining the independent nature of the external reality confronted by human experience, move in the opposite direction—reducing the creative and formative role of knowledge as far as possible and making it into a mere mirror that records ready-made realities outside itself, resulting in an unending entification even of relations, qualities, and so forth. This reference to the centrality of the mind must have been felt by the Pratyabhijñā masters to be a strong element of affinity, even though it was destined to have divergent developments. Bearing this in mind, one may be surprised by statements like that found in IPV, vol. 1, p. 43—*naiyāyikakramasyaiva māyāpade pāramārthikatvam iti granthakārābhiprāyaḥ "kriyāsaṃbandhasāmānya" ity ādiṣu uddeśeṣu prakaṭībhaviṣyati*[15]—which seem to have broader significance and refer not only to the more or less effective articulation of the *parārthānumāna*. The Pratyabhijñā seems to reject neither the Buddhist position nor the *naiyāyika* one, though they are antithetical. It accepts many concepts that the Buddhist logicians refute and that the Nyāya upholds, like the previously mentioned *kriyā saṃbandha sāmānya* (*dravya dik kāla*; see IPK, II.2.1) but it does so only after Buddhist criticism has rendered them untenable, recuperating them in a bound. Thus two attitudes essentially emerge. In certain cases positions pertaining to the Buddhists are accepted but to show that they become admissible in all their implications only if they are placed in a Śaiva frame of reference.[16] In others, Buddhist criticism is accepted to show that realities which on close examination prove to be irremediably contradictory and yet are demanded by *vyavahāra* become acceptable in a Śaiva context.[17] Through this subtle play of a declared basic disagreement with the doctrines of Buddhist logicians, a limited acceptance and purely instrumental (or thought to be so) use of them, the masters of the Pratyabhijñā end up by being somehow drawn into their orbit. The architecture of the Pratyabhijñā feels the effect of this. That many problems are posed, more or less unwittingly, in Buddhist terms to a certain extent prefigures their development and reduces possible alternative as regard solution.

To trace the features of this complex relationship in the filigree of the terse lines of the IPK and its commentaries, first and foremost one must try to reconstruct the terms of at least some of the various disputes to be found in it that deal with the principal *topoi* of logical-epistemological speculation. In doing so, one cannot fail to note, as a preliminary step, how the Pratyabhijñā has appropriated the typical terminology of Buddhist logic, to a markedly greater extent than the other schools. I am not referring to expressions such as the one encountered, *parārthānumāna*,[18] which, as we know, already had entered common usage from Praśastapāda onward, but, for example, to *svalakṣaṇa, arthakriyāsamartha, tādātmya, tadutpatti, svabhāvahetu, kāryahetu*, the various types of *anupalabdhi*, and so on. Some of these terms (e.g., *svalakṣaṇa*) may designate realities that do not completely coincide with those meant by the Buddhist logicians or that are valued differently (*arthakriyā*); others, like those connected with the inferential process, sometimes are expressly attributed to the Buddhists but more often are used freely in the course of their own argumentation.[19] But, whatever the case, it is the actual use of this terminology that indicates impregnation.

At the beginning of Āhnika III of the Kriyādhikāra[20] we come across this definition of *pramāṇa*:

> *idam etādṛg ity evaṃ yadvaśād vyavatiṣṭhate /*
> *vastu pramāṇaṃ tat so 'pi svābhāso 'bhinavodayaḥ //*
> *so 'ntas tathāvimarśātmā deśakālādyabhedini /*
> *ekābhidhānaviṣaye mitir vastuny abādhitā //*

> The means of knowledge is that thanks to which the object is situated in its own confines (*vyavatiṣṭhate*): "this thing, with these characteristics." This means of knowledge is an ever freshly arising light, correlated to a subject. This light, whose essence is the inner reflective awareness of that which is thus manifested, becomes, as regards the object without spatio-temporal limitations etc. and expressed by a single name, knowledge (*miti*) [provided it is] non-invalidated.

According to the Pratyabhijñā, therefore, there is no differentiation between the means of knowledge and its result (*pramāṇa—pramā* or *pramiti*), as also the Buddhists—but not only they[21]—maintain (see for example PS I.8b-11 and *vṛtti*, PV III.301-319, NBṬ pp. 79-86, TS 1343-60, etc.). The distinction between *pramāṇa* and *pramā*, the Buddhists say, is only the outcome of the analytic consideration of a reality, which in itself is one. The two terms thus foregrounded cannot in any case represent a relationship of cause and effect, because this would require an actual difference between the two terms, but at the most a relation of *vyavasthāpya-vyavasthāpana*, with a division of roles within the same reality.[22] And up to this point the Śaivas and Buddhists are mainly in agreement. A proof of this is that Abhinavagupta, in concluding his argumentation in the two commentaries,[23] which develops Utpaladeva's barely sketched position, quotes part of a verse by Dharmakīrti (PV III.308: *tadvaśāt tadvyavasthānāt*. On the contrary, the two positions differ on the concept of the "function, activity" (*vyāpāra*) carried out by the elements occurring in cognition. *Vyāpāra* is completely denied by the Buddhists, who consider every distinction on this basis purely imaginary (*utprekṣita*), so much so that, for example, an act such as piercing with an arrow may be analyzed in various ways, all equally legitimate, attributing to the bow the function (*vyāpāra*) either of *kartṛ*, or *karaṇa*, or *apadāna*.[24] But, above all, the impossibility of *vyāpāra* is the direct consequence of the doctrine of momentariness.[25] Cognition, therefore, only "appears" to be endowed with a function (*savyāpāram ivābhāti*). Abhinavagupta's reply refers implicitly to this statement by Dharmakīrti, which in turn depends on PS I.8cd: *savyāpārapratītatvāt pramāṇam eva sat*[26] (Abhinavagupta, as we have seen, just before had quoted with approval the third *pāda* of the same verse).[27] *Vyāpāra*, Abhinavagupta says, not only exists but constitutes the very essence of *pramā* and on this, according to the Śaivas, hinges the nondifferentiation of *pramāṇa* and *pramā*: *vyāpāra* is not a different reality from the subject that acts and from the instrument that is set in action.[28] All that already had been essentially contained in the laconic *pramātṛvyāpāraḥ*, which follows *pramitiḥ* in Utpaladeva's *vṛtti*. But, Abhinavagupta continues, that does not mean that *pramāṇa* and *pramā* are simply two ways of saying the same thing (*paryāyatvam*); the cognitive light, which is the essential nature of both, in the *pramāṇa* is turned toward the external object, whereas in the *pramā* it is turned inward as pure determinate awareness, contracted due to the influence of the object assumed in it, having the word as its essence.

It is precisely the inseparable connection between knowledge and the word that forms one of the nerve centers of both schools and a vantage point from which, yet again, to view this complex play of attraction and detachment that characterizes the positions of the Pratyabhijñā. Both Dignāga and Dharmakīrti substantially agree that *vikalpa-kalpanā* and *śabda* are very closely related, if not absolutely identical. The definition in PS I.3d, *nāmajātyādiyojanā*, is further elaborated by Dharmakīrti in the subtler and more comprehensive definition in NB I.5, *abhilāpasaṃsargayogyapratibhāsā pratītiḥ kalpanā*, which introduces the element of potentiality.[29] Utpaladeva definitely has this formulation in mind in the verse that opens Āhnika VI of the Jñānādhikāra:

> *ahaṃpratyavamarśo yaḥ prakāśātmāpi vāgvapuḥ /*
> *nāsau vikalpaḥ sa hy ukto dvayākṣepī viniścayaḥ //*
> [*vṛtti*] *prakāśasyātmany aham iti parāvāgrūpatvāt sābhilāpo 'pi svabhāvabhūtaḥ pratyavamarśo na vikalpa ity ucyate, sa hi pratiyoginiṣedhapūrvo niścayo na cātra pratiyogisambhavaḥ.*

The reflective awareness "I," which is the very essence of light, is not a *vikalpa*, although it is informed by the word. For a *vikalpa* is an act of determination which implies two alternatives.

The reflective awareness concerning the self, the reflection awareness "I," which constitutes the own nature

> of the light, cannot be called *'vikalpa'* even if it is essentially associated with a "discourse" (*abhilāpa*), since the word that informs it is the supreme word. Indeed, the *vikalpa* is a determination (*niścaya*) acquired through the negation of the opposite, and, as regards pure light, there is no possibility of the existence of something that is its opposite.[30]

The word, however, is not limited to pervading the sphere of discursive thought.[31] Following the teaching of that other great figure who conditioned the Pratyabhijñā, Bhartṛhari, it is placed at the very heart of reality as the supremely unifying element, it is the essence of all knowledge and sentience itself.[32] It therefore also informs sensation,[33] from which the Buddhist logicians, on the contrary, strictly excluded it. Direct perception is followed by the moment of determination (*adhyavasāya, niścaya*); it is worth dwelling on how this is conceived and valued in the two schools, because it constitutes the crux of the whole question. For this purpose the field must be extended to a consideration of the respective positions regarding the nature of the object of the *pramāṇa*. Let us return to the passage of the Kriyādhikāra quoted earlier, where one reads among other things: "as regards the object without spatio-temporal limitations etc. and expressed by a single name" (*deśakālādyabhedini / ekābhidhānaviṣaye* [. . .] *vastuny*). Thus, according to the Pratyabhijñā, the object of the *pramāṇa* is the single *ābhāsa*, which being disconnected from space and time is a *sāmānya* (cf. the *vṛtti sāmānyarūpe*); it is the object of a single word. A group of *ābhāsas*, including those of space, time, and form—endowed with a special individualizing force—is composed in the apparent unity of the individual thing, the *svalakṣaṇa*, with which we are confronted in everyday experience.[34]

If we then pass on to the respective position of the Buddhist logicians we find a diametrically opposed picture. The Buddhists make a sharp distinction between the objects of the two *pramāṇas*: the object of knowledge that appears to the senses is the *svalakṣaṇa*. What the Śaivas conceive as a secondary product they view as the supremely real and efficient, unitary and unrepeatable being; direct perception grasps it in its totality (cf. PV I.43: *ekasyārthasvabhāvasya pratyakṣasya sataḥ svayaṃ / ko'nyo na dṛṣṭo bhāgaḥ syād yaḥ pramāṇaiḥ parīkṣyate //* 'When the unitary specific nature of an object is perceived, what other part that is not perceived can there be that may be investigated by [other] means of knowledge?' and the first hemistich of the *saṃgrahaśloka* I.45: *tasmād dṛṣṭasya bhāvasya dṛṣṭa evākhilo guṇaḥ /* 'Therefore, when an object is perceived, all its qualities are automatically perceived').[35] However, it may be the object of determinate knowledge—which alone renders it communicable and places it within the sphere of human activities and conventions,[36] but at the price of the decomposition of its unity and the 'covering' (*saṃvṛti*) of the peculiar form of the object with the form of the cognition. The unity of the *svalakṣaṇa* shatters into a myriad of *dharmas*, each of which is grasped by a single act of determination (*niścaya, adhyavasāya*). This division into many *dharmas*, like the attribution of diverse multiple and unrepeatable entities to a single class or the division into particular and universal, though strictly speaking unreal are not arbitrary acts, however, because they still derive from the perception of a determinate individual reality and in a sense are a property of the thing itself; only a thing that possesses such a *svabhāva* may be grasped in this way (PVSV, p. 43: *taddharmatām evāvataranto vikalpā nānaikadharmavyatirekān saṃdarśayanti / na ca te nirāśrayās tadbhedadarśanāśrayatvāt / nāvastudharmatā tatsvabhāvasyaiva tathā khyāteḥ*).[37] These constructs do not so much mirror the thing in its reality as communicate the knowing mind's intentions. The *niścaya* cannot capture the particular in its totality but only enucleate one feature of it; various factors, such as mental acuteness, previous experiences, and so forth determine which of the many possible features (although the thing has in actual fact no parts) is grasped at different times (PVSV, p. 32: *yady apy aṃśarahitaḥ sarvato bhinnasvabhāvo bhāvo 'nubhūtas tathāpi na sarvabhedeṣu tāvatā niścayo bhavati / kāraṇāntarāpekṣatvāt / anubhavo hi yathāvikalpābhyāsaṃ niścayapratyayāñ janayati / yathā rūpadarśanāviśeṣe 'pi kuṇapakāminībhakṣyavikalpāḥ / tatra buddhipāṭavaṃ tadvāsanābhyāsaḥ prakaraṇam ity ādayo 'nubhavād bhedaniścayotpattisahakāriṇaḥ*[38]).

The two conceptions differ greatly but have a kind of cross correspondence that makes one think that the difference lies in the approach rather than in the content. For the Buddhist logicians (Dharmakīrti), the starting point is the particular (*svalakṣaṇa, bheda*); perception grasps it in its entirety but it also is inexpressible and uncommunicable, it may not be associated with words (unlike *kalpanā*); different *niścayas* may stem from this single perceptual content; each of them captures a (unreal but not unfounded) part of it and connects it with a word, which therefore denotes a certain *sāmānya* or rather the negation of what is other than that feature (PV I.50-51: *yāvanto 'ṃśasamāropās tannirāse viniścayāḥ / tāvanta eva śabdāś ca tena te bhinnagocarāḥ // anyathaikena śabdena vyāpta ekatra vastuni / buddhyā vā nānyaviṣaya iti paryāyatā bhavet //*; PVSV, p. 28: *tadviveka eva cānyāpohaḥ / tasmād tad api tanmātrāpohagocaram / na vastusvabhāvaniścayātmakam*).[39] For the Pratyabhijñā (Utpaladeva), each *pramāṇa* grasps an individual *ābhāsa* (which is a *sāmānya*), expressed by a determinate word, depending on a determinate reflective awareness[40] (*vṛtti ad* IPK II.3.2: *vimarśabhedānusāryekaikaśabdavācye; vṛtti ad* IPK II.3.5: *ekaikaś cāsāv ābhāsa ekaikena śabdena vyavahārārtham tattanniyatārthakriyārthibhir abhidhīyate*) or grasps—in the perception itself and not in a later act—a group of *ābhāsas* coordinated by the Lord's power of necessity according to *sāmānādhikaraṇya* (blue lotus); in this case the *pramāṇa* is oriented to the dominant *ābhāsa* and the perception remains unitary. In various passages of the IPK, Utpaladeva is concerned with safeguarding the unity of the thing that the division into multiple *ābhāsas* seems irremediably to break up. IPK II.3.3 and the relative *vṛtti* read as follows:

> *yathāruci yathārthitvaṃ yathāvyutpatti bhidyate /*
> *ābhāso 'py artha ekasminn anusaṃdhānasādhite //*
> *ekasminn eva caikapratyavamarśasāmārthyopapādite vastuni svecchāvaśād arthitvānurodhād vā naipuṇavaśād vāvabhāsabhedaḥ*

> In an object, though its unity is established by the unifying power of mind, various manifestations (*ābhāsa*) may be distinguished according to the inclinations, practical requirements and specific experience of the subject.
>
> In the object—though it is unitary, having been assumed as such on the strength of a single reflective awareness—there are different manifestations that are dependent on the will, practical requirements and experience of the subject.

Two themes peculiar to Dharmakīrti's thought are here clearly discernible. I already have dwelt on the first.[41] The second, which appears several times in the PV, is thus formulated in v. 109 of the Svārthānumānapariccheda and *svavṛtti*:[42]

> *ekapratyavamarśasya hetutvād dhīr abhedinī /*
> *ekadhīhetubhāvena vyaktīnām apy abhinnatā //*
> [. . .] *tad api pratidravyaṃ bhidyamānam api prakṛtyaikapratyavamarśasyābhedāvaskandino hetur bhavad abhinnaṃ khyāti / tathābhūtapratyavamarśahetor abhedāvabhāsino jñānāder arthasya hetutvād vyaktayo 'pi saṃsṛṣṭākāraṃ svabhāvabhedaparamārthaṃ svabhāvata ekaṃ pratyayaṃ janayanti* [. . .]

> Because it is the cause of a single reflective awareness, cognition appears as undifferentiated. Because they cause a single cognition, individual realities also appear as

undifferentiated.

> . . . That cognition, although it differs for each individual object, appears as undifferentiated, being by its very nature the cause of a single reflective awareness that establishes the nondifferentiation. Individual things, because they are the cause of a reality that is manifested as undifferentiated (cognition etc.) and is the cause of such a reflective awareness, owing to their very nature also produce a single cognition in which the forms merge, though in the absolute sense there is a differentiation of their own natures. [. . .][43]

Dharmakīrti uses this argument to account for the formation of the idea of class and universal that embraces a plurality of discrete realities which, strictly speaking, cannot be reduced to anything but themselves. The single particular realities become composed in an apparent unity through the same reflective awareness that by nature they are able to determine. Dharmakīrti concludes that it therefore is only the fact that they produce the same effects that constitutes the unity of things that are (in fact) differentiated (*tasmād ekakāryataiva bhāvānām abhedaḥ*). This theme already had been expressed and developed in a clear and rigorous way in PV III.73 and *svavṛtti*:[44]

> *ekapratyavamarśārthajñānādyekārthasādhane /*
> *bhede 'pi niyatāḥ kecit svabhāvenendriyādivat //*
> [. . .] *evaṃ śiṃśapādayo 'pi bhedāḥ parasparānanvaye 'pi prakṛtyaivaikam ekākāraṃ pratyabhijñānaṃ janayanti anyāṃ vā yathāpratyayaṃ dahanagṛhādikāṃ kāṣṭhasādhyām arthakriyām* [. . .]

> Some individual entities, despite the fact that they are differentiated, are determined by their very nature to bring into being a single reality, such as a single reflective awareness or a single object cognition.
>
> . . . Thus, different particular entities, such as *śiṃśapā* trees etc., despite the fact that they are not connected with one another, produce by their very nature a single, uniform recognition, or a different efficiency—depending on the orientation of the cognition—such as burning, building a house etc. carried out by wood.

The same effects are, therefore, first, the cognition that the thing because of its nature is able to give rise to, and, second, the determinate purpose that may be achieved thanks to this.[45] As

Kamalaśīla says later in his commentary on TS, everyday experience groups together completely heterogeneous and separate data, such as a certain shape, color, and so forth, on the basis of their combining to perform a single function (e.g., containing water) thus constructing the unity of a 'thing' (e.g., a jar).[46] IPK II.3.7 echoes, also in its formulation, Dharmakīrti's argumentation; the *vṛtti* furnishes an indispensable explicitation of it.

> *pṛthagdīpaprakāśānāṃ srotasāṃ sāgare yathā /*
> *aviruddhāvabhāsānām ekakāryā tathaikyadhīḥ //*
> *bhinnā pradīpaprabhā avibhāgenāvabhāsante nadīpravāhāś ca sindhubuddhau pānake ca te te rasāḥ tathāśauklyamahatvapaṭatvādyavabhāsāḥ parasparānupraveśakṣamāḥ na tu nīlapītādyavabhāsāḥ tattadekakāryaikadravyābhāsabhāvena kalpante pratyakṣa eva / tad etat sāmānādhikaraṇyam.*

> As in the case of the distinct rays of light in a torch and of the currents in the sea, thus in manifestations that are not in contrast with each other the notion of unity is produced by their appearing as unitary entities.
>
> The individual rays of light in a torch appear as an undifferentiated whole and the same holds for the currents of rivers in the notion of the sea and for the various flavours in the *pānaka*. Similarly, manifestations such as "white," "big," "cloth," and so on, capable as they are of interpenetrating, lend themselves in the direct experience itself to the manifestation of the various unitary things having a single, unitary effect. This does not happen with other series such as "blue," "yellow," etc. This is what we call "having the same substratum."

The context is different from that of Dharmakīrti's argument and very close to Kamalaśīla's: here the purpose is to explain how we may arrive at perceiving the apparent unity of the object from a multiplicity of *ābhāsas*. However, Utpaladeva's conclusion (*tad etat sāmānādhikaraṇyam*) and Dharmakīrti's (*tasmād ekakāryataiva bhāvānām abhedaḥ*) are strictly homologous.

In a long fragment of Utpaladeva's lost IP*Vivṛti*—that I have recently edited and translated—a section is devoted to the self-revealing nature of cognition. It concludes as follows:

> *siddhaṃ tāvat parasaṃvedyatāvyāpakedantāsvabhāvajaḍatāviruddhāhaṃprakāśavyāptatvaṃ svasaṃvidrūpatvasya / tena jñāne vyāpakaviruddhavyāptāyāḥ parasaṃvedyatāyā niṣedhaḥ*

> It has therefore been proved that being conscious of itself [on the part of cognition] is pervaded by the light of the I, which is opposed to insentience—and insentience, for its part, has the nature of "this," which pervades the property of being knowable by others. Thus it is possible to deny that cognition is knowable by others, because this property is pervaded by another that is in opposition to the pervading one (*vyāpakaviruddhavyāptāyāḥ*).[47]

What I wish to underline here is not the content of this statement—which would need to be dealt with separately (cognition as *svasaṃvedana* in fact is a well-known doctrine of the Buddhist logicians, although it is not limited strictly to them)—but the procedure Utpaladeva has used to demonstrate it. In fact, here we are faced with an argumentation (and a terminology) peculiar to the Buddhist logicians: the *anupalabdhi* as the *hetu* of a negative inference, here in the form of *vyāpakaviruddhavyāptopalabdhi.*[48] Moreover, it may be noted that this type is not found in any of the classifications of the *anupalabdhi* given by Dharmakīrti (in the PV, Pramāṇaviniścaya, Hetubindu, NB), it is not present in Dharmottara, it is not quoted by the Kashmirian authors Jayanta (840-900) and Bhāsarvajña (860-920),[49] and until now was thought to have first appeared in the relatively late Dharmottarapradīpa[50] by Durvekamiśra (late tenth-early eleventh centuries), who includes it in a classification comprising fourteen or sixteen forms.[51] The fact that the Pratyabhijñā constitutes a source of information on the logical-epistemological school of Buddhism contributes an additional interest to an examination of it from this point of view.

Notes

1. On the influence of the founder Dignāga, see Tucci 1971, pp. 191-192.

2. I am referring particularly to the well-known stanzas of the beginning (I.2) and the end (IV.286, only found in Miyasaka's edition) of the PV: *prāyaḥ prākṛtasaktir apratibalaprajño janaḥ kevalaṃ nānarthy eva subhāṣitaiḥ parigato vidveṣṭy apīrṣyāmalaiḥ / tenāyaṃ na paropakāra iti naś cintāpi cetaś ciraṃ sūktābhyāsavivardhitavyasanam ity atrānubaddhaspṛham //* 'Mankind are mostly addicted to platitudes, they don't go in for finesse. Not enough that they do not care at all for deep sayings, they are filled with hatred and with the filth of envy. Therefore neither do I care to write for their benefit. However, my heart has

found satisfaction in this [my work], because through it my love for profound and long meditation over [every] well spoken word has been gratified'; *anadhyavasitāvagāhanam analpadhīśaktināpy adṛṣṭaparamārthasāram adhikābhiyogair api / matam mama jagaty alabdhasadṛśapratigrāhakaṃ prayāsyati payonidheḥ paya iva svadehe jarām //* 'My work will find no one in this world who would be adequate easily to grasp its deep sayings. It will be absorbed by, and perish in, my own person, just as a river [which is absorbed and lost] in the ocean. Those who are endowed with no inconsiderable force of reason, even they cannot fathom its depth! Those who are endowed with exceptional intrepidity of thought, even they cannot perceive its highest truth' (trans. in Stcherbatsky 1930-32, vol. I, pp. 35-36). Mokṣākaragupta addresses him with the epithet *nyāyaparameśvara* 'Supreme Lord of Logic' (Kajiyama 1966, p. 125).

3. I am aware that the purely speculative aspect, dealt with in this chapter, does not exhaust the whole of the Pratyabhijñā teaching. On the doctrines of the Pratyabhijñā, see Pandey 1963, pp. 290-460; on its collocation within the Kaula tradition, see the observations of Sanderson 1985, pp. 203-204.

4. Cf. Masson and Patwardhan 1969, p. 34: "Another question that must go unanswered, though it is rich in possibilities, is Abhinava's debt to Buddhism. We simply do not know anything definite on this problem at all, though it is very tempting to speculate." See also, on the same page, note 1. See Gnoli 1960, pp. xxiii-xxvi.

5. It is PV III.282 *kāmaśokabhayonmādacaurasvapnādyupaplutāḥ / abhūtān api paśyanti purato 'vasthitān iva //*. The verse of the Śivadṛṣṭi is I.45 *dṛśyante 'tra tadicchāto bhāvā bhītyādiyogataḥ / tatra mithyāsvarūpaṃ cet sthāpyāgre satyatedṛśām //* (cf. Gnoli 1957, p. 22); see also Utpaladeva's *vṛtti: kāmaśokabhayādiyogāc ca te te bhāvāḥ puraḥ sphuranto dṛśyante.*

6. On the central role of Utpaladeva in the elaboration of Pratyabhijñā philosophy, see Torella, forthcoming A.

7. The privileged relationship with Dharmakīrti might be explained by the fact that he, unlike Dignāga, had accepted the legacy of Bhartṛhari (cf. Herzberger 1986, pp. 11-12), who constitutes one of the Pratyabhijñā's points of reference, from Utpaladeva onward.

8. Cf. Pandey 1963, pp. 147-150.

9. Ibid., p. 149; see also *Śivasūtravimarśinī*, p. 1.

10. Frauwallner 1961, p. 147; Stcherbatsky 1930-32, I 40-41.

11. Frauwallner, ibid., p. 148.

12. According to Abhinavagupta's testimony (Stcherbatsky 1930-32, I pp. 41-42). Stcherbatsky identifies a "Cashmere or philosophical school of commentators [of Dharmakīrti's works].'

13. On the figure and work of Śaṅkarānanda, see Gnoli 1960, pp. xxiii ff.; cf. also Stcherbatsky, ibid., I p. 42 and Bühnemann 1980.

14. Cf., e.g., vol. 2, p. 174: *prāmāṇikataraṃ manyaiḥ [bauddhaiḥ] tādātmyatadutpattī niyamanidānam upagate.*

15. Cf. ibid., p. 140: *parārthānumānaṃ hi śāstram / tatra ca pramāṇādi-ṣoḍaśapadārthatattvamayatvam eva paramārthaḥ*; see also IPVV, vol. 3, p. 182.

16. See, for instance, IPV, vol. 1, p. 308 (on *apoha*); IPVV, vol. 2, pp. 276-277 (on *śabdakalpanā*); IPVV, vol. 2, pp. 344-345, vol. 3, p. 205 (on *kāryakāraṇasiddhi*); IPVV, vol. 2, p. 371 (on *bādhyabādhakabhāva*), etc.

17. Cf. e.g., IPV vol. 2, p. 32: *ekānekarūpasya kriyādeḥ bāhyavāde viruddhadharmādhyāsadūṣaṇena anupapadyamānasyāpy avaśyaṃ samarthanīyaṃ vapuḥ.*

18. See note 15.

19. See also the description that Abhinavagupta gives of the *anumāna* in IPV, vol. 2, p. 84, which a Buddhist would agree with: *anumānajā tu pratītiḥ ābhāsāntarāt kāryarūpāt svabhāvarūpāt vā ābhāsāntare pratipattiḥ.* Abhinavagupta accepts the Buddhist conception en bloc, except that he inscribes it in the sphere of the Lord's power of necessity (ibid.: *vastvantarasya ca tena sākaṃ kāryakāraṇabhāvaniyamaḥ sāmānādhikaraṇyaniyamaś ca īśvaraniyatiśaktyupajīvana eva avadhāryo bhavati na anyathā*). He does the same elsewhere with the Buddhist doctrine of impermanence (IPVV, vol. 3, p. 214: *na bhāvasya kiṃcit nijaṃ nityam anityaṃ vā vapuḥ / īśvaras tu svasaṃvinmukure viśvam ābhāsayan kṣanikatām api ābhāsayatīti naḥ pakṣaḥ*).

20. The quotations from the IPK and *vṛtti* are drawn from my forthcoming (B) edition and translation.

21. Bandyopadhyay 1979, p. 43.

22. NBṬ, p. 82: *na cātra janyajanakabhāvanibandhanaḥ sādhyasādhana-bhāvaḥ, yenaikasmin vastuni virodhaḥ syāt / api tu vyavasthāpyavyavasthāpana-bhāvena / tad ekasya vastunaḥ kiṃcid rūpaṃ pramāṇaṃ kiṃcit pramāṇaphalaṃ na virudhyate.*

23. IPV, vol. 2, pp. 73-75; IPVV, vol. 3, pp. 71-72.

24. Cf. TS 1346: *ata utprekṣito bhedo vidyate dhanurādivat / utpādyotpādakatvena vyavastheyaṃ tu neṣyate //* and the relative *pañcikā*.

25. TSP, vol. 1, p. 488: *kṣaṇikatvena nirvyāpāratvāt sarvadharmāṇām.*

26. Cf. Hattori 1968, p. 28.

27. The whole verse reads as follows: *savyāpāram ivābhāti vyāpāreṇa svakarmaṇi / tadvaśāt tadvyavasthānād akārakam api svayam //.*

28. CF. IPV, vol. 2, p. 75: *kiṃ ca vyāpārarūpam eva phalaṃ vyāpāraś ca vyāpriyamāṇāt vyāpāryamāṇāt vā ananyākāra eva siddha iti abhedaḥ pramāṇaphalayoḥ.*

29. Cf. Hattori 1968, pp. 83-85. See the discussion in TS 1213 ff. and the relative *pañcikā*. Cf. also PV III.123: *pratyakṣaṃ kalpanāpoḍhaṃ pratyakṣeṇaiva sidhyati / pratyātmavedyaḥ sarveṣāṃ vikalpo nāmasaṃśrayaḥ //.*

30. Abhinavagupta, in commenting on this verse in IPVV, vol. 2, pp. 276-278, refers explicitly (following the *ṭīkā*) to the definition of the NB and also quotes two passages from Dharmottara, for which I have found only a summary correspondence in the edited text of the NBṬ. Another element worthy of consideration in the stanza and in the *vṛtti* is the conception of the determinate cognition (*vikalpa, niścaya*) as based on the exclusion of what is other. It reminds one of an important passage of the PV (I.48-49), where the *apoha*, which at first seemed only to concern the inferential process, also is extended to determinate cognition (*niścayajñāna*) that follows perception: *kvacid dṛṣṭe 'pi yaj jñānaṃ sāmānyārthaṃ vikalpakaṃ / asamāropitānyāṃśe tanmātrāpohagocaram //—[svavṛtti] yad rūpādidarśanānantaram aliṅgaṃ niścayajñānaṃ bhavati, tat katham asati samārope bhavad vyavacchedaviṣayaṃ bhavati, samāropaviṣaye tasyābhāvāt [. . .] // niścayāropamanasor bādhyabādhakabhāvataḥ / samāropaviveke 'sya pravṛttir iti gamyate // [svavṛtti] [. . .] tadviveka eva cānyāpohaḥ / tasmād tad api tanmātrāpohagocaram / na vastusvabhāvaniścayātmakam / tathā hi kasyacin niścaye 'py anyāsyāpratipattidarśanāt / tatsvabhāvaniścaye ca tasyāyogāt* (cf. Mookerjee and Nagasaki 1964, pp. 108 ff.). Cf. IPV, vol. 1, pp. 303-304: *vividhā kalpanā vividhatvena ca śaṅkitasya kalpo 'nyavyavacchedanaṃ vikalpaḥ, vividhatvaṃ ca vahnāv anagnisaṃbhāvanāsamāropanirāse sati bhavat, dvayaṃ vahnyavahnirūpaṃ samākṣipati*; see also IPK I.6.2-3.

31. Up to this point, in fact, the Pratyabhijñā and Buddhist logic agree, and the masters of the Pratyabhijñā are well aware of this (cf. IPV, vol. 1, p. 266: *bauddhair api adhyavasāyāpekṣaṃ prakāśasya prāmāṇyaṃ vadadbhiḥ upagataprāyaḥ eva ayam arthaḥ, abhilāpātmakatvāt adhyavasāyasya iti*).

32. IPK I.5.13: *citiḥ pratyavamarśātmā parāvāk svarasoditā / svātantryam*

etan mukhyaṃ tad aiśvaryaṃ paramātmanaḥ //.

33. IPK I.5.19: *sākṣātkaraṇe 'py asti vimarśaḥ katham anyathā / dhāvanādy upapadyeta pratisaṃdhānavarjitaṃ //* 'Even at the moment of the direct perception there is a determinate reflective awareness. How otherwise could one account for such actions as running and so on, if they were thought of as being devoid of determinate awareness?'; cf. IPV, vol. 1, p. 293: *sūkṣmeṇa pratyavamarśena saṃvartita-śabdabhāvanāmayena bhāvyam eva.*

34. Abhinavagupta refers explicitly (IPVV, vol. 3, p. 201) to two different positions as regards the nature of the *svalakṣaṇa.* For the one (which is also accepted by the Pratyabhijñā) it is formed by a collection of *ābhāsas* (*ābhāsanikurumbātmakasvalakṣaṇavāda*), for the other it is partless (*niraṃśasvalakṣaṇavāda*).

35. Cf. Steinkellner 1971, p. 198. This is valid for every *pramāṇa,* therefore also for the *anumāna* (cf. PV I.46 and *svavṛtti*). IPK II. 3.8 echoes this conception: *tatrāviśiṣṭe vahnyādau kāryakāraṇatoṣṇatā- / tattacchabdārthatādyātmā pramāṇād ekato mataḥ //* 'Regarding a nonspecific manifestation of "fire," a single means of knowledge knows what the effect or cause of it is, its being hot, its being denoted by this or that word and so on.' See also IPVV, vol. 1, p. 199.

36. Indeed it is precisely determinate knowledge, which is not itself a *pramāṇa,* that renders the perception for all intents and purposes a *pramāṇa* (NBṬ p. 84: *tasmād adhyavasāyaṃ kurvad eva pratyakṣaṃ pramāṇaṃ bhavati*).

37. Cf. Vetter 1964, p. 56.

38. The passage comments on PV I.58: *pratyakṣeṇa gṛhīte 'pi viśeṣe 'ṃśavivarjite / yadviśeṣāvasāye 'sti pratyayaḥ sa pratīyate //.*

39. Cf. Vetter 1964, pp. 48-49.

40. The *vimarśa* plays the role of "systematizer" (*vyavasthāpaka*) of reality that is strictly analogous to the role the Buddhists assign to *niścaya-adhyavasāya,* notwithstanding the different valuation (NBṬ p. 84: *niścayapratyayenāvyavasthāpitaṃ sad api nīlabodharūpaṃ vijñānam asatkalpam eva [. . .] akṛte tv adhyavasāye nīlabodharūpatvenāvyavasthāpitaṃ bhavati vijñānam*).

41. Cf. above p. 333 and note 38.

42. Cf. Steinkellner 1971, p. 190.

43. See also PV I.68-69: *pararūpaṃ svarūpeṇa yayā saṃvriyate dhiyā / ekārthapratibhāsinyā bhāvān āśritya bhedinaḥ // tayā saṃvṛtanānārthāḥ saṃ-*

vṛtyā bhedinaḥ svayaṃ / abhedina ivābhānti bhāvā rūpeṇa kenacit //.

44. Cf. Vetter 1964, p. 53.

45. It is a question of what have been called *pratiniyataśakti* and *sāmānyaśakti* (Mikogami 1979, pp. 80 ff.; Katsura 1984, p. 218).

46. TSP, vol. 1, p. 59: *ta eva rūpādayaḥ salilādidhāraṇārthakriyākāriṇaḥ samudāyo ghaṭa iti vyapadiśyante.*

47. Torella 1988, p. 28.

48. After Utpaladeva, Abhinavagupta also makes frequent use of this type of argumentation.

49. The *Nyāyamañjarī* (vol. 1, p. 53) and the *Nyāyabhūṣaṇa* (p. 288) refer to the classification in eleven forms, derived from the NB.

50. *Dharmottarapradīpa*, p. 140. Cf. Kajiyama 1966, pp. 151 ff.

51. The *vyāpakaviruddhavyāptopalabdhi* later is referred to by Mokṣākaragupta (between 1050 and 1202) in the *Tarkabhāṣā* (Kajiyama 1966, p. 85) and by Vidyākaraśānti (c. 1100) in the *Tarkasopāna* (Tucci 1956, p. 291).

Bibliography

Abbreviations

EW	*East and West*, Rome
IPK	*Īśvarapratyabhijñākārikā*
IPV	*Īśvarapratyabhijñāvimarśinī*
IPVV	*Īśvarapratyabhijñāvivṛtivimarśinī*
JIP	*Journal of Indian Philosophy*, Dordrecht
NB	*Nyāyabindu*
NBṬ	*Nyāyabinduṭīkā*
PS	*Pramāṇasamuccaya*
PV	*Pramāṇavārttika* (PV, vol. 1 = *Svārthānumāna*; PV, vol. 2 = *Pramāṇasiddhi*; PV, vol. 3 = *Pratyakṣa*; PV vol. 4 = *Parārthānumāna*)
PVSV	*Pramāṇavārttikasvavṛtti*
TS	*Tattvasaṃgraha*
TSP	*Tattvasaṃgrahapañcikā*
WZKSO	*Wiener Zeitschrift für die Kunde Süd- und Ostasiens*, Vienna

Texts

Abhinavagupta. *Īśvarapratyabhijñāvimarśinī* (see Bhāskara).

———. *Īśvarapratyabhijñāvivṛtivimarśinī*, ed. M. K. Shastri, vols. 1-3, KSTS 60, 62, 65. Bombay, 1938-43.

Bhāsarvajña, *Nyāyabhūṣaṇam*, ed. Svāmī Yogīndrānanda, Ṣaḍdarśana-prakāśanapratiṣṭhāna-granthamālā no. 1, Varanasi: 1968.

Bhāskara. *Bhāskarī. A Commentary on the Īśvarapratyabhijñāvimarśinī of Abhinavagupta*, vols. 1-2, ed. K. A. S. Iyer and K. C. Pandey. The Princess of Wales Sarasvati Bhavana Texts Nos. 70 and 83. Allahabad, 1938-1950.

Dharmakīrti. *Pramāṇavārttika-kārikā* [Sanskrit and Tibetan], ed. Y. Miyasaka, *Acta Indologica* 2 (1971-72).

———. *Pramāṇavārttika with the Commentary 'Vṛtti' of Acharya Manorathanandin*, critically ed. Swami Dwarikadas Shastri. (Varanasi 1968).

———. *Pramāṇavārttikam. The First Chapter with the Autocommentary*, text and critical notes by R. Gnoli. Serie Orientale Roma 23. Rome: ISMEO.

———. *Hetubindu* (see Steinkellner 1967).

Dharmottara. *Nyāyabinduṭīkā* (see Durveka Miśra, *Dharmottarapradīpa*).

Durveka Miśra. *Dharmottarapradīpa [being a subcommentary on Dharmottara's Nyāyabinduṭīkā, a commentary on Dharmakīrti's Nyāyabindu]*, ed. Paṇḍita Dalsukhbhai Malvania. Revised 2d ed. Patna: Kashiprasad Jayaswal Research Institute, 1971.

Jayanta, *Nyāyamañjarī*, ed. Pt. Surya Nārāyaṇa Śukla, parts 1 and 2, Kashi Sanskrit Series 106. Varanasi: 1969-71.

Śāntarakṣita. *Tattvasaṃgraha with the Commentary 'Pañjikā' of Kamalaśīla*, 2 vols., critically ed. Swami Dwarikadas Shastri. Bauddha Bharati Series 1. Varanasi: 1981.

Utpaladeva. *Īśvarapratyabhijñāvṛtti*, critical ed. and trans. R. Torella, Serie Orientale Roma. Rome: ISMEO, forthcoming.

Studies

Bandyopadhyay, N. 1979 "The Buddhist Theory of Relation between *pramā* and *pramāṇa*, 7." *JIP*, 7, no. 1.

Bühnemann, G. 1980, "Identifizierung von Sanskrittexten Śaṅkaranandanas." *WZKSO*, 24.

Frauwallner, E. 1961, "Landmarks in the History of Indian Logic." *WZKSO*, 5.

Gnoli, R. 1957. "*Śivadṛṣṭi* by Somānanda." *EW*, 8.

———. 1960. See Dharmakīrti, *Pramāṇavārttikam. The First Chapter with the Autocommentary.*

Hattori, M. 1968. *Dignāga, On Perception, Being the Pratyakṣapariccheda of Dignāga's Pramāṇasamuccaya*, Harvard Oriental Series No. 47. Cambridge, Mass.

Herzberger, R. 1986. *Bhartṛhari and the Buddhists. An Essay in the Development of Fifth and Sixth Century Indian Thought*, Studies of Classical India 8. Dordrecht.

Kajiyama, Y. 1966, "An Introduction to Buddhist Philosophy. An Annotated Translation of the *Tarkabhāṣā* of Mokṣākaragupta." *Memoirs of the Faculty of Letters. Kyoto University*, 10.

Masson, J. L., and M. V. Patwardhan. 1969. *Śāntarasa and Abhinavagupta's Philosophy of Aesthetics.* Bhandarkar Oriental Research Institute. Poona.

Mikogami, E. 1979. "Some Remarks on the Concepts of *arthakriyā*." *JIP*, 7, no. 1.

Mookerjee, S., and H. Nagasaki. 1964. *The Pramāṇavārttikam of Dharmakīrti. An English Translation of the First Chapter with the Autocommentary and with Elaborate Comments [Kārikās I-LI]*. The Nava Nālandā Mahāvihāra Research Publication, vol. 4. Patna.

Pandey, K. C. 1963. *Abhinavagupta, An Historical and Philosophical Study.* 2d edition Banaras: Chowkhamba Sanskrit Series Office.

Sanderson, A. 1985. "Purity and Power among the Brahmans of Kashmir." In M. Carrithers, S. Collins, and S. Lukes, *The Category of the Person.* Cambridge, Mass.: Cambridge University Press.

Stcherbatsky, T. 1930-32. *Buddhist Logic*, 2 vols. Bibliotheca Buddhica 26. Leningrad (reprinted New York, 1962).

Steinkellner, E. 1967. *Dharmakīrti's Hetubindu*, Part 1, Tibetischer Text und rekonstruierter Sanskrit-Text; Part 2, Übersetzung und Anmerkungen. Vienna: Österreichische Akademie der Wissenschaften.

———. 1971. "Wirklichkeit und Begriff bei Dharmakīrti." *WZKSO,* 15.

Torella, R. 1988. "A Fragment of Utpaladeva's *Īśvarapratyabhijñā-vivṛti.*" *EW,* 38.

———. Forthcoming A. "Importanza di Utpaladeva." *Atti del IV Convegno Nazionale di Studi Sanscriti.* Turin.

———. Forthcoming B. See Utpaladeva, *Īśvarapratyabhijñāvṛtti.*

Tucci, G. 1956. *Minor Buddhist Texts,* Part I. Serie Orientale Roma 9. Rome.

———. 1971. "Bhāmaha and Diṅnāga," (*Indian Antiquary* 59, 1930), reprinted in *Opera Minora,* Università di Roma, Studi Orientali pubblicati a cura della Scuola Orientale, 6. Rome.

Vetter, T. 1964. *Erkenntnissprobleme bei Dharmakīrti.* Vienna: Österreichische Akademie der Wissenschaften.

INDEX OF SANSKRIT TERMS

INDEX OF NAMES AND SUBJECTS

www.ingramcontent.com/pod-product-compliance
Lightning Source LLC
LaVergne TN
LVHW010944271026
851073LV00023B/245